Decisive Battles of the English Civil Wars

Decisive Battles of the English Civil Wars

Myth and Reality

Malcolm Wanklyn

Pen & Sword
MILITARY

First published in Great Britain in 2006
Reprinted and revised in 2014 by
PEN & SWORD MILITARY
an imprint of
Pen & Sword Books Limited
47 Church Street
Barnsley
S. Yorkshire S70 2AS

Copyright © Malcolm Wanklyn, 2006, 2014

ISBN 978 1 78346 975 8

The right of Malcolm Wanklyn to be identified as Author of this Work has
been asserted by him in accordance with the Copyright, Designs and Patents
Act 1988.

A CIP catalogue record for this book is available from the
British Library

Printed and bound in England
by CPI Group (UK) Ltd., Croydon, CR0 4YY

Pen & Sword Books Ltd incorporates the imprints of Pen & Sword
Archaeology, Atlas, Aviation, Battleground, Discovery, Family History,
History, Maritime, Military, Naval, Politics, Railways, Select, Social History,
Transport, True Crime, and Claymore Press, Frontline Books, Leo Cooper,
Praetorian Press, Remember When, Seaforth Publishing and Wharncliffe.

For a complete list of Pen & Sword titles please contact:
PEN & SWORD BOOKS LIMITED
47 Church Street, Barnsley, South Yorkshire, S70 2AS, England.
E-mail: enquiries@pen-and-sword.co.uk
Website: www.pen-and-sword.co.uk

Contents

Illustrations

Preface

This is the second of three books that focus on various aspects of the military history of the wars fought in Britain and Ireland in the middle years of the seventeenth century. The first, *A Military History of the English Civil War 1642–1646: Strategy and Tactics*, co-authored with Frank Jones and published by Pearson/Longman in 2004, concentrated overwhelmingly on removing a hundred years of historians' concretions from the strategic narrative of the English Civil Wars. The third, *The Warring Generals*, to be published by Yale University Press in 2007, will endeavour to assess the experience of generalship in the various British wars of 1642–51, and also the personal and collective responsibility of the army commanders for the wars' outcomes. This book will examine the way in which historians have written about the battles of the English Civil Wars in the context of recent anti-Modernist doubts concerning the feasibility of reconstructing what happened in past time. However, it is not a postmodernist text. Indeed, an underlying theme is that the claim that the study of History cannot produce factual information about what happened in the past is a fallacious one. Nevertheless, some of the terms and concepts used in the more accessible postmodernist texts, and some of the insights they contain, are of value in shedding a harsh but necessary light on the ways in which military historians practise their craft.

Chapter 1 justifies the choice of the battles, and explains why accurate narratives of battles are essential if the significance of the purely military explanations of how the wars ended as they did are to be adequately evaluated. Chapter 2 discusses in general terms the problems involved in constructing accurate battle narratives from the various types of primary source material military historians use. Chapter 3 examines the potential pitfalls facing historians who write about seventeenth-century warfare, and proposes ways in which narratives of what happened on the Civil War battlefield can be improved.

In the main section of the book seven decisive battles are discussed with two chapters being devoted to each battle. The first chapter places the battle in its exact historical context, deconstructs the sources for the battle, and attempts to reconstruct and repopulate the landscape over which it was fought. The second comprises a narrative of the battle written in accordance with the procedures and protocols set down in Chapter 3. The concluding chapter re-emphasizes the hypothetical nature of narratives of the seven battles. It also suggests some changes in military doctrine which took place during the English Civil Wars and which help to determine their outcome.

I would like to thank my colleagues John Benson and John Buckley for reading various chapters; my university and the British Academy for providing the financial support without which visits to distant archives and distant battlefields would have been impossible; Rupert Harding for his very sound editorial advice and Susan Milligan for copy-editing; the staff of the Libraries and Record Offices I have visited for their assistance; the City Campus Learning Centre, Wolverhampton University, for giving permission to include de Gomme's sketch of the deployment of the Royalist army at Naseby (Plate 16) from their copy of Volume 3 of E.G.B. Warburton's *Memoirs of Prince Rupert and the Cavaliers;* the Shropshire Record Office and the Berkshire Record Office for allowing brief extracts from their archives to be used in a similar manner (Plate 11 and 13 respectively); English Heritage for permission to include our photograph of the gatehouse at Donnington Castle; the farmer at Hinton Ampner who allowed me to take photographs on his land; and friends inside and outside the university who have kept up my spirits during the year 2005, most particularly Mike Dennis, Patrick McGraghan, Toby McLeod, Roger Page, Jim Quinn, Charles Singleton, and the happy band of colleagues with whom I share office space - George, Glyn, Martin and Tony. Finally, I thank my wife Jean for employing her photographic skills on my behalf, and Matt Rogers for drawing the maps.

After Thoughts

Since 2006 no new primary sources have entered the public domain covering the battles described below. I have therefore left the battlefield narratives as they are apart from modifying my position on the deployment of the Parliamentary infantry at Naseby in the light of David Blackmore's excellent discussion of the size of the regiments based on his research into New Model Army pay warrants. I do, however, have concerns that two of the really fine accounts of Civil War battles published since 2006 reject the sequence of events to be found in first-rate primary sources. In his narrative of the First Battle of Newbury to be commended for its employment of inherent military probability to fill in the gaps in the sources, Jon Day in *Gloucester and Newbury 1643* (Pen and Sword, 2007) places the engagement of the Red Regiment of the London Trained Bands in the afternoon rather than in the morning despite what three participants had stated in accounts peinted within a fortnight of the battle. Second, Martin Marix Evans in *Naseby 1645* (Osprey, 2011) places the abortive charge of the King's Lifeguard in a stand-off that took place after the battle had ended rather than in the middle of the fighting, despite Sir Edward Walker's evocative description of the charge written for the king to vet, which places it firmly at the time of the collapse of the royalist left wing. I also remain totally convinced that any conflict between first-rate written testimony and archaeological evidence is a matter for debate and should not invariably be settled in the favour of the latter.

Chapter 1

Introduction

The central question of the 1640s frequently ignored or marginalized by historians is why Parliament won the Great Civil War of 1642–6 and the Second Civil War of 1648–9. Attempts to answer the question tend to be strongly determinist in nature, stressing the overwhelming preponderance of resources that Parliament enjoyed over the forces that supported the king. The argument that lack of resources made it inevitable that Charles I would lose the First Civil War once the campaigns of 1642 and 1643 had ended indecisively has been challenged elsewhere, and combined with a plea for the more purely military explanations to be re-examined. In *A Military History of the English Civil War* Frank Jones and I developed a revised narrative focusing on how strategic decisions influenced the ebb and flow of the fighting in the First Civil War.[1] Subsequently Stanley Carpenter examined the significance of military leadership in determining the outcome of some of the campaigns in the North of England theatre of war between 1642 and 1651.[2]

Neither Wanklyn and Jones nor Carpenter paid much attention to the battles, but in the last resort it is how military force was used in the decisive engagements that ultimately decided which side won the war. This book will therefore focus on those battles that constitute significant turning points in the Civil Wars. But why is a new set of battlefield histories needed after so many have been written over the past 120 years, beginning with S.R. Gardiner's *History of the Great Civil War*?[3] The answer is not that major new sources have emerged, but rather that the methodologies employed by most of the authors for most of the time have produced narratives of campaigns that are unsatisfactory in a number of ways. In particular what has been written about what happened on the battlefield is often questionable at best, and sometimes erroneous. In addition, discussion of the landscape over which the battles were fought is often perfunctory and sometimes wrong-headed.

But which were the most significant battles? In the case of Edgehill, the First Battle of Newbury, Cheriton, and Naseby, the campaigns in which they occurred were acknowledged at the time as turning points in the war. In the case of Preston, a draw or a Scottish/Royalist victory would have transformed the Second Civil War from a series of isolated blazes into a major conflagration. The Second Battle of Newbury is more problematic, but if the creation of the New Model Army is seen as a major direct military reason for Parliament's victory in the field in the following year (indirect reasons being strategic and tactical errors made by the king and his generals and military advisers) then it too was decisive. Marston Moor is more problematic to me than it is to others.[4] More soldiers fought at Marston Moor than in any other battle; it brought Cromwell's Ironsides to the fore as potential war-winners; and the victory of the Parliamentary armies and their Scottish allies marked a very important stage in driving the Royalists out of the north of England. On the other hand, the Allied generals and their political masters allowed the strategic advantages that might have accrued from the victory to slip through their fingers. Indeed it could be argued that for the next year or so the king used resources from the north more effectively than did his enemies. Nevertheless, it would be perverse of me to exclude Marston Moor given the prominent place it enjoys in books on battles written by others. I have, however, excluded Langport. Years ago I would not have done so, but a Royalist military revival after Naseby depended on combining infantry from South Wales and the south-west of England with veteran cavalry regiments, some of which had fought at Naseby and some of which had not. This was a most unlikely scenario. Even if the New Model Army quartered in Somerset in July 1645 was as short of food and fodder as Sir Thomas Fairfax claimed it was, it seems highly improbable that a concentration of Royalist forces could have been achieved without one or other element being held back, picked off, or diverted elsewhere by Allied forces that were converging on Wales and on the south-western peninsula from elsewhere. I also do not see Winceby as being decisive in blunting the northern prong of the king's so-called threefold attack on London in 1643. In August and September the Marquis of Newcastle would not leave the north without capturing Hull. In October with Hull still defiant, and with a Scottish invasion only weeks away, a move southwards would have seemed even more foolhardy even if that part of his army stationed in Lincolnshire had managed to inflict a defeat on Cromwell and Fairfax.[5] Finally, I would exclude the Battle of Worcester. This may seem illogical as Preston is included, but I see the so-called Third Civil War of 1649–52 as nothing of the sort so far as England was concerned.[6] What happened at Worcester was not a battle between Englishmen fighting for different political and/or religious systems, but the defeat of a Scottish invasion brought about not just by the New Model Army under Oliver Cromwell's leadership, but by the nation in arms. Also on the battlefield at Worcester, or on their march there, were volunteer regiments from the English counties intent on driving out the Scots. Only in north-west

England was there any real sign of a resurgence of support for the monarchy, and that was easily suppressed.[7]

Before trying to understand the outcome of a battle – and I emphasize the word try – the first stage must be to identify what happened during the course of that battle as far as the sources allow, that is to construct as accurate a narrative as possible. This is much more problematic than is often supposed. The further back in time, the more incomplete is the contemporary evidence that survives. However, reconstructing what happened on Civil War battle-fields is not such an uncertain process as it is with battles fought in the Middle Ages, when much of the so-called factual information comes from monkish chroniclers who were reliant on second-hand information at best, and who interpreted what they had heard in relation to their Church-centred, moralistic view of the world. Nevertheless, the gaps in the evidence relating to Civil War battles are significant ones. I would like, for example, to be able to examine contemporary sketches showing how the Earl of Essex's army was deployed at Edgehill and how both armies were deployed at Cheriton. It would also be most useful to have to hand an account of Edgehill written by somebody who fought in Charles Gerard's or Henry Wentworth's brigade, a fully worked-up version of Prince Rupert's memoirs, and a trio of letters written by Oliver Cromwell describing in detail the battles of Marston Moor, Second Newbury and Naseby. However, a much bigger problem is caused by the imperfections in the evidence that has survived to the present day, and by the ways in which historians have sometimes used and abused it.

Part I

Recapturing the Past

Chapter 2

Civil War Battles
The Primary Sources

It is self-evident that what the present thinks it knows about the past is dependent upon the information about the past that has survived into the present. This corpus of 'knowledge' is not fixed. It expands over time as additional primary sources are discovered or brought into the public domain, and as new techniques are devised for accessing or interpreting them. Nevertheless the primary sources, which military historians of the seventeenth century can use today, or may be able to use in the future, constitute only a tiny fraction of the information concerning the Civil Wars that once existed. Much is lost forever, such as letters and administrative records destroyed because they might become incriminating or because they took up too much space; evidence lodged in the memories of those who fought in the battles that was not subsequently written down; and the landscape and archaeology of battlefields that have since been built over. Moreover, the 'traces of the past' that do survive are often incomplete in themselves. For example, much of Prince Rupert's incoming correspondence exists, but very few of his outgoing letters, whilst most Devonshire and Wiltshire maimed soldiers' petitions have been preserved, but very few for Somerset and Dorset.

The historian's traditional role has been to use such traces of the past to recount what happened in past centuries and then to try to explain it. The narratives thus created are expected to conform to the laws of logic in terms of evidence and argument, and also to take cognisance of narratives already in existence. Not surprisingly, new narratives tend to be diffused with qualifications and caveats, but the flow of the argument is often interspersed with short bursts of triumphalism as earlier narratives are shown to be faulty in some respect or other. In the closing years of the twentieth century persistent criticism of History's ability to establish what happened in the past and why, often described as postmodernist, has made the present generation of historians even more cautious. For, as Keith Jenkins has reminded us, it is not the past itself that historians reconstruct in their writings, but a representation of the past that is firmly lodged in the present, as its backbone is not the traces of the past but a story line devised by the historian, which will be influenced to a large extent by her or his life experience. The traces of the past illustrate the story line; they do not predetermine or preordain it.[1] Indeed the traces of the past are totally subordinate to the writer's will. Historians will choose what they deem supportive of their story, and either ignore the rest, or else use the tools of rhetoric to belittle its significance, particularly if it conflicts with or challenges their argument in any way. Each narrative is therefore no more than a version of the past that owes as much if not more to the writer than to traces of the past embedded in it. This critique of History's ability to bring factual knowledge of the past into the present helps explain why I felt it necessary to write this book, though much of the argument will focus not on appraising critiques of my profession's pretensions to establish 'the truth' about the past, but rather on the current defects in the practice of writing battlefield narratives. The ways in which military historians of the English Civil Wars have gone about their business will be discussed in greater detail in Chapter 3, but first it is necessary to look very carefully at the extent to which primary sources can be regarded as factual – that is gobbets of knowledge about what happened in the past – or something subtly different.

Traces of the past come into existence at the instant that the present becomes the past (as in the case of much of the archaeological record) or not long afterwards (as in the case of much of the written record). Very occasionally traces of the past predate what they describe, as in the case of a sketch of how an army was to be deployed in a forthcoming battle. This illustrates, albeit in a very narrow way, that traces of the past are not necessarily a 'truthful' record of what happened on the battlefield, as it is unlikely to be clear from the sketch whether the eventual deployment was exactly as depicted in the sketch, or whether the plan was modified to take into account, for example, the physical characteristics of the battlefield. At the other extreme some descriptions of battles were not written down until many years after the event, often as part of an autobiography or an authorized biography. Despite what some of their authors claimed,[2] the chief purpose of such texts, and indeed of letters and diary entries written soon after the battle, was not to provide future historians with a dispassionate record of what happened in the past, but to address the needs of the 'then present', which are discussed below.

Scepticism with regard to the objectivity of battle accounts is not new. The Duchess of Newcastle wrote of many 'who have written of the late Civil War with but sprinklings of truth like as heat drops on a dry, barren ground knowing no more of the transactions of those times than what they learned in the Gazettes, which for the most part out of policy to amuse and deceive the people contain nothing but falsehoods.'[3] Sir Richard Bulstrode was more specific:

> There is always great difference in relation of battles, which do usually according to the interests of relators; when it is certain that in a battle the next man can hardly make a true relation of the actions of him that is next him, for in such a hurry and smoke as in a set fight [field] a man takes notice of nothing but what relates to his own safety, so that no man gives a clear account of particular passages.[4]

But Sir Richard was only scratching the surface. Indeed, he may have only been describing difficulties in the act of observation, as the word 'interests' appears from its context to have the very specific meaning of what the relater himself did or did not experience. Whether consciously or unconsciously, however, Sir Richard was pointing towards a much wider truth about primary sources – they are not always what they seem.

The Provenance of Printed and Manuscript Sources

In most cases the authenticity of primary sources is self-evident, but if only a printed version exists, there must always be a shadow of doubt. The *Memoirs of a Cavalier* by Daniel Defoe is a salutary example of the need for caution. It was cited in historical works as late as C.V. Wedgwood's *The King's War* in the belief that Defoe might have drawn on a genuine memoir no longer extant, as he had done in the case of his *Robinson Crusoe*.[5] Nowadays the text is recognized as being entirely fictitious other than where Defoe rifled accounts of the war already in print. More recently the discovery of part of the manuscript of Edmund Ludlow's *Memoirs* has shown how radically the text was altered by its late seventeenth-century editor.[6] Unfortunately, the manuscript does not cover the Civil War period, but there is little doubt that much of Ludlow's account of the Battle of Edgehill could have been written from material available in books and pamphlets in the 1690s. In the case of the *Memoirs of Sir Richard Bulstrode*, first published in 1721, Sir Charles Firth realized over a hundred years ago that the editor had filled out genuine memoir material with passages from Clarendon's *History of the Great Rebellion* and Sir Philip Warwick's *Memoirs* in order to create a marketable product.[7] However, the manuscript covering the period up to the summer of 1644 has recently been located, and from this it is clear that all the editor did was to simplify the language; only on rare occasions did he alter the meaning.[8] Another problematic memoir is that of John Gwyn, discovered in an Irish country house in the early years of the nineteenth century and edited for publication by Sir Walter Scott. It probably contains some genuine memoir material, but to what extent cannot be judged as the original manuscript no longer exists. However, I have very strong misgivings about its authenticity given that Gwyn, who claimed to have been at both the First and the Second Battle of Newbury, was under the delusion that they had been fought on the same piece of ground.[9]

Contemporary journals and pamphlets provide different examples of dodgy traces of the past. Weeklies published in the immediate aftermath of the battles sometimes seem to draw on genuine material not to be found in any other source, but there is always a doubt as to their provenance as editors were only too happy at times to publish complete fictions, such as the reports of a major encounter between the armies of the king and the Earl of Essex taking place at Shrewsbury some weeks before the Battle of Edgehill.[10] Amongst the individual pamphlets printed in London in the 1640s are quite a number of descriptions of battles written by officers who had taken part in them, but there are also several which are anonymous or whose authorship is concealed by initials or by a pseudonym. Historians tend to incorporate such works into their narratives without giving a second thought as to their authenticity, but some are almost certainly journalistic fabrications dressed up in such a way as to appear authentic, the most notorious example being *The Bloody Battle of Preston.*[11] In this book such texts will be carefully appraised and rejected if there is still doubt about their authenticity.

The only major manuscript source about which there is similar concern is Prince Rupert's Diary, an unhelpful title in that it is not a diary and it was written for, not by, the prince.[12] The longer of the two documents is the photocopy of a manuscript written in a late seventeenth-century hand describing his military experiences in the Civil War. Although no more than an early draft, it appears to have been corrected and added to by Rupert. As the 'Diary' was discovered in the family archive of the Bennets of Pythouse, Wiltshire, one of whose members had been Rupert's secretary in the 1680s, and as King James II appears to have read parts of it before writing his own memoirs, there is little doubt as to its authenticity.[13] The same cannot be said of the second document, which includes some short additions to the Diary and some brief precis of letters written to the prince, as the version in the public domain was typed on a manual machine manufactured in the middle years of the twentieth century.[14] However, the vocabulary and the syntax conform well with the Diary; it does not contradict anything that is to be found in any other primary source; there is no obvious motive for somebody living in the mid-twentieth century to go to the trouble of writing such a disorganized yet narrowly focused document; a subheading states that the notes were taken from a 'marble bound paper volume'; and the text has been corrected in ink, which suggests that the typist was working from a genuine seventeenth-century document but was not proficient in reading seventeenth-century handwriting. For these reasons I feel reasonably certain that the typescript is the copy of a manuscript roughly contemporary with the Civil War, but now lost, destroyed, or no longer in the public domain.

Fact and Fiction

Edward Hyde, Lord Clarendon's *History of the Great Rebellion* and *Auto-biography* are the source of sources on the English Civil Wars, brilliantly written and at first, or even second glance, highly convincing accounts of the events and personalities of mid-seventeenth-century England. Moreover, the author was a moderate in politics, and as such likely to have viewed the period through which he lived with a dispassionate eye. However, Clarendon's could never be described as an even-handed account; moderation and lack of prejudice are not necessarily two sides of the same coin. Instead his writings are a subtle attempt to enhance the reputations of his friends and to blacken those of his enemies, most particularly the young generals who had fought for the king, Princes Rupert and Maurice and George Goring.[15] Fortunately for military historians Clarendon did not destroy the evidence that he had obtained from others prior to writing, and then ignored or distorted when he put pen to paper. However, the evidence for such behaviour was hidden away in the Hyde family archive and then in the Bodleian Library. It therefore had no effect on sales to the elites of eighteenth- and nineteenth-century England for whom reversion to civil strife was a deep-seated worry and moderation in politics perceived as a great virtue. Its very success meant that Clarendon's account of the war was the dominant narrative until the publication of Gardiner's *History of the Great Civil War* late in Queen Victoria's reign, and even today its reputation is still largely untarnished outside a small group of academics specializing in seventeenth-century British history[16], but surprisingly, given that Clarendon was present at only one battle, Edgehill, military historians of the English Civil Wars continue to use his books uncritically.[17]

There are many other reasons why a primary source is not necessarily an entirely accurate record of what happened in the past. Quite frequently uncertainty about factuality is acknowledged by the writer. Sir Hugh Cholmley, for example, when attempting to explain the sudden Allied attack that began the Battle of Marston Moor, reported that it was in response to intelligence given by a Scottish deserter 'as some conjecture'.[18] Sometimes, however, uncertainty is hidden, but can be uncovered by historical method. This is particularly the case with generals' reports on battles in which they had fought. Cromwell's information about the enemy's movements before the Battle of Preston, for instance, was clearly not as accurate or as precise as he suggested in his post-campaign letter to the Speaker of the House of Commons, as other sources tell a different tale.[19]

Less frequently the writer of a primary source hides her or his lack of knowledge behind a generalized statement, which, though dressed up as something profound, is based on very shaky evidence at best. Lord Digby, in the official account of the First Battle of Newbury, for example, stated 'without partiality' that the Parliamentary army lost three times as many men as the Royalists. However, he had no means of ascertaining this, as the king's army only overran the enemy positions on Wash Common, and then only briefly.[20] Misinformation could also arise in circumstances where a contemporary writer needed to produce an explanation that would convince his readers. The two members of the Committee of Both Kingdoms accompanying Parliament's armies in the south of England in October 1644 faced such a problem when the Second Battle of Newbury ended inconclusively, despite the presence on the battlefield of the victors of Marston Moor, Oliver Cromwell's cavalry. They chose to blame enemy artillery, and their reasoning was probably based on the knowledge that most of the rest of the Committee would be aware that a single cannon ball could kill several men at once. They therefore emphasized that Cromwell's men, a stationary target whilst they were deploying, had been discomforted by heavy fire from Royalist artillery pieces sited at Donnington Castle on the north side of the battlefield. However, the small number of artillery pieces actually deployed at Donnington, their slow rate of fire, and the short length of time the cavalry were exposed to it, makes it unlikely that incoming fire was the principal explanation of why the Eastern Association cavalry under-performed at Newbury.[21]

Other blemishes that can characterize traces of the past are more clearly accidental rather than deliberate in origin. In the first place, what traces of the past record as fact may not be fact at all, but fiction resulting from faulty observation, poor memory, or errors made by informants. Writers, for example, occasionally confused left with right or placed events in the wrong order. It might be thought that such errors would be common in texts written long after a battle, but this was not necessarily so. The account of Marston Moor by 'Captain Stewart' published in London a fortnight after the battle, for example, confused infantry and cavalry when describing the problems faced by the right wing of the Allied army, though whether this was the writer's fault or that of the London editor who produced the printed version is uncertain, as only the printed version exists today.[22] Similarly Arthur Trevor, who had been close to the battlefield but not actually present at the battle, sent incorrect information about Prince Rupert's role in a letter to the Marquis of Ormond written the day after the battle. According to Trevor, the prince had fought on the victorious Royalist left wing when he had actually fought on the defeated right.[23]

Second, as with the Committee members reporting on the Second Battle of Newbury, the material the writer selects will reflect the nature of the person or audience he is addressing. Although his or her account is unlikely to be a complete pack of lies, the desire on the one hand not to place oneself in a bad light with one's superiors and on the other to gain the maximum credit for any successes, sometimes shines through very strongly. Rupert's Diary, for example, gives every sign of being self-serving. In the descriptions of the Battles of Edgehill, Marston Moor and Naseby, the main intention seems to be to blame others for what went wrong, most particularly Lords Digby and Byron. The only explanation I can give for this is that the prince knew that

Clarendon had completed his *History of the Great Rebellion*, and that he must be ready to challenge the inevitable attack on his military reputation[24] in print. But Clarendon's work was not published until 1704 and by that time both Rupert and his secretary were dead.

Alternatively, if the intention was that the report should be printed and sold, the writer might gear her or his story to their audience's interests in order to achieve the best possible sales. Typically, if a news story was intended for publication in London, it might concentrate on the performance of London regiments, as did Sergeant Henry Foster's account of the First Battle of Newbury.[25] Alternatively, the writer's main purpose might be to amuse or to divert the reader, or to get across a certain moral, political or religious message. Arthur Trevor's letters, for example, are all slightly tongue-in-cheek interspersed with colourful turns of phrase, such as the leading citizens of Shrewsbury being described as the 'foggy burghers of this town', with interesting rumour on occasions being dressed up as something rather stronger,[26] whereas some of Cromwell's letters, most particularly those written after Marston Moor and Naseby are the righteous and impressionistic rants of a man high on the stimulant of victory and therefore better evidence of his state of mind than of what had happened on the battlefield. Finally, the language used might be toned down for fear of upsetting the readers' sensibilities. Sir Edward Walker's description of Prince Rupert's strategic ideas at the start of the 1645 campaign as 'greedy' in the manuscript version he gave Lord Clarendon was replaced by a euphemism in the printed version,[27] whilst Lionel Watson's account of the departure of half the Allied army from the battlefield of Marston Moor was similarly changed from flight to retreat.[28]

In private memoirs not intended for publication the author had greater opportunity to indulge in hyperbole, especially if he or she was a loyal servant writing for their master or their master's family. Examples of this include the lives of Lord Bellasis and Colonel John Birch compiled by their secretaries Joshua Moone and Henry Roe. Moone wrote what was in essence an auto-biography, as he drew not on his own notes but on his master's memory of events. Not surprisingly the text contains very little about the performance of Bellasis's infantry brigade at Edgehill and the First Battle of Newbury, where it apparently performed badly, but waxes lyrical about its role in the storming of Bristol, where it had done well. In Roe's work, on the other hand, a true biography, not dictated memoirs, his master is portrayed as a military paragon whose advice to his superiors was invariably correct.[29] A similar type of source in which critical faculties are suppressed is the convoluted and repetitive autobiographical jottings of Sir Phillip Monckton, which were set down on paper at the time of the anti-Catholic frenzy of Charles IIs reign, but in this case the recurrent theme is that the Royalists would have won the war if the general officers had only listened to Monckton's advice.[30]

On only a very few occasions do traces of the past blatantly reveal the existence of what today would be described as spin. An illustration can be found in the discussion of the mishandling of the media in the Scot Robert Baillie's letters relating to the Battle of Marston Moor. Officers of the Eastern Association Army, who favoured religious toleration for most English Protestants rather than the imposition of a strict Presbyterian system of church government, which was the Scots' principal war aim, managed to get their account of the battle to London first. The fact that it underplayed the role of the Scottish army in the Allied victory infuriated the Scottish leadership, particularly as one of the Scots' English Presbyterian supporters, Simeon Ashe, had written in a similar vein. The final letter in the series included a strong recommendation that any subsequent reports on the campaign written by Ashe should be vetted prior to publication to ensure that they followed the party line.[31]

On most occasions, however, the existence of spin can only be inferred, as for example in the accounts of the Second Battle of Newbury written immediately after the battle by the generals and politicians who accompanied the Parliamentary forces. Disputes about who was to blame for the tactical mishandling of the battle were kept under wraps, probably because all saw the value of maintaining a common front: the chance of administering a killer blow during the campaign had been postponed, not lost forever.[32] Only after a second failure to destroy the enemy on the same battlefield two weeks later did the consensus break down and recriminations start to fly.

However, there is a factor that may serve to partially allay fears concerning the factuality of traces of the past. In the seventeenth century there were sanctions operating against the purveying of outright lies: fear of the Lord and the concept of honour that animated the upper classes. A falsity put down in print, particularly if dressed up as fact and likely to be damaging to the reputation of another person or persons, was a grievous sin that would hazard one's hope of everlasting life and result in loss of honour in this life if it was publicly shown to be untrue. It is important to bear both these points in mind when considering the veracity of a source, as they are no longer embedded in today's political culture. However, the extent to which Christian belief acted as a real deterrent is a matter of great uncertainty. In cases where factional infighting was bitter as, for example, in the rumpus over who was responsible for the disappointments of the Second Newbury campaign mentioned above, truth flew out of the window as the commanders involved sought to protect their own military reputations by blaming others. In so far as honour is concerned, the failure of memoir writers to publish their work may reflect the fact that it was so partisan and self-regarding that it was bound to attract unfavourable comment. Indeed the only memoir to be published in the immediate aftermath of the Restoration, the Duchess of Newcastle's life of her husband, deliberately avoided criticizing Newcastle's fellow Royalist generals and politicians. The other major accounts of the Civil War period written by Clarendon, Ludlow, Rushworth, Walker, Warwick, Whitelock and Bulstrode were only published after their deaths when losing honour amongst their peers and fear of God's wrath were no longer issues. However, the strict censorship that persisted from the Restoration until the Glorious Revolution may have been a more important factor in delaying publication. It is probably significant that the only long set of memoirs apart from Newcastle's to be published before 1689, Joseph Bampfield's *Apologie written by Himself*, saw the light of day in the Netherlands.[33]

Reading and Interpreting Written Traces of the Past

The extent to which traces of the past are able to transmit accurate information from the time of the Civil Wars to the present day is thus partly the result of the circumstances in which they were created, but it is also partly determined by mishaps that can happen between the act of writing the text and that text acquiring some meaning in the mind of the reader. Some mishaps are in essence errors in translation, for traces of the past that exist as seventeenth-century manuscripts need to be decodified before they can be read. The letter forms in use at the time are different from those in use today. Moreover, they are by no means standard, spelling is wayward, abbreviations are very common but not always signalled as such in the text, and the manuscript itself, if a draft, is often full of crossings out, interpolations, smudges and gaps, which militate against ease of reading. Capital letters are the most frequently misread, as for example in the case of Colonel Luke Holtby, mentioned in Rupert's Diary in November 1644, who appears as Tuke Haldby in Warburton's *Memoirs of Prince Rupert and the Cavaliers* and as Tuke Heleby in Morrah's biography of the prince.[34] This is only of minor significance, but S.R. Gardiner's misreading of Farum as Farnham rather than Fareham in a letter written by George Goring to Prince Rupert early in 1645 implied that Goring had just captured one of the principal Parliamentary garrison towns in southern England, rather than that his army was quartered thirty miles to the south close to Portsmouth, an even more important stronghold, which he probably had some hopes of capturing by stealth.[35] Similarly historians' attempts to describe the landscape over which the Battle of Marston Moor was fought have been frustrated by an early nineteenth-century reading of the word 'slow' (a ditch or area of wet ground) in Sir Phillip Monckton's account as 'glen' (a valley).[36]

Second, communication between the seventeenth and the twenty-first century is inhibited to a certain extent by changes in vocabulary. Words like field and pass, for example, had different meanings then from what they have today, whilst others like sleek do not appear in modern dictionaries. Another difficulty in reading most prose written in the mid-seventeenth century or earlier is that it is not written in short sentences interspersed with commas but in Latinate periods, often a hundred words in length, in which punctuation marks, if used at all, are often employed in an inconsistent and idiosyncratic manner. The result can be highly unsatisfactory. The writer loses his or her way amongst the subordinate clauses or fails to indicate clearly to which noun a pronoun refers; readers are left perplexed, faced as they are with choosing between a number of alternative readings.[37]

Another reason for the inaccurate transmission of information from the seventeenth century, which particularly applies to correspondence between officers, is that the writer presumes knowledge on the part of the person he is addressing which is now lost. The natural reaction of the historian in such circumstances is to try to fill the gap in knowledge by inference or by correlation with other traces of the past, and then, if the source is published, to annotate the text in order to assist the readers. Thus, in his reproduction of Thomas Stockdale's account of the Battle of Marston Moor, Peter Young appended the phrase 'Sir William Blakiston' in square brackets to the brief description of the charge by an unnamed brigade of Royalist horse against the centre of the Allied army.[38] The use of square brackets is the normal convention to indicate editorial intervention in the script, but readers may not be aware of the convention and assume that it was Stockdale who put the phrase in parentheses. Moreover, the identification of the brigade with Sir William Blakiston is not certain. It is dependent on accepting Bernard de Gomme's depiction of the deployment of the Royalist regiments at Marston Moor not as a pre-battle plan but as a representation of the way in which they were actually deployed on the day.

There are other types of modern, as opposed to contemporary, or near contemporary editorial interventions that have the potential to disrupt the way the present sees the past. One involves cutting the length of the primary source prior to publication. As a result, what the reader sees in print is what the editor considers to be the most important parts of the document. He or she may, for example, choose not to include the signatories of letters, but such names could be of considerable interest to historians who are attempting to reconstruct Civil War army lists.[39] Alternatively an editor may decide to delete whole passages. Warburton in *Memoirs of Prince Rupert and the Cavaliers*, for example, left out most of George Digby's letter to Prince Rupert written two days before the Second Battle of Newbury because it was written in code.[40] Editors may also mistakenly publish a garbled version of a primary source because they failed to locate the original version. An easily readable manuscript account by Sir Phillip Monckton of his experiences at the Battle of Marston Moor can be found in the British Library. However, successive editors of the source have misled historians by reproducing instead a truncated and inaccurate transcription that was printed in the Annual Register for 1811.[41] The examples cited above largely date from the period before standard conventions for editing came into general use, but other editorial errors, such as carelessness, are an omnipresent problem. Money's transcriptions of two of the principal Royalist reports of the first Battle of Newbury, for example, are full of minor mistakes.[42] Here, however, it is perhaps those who use Money as a short cut who are principally at fault. The original manuscripts are widely known and easy to read.

However, even the fullest and most painstaking edition of a primary source can unwittingly lead the reader and the researcher into error. The Roundway Press studies of Civil War battles contain accurate transcriptions or reproductions of primary sources relating to the battle. Some were left out, as is fully apparent from the footnotes to Peter Young's book on Edgehill. Nevertheless, recent accounts of the battle only use those that were reproduced in full.[43] In this case, it is the writers of such accounts who are to blame, but sometimes it is the editor's introduction to the source that is at fault for encouraging readers to read the source in a certain way. This is frowned on in current guides for editors such as R.F. Hunniset's *Editing Records for Publication*,[44] and is therefore less blatant than it used to be as, for example, in the mid-nineteenth century in the works of Thomas Carlyle and Eliot Warburton,[45] but the way in which the documents are chosen, explained and codified can lead the reader inadvertently towards one particular interpretative path. My edition of Worcestershire Landed Gentry Probate Inventories, for example, used a materialist model of social structure in the selection of inventories to include, rather than currently more fashionable culturally determined models. It also reproduced the inventories in order of date rather than in accordance with status, thus pointing the reader towards looking for change over time rather than for differences between the possessions of knights and those of mere gentlemen.[46] However, being led by the nose in one interpretative direction is much more of a problem when the traces of the past are not freestanding documents but extracts taken from many primary sources and then strung together with pieces of text to form a battle narrative.[47]

Summing up, the act of reading a printed primary source is superficially easy, but comprehending it is difficult and time-consuming. Traces of the past need to be read over and over again if the seventeenth century is to communicate, however imperfectly, with the twenty-first. That is the only way in which the information the author intended to convey to the reader can be understood, albeit partially. There is also the need to query the text. To what extent is the piece of writing positioned? Has it been tampered with? If there are several versions, how and why do they differ from one another? This process, which could be described as an elementary type of deconstruction, is necessary as part of an informed discussion of the extent to which the writer is likely to have produced a fictive, as opposed to a factual, account, for posterity. A definitive verdict on the factuality of every clause or phrase in a source is, of course, impossible, but if the precautions listed above are not taken, the twenty-first-century narrative will be a less accurate representation of what happened in the past than it could or should be.

Landscape and Archaeology

The landscape over which a battle was fought had a major impact on how it was fought. Traces of the past therefore often mention features in the landscape, but they tend to be brought into the argument as much to explain why the battle did not develop in the way it should have done as to help the reader's understanding. Not surprisingly, attempts to conflate all the traces of the past relating to an important feature, such as the ditch that lay between the armies at Marston Moor, often grind to a halt in a morass of conflicting information. Other types of primary evidence, such as contemporary maps and diagrams, display similar defects in supplying the present with an unambiguous picture of the mid-seventeenth-century landscape. In the first place the countryside in 1642 had not been comprehensively mapped other than at a scale of about five miles to the inch, which is far too small to be of help to the military historian in trying to reconstruct a Civil War battle. The earliest maps to be drawn to a scale large enough to be useful were not published until the middle years of the eighteenth century. They frequently delineate cultivated land as opposed to heath, moor and marsh, but only Rocque distinguished systematically between heath land, open field and enclosed landscapes.[48] The big problem for the historian in using such maps, however, is not the accuracy of the detail, but the fact that a lot had happened to the landscape in the intervening hundred years. Much of the parish of Long Marston, for example, was enclosed just before Thomas Jeffereys completed his research for the first large-scale map of Yorkshire in the late 1750s.

The only engraving to accompany a contemporary narrative is Streeter's depiction of the armies as they were deployed at the start of the Battle of Naseby, which accompanied Joshua Sprigg's *Anglia Rediviva* published in 1647. Its shortcomings are discussed in Chapter 14.[49] All that needs to be said for the moment is that Streeter spread the New Model Army across three miles rather than a mile and a half of the Northamptonshire countryside for what were almost certainly presentational reasons. If he had portrayed the deployment accurately, his map of the battlefield would have been exceedingly cluttered, as indeed the battlefield had been in reality. The only other near contemporary depictions of Civil War battles are de Gomme's four water-colours produced in their final form after the Restoration, but he is primarily concerned with showing how the Royalist armies were drawn up. Only in the case of Marston Moor and the so-called Third Battle of Newbury does he provide any information about physical features on the battlefield itself that are not obvious from the written accounts.[50]

Methodologies developed by geographers, environmental scientists and local historians for recovering past landscapes from the landscape that exists today, such as dating hedgerows by the number of species they contain, and determining past land use via soil surveys and pollen analysis, are insufficiently precise to shed much light on a short time period like that of the English Civil

Wars. However, the depositing of estate archives in county record offices since the Second World War has facilitated the reconstruction of the mid-seventeenth-century landscape using traditional methods. Large-scale maps dating from the period 1600 to 1720 which often accompany surveys are not particularly uncommon, but the only one known to exist today that depicts a Civil War battlefield was drawn with the sole purpose of showing the exact location of the pieces of land in the open fields of the parish of Naseby owned by the lord of the manor.[51] It is therefore most disappointing in the information it provides about tracks and heath land, and it does not extend over that part of the battlefield which fell within the bounds of Sibbertoft parish. The early seventeenth-century survey of the Bishop of Winchester's lands in Cheriton is a little more informative despite not being accompanied by a map, but it focuses on the enclosed land of the parish rather than on the area covered by Cheriton Wood where the fighting began.[52] Eighteenth-century maps of parishes, such as that of Radway, which covers part of the Edgehill battlefield and predates enclosure,[53] maps and surveys that accompanied the Parliamentary enclosure of Newbury, Speen and Enbourne, and tithe apportionment maps of the late 1830s and early 1840s, are all of considerable value, particularly when they contain clues concerning the position of topographical features that had disappeared by the time of the publication of the first six inch to the mile maps in the 1880s.[54] However, even the one inch to the square mile Ordnance Survey maps produced some fifty years earlier are useful in that they depict a stage in the evolution of the landscape that predates extensive urbanization.

Some work on battlefield landscapes has been published, but the end result is a little disappointing. The best is contained in recent works on Naseby and Edgehill,[55] but overall the authors' conclusions tend to be interesting rather than convincing because of the partial and problematic nature of some of the evidence on which they draw. Archaeology is a different matter altogether. Already a new version of the closing stages of the Battle of Naseby based on field archaeology alone is becoming close to an orthodoxy,[56] and much is promised from a more comprehensive analysis of finds from the battlefield at Edgehill. However, it is vitally important not to be so led astray by enthusiasm for the new as to forget to appraise the archaeological data as systematically as written traces of the past.

First, as implied above, many Civil War battlefields can no longer be subjected to a rigorously scientific archaeological investigation. The sites where the first encounters took place at Preston and at First and Second Newbury, for example, have largely been built over, whilst a Royal Ordnance Department depot and staff living accommodation cover the Parliamentary position at Edgehill. Second, the only artefacts to occur in considerable numbers in an archaeological context are musket balls.[57] Being made of lead, they survive well under the ground, but can be dissolved by tannic acid if immersed for too long in peaty soil. This may be a factor in explaining why there are few musket balls in that part of the Marston Moor battlefield where written sources suggest the main infantry encounter took place.[58] However, the soils covering other battlefields discussed in this volume are not inimical to the survival of objects made of lead. Third, artefacts discovered as a result of field walking or metal detecting do not come from a pristine archaeological setting but from one that has been disturbed time and time again over the past 350 years. Even in the case of battlefields that are still largely farmland, such as those of Naseby and Cheriton, diagrams recording the distribution of musket balls do not necessarily show a pattern that is truly representative of all those fired on the day.[59] Many, for example, will have disappeared from the battlefield since the 1640s through human activity. The most accessible parts will have been systematically stripped over the centuries by farm labourers and children of the village, and the musket balls sold to visitors, retained as keepsakes, deposited elsewhere, or melted down and converted into something more useful. However, in other parts of the battlefield, most particularly those under permanent grass, the archaeology may hardly have been touched, but locating musket balls in such circumstances is much less easy than in the case of arable, as field walking will yield nothing and basic metal detecting not much more.

There are other reasons why musket balls may not be where they first came to rest after having been fired. Those that finished up on a slope will tend to drift downhill over time under the influence of gravity, a process known as 'creep'. In addition, a heavy concentration of finds consisting almost entirely of musket balls that have not been distorted by hitting a target will indicate the last resting place of an overturned munitions wagon, not heavy incoming fire. Similarly, small deposits of musket balls found along escape routes from the battlefield do not necessarily indicate encounters between the pursuers and the pursued. They may merely be evidence of individual strategies for survival as escapees got rid of their cumbersome bandoliers, which might still contain a dozen or more musket balls.

Moreover, plotting musket balls on a diagram of a battle that excludes those which might represent the contents of an overturned wagon, those that might have 'crept' away from their original position, and those that might have been discarded by musketeers as they fled from the field, is not that informative as to where the principal firefights took place. First, although it is possible to estimate roughly how far away from a concentration of musket balls the musketeers responsible for the incoming fire are likely to have been, the historian can discover nothing about the target at which the fire was being directed. Second, the final resting place of those balls that penetrated the flesh of men or horses is likely to have been off the battlefield or in a burial pit rather than in the place where the wound was inflicted. Third, musket balls that hit a solid target are more likely to have disintegrated completely over the centuries than those that did not, as the more irregular surface area of the former would have made them more susceptible to decay. Finally, some of the published maps of the distribution of musket balls are insufficiently precise as they fail to distinguish adequately between those that had hit a target and those that probably had not, or between musket balls and other battlefield artefacts. Even so, however careful and scientifically sensitive the field archaeology has been, the distribution maps that are drawn subsequently can only give a rough indication of the spread and density of musket fire. Conclusions drawn from such maps should therefore be described as hypothetical, not factual, in that they depict what survives today, not what was there in the mid-seventeenth century. As with exercises in the statistical manipulation of traces of the past, so fashionable with professional historians in the 1960s and early 1970s, field archaeology conducted on battlefield sites will tend not to answer questions, but to create new ones. These in their turn can best be addressed by integrating the research methods of the archaeologist with those of the historian.

Somewhat similar caveats apply to the contribution of re-enactors to the understanding of the English Civil Wars.[60] Their work in reconstructing what happened on the battlefield is not merely a pastime in which men and women dress up in period costume and threaten to do serious damage to one another. It is truly a branch of experimental archaeology in that it tells the world what was or was not possible with the weapons available in the mid-seventeenth century. As such, it is a most valuable adjunct to the historical process. Its emphasis on the importance of drill in enabling battalions of infantry to function effectively is very important. Its role in raising the profile of the infantry is equally important.[61] However, care must be taken when trying to recreate what happened on a battlefield or in lesser encounters to ensure that the whole process is not straitjacketed by what was written in military treatises that were in print in the early 1640s. The complex drill sequences described and illustrated in such books were an ideal, as the great captains of the time realized. The extent to which parade ground drill worked in practice once the battle was under way is a matter of considerable uncertainty. There is certainly some evidence that it did have a place on the Civil War battlefield, but Walter Slingsby's description of the firing by ranks by Lord Hopton's regiment at Cheriton, and accounts of the success of the London Trained Bands against Royalist cavalry during the Gloucester and Newbury campaign in 1643, may represent the exceptions rather than the rule.[62] Once the two battle lines became locked in hand-to-hand conflict, the ability of individual brigades or battalions to operate as mobile castles would have come to an end. However, when uncommitted formations entered the fight to unscramble such mêlées, the effects of properly managed musketry fire could be devastating.[63]

Conclusion

Thus traces of the past present the historian with three different types of information. The first is factual, such as that the First Battle of Newbury was fought on 20 September 1643, or that Lord John Stuart was mortally wounded at the Battle of Cheriton, both of which were attested time and time again in sources written at the time. The second is fiction, such as the description of the Earl of Caernarvon's deathbed scene in Daniel Defoe's *Memoirs of a Cavalier*. However, the majority of the traces of the past cannot be placed in one category or the other, and these will be described as opinion. The first two categories are absolutes – fact is fact and fiction fiction. The third, however, is a variable perhaps best pictured as a sliding scale between fact and fiction. Historians can and do spend much time discussing whether specific traces of the past are in the wrong place on the scale. However, although I may argue strongly that something in the second category is true or false, my view can be no more than a hypothesis unless I am able to show that the case for so doing is incontrovertible.

Chapter 3
Civil War Battles
Narrative

Characteristics of the Narrative Form

History is not the past, it is what historians write about the past using the traces of the past that have survived into the present. Reconstructing what happened in a battle, as with reconstructing other historical occasions or events, entails placing the traces of the past into a narrative that describes what happened, the usual objective being to explain how the battle ended as it did. The narrative is not an act of resurrection. It cannot bring the past back to life, even though this is a very common accolade given to a fine piece of historical writing. It also cannot be definitive, given how little evidence survives from the past and the uncertainties that surround much of what does.

The process of writing a historical narrative can be seen as similar to the work of a jeweller, who threads beads, the traces of the past, onto a string, the historical argument, to create a necklace, the narrative. In doing so, the jeweller will draw on expertise acquired during her or his apprenticeship and training. A historian will similarly draw on a corpus of knowledge derived from research, and on a pool of skills in using language and evidence acquired through study, instruction and practice, to construct a convincing narrative. The jeweller will need to sell the necklace to cover costs, and she or he will draw on their business acumen to make its appearance and price as attractive as possible to potential customers. Similarly, a historian will tailor his or her narrative to the audience for which it is intended, be that audience non-historians, who might be encountered when addressing, for example, a Rotary Club meeting, or top professionals such as the editorial committee of a learned journal. Finally, aesthetic judgement and a range of other factors will serve to differentiate one jeweller's necklace from another, even if they are aiming their product at a specific, narrowly defined sector of the market. In the same way, historians, even if they use identical traces of the past and read identical secondary sources, will not produce identical accounts of the same battle because of differences in their life experience, family background, gender, education, religion, leisure interests, and so on.[1] A strong attachment towards Gladstonian Liberalism and his earlier commitment to the Irvingite brand of Protestant Nonconformity,[2] for example, probably help to explain S.R. Gardiner's hero worship of Oliver Cromwell, which pervades and to some extent distorts his narrative of the First Civil War. His description of the victory of Cromwell's cavalry on the left wing of the Allied army at Marston Moor makes it sound a comparatively easy task. A check administered by Prince Rupert's second line and reserves was only momentary. Thereafter Cromwell's troopers and their Scottish allies steadily pushed back Rupert's previously undefeated cavalry, at last 'scattering them like a little dust'.[3] Other historians, however, using a wider set of traces of the past, describe a static, hard-fought fight lasting half an hour or so.[4]

A multiplicity of different narratives is not a recipe for peace and calm in a subject most of whose practitioners have a modernist faith that research, if properly conducted, will result in progress towards fuller, if inevitably incomplete, knowledge of what happened in the past. Assaults on narratives written by others normally focus on such matters as errors in the logic of the argument or deficiencies in the evidence underpinning it. Alternatively, the critic may draw on skills acquired in another profession to suggest new insights into old problems, as in the case of army officer historians of the English Civil Wars from Colonel Ross to Sir Frank Kitson. Achieving a balance, however, is difficult, particularly if one of the three causes of conflict between human beings identified by Thomas Hobbes lies somewhere in the background: 'every man looketh that others should value him at the same rate he sets upon himself.'[5]

In the first book to give due weighting to non-written traces of the past in its analysis of a Civil War battle, Scott, Turton and Von Arni's study of Edgehill, there are slight hints of Hobbes's aphorism in remarks to the effect that it is fashionable to belittle the thoughts of re-enactors, and that the authors have some concern that their opinions might not be acceptable to more traditional or more enlightened readers. Their declared aim is to raise the study of archaeology and the landscape to an equal footing with documentary analysis in researching what happened on the Civil War battlefield. They nevertheless promise a synthesis of the three methodologies,[6] and it is only on very rare occasions that they fail to achieve a judicious balance. One such example is their discussion of whether the Royalist infantry was deployed in five or in nine brigades as it advanced towards the enemy line at the start of the battle. Here they use their reading of the landscape to prioritize one written source and to explain away two others, in my opinion incorrectly.[7]

A further fruitful cause of discord between narratives principally relates to the different ways in which individual historians read traces of the past. Variant readings that are the accidental effects of the decoding process have been described in Chapter 2. The rest occur at the final stage in the transmission of information from the past to the present when the reader is attaching meaning and significance to passages in the primary source. This will duly inform decisions about if, where, and in what form the traces of the past are to be incorporated into the narrative. Here, judgement can sometimes go astray as, for example, when the narrator experiences a moment of blindness caused by the intense light generated by a new hypothesis.[8] However, the most common cause of discord between historians lies in the nature of language itself. It is now an axiom in the Humanities that language is an inexact means of communication between people who are contemporaries. How much more so then is communication a problem when it has to take place across both time and space? In such circumstances it is scarcely surprising that two researchers using the same set of primary sources will often reach very different conclusions neither of which is necessarily superior to the other.[9]

My intention, however, is not to imply in any way that all readings are equally valid. It is perfectly possible for one reading of a text to supersede another as a result of new research. For example, my appraisal of the evidence that S.R. Gardiner used to explain the king's strategy for 1643 in terms of a threefold advance on London showed that one of his two sources had been incorrectly read and that the other related to a different year.[10] Thus traces of the past do help to alter the way in which the present sees the past. However, for much of the time the flow is in the opposite direction. The now-present uses traces from the past to create new narratives which are very much positioned in that present, and which could not have been written at any other time in the way that they were in terms of the language used, the concepts employed, the preconceptions and knowledge assumed, and the conventions that underpin the argument. What is politically correct or academically fashionable in one generation, for example, is not so in another.

Although some narratives of Civil War battles are no more than rearrangements of familiar primary and secondary materials, most historians aspire to a more positive role and endeavour to impose their own inter-pretation on the past. This is commendable, provided that the point at which the narrative heads off into the realms of hypothesis is clearly indicated in the language used, and that historians are as careful in appraising the traces of the past that support their hypotheses as they are in drawing attention to the shortcomings of the writings of others in this respect. It could, for example, be argued that Stuart Reid falls into this trap in his account of the fighting on the Royalist right wing at the Battle of Marston Moor.[11] He begins very convincingly by expressing misgivings about both Prince Rupert's claim that Sir John Byron counter-charged Cromwell's Eastern Association cavalry instead of remaining on the defensive as ordered, and assertions made in accounts written by Northern Royalists that Rupert's regiments fled quickly from the battlefield. However, he then continues with a forthright reiteration of the long-established view that it was the intervention by Cromwell's third line of horse, comprising 900 or so Scottish cavalry led by David Leslie, which eventually decided the day. However, Leslie's charge is not a historical fact by the strictest definition of fact. Indeed, what actually happened in the cavalry engagement on the Royalist right wing provoked great controversy within days of the battle and again several years afterwards.[12] Reid then ends by stating that Leslie took some time to make his presence felt because he was initially involved in an encounter with some Royalist infantry.[13] However, the fight with the infantry is only described in a single account written soon after the battle, the one usually described as Captain Stewart's, and the officer who wrote it did not have first-hand knowledge of the encounter, as he fought on the opposite wing.[14] Moreover, the encounter could not have taken place as Reid describes because of the relative position of the two bodies of men. The Scottish cavalry regiments were to the rear and well to the left of the place where the enemy foot were deployed. To get at them Leslie's men would have had to force their way through their own infantry.

If it is extremely important not to be swept away by the persuasiveness of one's hypotheses, so is it equally important not to go to the opposite extreme and rely excessively on the work of other historians. Amongst Civil War historians, trusting in the professional skills and the integrity of distinguished forebears is too widespread. It is still common practice, for example, when requiring information concerning what happened when, to place complete confidence in the works of S.R. Gardiner, but he made mistakes.[15] One should, of course, be fully informed about what others have written, but it is essential to check not only the logic of their argument, but also the provenance, accuracy and relevance of the traces of the past that underpin it, as every historian, however distinguished, is capable of weak scholarship on occasions. What can happen if one is too trusting is well illustrated by the myth that has accrued around Sir Thomas Fairfax's personal contribution towards the tactical decisions that secured victory for the Allied armies at the Battle of Marston Moor. The canonical version runs as follows. After the Allied right wing, which he commanded, had been put to flight by the king's Northern Horse, Fairfax rode through the ranks of victorious Royalists to bring news of the disaster to Oliver Cromwell, who had just routed the other wing of the Royalist army. As a result Cromwell put in train a second cavalry action that decided the battle and with it the fate of the north of England. Sir Clement Markham was the first historian to propose this sequence of events and, despite some slight equivocation on Gardiner's part,[16] almost every narrative of Marston Moor written since has followed Markham's lead.[17] Fairfax may indeed have been the messenger, but it seems unlikely for two reasons. First, it is odd that primary sources written by Allied commanders are silent on this point, whilst paying great attention to Sir Thomas's escape from the collapse of the Allied right wing. Second, it is even odder that Fairfax himself did not mention it in his own writings. Sir Thomas was famous for his modesty but not when his own military reputation was at stake. For instance, he took umbrage at the notion, mentioned by Thomas Fuller, that his wing had fled without a fight and added a note to his memoirs to that effect.[18]

Methodology

The first step in writing a battle narrative must be to collect together all the traces of the past relating to the battle being investigated. This may seem obvious, but it is quite clearly not. Three recent accounts of the First Battle of Newbury, for example, would have benefited enormously from looking at Prince Rupert's Diary, parts of which Peter Young reproduced in his books on Edgehill and Marston Moor, together with clear directions as to where it was to be found.[19] The traces of the past must then be read again and again throughout the process of research and writing. This process of continuously addressing the traces of the past should continue into the writing phase and beyond, as even at the last moment reading them in a different order or under different circumstances can produce new insights even in a source with which one is extremely familiar. However, repeated reading will not necessarily produce results in the short run or even in the medium term. In my own case, the first inkling that Adair might have been substantially correct about the site of the Battle of Cheriton, and everybody else wrong including me, came from rereading for the umpteenth time Lord Hopton's account of the battle, which I have used in teaching and research for over forty years.

The most logical next step in writing a narrative is to use the traces of the past to endeavour to establish a timeline recording the order in which events occurred from the start of the battle until fighting ceased.[20] In the strictest sense this is not usually possible. Traces of the past rarely attempt to estimate the duration of the various stages of a battle, and when they do there is often a wide measure of disagreement between them.[21] This is not surprising, given what happens to individuals' perceptions of the passage of time in periods of acute stress, but there are often major discrepancies between primary sources even as to the hour of the day a battle began. Only in the case of the First Battle of Newbury and the Battle of Naseby is there a very clear agreement about when the fighting started. In the case of Marston Moor, the times mentioned in primary sources range from mid-afternoon to mid-evening, a period of some three and a half hours. In the case of the Second Battle of Newbury the variation is only an hour and a half, that is between 2 p.m. and 3.30 p.m., but the time at which the fighting began is crucial to discussions as to whether the battle was winnable before nightfall on a late October day.[22]

If, however, the measurement of time is an inexact science in so far as witnesses of most Civil War battles are concerned, this does not invalidate the timeline technique as a means of reconstructing the narrative framework.

The order in which events occurred is often of far more significance than the exact time, and fortunately many contemporary accounts of battles have a chronological framework. However, they do not necessarily provide a comprehensive and coherent chronology of the battle from beginning to end. Some focus on the experiences of a single unit for part of the time like, for example, Sergeant Foster's account of the First Battle of Newbury.[23] Others describe what happened on one sector of the battlefield from beginning to end and then repeat the process with another, as in the official Parliamentary accounts of Edgehill and the First Battle of Newbury and Joshua Sprigg's account of Naseby.[24] Finally, some participants place events in the wrong order, as is the case with Captain Stewart's account of the Battle of Marston Moor mentioned above.[25] Nevertheless, by using the procedures listed in the final section of this chapter it is usually possible to establish a timeline that is very largely factual for the first and last stages of the battle, even if the order of events in the middle part of the battle, when most participants were thoroughly preoccupied with their immediate surroundings, is often unclear.

The next step is to flesh out the timeline. A comparison has often been drawn between this stage in the process of writing a battle narrative and trying to complete a jigsaw puzzle,[26] but it is a false one. Admittedly traces of the past superficially resemble jigsaw pieces in their diversity and in the multiplicity of ways they seem capable of being interconnected, but underlying the analogy is an assumption that the pieces were once part of a larger picture that can be reconstructed provided they are put together in the right way. This is not true of the historical process. As explained above, the past cannot be reconstructed in its entirety, as we do not have all the pieces, and the pieces we do have are not necessarily true representations of the past. Also, the historian, when attempting to reconstruct what happened in a battle, does not have a small version of the full picture from which to work, but instead a large number of partial and conflicting narratives, some written by contemporaries, some by historians.

As some of the traces of the past are factual, some probably fictional, and the majority impossible to place in one category or the other, it should not be surprising that trying to slot them together jigsaw-fashion can quickly lead to an impasse, with one source suggesting that such and such happened and another something rather different. With much subtle use of language, a small discrepancy may be papered over or explained away, but what is to be done if the incompatibility is so great that the two sources cannot be reconciled? The most tempting procedure in such circumstances is to prioritize the source that fits more comfortably into one's preferred narrative, and then either to discredit the other or else to ignore it altogether. In Young and Holmes's description of the cavalry action on the Royalist right wing at Marston Moor, for example, the notion that Leslie's charge discussed above decided the matter is taken as fact. There is no comment to the effect that Lionel Watson's account of the battle, which is used as supportive evidence in the preceding sentence, does not mention it at all.[27]

Having collected the traces of the past, they need to be structured in such a way as to tell a tale. The temptation is to allow the traces of the past to bear the strain by constructing a narrative made up of large chunks of primary source strung together by small passages of texts.[28] This is a highly questionable procedure. In the first place, as stated in the previous chapter and earlier in this chapter, the passages put in quotation marks may be open to a variety of interpretations. Second, quotations from contemporary texts can give a spurious validity to the argument, as they are as likely to be positioned as any modern text. A degree of deconstruction is almost certainly needed even if the quotation is merely describing what happened. By incorporating raw seventeenth-century prose into the narrative without a measure of critique, the author is guilty of avoiding his responsibility.[29]

A less risky way of achieving a balanced narrative is to separate out the traces of the past that clearly belong to a specific stage in the timeline. It will then become apparent that some of the sources are mutually supportive and others not. With two or more saying the same thing, the relationship between the narrative and what actually happened on the battlefield becomes very much closer, as what was initially opinion, in that it derived from a single trace of the past, converges on fact through a process of cross-referral. There is, however, one extremely important caveat. For opinion to move towards becoming fact in this way, it is essential, particularly if only two sources are involved, that they are not in any sense dependent upon one another, the most likely example of interdependency being if the more recent of the two sources in terms of date had access to what his or her precursor had written. If there is any suspicion of this, then opinion must remain opinion.[30] The best type of supportive evidence is therefore an account written on the same day by somebody who fought in the battle on the other side. Conversely, a piece of evidence, however well regarded, which is not validated by another trace of the past, cannot be treated in the narrative as if it were factual. It is opinion, and a form of words must be used to identify it as such and to indicate where it stands on the spectrum between fact and fiction. Finally, if two traces of the past tell different tales, they must both be classed as opinion and their respective merits discussed in the narrative. Neither can be dismissed as fiction, however famous or respected its counterpart might be, until additional pieces of evidence come to light that serve to validate one or the other.

By such means a narrative can be compiled that gives due weighting to what is fact and what is opinion without doing injustice to either, but inevitably there will be gaps in the narrative in places where no traces of the past have survived into the present. To fill these Colonel A.H. Burne applied a technique that he described as inherent military probability (i.m.p.). Having discarded evidence concerning battles that is exaggerated, distorted due to misconceptions, or even deliberately fabricated, 'there is not much pure grain left. ... Something more is required if the battle is to be depicted with any precision and detail'. Burne's method was to begin with what seemed to be undisputed facts, then to try to supplement them by placing himself in the shoes of each commander in turn and asking himself what he would have done in the circumstances given the landscape over which the battle was fought. He then compared his hypothesis with the 'pure grain' to ascertain if it was or was not compatible with it. If it was compatible, he then repeated the process 'with the next debatable or obscure point in the battle'.[31]

This is a sensible way of using one's own professional expertise to develop new hypotheses, even though Burne's use of the word 'precision' is a cause for some concern, as it suggests that conclusions that emerge from i.m.p.-type reasoning will be regarded as factual rather than hypothetical. However, a careful reading of Burne's books shows that, once one gets used to the brusqueness of his language, the argument tends to be cautious rather than dogmatic when he uses i.m.p. to fill gaps in primary sources or to explain away discrepancies between them. If his example is followed, there can be no quarrel with using inherent military probability as a technique for developing hypotheses concerning what might have happened on the battlefield.

Another way of plugging gaps in the narrative is much more problematic, the use of analogies drawn from contemporary military textbooks or from what happened in other battles of the mid-seventeenth century. This technique is fine if, like i.m.p. as used by Burne, it is confined to the formulation of new hypotheses, but it is wrong to assume that the same circumstances will recur or that theory concerning the conduct of war is a superior kind of knowledge when it is confronted by traces of the past that suggest something different. For instance, in two recent narratives of the First Battle of Newbury evidence provided by eyewitnesses on both sides concerning the deployment of the Parliamentary cavalry is ignored, perhaps because it does not conform to what is found in some military manuals or to how Civil War armies were deployed at Edgehill, Naseby and Marston Moor.[32]

Maps and Illustrations
Books on the English Civil Wars make extensive use of maps and battle plans to illustrate, or in the case of the recent work written by Frank Jones and myself, to serve almost as a substitute for a written narrative. However, the fact that words are only to be found in the heading, the key, and the occasional personal name or physical feature does not mean that maps and battle diagrams are in any way free from the kinds of criticisms made of written texts, be they traces of the past or the work of historians. In the first place, although the template, that is the map on which the historian places military formations, may appear not to be the historian's construct, it is exactly that in the sense that she or he

chooses what to include and what not to include – towns, rivers, roads, hills, wet lands, contour lines, parish boundaries, hedge lines and so on. These may be factual in one respect, in that their spatial relationship to one another is fixed by something other than the historian's will. However, the selection of features to include or exclude will depend upon the nature of the narrative she or he has written, and this is obvious from the widespread use of the term illustration to describe materials that are designed to help the reader understand the text. Moreover, maps like written narratives can include elements that are matters of opinion, and, as in written narratives, they may not always be signposted as such. In various representations of the Battle of Cheriton in secondary sources, for example, the Royalist cavalry brigades are allotted various positions to the left and rear of their infantry that have no foundation in primary sources.[33]

Finally, as with written sources, maps that accompany military histories of the English Civil Wars sometimes contain errors. For example, a recent account of the First Newbury Campaign includes one purporting to represent the areas of England controlled by the forces of the king and those of Parliament in September 1643, but it is merely a redrawing of a map of May 1643 from Gardiner's *History of the Great Civil War*, when the Royalists controlled much less territory, with the added error that Birmingham is depicted as if it was in Royalist hands.[34] Similarly, a recent account of fighting in the north of England in 1644 has Sir Thomas Fairfax advancing to the relief of Nantwich from Leicestershire rather than from Lancashire.[35] Definitive maps of the battlefield are thus as much of a delusion as definitive narratives; what they do or do not include is dependent on the will of the historian.

Conclusion

In the last two chapters various procedures have been discussed for ensuring that battle narratives are as accurate a record of what happened on the battlefield as possible, whilst recognizing that definitive narratives are an impossible dream, given the factual shortcomings of primary sources and the effects of the narrators' own prejudices and idiosyncrasies. These procedures are listed below.[36] Sadly, there is nothing particularly new about any of them. They are merely examples of good practice and quality control that should be applied universally to the study of the past.

1. Most information to be found in traces of the past is opinion, not fact.
2. When dealing with a trace of the past that is opinion, its position on the sliding scale between fact and fiction should be determined by cross-referencing with other traces of the past that have not influenced it and not been influenced by it.
3. When two primary sources tell different stories about the past, neither can be regarded as factual, but strenuous efforts should be made to rank them in terms of their probability.

4. Very close attention must be paid to the language used by the writer of the trace of the past in order to ascertain exactly what information she or he hoped to implant in a reader's mind. This will require the source being read over and over again across the whole period in which the narrative is being researched and written.
5. Particular care should be taken to use the earliest form of a primary source when selecting evidence to be included in the battle narrative.
6. Every effort should be made via textual and cross-textual analysis to assess the likelihood that the writer or the editor of the source has given a particular spin to the text.
7. In the battle narrative any evidence used to underpin the argument that is not factual in nature must be accompanied by a form of words showing that it is opinion.
8. Non-written sources must be subjected to the same degree of rigorous critical examination as written ones.
9. Military theory, whether culled from seventeenth-century publications or from secondary sources, should be regarded as an aid to understanding and a seedbed for the development of new hypotheses, not as material of a factual nature for filling in gaps in the narrative.
10. Battlefield plans that accompany the narrative must be accurate and be presented in such a way as to enable the reader to distinguish at a glance between what is factual and what is opinion.

Part II

The Decisive Battles of 1642 and 1643

Chapter 4

The Battle of Edgehill
Context, Landscape and Sources

Context

The Great English Civil War broke out in June 1642. The issues that caused the deep fissure in English society were well recognized at the time as being directly or indirectly religious in nature. Many followers of the king wished to maintain the forms of worship as established in Queen Elizabeth's reign and to preserve government of the church by bishops; many followers of Parliament wanted a more or less radical reform of the Church. Those who were terrified of a Catholic conspiracy to overthrow the Protestant Reformation in England tended to see Parliament as a more reliable defence than the king, who had a Catholic queen and a number of Catholic courtiers and favoured a form of High Church Anglicanism. Similarly, many Catholics saw the king as likely to be less of a danger to the practice of their faith than Parliament. It has also been argued, much less convincingly, that those who enjoyed elements of popular culture disliked by Protestant radicals as occasions for sin or Romish survivals saw the king as more likely than Parliament to allow them to continue their traditional practices. Another factor in the pattern of allegiance in 1642 was the extent to which the king was or was not seen as a threat to the liberties of his subjects with regard to equality before the law and freedom from arbitrary taxes. However, these are generalizations driven by what was written down at the time and what survives today. The extent to which such considerations were superseded at the level of the individual by considerations of self-interest and self-preservation in individual circumstances cannot be known. Towns happily switched from neutrality to enthusiastic support as soon as an army arrived in their vicinity, whereas the evidence for the very poor in the only English community for which we have a near contemporary analysis of those who fought for King or Parliament, Myddle in Shropshire, is equivocal. The men who joined the king's army in 1642 were just the kind of people the village elite would have put pressure on to leave the parish, as they were an actual or potential charge on the poor rate. On the other hand they themselves may have seen volunteering for the army as a way of escaping from the bottom of the social heap.[1]

Charles I drew soldiers from the north of England and the East Midlands to his headquarters at Nottingham; Parliament drew theirs primarily from London and its environs. However, the king's attempts to move into the central Midlands were frustrated in August by the resistance of Coventry and the timely arrival of a corps of the new Parliamentary army. He therefore marched his troops westwards to Shrewsbury, an ideal place of rendezvous for Royalist regiments raising in Wales and the north-west of England. Parliament's commander, the Earl of Essex, thereupon moved his field army from Northampton to Worcester. Up to that point Essex had done well by using contingents from the field army to secure the counties of the south of England, the Thames valley and the central Midlands. The king had done less well, with only the extreme north of England totally secure, and troops apparently coming in less easily to his army than to Parliament's.[2] However, having established a corridor of garrisons between Worcester and the Welsh border to prevent troops from South Wales and the south-west joining the king, Essex sat back and tried negotiation. Nothing further was done to intercept the king's regiments marching to Shrewsbury, possibly because of the psychological shock caused by Prince Rupert's victory at brigade level over horse and dragoons from Parliament's field army at Powick just to the south of Worcester on 23 September.

In mid-October, as its last detachments converged on Shropshire from the north-west and south Wales, the king's army began its advance. By sending troops to the south and the north of Birmingham Charles managed to confuse Essex as to his intentions, with the result that when it became clear that Charles was advancing towards London rather than down the Severn valley or back into the East Midlands, the Parliamentary army was a day's march behind. Blundering out of Worcester in pursuit, Essex's advance guard ran into troops from the Royalist rearguard at the small town of Kineton between Warwick and Banbury on the evening of Saturday 22 October. Deciding that this gave him a good chance to do battle in favourable circumstances, the king ordered his troops to backtrack and assemble the following morning on Edgehill, an escarpment two miles long and some 700 feet above sea level running in a north-east/south-west direction and overlooking the flat lands of central Warwickshire.[3] Meanwhile Essex drew up such of his army as had arrived in a position covering Kineton.

Landscape

The Battle of Edgehill was not fought on Edgehill. Neither was it fought in and around the small town of Kineton, which lay three miles to the north-west, despite the fact that this was a common name for the battle in the seventeenth century. Instead it was fought in a large tract of open country between the two,

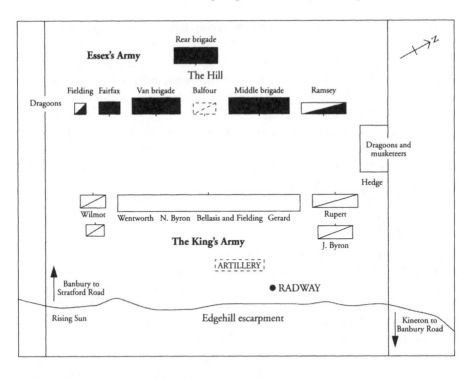

Key

☐ Royalist Infantry

▨ Royalist Cavalry

■ Essex's Infantry

◣ Essex's Cavalry

⌐ ⌐ Location uncertain

Map 1. The Battle of Edgehill

known at the time as the Vale of the Red Horse. Part of this was hay meadow and arable belonging to the parishes of Radway and Tysoe. Most of the rest was arable belonging to the parishes of Kineton, Oxhill and Radway, which by mid-October was ploughed ready for the next growing season.[4] There was probably some poorer quality land on the western fringes of the battlefield, as indicated by later field and farm names such as Starveall, Moorlands and Hardwick Gorse. Unlike the rest of the battlefield, this area was probably not farmed in a systematic way but simply used as rough grazing, and as such full of brambles and other types of undergrowth capable of disrupting the movement of formations of horse and foot. However, it is not the case that the entire ground over which the battle was fought was of this nature, as claimed by the authors of a recent book on Edgehill: that is, lowland and upland heath and 'open moorland' for the most part.[5]

About 200 yards to the west of the Kineton–Banbury road (the B4086) and midway between the Edgehill ridge and Kineton, there is a slight elevation in the ground which runs parallel to the ridge for the space of about a mile.[6] At the time it was described as 'a little round rising hill'. Today the rise is so slight that it is difficult to discern on maps and on the ground,[7] but it can be seen quite clearly in the distance from the Leamington to Banbury railway line. On and around this smallest of elevations the whole of Essex's army drew up before the start of the battle.[8] Seeing them adopting such a position, the Royalists descended into the vale, drew up in battle formation as described below, and advanced towards them.[9]

The Edgehill battlefield was the most open of all the major Civil War battlefields, with few physical features to give advantage to the attacker or the defender. Only in the extreme eastern part close to the Kineton–Banbury road were there small, hedged fields, probably in the location described in later maps as Radway grounds.[10] Various streams are marked on modern maps, but they cannot have posed much of a problem for the Royalists as they advanced. They were all very close to their source and therefore carried little water. The extent to which the area was boggy is not known, but it is probably significant that contemporary sources do not mention waterlogged ground as they do at Marston Moor and Naseby. Hedges on the extreme east of the battlefield, hedges and brambles on the extreme west, and a ditch towards the eastern side, provided the only obstacles to military operations.[11] The small tracts of woodland that are a prominent feature of the 'small, rising hill' today appear not to have been there in the seventeenth century.

Historians tend to place both the left wing of the Parliamentary cavalry and the right wing of the Royalist cavalry straddling the Kineton–Banbury road.[12] This is a mistake that probably originates in the depiction of the battle in Henry Beighton's map of Warwickshire of *circa* 1730. A contemporary description of the battle states that the left wing of Essex's cavalry was drawn up on the 'little round rising hill' itself. This was confirmed by Lord Bernard Stuart in a letter written straight after the battle. He commanded the King's Lifeguard stationed on the extreme right of the Royalist army, but described his troop as riding uphill towards the enemy. If his charge had been to the east of the B4086, he would have been riding on the flat or even slightly downhill.[13]

There are other signs that the Parliamentary army was deployed some way to the west of where they are depicted in every modern plan of the battle. First, Bernard Stuart's troop passed through or close to several hedges in their advance towards the enemy. Radway was not enclosed until the middle of the following century. Before then, its only hedges were as depicted in Map 1. Second, Richard Bulstrode, who, like Stuart, fought in a regiment on the right wing, described preparations for an advance towards Kineton on the day after the battle as commencing at Rising Sun, a mile to the west of where the battle was fought. If his regiment had been deployed to the east of the Kineton–Banbury road, he would have described the distance as two miles or more, not one.[14]

However, although the battlefield was largely featureless, giving little advantage to either side, the landscape that surrounded it was of considerable influence on the outcome of the battle. As has already been written, Edgehill served as a convenient rendezvous for the regiments of the king's army, which prior to the battle had been scattered across a hundred square miles of countryside between Kineton and Banbury.[15] The escarpment provided a refuge for formations that had retreated or been broken by the enemy, and on the following day it was an excellent vantage point from which to view the movements of the enemy. As for the Earl of Essex, the undulating and thickly wooded country between Stratford-upon-Avon and Kineton may explain the slow progress of his rearguard. It may also explain why some of his cavalry troops approaching the Vale of the Red Horse from the west seem to have found it difficult to ascertain exactly where the fighting was taking place.[16]

Sources

There are numerous descriptions of the Battle of Edgehill compiled by men who were present on the day. Some are full accounts, others merely record one or two incidents experienced by the writer. Ten were written within a month; some after a lapse of many years. Even so, there is still insufficient information to be absolutely certain about what happened in the final stage of the battle. The principal reason for this is that almost all were written by cavalry officers or civilians, only three by infantry officers and one of these is exceedingly short. As for the other two, neither can be regarded as a completely credible description of what happened. The first is a speech by the Parliamentarian Lord Wharton, who had just had the disagreeable experience of seeing his regiment run away at the start of the battle. It has all the benefits of immediacy, but Wharton's language suggests that he was in a state of shock and acutely aware that his audience would turn against him if he did not choose his words carefully.[17] The second, that of the Royalist brigade commander John Bellasis, was put together many years later by Joshua Moone, his secretary, using oral testimony written down between 1649 and 1651 when Bellasis was a prisoner in the Tower of London. It contains some interesting pieces of information about the Royalist army, but they are not totally consistent with what is to be found in descriptions written straight after the battle, and on one occasion Moone or Bellasis confuses left with right. There are therefore quite strong grounds for doubting the accuracy of the account, particularly with regard to incidents in which Bellasis himself was directly involved, as memory in such circumstances can be wittingly or unwittingly selective.[18]

In other respects Edgehill is not a difficult battle to reconstruct, as Royalist and Parliamentary sources tell a very similar tale of the overall progress of the battle. If one did not know which side the writers supported, it would be quite easy to mistake the official Royalist account for the official Parliamentary one and vice versa.[19] The detail does, of course, differ from account to account, but although most accounts are focused on putting their own side in the best possible light, they are also critical of mistakes that were made by the commanders. Possibly all of this is a sign that the writers were not yet used to managing their material in such a way as to extract the maximum value out of it for their side or for their particular faction within it. The only major inconsistency between the two is that the Parliamentary accounts do not follow the Royalists in describing a significant cavalry engagement on the western side of the battlefield between troops led by Lord Fielding and Henry Wilmot. Once the war was over, however, Royalist writers changed their tune. Both Prince Rupert and James II describe Wilmot's wing as routing dragoons not cavalry, though it is possible that the king had a sight of Rupert's Diary before writing his memoirs.[20]

Later works, however, contain problematic elements. Lord Bellasis's memoirs have already been discussed, whilst Sir James Hinton's are so ill-informed as to be useless for anything other than the story of the escape of Charles I's two sons, and even that is problematic.[21] Prince Rupert's Diary is keen, as always, to absolve the prince from blame, whilst Lord Clarendon, as always, is consistent in his criticism of the prince.[22] The future King James II was also on the battlefield as a child. However, the observations in his memoirs are not those of a child, but of a former officer, who had fought in the French army under Turenne. Not surprisingly they are shot through with insights drawn from his military career.[23] The account of Sir Robert Walsh is primarily concerned with celebrating his feat of honour in recapturing the Royal Standard, but otherwise it adds nothing of substance to the biography of the other claimant, Sir John Smith, when discussing fighting on the western side of the battlefield.[24] Then there is the exciting account in Edmund Ludlow's memoirs. Ludlow fought in the Earl of Essex's Lifeguard of Horse, which played a significant part in extracting a draw from the jaws of almost certain defeat. However, this passage is almost certainly a later forgery, as in content, if not in language, it follows very closely Nathaniel Fiennes's account of the battle printed a few weeks after the battle.[25] Unfortunately the original does not survive to check it against, but the manuscript of Sir Richard Bulstrode's does. In this case the eighteenth-century editor altered some of the vocabulary but added and subtracted very little. Occasionally, however, the changes are of some significance: the king's infantry descended Edgehill by covered, not several, ways; and 'when we returned from following the enemy the night came soon upon us' is split in two by the phrase 'by the too great heat of Prince Rupert'.[26]

There are no contemporary drawings of the Edgehill battle. All we have is Bernard de Gomme's watercolour discovered in the Royal Archives at Windsor in about 1950. This was almost certainly completed nearly twenty years after the battle. Unlike his other sketches of Civil War battlefields, the enemy formations are not depicted, possibly because he was not himself at the battle. The comment on de Gomme in the margin of Rupert's Diary – 'Mr de Gomez can give us the battle of Edgehill' – only indicates that he had the knowledge of how to do so, nothing more.[27]

De Gomme's depiction of the deployment of the Royalist cavalry regiments is confirmed in general by other sources, but this is not the case with the infantry. The plan shows the foot regiments drawn up in five brigades with three in the front and two in the second line, in such a manner that the latter could fill the gaps between the brigades in the front line if necessary, that is, in what is popularly referred to as the Swedish manner. However, one wonders if the Royalist infantry was deployed exactly as depicted. In the first place, under the Swedish system regiments were disaggregated in order to create the complex fourfold division of pikes and muskets required, yet there is plentiful evidence to show that some at least of the Royalist foot regiments operated as units during the battle. Second, the plan does not include three regiments that were with the army on the march to Edgehill, two of which are known to have fought at the battle.[28] Third, two contemporary accounts of Edgehill, one Royalist and one Parliamentarian, specifically mention the Royalist infantry as being drawn up in nine, not five, bodies.[29] This would allow for eighteen regiments if they were brigaded in pairs, and that is almost the exact number known to have been in the king's marching army in late October 1642.[30] The nine-brigade scenario may also explain why the Royalist foot regiments which suffered the highest losses amongst their leading officers appear to have been in pairs, the Lifeguard and the Lord Lindsey's regiments, and Sir Edward Stradling's and Thomas Lunsford's, for example.[31] It would therefore be best to describe de Gomme's map as a guide to how the Royalist infantry was deployed at Edgehill but nothing more.

Chapter 5
The Battle of Edgehill
Narrative

According to de Gomme's plan, the Royalist infantry at the start of the Battle of Edgehill were drawn up in two lines in a chequerboard formation, which enabled the brigades in the second line to move forward into the gaps in the first line to form a continuous front if necessary when battle was joined. The first line consisted of the brigades commanded by Henry Wentworth, Richard Fielding and Charles Gerard; those in the second row were commanded by Sir Nicholas Byron and John Bellasis. All appear to have been roughly equal in size with three regiments in four of the brigades and four in the other.[1] However, they may on the day have been drawn up in nine rather than five bodies. This is what is clearly stated in Moone's biography of Lord Bellasis and in the *Official Parliamentary Account* of the battle.[2]

Scott, Turton and Von Arni favour the five-brigade formation.[3] Their argument runs as follows. Thanks to the convoluted nature of the countryside separating the two armies, the Parliamentary commanders could only see the Royalist front line as it advanced towards them, and this they would have described as being made up of 'nine great bodies',[4] as each brigade consisted of a stand of pikes flanked by two sets of musketeers. However, the battlefield at Edgehill was not like that at Marston Moor, where a dip in the slope along which the Allied armies deployed was deep enough to hide some of their troops from the Royalists on the flat moorland below. The rise in ground between the base of the Edgehill ridge and the low hill on which the bulk of the Parliamentary army was drawn up is a smooth, gentle slope.[5] Observers on the summit of the low hill would therefore have been able to see both lines of enemy infantry as they advanced towards them, that is fifteen bodies, not nine. Second, it seems unlikely that Essex's staff, which included a number of professional soldiers, would have seen the three components of a brigade as being anything but a single body of infantry. Third, the wording of the

Official Account – 'their foot which appeared to us divided into nine great bodies came up all in front' – gives a strong impression that the writers were describing the whole of the Royalist infantry.[6] However, this is not a case where a cross-reference between two accounts written by observers with different perspectives (the *Official Account* and Bellasis's biography) permits a third account (de Gomme's depiction) to be denied a place in the narrative and cast into outer darkness. Moone may have had a sight of the *Official Account* at the writing-up stage and used it to plug a gap in his master's reminiscences, and his choice of words does not rule this out entirely. In the current state of knowledge all three traces of the past are opinion, the discrepancies between them being both inexplicable and irreconcilable. I have therefore ducked the issue in my illustration by drawing the Royalist infantry as a single line.

Although no equivalent plan exists of the Earl of Essex's army, contemporary accounts of the battle enable its infantry deployment to be reconstructed with some degree of confidence. Clearly it was a defensive formation. The reasons for this are unclear. Possibly the earl did not want to be held responsible for attacking the king; possibly he was waiting for the remainder of his army to catch up, after which he would have redeployed it in an attacking formation. Whatever the cause, it provided the first of many occasions on which his generalship was questioned, with Nathaniel Fiennes expressing surprise that he had not attacked the Royalists before they deployed whilst they were trying to make their way down the steep slope of the Edgehill ridge.[7]

The earl's twelve infantry regiments were grouped into three very large brigades of between 3,000 and 4,000 men, described as the van, the middle, and the rear. However, although they were the size of a classic Spanish *tercio* and were described as such by one eyewitness, they consisted of regiments able to act independently of one another, not a mass of pikemen twenty deep flanked by musketeers similarly deployed.[8] The van comprised the regiments of Lord Say and Sele, Lord Robartes and Sir William Constable, the middle the regiments of Charles Essex, Lord Mandeville, Lord Wharton and Sir Henry Cholmley. Sir William Fairfax's regiment is described as being in the van brigade in most accounts, but in the battle in another. Both brigades were positioned in the centre of the Parliamentary position on the Edgehill side of the small rise in the ground mentioned above, with the van to the right and the battle to the left. The rear brigade, comprising the regiments of Lord Brooke, Thomas Ballard, Denzil Holles and the Earl of Essex himself, was placed in reserve on the reverse slope, possibly protecting those heavy artillery pieces that had managed to arrive on the battlefield in time.[9]

Most of the Royalist cavalry were on the right wing. They were drawn up in two parallel lines facing the enemy. The first, under Rupert's personal command, comprised the twenty-one troops of horse of his own, Prince Maurice's and the Prince of Wales's regiments and the King's Lifeguard; the second, under Sir John Byron, consisted solely of his regiment's six troops. The remainder of the cavalry, comprising between twenty-one and twenty-three troops, was on the left wing, under the overall command of Commissary General Henry, later Lord, Wilmot. They were drawn up in a similar manner, with the first line comprising Wilmot's, the Earl of Caernarvon's, and Lord Grandison's regiments being the stronger of the two. The second line, under the command of the Earl of Caernarvon or Lord Digby, comprised eight troops at most of Digby's and Sir Thomas Aston's regiments. However, although on both wings the regiments in the second line were described as the reserve and instructed not to take part in the initial attack but await instructions, in de Gomme's watercolour there is only a very small gap between the two lines. If this was indeed correct, there was no true Royalist cavalry reserve stationed well behind the main battle line able to intervene on the battlefield wherever and whenever necessary. The King's Lifeguard should have been in that position, but they had begged to participate in the first charge, and the king had weakly agreed to their request. The only horse that remained to defend the heavy cannon and the non-combatants, including the king's two elder sons, was the troop of gentlemen pensioners, fifty or so strong. This failure to retain a true reserve almost certainly lost Charles the chance of winning a decisive victory.[10] However, the king's generals expected to attack and overwhelm the enemy. They were not prepared to wait to be attacked, and this probably explains the unreservedly offensive formation they adopted.

Most of the Parliamentary cavalry, probably twenty-four troops of horse, were drawn up under Sir James Ramsey's command on the left flank of Essex's middle infantry formation and slightly to its front. They were supported by dragoons and 500 or so musketeers drawn from two regiments belonging to the rear brigade. These lined the hedge on the eastern flank of the battlefield as described above. Some musketeers were also stationed between the cavalry regiments in the Swedish manner to provide additional firepower. Parliamentary sources written immediately after the battle allege that the decision to concentrate so many cavalry on the left wing was taken because Essex and his military advisers knew that this was where the bulk of the Royalist cavalry was stationed. However, they could not have been sure of this until just before fighting commenced.[11]

According to Nathaniel Fiennes, there were only three regiments of cavalry on the right wing of Essex's army, the Earl of Essex's and Sir William Balfour's in the front line and Lord Fielding's in the second.[12] They comprised at least sixteen troops of horse and were supported, as on the left, by several companies of dragoons.[13] However, this was probably how they were first deployed. By the time the battle started, some or all of the troops in the first line must have been elsewhere with Sir William Balfour.[14] Finally, there were the two troops of cuirassiers described as the Earl of Essex's and the Earl of Bedford's Lifeguard, the first commanded by Sir Phillip Stapleton, who was also colonel of the Earl's regiment of horse. In the case of Essex's Lifeguard, Ludlow claims that it was on its own somewhere directly behind the van brigade, a point his editor did not take from Fiennes.[15] This may be editorial fill-up, but there is some slight support for the statement in Bulstrode's description of the Parliamentary foot at the start of the battle as being 'lined with horse behind them with intervals betwixt each body for their horse to come up if required'.[16] The whereabouts of Bedford's troop is not known.

All that remains to discuss is the whereabouts of regiments missing, or allegedly missing, from the battlefield. Three regiments of Essex's foot were in garrison at Worcester and Hereford. Two had been detached during the march to strengthen the defence of Coventry and Banbury, and two others, together with Lord Willoughby of Parham's regiment of horse, were several hours' march behind the main army escorting the remainder of the artillery along the road between Stratford-upon-Avon and Kineton. One troop of horse was at Banbury, whilst several other troops were scattered across the south Warwickshire and east Worcestershire countryside attempting to catch up with the army.[17] The absence of foot from the battlefield was not a problem. Though denied by two recent accounts of the battle, the twelve regiments present almost certainly outnumbered the king's infantry by a considerable margin.[18] This was not the case with the horse. At his army's first night's stop after leaving Worcester, Essex himself claimed to have sixty-one troops of horse under his direct command. If he had had that many troops at Edgehill, his cavalry would have outnumbered the king's by between 500 and 1,000 horse. But when he drew up his army on the morning of 23 October he only had between thirty-five and fifty troops.[19] Essex maintained that he failed to assemble his full strength because of the remarkable speed of his march, an unlikely story. If Keightley's and Fiennes's accounts are typical, they were involved in all kinds of missions and under little if any overall control.[20]

The king's army, on the other hand, was almost as strong as it could have been in late October 1642. None of his infantry regiments was on garrison duty, but, as stated above, three are missing from de Gomme's plan of the battlefield. One, the Earl of Northampton's, may possibly have been stationed, as Peter Young suggested, on the reverse slope of the Edgehill ridge to deter the Banbury garrison from launching an attack on the rear of the king's army, but this is based on nothing more than inherent military probability and the earl's close association with Banbury. However, the other two certainly fought at Edgehill. William Alderton, a soldier of Earl Rivers's regiment, received a pension from the Cheshire Quarter Sessions Court after the Restoration. Attached to his petition was a letter written by John Boys, the regiment's lieutenant colonel, to the effect that Alderton had been at Edgehill. Anne

Chantler, the widow of another Cheshire soldier, also claimed that her husband had been at Edgehill under Major Peter Walthall in Richard Fielding's regiment. Her petition was signed by Sergeant Randle Whittaker, who had fought in the battle in the King's Lifeguard of Foot.[21]

As the king's infantry flanked by cavalry advanced from its position below the edge towards the Earl of Essex's army on the little, round hill, the Royalist dragoons chased the enemy musketeers and dragoons from the hedges lining the eastern side of the battlefield. The first line of cavalry regiments on the right wing led by Prince Rupert then advanced towards the enemy left wing at a fair pace knowing that they would not be raked by flanking fire as they moved forwards. Sir James Ramsey's tactics were not for his horse to counter-charge. They were to receive the enemy in a stationary position with a concentrated burst of fire from their pistols and carbines delivered at close range and strengthened by that of the musketeers drawn up between the squadrons. Though charging up a slight incline and having, according to Lord Bernard Stuart, to cross a number of hedges before reaching the enemy, the Royalists quickly routed the whole of the cavalry facing them.[22] The speed of their success elicited numerous comments. Some writers pointed to the Royalists reserving their fire until point of contact, as instructed by Prince Rupert just before they charged, whilst the Parliamentary troopers met them not with a concentrated barrage but with a ragged fusillade, some of which was delivered before the enemy came into range. Others cited the demoralizing effect on the Parliamentary horse of the defeat that some of their regiments had suffered at Prince Rupert's hands at Powick some weeks earlier, which was compounded by the desertion of a whole troop of Parliamentary horse on Ramsey's wing at the moment the Royalists charged.[23] Some did not mince their words. A chaplain in Essex's army attributed the debacle firstly to the cowardice of Parliament's horse and secondly to the bravery of the Royalists.[24]

The second line on the Royalist right wing followed Rupert into the attack. The Prince's verdict was that 'they should not have done being the reserve'.[25] Many other contemporary writers, from the author of the *Official Account* to Clarendon, Warwick and James II after the Restoration, pilloried the commanders of the second line for their precipitate action,[26] but a possible reason why Byron on the right wing behaved as he did may have been the behaviour of a troop of Parliamentary turncoats commanded by Sir Faithful Fortescue. Fortescue had raised his men for service in Ireland, but was forced to take up a commission in Sir William Waller's regiment. He came to an understanding with Rupert that he and his men would desert as soon as the cavalry engagement began. The first line of the Royalists knew it, and rode around Fortescue's men as they fired their pistols into the ground, but the second had not apparently been informed. What they saw in front of them were Rupert's horse disappearing into the distance, and a troop of Parliamentary horse in the foreground that had either broken through the ranks of Rupert's men, or else had managed to avoid them. In such circumstances Byron would have seen it as his duty firstly to charge that troop, which he did, inflicting considerable casualties, and then to follow his general, believing, on the evidence of his encounter with the renegades, that Rupert would need support to complete the task of routing the enemy left wing.[27]

The middle brigade of Parliamentary infantry under Colonel Charles Essex, stationed slightly in front of Ramsey's regiments of horse, cut and run at about the same time. According to Nathaniel Fiennes and another account published in London straight after the battle, it fled from the field in disorder at about the same time as the cavalry broke, though Lord Wharton's account argued that the brigade fled during the course of the cavalry engagement, whilst the *Official Account* blamed the cavalry for running over them as they fled. Several sources, however, agree that infantry regiments took to their heels before they came into contact with the enemy foot.[28] A recent account of the battle presents a very interesting hypothesis as to how the collapse might have occurred, with first the dragoons and then the cavalry disrupting the ranks of the middle brigade, whilst they were being fired on by the musketeers of two if not three Royalist brigades.[29] The regiment on the left of the rear brigade, Colonel Holles's, was also apparently ridden over by both sets of cavalry but without being broken up and dispersed. Holles's personal example (according to Holles) steadied his men, but the regiment probably benefited from having a much higher ratio of pikemen to musketeers, as before the battle several hundred musketeers had been commanded away to strengthen the firepower of the cavalry on the left wing. Holles also claimed to have stopped three troops of Parliamentary cavalry in their flight.[30]

On the western side of the battlefield both lines of Royalist horse, assisted by dragoons, also charged the enemy, but what they actually achieved is surrounded by uncertainty. Several Royalist accounts written immediately after the battle describe Wilmot's command as routing the enemy horse facing them as comprehensively as Prince Rupert had done on the other wing, and also a regiment of foot, namely Fairfax's.[31] However, later descriptions paint a less clear picture. Walsingham's biography of Sir John Smith can be read in such a way as to suggest that, in their headlong rush towards Kineton, Wilmot's men failed to encounter any enemy cavalry, whilst Prince Rupert's and King James II's accounts of the battle describe Wilmot's horse as overcoming dragoons, not cavalry.[32] Nathaniel Fiennes's account, the only one written by somebody who fought on the opposing wing of the Parliamentary army, does not resolve the matter. Having described the right wing as comprising three regiments, Sir William Balfour's and the Earl of Essex's in the van and Lord Fielding's in reserve, he then suggests that his regiment, Sir William Balfour's, did not see Wilmot's men, a point confirmed by the official Royalist account of the action. However, the really interesting thing about Fiennes's report is his comment that after the battle he could not believe a prisoner's claim that the Parliamentary right wing had faced four regiments of enemy cavalry. His estimate was 'some few' and the *Official Account*'s ten troops.[33] In fact there were as many as twenty troops belonging to five regiments. As Fiennes had no reason for being economical with the truth given the successes of Balfour's regiment during the battle, it seems highly likely that Balfour did not see Wilmot's charge rather than, as Scott, Turton and Von Arni assert, that he deliberately moved his force out of the way when he saw the Royalist left wing descending the Edgehill ridge and realized that he was outnumbered.[34] Moreover, if he could see Wilmot's men, why did they not see him taking evasive action and respond accordingly, but Sir Philip Warwick's claim that Wilmot deliberately avoided the enemy because he did not want the king to win a decisive victory is almost certainly an example of hindsight based on his knowledge of the general's intrigues two years later.[35]

Reading between the lines of Fiennes's and the *Official Parliamentary Account*, it seems likely that Wilmot's regiments routed Lord Fielding's regiment of horse and possibly part of the Earl of Essex's, a regiment or so of dragoons, and Sir William Fairfax's regiment of foot.[36] The likelihood, as Fiennes strongly implies,[37] is that Balfour's force neither saw nor was seen by the enemy because at some time prior to the outbreak of fighting it was ordered to move elsewhere to be replaced on the right wing by Fairfax's regiment of foot. Such a move would be more understandable if, in direct contrast to Scott, Turton and Von Arni's hypothesis, Balfour believed that the enemy horse facing him were few in number, that the hedges and brambles on the western part of the battlefield would be sufficient for the dragoons supported by a regiment or so of cavalry and infantry to fend off any Royalist attack, and that he could spare half his troops of horse for service elsewhere on the battlefield where they were more clearly needed.

If this was indeed the case, where was Balfour's force when Wilmot struck? Historians who place it directly behind the regiments of the van brigade beside Essex's Lifeguard are probably mistaken.[38] In the first place, if Fiennes's account is correct, the two bodies of Parliamentary horse still on the battlefield after Rupert and Wilmot's charges were not aware of one another's existence until much later in the battle. Second, if Balfour's force had been behind the centre or the left of the van brigade, it would have been in a position to wheel to the right and attack Wilmot's regiments in the flank as they passed by on their way to Kineton.[39] If, on the other hand, Balfour's force had been far to the west of the van brigade on Herd Hill, for example, and was missed by Wilmot's men for that reason, it would have been in the wrong position from which to launch its first, very successful attack on the Royalist infantry.

Two other possibilities remain. First, once Essex's generals were aware of the strength of the cavalry on Prince Rupert's wing of the Royalist army, they may have decided that Balfour's force should be withdrawn from the left wing to reinforce Sir James Ramsey. This may explain why one early Parliamentary account of the battle stated that the left wing comprised eighteen or nineteen troops of horse rather than the twenty-four cited by other accounts.[40] However, if this had been the case, Balfour's force cannot have reached the left wing before the cavalry fight began or else it would have been routed along with the rest. Even if it had been halfway there and behind the small hill close to where Essex's reserve brigade had been deployed at the start of the battle, it would not necessarily have been out of harm's way when Wilmot charged. Walsingham claims that the left wing of the Royalist cavalry did not head straight for Kineton but took a line further to the east around the rear of the hill, where they dispersed the remnant of Lord Wharton's and Charles Essex's regiments of the middle brigade as they fled from the battlefield.[41]

My preferred hypothesis is that Sir William Balfour had moved his force into the gap between the Parliamentary van and central brigade just before the cavalry engagements began, in the belief that what would take place at the western edge of the battlefield would be merely an encounter between dragoons. By then it would have been obvious that some of the enemy infantry brigades were also on the attack and might be able to exploit the gap between the two brigades unless he did something about it. The persistent Royalist use of the term reserve to describe Balfour's force indicates that it acted in one of the textbook roles for a reserve, namely plugging a gap in the line when it occurred.[42] Indeed the timeline of events makes it possible that Balfour's first charge took place at the very start of the battle before the cavalry actions had been fully resolved on either wing.[43] In such circumstances his men would not have been 'in the corner of a field undiscovered' when Wilmot made his breakthrough, but already either in the thick of the fighting or about to be.[44] If so, this is an important subtlety in the use of language that needs to be noted at this stage in compiling the battle narratives, namely that the term wing indicates a force that would have fought in that position in a textbook battle in open country, but which is still used as a descriptor if they are deployed elsewhere because of the physical nature of the battlefield.

Within half an hour of the start of the battle, with Essex's right wing cavalry and the troops stationed on his left wing routed, and one of his three brigades of infantry also in flight, all looked lost for the Parliamentarians. In the circumstances the Lord General must be praised for keeping his head and making the most effective use of the forces he had left. He ordered the reserve brigade to move into the front line taking the place of the middle brigade. By that time the van brigade was involved in a desperate encounter with what was probably the best equipped of the Royalist infantry brigades, that commanded by Sir Nicholas Byron, comprising the King's Lifeguard and the Earl of Lindsey's regiment, supported, according to de Gomme, by the small regiment of Sir John Beaumont.[45] Whether or not the attack by Byron's brigade had been authorized is unclear from the Royalist sources, but if that brigade was intended to spearhead the Royalist infantry assault it was in the wrong place in de Gomme's depiction of the battle, that is, in the second not the first line.

Lindsey's insubordination, if that was what it was, has been seen as a response to what had happened at the council of war earlier in the day when, after a series of slights stretching over several weeks, the Lord General had to all intents and purposes been superseded by Rupert, his wish to deploy the Royalist infantry in the Dutch manner having been overruled by the king on the prince's advice. By performing some conspicuous act of valour, Lindsey could recover both his reputation and his honour. His aim was no less than to destroy the Earl of Essex's regiment, which he believed to be in the Parliamentary van directly to his front.[46] But this explanation of Lindsey's behaviour is only to be found in Clarendon's *History of the Great Rebellion* and is almost certainly yet another attempt to blacken Rupert's name.[47] Other accounts describe Lindsey as deferring with good grace or resentment to General Ruthven because of his extensive experience in Swedish service, not as grudgingly giving way to Prince Rupert.[48] It may, however, then seem odd for the Lord General to be allowed to fight at the head of his regiment unless he was resentful or uncooperative, but there was little else for him to do. There were no infantry reserves to feed into the battle at the most appropriate moment, and Rupert had supreme command over the cavalry. It was also normal practice for most commanding officers in the seventeenth century as from time immemorial to lead from the front rather than manage the battle from the reserve line.[49]

The assault by Sir Nicholas Byron's brigade against the van brigade of Essex's army was directed against two regiments, Lord Robartes's and Sir William Constable's; the third regiment, Sir John Meldrum's, which was to their right, was probably held in check by Henry Wentworth's brigade, which directly fronted it, thus preventing its wheeling to the left to attack Byron's flank. The assault began in the customary manner with a barrage of musket fire, which was met by a counter barrage, which one source says lasted until the musketeers ran out of ammunition. This softening up operation was then followed by an assault by the Royalist pikemen, and the two brigades indulged in 'push of pike' for an indeterminate length of time with neither giving way. The impasse was resolved by the intervention of Essex's Lifeguard of Horse, which appears to have made its way through a gap between the two regiments under attack and Sir John Meldrum's, and attacked Byron's brigade in the flank. Although not powerful enough to break the Royalist brigade, the charge was sufficiently powerful to force the king's regiments to disengage and draw back a short distance. What the rest of the Royalist infantry were doing at this point is unclear. If James II is correct, all the infantry drew up within musket range of the enemy and opened fire 'even till night', but another Royalist source claims that one brigade did not play any part in the battle until much later in the day, whilst a Parliamentary source asserts that the brigades on the left of the Royalist line were in advance of the rest.[50] Unfortunately the uncertainty cannot be resolved by field walking and metal detecting as the musket balls fired by the Royalists would have landed exactly where the royal ordnance factory is now situated.[51]

Having relieved the pressure on Parliament's infantry, Essex's Lifeguard made for the rear, and probably took up a position defending some of their artillery pieces. To the Lifeguard's alarm, a body of cavalry emerged out of the Royalist ranks heading in their direction. They fired a round of case shot at them, thinking that they were about to face the *coup de grâce* from the Royalist reserve, but soon discovered that riding towards them were the other troops of Parliamentary horse still on the battlefield, Balfour's force, which had just conducted a most successful operation against the king's infantry position.

If, as suggested above, Balfour's force had moved into line between the van and the centre brigade of Essex's army just before the battle began, they would have found themselves facing the four regiments of Richard Fielding's infantry brigade, if what is depicted on de Gomme's watercolour is correct. What happened next is largely taken from the *Official Account* and from the account written by Nathaniel Fiennes, who took part in the charge. It is not clearly and specifically identified in any of the Royalist accounts, which focus on the role of Balfour's force in the later defeat of two regiments in Sir Nicholas Byron's brigade.[52]

The Parliamentary narratives are clear and straightforward, though with some differences in the detail. Balfour's force charged Fielding's brigade, captured the brigade commander, and broke a regiment of Greencoats, probably Thomas Lunsford's, and another regiment, which were identified as Bluecoats by Lord Wharton, presumably Sir Edward Stradling's, which suffered considerable casualties amongst its officers. However, they did not destroy the whole brigade. A letter written to the commissioners of array for Cheshire after the battle described Fitton's regiment as 'the last on the field that retreated, which the king took especial notice of'.[53] It is also perhaps significant that only a single officer was wounded and that none of the twenty soldiers from Fitton's regiment who petitioned the Cheshire Quarter Sessions court for pensions after the Restoration on account of wounds suffered during the war claimed to have been wounded at Edgehill.[54] It is not known what happened to the fourth regiment, Richard Bolle's.

Balfour's force then drove onwards attacking the king's heavy artillery and killing a number of gunners, but having no means of disabling or driving away the captured artillery pieces, they retired to their own lines, taking a slightly different route, which took them close to Byron's infantry brigade.[55] They were not fired on by Byron's musketeers, who mistook them for the king's cavalry reserve advancing to the attack. Some of the King's

Lifeguard even shook them by the hand as they passed.[56] Their next encounter with Balfour's force was to be much less friendly.

How had this serious penetration of the Royalist infantry position come about? The sources tell us very little. However, a possible pointer is provided by the report sent to the Marquis of Ormond to the effect that Balfour's force 'took advantage of some little disorder in our foot'.[57] At that stage of the battle this is most unlikely to have been because they were already in direct conflict with Essex's infantry. Possibly the disorder resulted from being required to carry out a drill more complicated than advancing in a straight line, such as wheeling to the left to take Essex's van brigade in the flank at the very moment it was being attacked head-on by Sir Nicholas Byron's brigade. If this was the case, Balfour's force cannot have charged at the very start of the battle, but only after the centre brigade of Essex's army had fled. Otherwise the Royalist infantry would have been unable to execute a turning movement. This is no more than speculation based on inherent military probability, but there is some support for the timing in Parliamentary sources. Fiennes describes Balfour's force routing one Royalist regiment without infantry support but the next one with infantry support. Presumably the first success occurred before the rear brigade reached the front line, the second afterwards. Another makes a distinction between the flight of the centre brigade 'at the very first' and Balfour's group's charge 'in the beginning of the day', but as the two passages are several hundred words apart in the narrative, the fine distinction was probably not intentional.[58]

The next stage in the battle saw the destruction of Sir Nicholas Byron's brigade in what was almost certainly a second attack by Parliamentary infantry and cavalry rather than a continuation of the first.[59] In this attack the van brigade seems, surprisingly, to have played a passive role, possibly because it was exhausted by the first encounter or out of ammunition. Instead, two components of the rear brigade, Lord Brooke's and all or part of the Lord General's regiment, assaulted the Royalists in the flank, whilst Balfour's force and Essex's Lifeguard attacked it from a different direction or directions. After a fierce fight of uncertain duration, the concerted fire of the Parliamentary infantry severely disrupted the ranks of Byron's brigade enabling the cavalry to surge in and break up the formation. Both large regiments in the brigade, the Lifeguard and Lord Lindsey's regiment, suffered heavy casualties, particularly amongst their officers; the two colonels, Lindsey and his son, were wounded and captured; and the Royal Standard was seized after its bearer, Sir Edmund Verney, had been killed, apparently by one of Essex's Lifeguard.[60] Those who survived fell back in some disorder towards the Edgehill ridge.

According to both Royalist and Parliamentary accounts, the defeat of Byron's brigade caused the rest of the king's infantry to retreat, but some fell back further than others. The most determined stand was that taken by the regiments on the extreme right of the Royalist position, most particularly the brigade commanded by Charles Gerard, which fell back in good order. Having had a quiet opening to the battle thanks to the flight of Parliament's middle brigade, Gerard's musketeers would still have been well supplied with ammunition. Moreover, the brigade as depicted by de Gomme consisted of regiments that had been with the army since Nottingham, and they were presumably better trained, and possibly better armed, than any brigade other than Byron's. Gerard's men took up a good defensive position behind a ditch where, supported by artillery pieces and dragoons, they held out against enemy attack until nightfall.[61] Most historians place Gerard's brigade on the Radway brook to the north-east of the village, but this is probably incorrect, as in order to get there they would have had to execute a wheel to the left, a difficult manoeuvre to perform whilst withdrawing without losing formation. Moreover, both Royalist and Parliamentary accounts describe the right of the Royalist infantry as falling back on the main Royalist artillery position, which the sources describing Balfour's first charge place to the rear centre of the Royalist line of battle.[62] I would therefore suggest that Gerard's brigade made its stand behind Green Ditch, marked on the pre-enclosure map as just to the north-west of Radway village.[63]

Of the remaining brigades Sir Nicholas Byron's had, of course, been overrun and there is no record whatsoever of what happened to John Bellasis's. He himself, but not his brigade, seems to have fought with the Earl of Lindsey, which suggests that it might have withdrawn early from the fight. There is no mention of this in any of the accounts, but Bellasis's biographer tended to leave out embarrassing incidents, as in his account of the First Battle of Newbury.[64] Alternatively, de Gomme's watercolour is incorrect and the two brigades were adjacent to one another rather than separated by Fielding's. This would make sense of the claim that Fitton's regiment was somehow associated with Gerard's defence of the artillery as night fell and that it was the last to leave the battlefield. It would also have allowed Bellasis and his brigade to fall back with the rest of the Royalist infantry line on Byron's defeat.[65] There is, however, no evidence to support a recent assertion that one regiment in Bellasis's brigade 'was under heavy pressure and gave more ground than the rest'.[66]

But what of the fate of the fifth brigade on de Gomme's map, Henry Wentworth's, stationed on the extreme left of the Royalist infantry position beyond Byron's? As Parliamentary accounts clearly refer to two bodies of Royalist infantry holding out until nightfall, Young suggested tentatively that Wentworth's brigade fought until the end, having conducted a fighting retreat in parallel with Gerard's brigade.[67] His hypothesis rested upon a statement by Lord Bellasis to the effect that the survivors of Byron's brigade fell back on the brigade to their left, which was intact as it had not taken part in the fighting. However, this evidence is not very convincing. Bellasis's biographer sometimes had trouble in locating units on the battlefield. In the previous sentence, for example, he had placed Byron's brigade on the right of the king's army rather than towards the left. If both are reversed, Wentworth's brigade disappears from the picture, and Byron's fell back on the brigade to its right, presumably what was left of Fielding's, Fitton's regiment and possibly Bolle's, about which nothing at all is known other than that none of its officers are mentioned as being casualties.[68]

Other pieces of evidence also suggest that Wentworth's brigade was not the one on which Byron's brigade fell back. One Parliamentary account makes it clear that the two Royalist infantry formations that were still on the battlefield when night fell were adjacent to one another, not well over half a mile apart, as would have been the case if they had been Wentworth's and Gerard's brigades. The largest regiment in Wentworth's brigade, Sir Thomas Salusbury's, which had been raised in Denbighshire, was acknowledged not to have performed well at Edgehill. Its colonel claimed at the 'Battle' of Brentford, the next engagement in which it participated, that it needed to show conspicuous bravery in order to redeem the honour of the Welsh. There is some support for this in the account written by T.C., a chaplain on the Parliamentary side, who referred to the shameful retreat of the Welsh and northerners. However, his comment could equally well apply to Fielding's brigade, which included south Welsh and Cheshire regiments, or to more than one brigade. Finally, James II, having described the action in which Byron's brigade was mauled, commented that the victorious enemy were halted in their tracks by cannon fire, presumably from Gerard's position. This then 'gave those regiments on the left hand which had given ground time to put themselves once more in good order'. The description, however, may have applied to the whole of the left of the Royalist infantry, that is both Wentworth's and Byron's brigades but, to be fair to Wentworth's men, they may only have fallen back after suffering heavily in a firefight with the regiment facing them, Sir John Meldrum's. Lord Molyneux's regiment in particular is supposed to have suffered quite heavy casualties amongst its rank and file at Edgehill, whereas the Welsh may have had fewer muskets than the rest of the king's infantry and become demoralized when unable to retaliate against an enemy that was well supplied.[69]

The two bodies of Royalist foot that remained on the battlefield at nightfall were therefore likely to have been either the two components of Charles Gerard's brigade (if the Royalist infantry were drawn up in nine bodies) or Gerard's brigade and that part of Fielding's brigade, which included Fitton's regiment (if de Gomme's plan is correct and they were drawn up in five bodies). Powerful evidence that Fitton's regiment was with Gerard is provided by the inscription on his funeral monument in Gawesworth church, Cheshire: 'as commander of the royal artillery he shattered the rebel squadrons with his artillery fire',[70] an incident that can only have taken place at the end of the battle. If de Gomme's depiction is correct, then three and a half of the five or seven out of the nine Royalist infantry brigades had quitted the battlefield or been destroyed during the course of the battle. Only two brigades, Sir Nicholas

Byron's and Charles Gerard's, had put up a fight, and one had been destroyed. The words of Nathaniel Fiennes concerning the cavalry can therefore be equally well applied to the infantry: 'some of both sides did extraordinarily well and others did as ill.'[71]

By the last hour of daylight both sides had fought themselves to a state of exhaustion. Parliamentary sources claim that the formations of Royalist foot that were still intact only escaped being destroyed because Balfour's cavalry were too tired to charge. It was also claimed that the two remaining Parliamentary infantry brigades had run out of ammunition, possibly because the Royalist horse dominated the area between Kineton and the battlefield, thus making it difficult to bring ammunition wagons forward.[72] Another consideration may have been the need to show caution as the situation on the battlefield began to change. By 5 p.m. the victorious Royalist cavalry belonging to both wings were beginning to return in considerable numbers. They were able to rescue captured officers like Richard Fielding, commander of the central brigade; they recaptured the Royal Standard; they may even have had a successful clash with some of Balfour's cavalry. The Parliamentarians, on the other hand, claimed to have successfully attacked five troops of the returning enemy horse and routed them, but as it was almost dark little credence should be placed in the alleged scale of such encounters. The Royalist officers who had regained their own lines also cited the darkness as one reason for not making a final charge against Balfour's horse, which could be dimly discerned between Essex's two remaining brigades of foot. The second justification was that it was not possible to get the horse back into close order before nightfall. Clarendon, the quintessential armchair general, implied that the cavalry officers were shirking their duty. However, an assault by disorganized cavalry on the Parliamentary horse could have ended in disaster if not immediately successful, as the two enemy infantry brigades would have turned inwards to pour fire into the mêlée; and instant success would have been an unlikely result of an attack delivered by a disorganized mob.[73]

Overall, the battle was clearly a draw. It has always been the habit of historians to praise the Royalists, the cavalry for their initial success, the infantry for their fortitude, but Essex's army had a lot to be proud of. Those troops that had not left the field in the first half-hour fought extremely well, that is the infantry of the van and reserve brigades and the remaining cavalry. Balfour may only have had five troops of horse under his command, but he moved them about the battlefield with great skill, whilst Essex was almost certainly personally responsible for the manoeuvre that broke Byron's brigade. The extent to which Balfour was obeying Essex's instructions or acting under his own initiative cannot be ascertained. Sir Charles Firth alleged that Oliver Cromwell observed the way in which Balfour conserved his forces and drew on the experience in formulating his own battlefield tactics. This was probably not the case. Cromwell's troop was not part of Balfour's force, and none of

Cromwell's subsequent successes on the battlefield employed the tactics Balfour had used at Edgehill, which relied on the careful, even delicate, management of a small force of cavalry of less than brigade strength. Cromwell's skill lay in husbanding large bodies of horse so that they could be used appropriately as the battle progressed. To use a metaphor drawn from fencing, Balfour used an epée, Cromwell a cutlass.[74]

Chapter 6
The First Battle of Newbury
Context, Landscape and Sources

Context

Almost a year passed before there was a second battle between the field armies, although they had come very close to it on two occasions. The Edgehill campaign had culminated in a Royalist advance on London. The king's army captured Banbury, Oxford and Reading in quick succession without having to strike a blow, but on 13 November at Turnham Green, some four miles to the west of the capital, it came face to face with Essex's army reinforced by the Trained Band regiments of the city of London.[1] The king's advisers persuaded His Majesty that attacking so large a force was too much of a risk, and the Royalists fell back on Reading and Oxford. Oxford was to remain Charles's headquarters for the rest of the war.

In the following April Essex set siege to Reading with his field army reinforced by a brigade of the London Trained Bands and a corps of the new Eastern Association army under Lord Grey, which had been raised in East Anglia during the winter. The king's unsuccessful attempt to relieve the town ended in a firefight at Caversham Bridge followed by retreat. For the next two months there was stalemate on the Thames valley front. Essex's army, ravaged by disease, manoeuvred around the eastern approaches to Oxford but could not bring the Royalists to battle. The king, on the other hand, was too weak to attack the Parliamentary army, having almost exhausted his supplies of ammunition in the failed expedition to Reading. Nevertheless a cavalry encounter at brigade level at Chalgrove on 18 June was a significant victory for Prince Rupert.

Victories in the north and west of England in late June and early July and the arrival of two large munitions convoys from the north escorted by several thousand troops enabled the king to take the offensive. With the aid of his Western Army, troops from Cornwall, Wiltshire and Somerset raised during the winter and the spring by Sir Ralph Hopton and the Marquis of

Hertford, the king's field army under Prince Rupert was able to capture Bristol by assault, but the infantry losses sustained as a result forced Charles to abandon plans to advance once more on London until he had been joined by further reinforcements. In the meantime the Western Army was sent home to recruit and complete the conquest of the south-west peninsula, whilst the field army set siege to Gloucester, the capture of which would complete Royalist control over the Severn valley.

Parliament's response was to order the Earl of Essex to relieve Gloucester with an army supplemented by regiments from London, Kent, Hampshire and the East Midlands. With a force consisting exclusively of cavalry, Prince Rupert was unable to prevent Essex's army from reaching Gloucester via the northern Cotswolds, but the earl's progress was slow enough for the besieging Royalist infantry to disengage before he could surprise them in their siege works. As the earl's army began its march back towards London, the king's army set off in pursuit. Initially Essex wrong-footed the king by taking a more southerly route over the Wiltshire Downs. His intention was to reach the Bath road, today's A4, at Hungerford in the Kennet valley and then to head at full speed via Newbury towards enclosed country that began about six miles to the west of Reading. Once there, his infantry could repel any attack the Royalists launched against the rear of the army. However, in a major cavalry engagement at Aldbourne Chase on the downs to the north of Hungerford on 18 September the Royalists rattled Essex's confidence that he could reach safety via the Bath road. He therefore ordered his army to cross the Kennet at Hungerford and make for Newbury by a slower but less open route. However, when his quartermasters reached Newbury on the afternoon of 19 September to prepare overnight billets, they found that Rupert had arrived there first with the vanguard of the king's cavalry, seizing the bridge over the Kennet that gave access to the Bath road and a large quantity of provisions that had been collected locally to feed the Parliamentary army. The quartermasters withdrew, and Essex's men bivouacked for the night in enclosed country two miles or so to the west-south-west of Newbury in and around the villages of Enbourne and Hamstead Marshall.[2]

The remainder of the king's army, having approached Newbury from the direction of Wantage, crossed the Kennet and occupied the town itself and the low ground immediately to its west and south.[3] The Royalist generals then pushed a small advance guard up the Andover road, which leaves Newbury in a south-westwardly direction and, after a mile or so, crosses a chalk plateau known as Wash Common situated at an altitude of some 200 feet above the river plain. The advance guard quartered on the plateau for the night, probably to the east of the Andover road, but patrols were apparently sent out to keep an eye on the movements of the enemy. These ranged as far as the western edge of the plateau facing Enbourne, where Essex's troops spotted them before nightfall.[4]

Landscape

The countryside over which the First Battle of Newbury was fought largely disappeared under housing during the course of the twentieth century. The town has expanded massively to the south and west encompassing almost the whole of Wash Common, apart from a small piece of open land with some tumuli on it towards the top end. However, beyond the western edge of the Common, there has been very little development. The countryside is still made up of hedged fields. Only along the road to Enbourne does the viaduct carrying the Newbury bypass disrupt the view. Nevertheless, despite all these changes, contemporary descriptions of the battle can very largely be married up with the earliest large-scale maps of the area.

Between the Earl of Essex's army and that of the king lay a tract of country bounded on the north by the Kennet, on the east by the Newbury to Andover road, and on the south by the little River Enbourne. Close to the River Kennet it was no more than half a mile wide, in the south between two and three miles. The most conspicuous feature within it is an escarpment, the middle section of which follows the western edge of Wash Common.[5] The feature, however, does not run due north–south. It is, in fact, shaped like a crescent moon but with spurs of unequal length. The short spur, part of which was described by the Royalists as a round hill, runs roughly parallel to the Kennet and to the lane from Hungerford to Newbury through Enbourne along which Essex's army had marched on the day before the battle. The other, longer spur a mile or so to the south separates the valley of the River Enbourne, which marks the southern limit of Wash Common, from the area where the Parliamentarian army had bivouacked. In two contemporary accounts the entire crescent is described as Biggs Hill.[6] Unfortunately by the nineteenth century only part of the southern spur was known by that name, a source of confusion to later historians.

The area over which the principal engagements were fought was a complex one. Beyond the northern spur there was a large area of open ground about half a mile in length and a quarter of a mile wide. Although bordering the Kennet, it appears to have been meadow rather than marsh. It was described by Lord Digby as a big field, and by another writer as a large place.[7] Through it passed the track that led from Newbury to Hungerford mentioned above and known as Enbourne Lane. At its western boundary began the enclosures in which the Parliamentary army had spent the night, but this feature in the landscape extended all along the slope of the northern spur of the crescent facing the Kennet past Newbury itself and at least as far as the Basingstoke road. Some secondary sources see this ribbon of land as being similar in nature to the *bocage* country across which American and some British forces fought the Normandy campaign 300 years later.[8] However, early maps, the first of which dates from the mid-eighteenth century, depict the enclosures facing the Kennet as quite large fields, and therefore not entirely unsuitable for cavalry actions. This

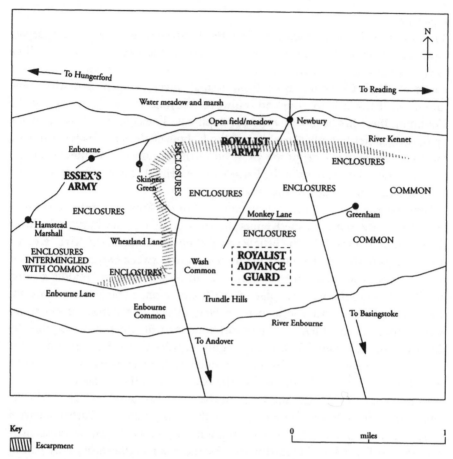

Map 2. The First Battle of Newbury (dawn)

is confirmed by an account written by a senior Royalist cavalry officer, which describes one of the fields as occupying most of the so-called Round Hill and being large enough to accommodate 1,000 infantry at its furthest end.[9] Nevertheless, the hedge lines provided ideal positions from which musket and artillery fire could be directed against an attacking force.

To the south of the enclosures was a belt of open chalk down stretching from Holt Common and Crockham Heath on the Newbury to Hungerford Lane west of Enbourne via Enbourne, Wash and Greenham Commons and Crookham Heath to Aldermaston where the enclosed country Essex was so keen to reach began, a distance of some ten miles. For much of its length the open land followed the course of the River Enbourne, which joined the Kennet about four miles to the east of Newbury. How serious a barrier the Enbourne was to the fighting it is impossible to say. Today it is a mere trickle for most of the year, but the fact that no units from either side attempted to cross it during the battle does not necessarily mean that it was a serious obstacle in the seventeenth century. The southern boundary of the battlefield was probably fixed by what are described in a nineteenth-century map as the Trundle Hills, an area towards the southern extremity of Wash Common, which is characterized by steep undulations in the ground that would have made it very difficult for bodies of infantry and cavalry to maintain formation.[10]

Although the area where it had quartered for the night made it easy to repel attacks from the direction of Newbury, Essex's army was nonetheless in a position of some peril on the evening of 19 September. Shortage of supplies was not the only reason why the Lord General could not simply wait for Parliament to set in motion a relief force under the command of his rival, Sir William Waller.[11] If Rupert's cavalry were able to deploy in strength on Wash Common, they could push westwards down the Enbourne valley until they reached the Hungerford–Newbury Lane where it crossed Crockham Heath, a mile or so to the west of Enbourne, thus cutting off the Parliamentary army's only avenue for retreat. Before nightfall Phillip Skippon, Essex's major general of foot, had apparently seen the problem and taken steps to counter it by stationing troops in a linear formation along the lane rather than bunching them up around Enbourne.[12] This, however, was only a temporary expedient. Essex had something far more ambitious in mind for the following day, which involved resuming the march towards Reading, not waiting for the Royalists to attack.

The most obvious line of advance was for Essex to push further down the lane from Enbourne to Newbury, secure the bridge over the Kennet, and resume the march down the Bath road towards London. However, when his troops entered the flat area beside the river where the bulk of the king's army had spent the night, they would enter a killing ground. The lane itself was so narrow that only six soldiers at a time could march abreast along it. As a result when they tried to deploy in battle formation on the open ground at the lane's end, they would only be able to do so in penny numbers, whilst subject to cavalry attack supported by the massed firepower of the enemy musketeers and artillery.[13] Moreover, there was no easy way for Essex to circumvent the problem by getting his troops across the Kennet short of the bridge. Although the army's starting point would be within its own quarters, and thus very largely protected against incoming fire, the king's commanders could easily move troops and artillery over Newbury bridge and down the Bath road to oppose the crossing, which would be slow as there was no ford across the river at that point. Moreover, even if Essex succeeded in getting his men to the north bank of the Kennet, their progress would still be slow, as they would be faced by the task of negotiating several hundred yards of waterlogged ground and then a short but steep incline to reach the road.[14] Finally, the artillery would have to be left behind, a major humiliation for a seventeenth-century army. For the Parliamentarians therefore attempting to cross the river would probably have led to a longer engagement than a direct attack down Enbourne Lane, but it would probably have ended in as bloody a massacre.

The only other alternative was to attempt to bypass Newbury by a broad sweep to the south of the town, but this would entail moving through the long, thin belt of open land described above. Here it would be possible to make good progress, but the Royalist cavalry would be a formidable opponent. Not only do they appear to have outnumbered Essex's mounted troops by a considerable margin, the king's generals, unlike at Stow-on-the-Wold and Aldbourne Chase, would be able to bring up musketeer and light artillery support onto the heath using the roads that left Newbury for Andover and Basingstoke. However, if the Royalists were not expecting such a move, or if Essex was able to distract them by threatening a parallel advance down Enbourne Lane, the ensuing logjam in Newbury, as the king's infantry and artillery tried to get from one side of the town to the other when the true direction of the Parliamentary advance became apparent, might at best give his army time to reach the safety of the enclosures at Aldermaston almost unscathed. At worst he ought to be able to save part of his army, given the discipline both his cavalry and the infantry had displayed when attacked by Royalist cavalry on the way to and from Gloucester. However, the degree of success would depend on how quickly the king's army was able to mount a combined arms attack in force on the heath land to the south and east of Newbury.

The Sources

The First Battle of Newbury has the distinction of being both the longest battle of the English Civil War and the one that historians have found the greatest difficulty in describing. However, General Kitson is perhaps exaggerating when he claims that the sources are 'so diverse and contradictory as to make any reliable description of it impossible'.[15] Admittedly there is no contemporary plan of the battle, and the documentary evidence makes it impossible to identify the position of every regiment on the battlefield, but accounts of the more significant developments written by participants on both sides very largely dovetail with one another, though, as with most other Civil War battles, the evidence that survives is much fuller for the first few hours of the engagement. Also there appears to be some ambiguity in the use of the terms 'hill' and 'valley', but a careful reading of the source material makes it nearly always possible to establish a timeline, and also to be almost totally certain as to which part of the battlefield a specific passage relates to.

The official Royalist account written by Lord Digby took the form of a letter to a lord dated 22 September, that is, two days after the battle.[16] Digby's writings about military matters later in the war need to be very carefully appraised, but this one is less likely to have been driven by a personal agenda.[17] The rivalries within the Royalist High Command, principally that between himself and Prince Rupert for the king's ear, were yet to develop. Also he was not yet a main actor. Immediately afterwards he succeeded Lord Falkland, killed at Newbury, as one of the two Secretaries of State, the other being Sir Edward Nicholas, but at the time he wrote the account he was still no more than an important courtier and a colonel of horse. However, Digby's account has two important shortcomings. In the first place it was intended as a reflection on the battle's outcome, not a blow-by-blow description of what happened. Second, Digby himself almost certainly spent the whole day in the Kennet valley, where there was little fighting. As a result the detail, as opposed to the generalizations, concerning what occurred elsewhere on the battlefield is not always completely accurate. The key theme is the bewilderment and bafflement that he believes his readers must feel at the failure of the king's army to destroy Essex's army, having caught it in a trap. He therefore concentrated on explaining how the battle developed in the ways that it did, but the account reads like a piece of special pleading against the charge that the Royalists should not have attacked but waited for the enemy to surrender or scatter, thus preserving the lives of the hundreds of officers and men killed during the battle. Digby made two substantive points. First, he claimed that Essex's heavy artillery, having occupied Round Hill, was able to inflict such a heavy bombardment on the king's army quartered in the low-lying ground to the west of Newbury that, if the Royalists had not attacked that position, the king would have been forced to withdraw, thus allowing the Parliamentarians to cross the bridge over the Kennet and so escape to Reading. He also claimed that the king's generals had been tempted to attack the other flank of the enemy army, because it had been drawn up in an exposed position on open common at some distance from the rest of Essex's troops. The first contains an element of truth, the second does not, but to be fair to Digby he, like many others at the time and since, failed to understand what Essex's operational plan was, and it was this which very largely determined how the battle developed.

Digby's account, however, is far closer to reality than Lord Clarendon's, as it shows considerable awareness of what happened where on the battlefield, even though he then used that information to support an argument that was largely fallacious. Clarendon claimed that the Royalist council of war had decided to remain on the defensive and wait for Essex to attack, but there is no supportive evidence for this in any of the other Royalist accounts.[18] Moreover, he twisted Digby's words so as to change a tentative suggestion that the battle began by accident when part of Essex's army took up an exposed position in open country, into a denunciation of the impetuosity of some of the king's younger officers holding high commands for attacking the enemy positions and getting themselves into serious trouble. To rescue them, more and more troops were committed until it became impossible for the king to avoid fighting a pitched battle in circumstances that favoured the enemy. Finally, Clarendon criticized the Royalist generals for not bringing their artillery into action until very late in the day, something that most other accounts strenuously deny. To be fair, the heavy cannon were probably kept on the flat ground near Newbury until the late afternoon when the chance of a major attack down the Enbourne road had finally disappeared, but according to Foster field artillery were in action from the start on Wash Common.[19] Some of this compendium of half-truths may be attributed to the fact that Clarendon himself was not present, and as a result was misinformed. However, the fact that he failed to make any substantial use of Lord Byron's description of the fighting on Round Hill, even though he had commissioned it, suggests that it was the overall message, not writing a complete narrative, that was the more important consideration.[20]

Unlike the accounts written by Digby and Clarendon, those written by officers who fought in the battle are very narrow in focus. The first, which is anonymous, was penned immediately afterwards as a defence against the charge of allowing Essex's men to occupy and then hold onto Round Hill in the first hour of the action. For the remainder of the day the writer remained in the Kennet valley on the king's orders to counter any attempt by the enemy to advance towards Newbury along Enbourne Lane.[21] Another, written by Lord Byron four years after the event, is a detailed description of a second attempt to capture Round Hill and its environs, but it stops at about midday. The author also flatly declined to make any comment upon what happened elsewhere on the battlefield.[22] The deficiency is supplied to some extent by the description of the battle in Prince Rupert's Diary. This contains some fascinating detail that has never been used before, but as with so much of the Diary it is only a string of observations in little more than note form focusing on what the prince advised and the effectiveness of the operations in which he himself was involved.[23] However, the incidental information concerning Newbury contained in the two documents that make up the Diary dovetails quite neatly with information to be found in several of the other accounts, and there is no evidence from the text that the author drew on such accounts in writing the Diary. Finally there is the biography of Sir John Digby of Goathurst, a colonel of horse, written by Edward Walsingham in 1645, which provides some detail about the cavalry fight on Wash Common, but it is a work of piety which displays far more interest in the good Catholic deaths of the Earl of Caernarvon and Colonel Morgan than in the ebb and flow of the battle.[24]

Two other sources, the narrative of Joshua Moone, Lord Bellasis's servant, and the memoirs of John Gwyn, were written from the point of view of the infantry that fought on Wash Common and its environs.[25] Moone in particular provides some interesting snippets of information, but neither contains the slightest hint of the charge made in Royalist and Parliamentary accounts alike that the king's foot soldiers, most particularly Bellasis's own brigade, refused to attack the enemy infantry and artillery lining the hedges along the common's western edge.[26] Finally there is the description of the battle in *Mercurius Aulicus*, the Royalist weekly journal published in Oxford.[27] This appears at first glance to be nothing more than a shortened version of Lord Digby's account, but that is not the whole story. The writer had certainly seen a version of the official Royalist account, but the middle part of the description goes beyond what Digby wrote by claiming that the Parliamentary defensive position was so strong that the king's troops were forced to fight in order to gain the ground on which to deploy for battle. This sounds very profound, but it is probably a *bon mot* devised by the writer rather than a soundbite from a member of the Royalist council of war. It makes no sense whatsoever in the mouth of a senior commander.

Of the Parliamentary sources the most informative by far is the *Official Account* of the battle published a month or so later.[28] Its prime intention was to kill off a number of rumours and criticisms, of which the most serious were that the cavalry had run away and ridden over their infantry as at Edgehill, that some of the London regiments suffered disproportionately heavy casualties because of faulty orders, and that the Scottish officers in the army had not pulled their weight.[29] This is made clear in general terms in the first sentence of the first paragraph:

> The fight of Newbury hath been of late the subject of some pens who, had they loved truth as well as elegancy, and laboured by plain and particular narrations to describe the action, as much as they have done by false glosses and shadows to disguise it, had been historians good enough to have informed the people, and saved the labour of any other pen; but howsoever we shall not waste a line in way of confutation or picking out any false stitches which they have sewn, but only present to the world our own positive piece of truth so plainly wrought that perchance the contrary, set by it, may be forced to blush through all her painting.

The fact that its publication coincided with the earl's successful campaign to place Sir William Waller's army firmly under his jurisdiction and immediately after the conclusion of an alliance with Scotland, which was not universally popular amongst moderates in the House of Commons and the House of Lords, is probably not a coincidence. Great care was taken in trying to explain to a lay readership what had happened on the battlefield, and there is no obvious attempt to gloss over or hide anything other than the important point that what had probably been the Earl of Essex's operational plan for the day had failed.

Equally clear, though more narrowly focused, is Sergeant Henry Foster's account of the outstanding defensive role played early in the day by the Red and Blue regiments of the London Trained Band regiments in the fighting that took place at the southern extremity of the Parliamentary line of battle.[30] Nevertheless, two writers have recently misread Foster's words, probably because the place where he said the regiments fought does not conform with what they see as fundamental seventeenth-century military doctrine, namely that cavalry invariably fought on the wings.[31] However, like Lord Byron's account of fighting on Round Hill, Foster stops at midday. The reasons for this are discussed below.[32]

The diary of Walter Yonge, MP for Honiton, describing proceedings in the House of Commons, contains a précis of two reports made to the House by Essex's officers, one of whom, Sir Phillip Stapleton, had commanded the right wing of the cavalry in the absence of Sir William Balfour.[33] They focus on the reporter's own experience of the battle, and also the interest (in both senses of the word) of the diarist. Both contain a few points that may have been deliberately omitted from the official version, and these will be evaluated in their appropriate place in the battle narrative, but as a source they are less important for understanding the First Battle of Newbury than, for example, Sir Arthur Haselrig's report to the House of Commons on the Battle of Cheriton, as a version of Stapleton's report was published in the London weekly journals.[34]

Robert Codrington's biography of Essex published immediately after his death in 1646, however, is little more than a collation of the newspaper and pamphlet accounts of the battle dressed up in his own flowery, but occasionally very effective, language.[35] The Parliamentary troops, for example, incapable of sleep on the eve of the battle, 'observed the silent marches of the stars, and the moving scene of heaven'. The only possible pieces of original material relate to Essex's wearing of a large white hat to the consternation of colleagues worried about his safety, and some generalizations about the last hour of the battle. The first does not sound like literary invention. The second may be from an account that no longer survives, but may equally well be a fill-up by the author when he discovered his sources had little to say about the closing stage of the engagement.

Finally, there are at least twelve accounts in London newspapers that precede in date the publication of the official account and that written by Sergeant Foster.[36] These were all published during the last week in September, and contain snippets of information but also comments on the battle and the campaign, some of which were critical of the Parliamentary army. This explains the preamble to the *Official Account* quoted above. Only one is a blow-by-blow narrative of the battle, and it is particularly useful as it confirms some of the points made in the *Official Account* and in Foster's narrative, but using language suggesting very strongly that it had not been read by the writers of the two later accounts and incorporated into their narratives. The other that is of significant value reproduces extracts from a letter written by a soldier who, it can be inferred, fought in the Blue regiment of the London Trained Bands. This contains information that conforms well to what is to be found in Sergeant Foster's account.[37]

Chapter 7

The First Battle of Newbury
Narrative

At first light Essex pushed forward the vanguard of the Parliamentary army composed of his own large regiment of foot, two of his brigades of regular infantry, and part of a third comprising the Red and the Blue regiments of the London Trained Bands, in all probability between 4,500 and 5,000 foot supported by field artillery. Not far behind came what the *Official Account* written by Essex's senior commanders described as the right wing, six regiments of cavalry, some dragoons, and a number of detached troops of horse. Also following in the infantry's wake were the heavy artillery pieces. The vanguard's first task was to climb the escarpment and deploy on Wash Common.[1]

To their left in the Kennet valley Essex placed a small body of infantry, the forlorn hope, also supported by field artillery, which took up a defensive position behind the hedge that separated the enclosures around Enbourne from Digby's large field. Its task was apparently to prevent the Royalists using the track to Hungerford to disrupt the Lord General's operational plan. Behind the forlorn hope, probably on the hill at Enbourne where they had spent the night and where they could easily be seen by the Royalists massed in the large field, were Essex's remaining ten infantry regiments, also probably 4,500 to 5,000 strong, and described in Digby's account as the Grand Reserve.[2] As long as they remained there, the Royalists could not rule out a major push down the Kennet valley towards the town. The Grand Reserve was also well placed to go to the forlorn hope's assistance if it came under attack, but Essex's plan was probably for it to serve as the main battle, that is the central section of the Parliamentary army, during its march eastwards. The whereabouts of the so-called left wing of the cavalry under Colonel John Middleton cannot be ascertained from the primary sources. Barratt's, Seymour's, Reid's and Roberts's battle plans show Middleton's regiments deployed in the conventional manner in the Kennet valley behind and on the flank of the forlorn hope, but this is an example of inappropriate extrapolation from military theory to battlefield practice when there is a gap in the traces of the past.[3] If the left wing did spend their day in close company with the forlorn hope, they seem to have kept a very low profile. The account of the only attack by Essex's forces in the Kennet valley implies very strongly that infantry alone was involved.[4] Similarly, Middleton's regiments do not seem to have played any part in countering the only serious attack on the forlorn hope from the large field. This was apparently driven back by cannon and musket fire but not followed up by a cavalry charge as the Royalists retreated. The *Official Parliamentary Account* confirms that the left wing of horse played little part in the battle, claiming that it was only able to operate in small parties because of the enclosures.[5] However, the sentence mentioning Middleton's men is couched in the form of an explanation. It does not assert that they were associated in any way with the infantry battalion defending the 'pass' where the lane from Newbury to Enbourne entered the enclosures. In fact they could as easily have been deployed between Enbourne and Hamstead Marshall to block any attempt by Rupert's cavalry to attack the rear of Essex's army using the corridor of open country that stretched around the south of Newbury as far west as Crockham Heath.

Essex himself and his acting lieutenant general, Sir Phillip Stapleton, led the vanguard leaving Phillip Skippon, major general of foot, to manage the Grand Reserve, the forlorn hope and, presumably, the left wing of the cavalry.[6] Access to Wash Common from Enbourne and Hamstead Marshall was provided by three tracks. Skinners Green Lane, the most northerly, ascended the northern spur of the escarpment from the west-south-west, with the happy result that troops passing up it could not be seen by the enemy from their quarters in the Kennet valley. The lane passed over Round Hill, the tip of the northern spur of the escarpment, and soon afterwards entered Wash Common at its north-western corner. Here it joined the Newbury–Andover road, which followed the southern edge of the enclosures as far as its junction with Monkey Lane. The main road then made a right-angled turn plunging down the escarpment to Newbury, whilst Monkey Lane continued in an easterly direction as far as the western edge of Greenham Common. The gradient was not all that daunting apart from a short stretch midway up the escarpment where there is now a bend in the road.

The second, Wheatlands Lane, reached the top of the escarpment after a shorter but even steeper climb. It entered the common very quickly there-after about 250 yards to the south of Skinners Green Lane, but came to an end at a T junction with the Newbury–Andover road. The third lane, which began as Enbourne Street Lane or Biggs Hill Lane and ended as Bell Hill Lane, was some way to the south. Running in an easterly direction from the enclosed country between Hamstead Marshall and Enbourne, it entered open land at Enbourne Common about 1,200 yards to the west of the old

Newbury–Andover road, which it joined about 750 yards to the south of the Wheatlands Lane junction.[7] The journey from Parliament's quarters to Wash Common was much longer by this route than via the other two lanes, but the gradient was far less as Enbourne Street Lane skirted the southern spur of the crescent for much of the way.[8]

Essex's vanguard attained their first objective without encountering any opposition. His own regiment secured Round Hill and possibly the entrance to Wash Common at Skinners Lane Head. Colonel Barclay's and Holbourne's brigades breasted the escarpment to the south, probably by way of Wheatlands Lane, and deployed initially on the edge of the common rather than behind the hedges that followed the western side of the Newbury–Andover road. The two London Trained Band regiments had further to march, but when they heard firing away to the north,[9] they apparently hurried forward, almost certainly along Enbourne Street Lane, leaving their field artillery to proceed as best it could. By 8 a.m. they too were deployed in open ground, possibly close to where Wash Common and Enbourne Common joined.[10] Thus the Parliamentary front line stretched for about 1,000 yards in a north–south direction, but with gaps between the various components.

The position of the Red and Blue regiments of the London Trained Bands on the battlefield and the time at which they came into action have been incorrectly represented in most recent accounts of the battle.[11] However, there is no doubt whatsoever that they were initially deployed early in the morning on the extreme right wing of the Parliamentary line, not taken from the Grand Reserve early in the afternoon to defend the place where Skinners Green Lane enters Wash Common.[12] This is clearly stated in Sergeant Foster's narrative, and confirmed quite independently in the letter written by the soldier who fought in the Blue regiment.[13] Other accounts of the battle provide supplementary information of a circumstantial nature. Both Digby and Rupert, for example, claim that there were three brigades of Parliamentary foot on the heath, whilst the *Official Parliamentary Account* confirms Sergeant Foster's statement that the trained bands were amongst the first to be in action. Finally, it is most unlikely, given the climate of opinion prevailing in London in late September/early October 1643, that Foster and the anonymous soldier of the Blue regiment would have been careless in reporting where on the battlefield their units had fought. Not only would Londoners have been very interested in the recent performance of their own regiments, there were also tales of incompetent leadership circulating that were causing alarm.[14]

With the vanguard of the infantry in place, the artillery and cavalry could begin their advance. The heavy artillery started its ascent of Skinners Green Lane as soon as Essex's regiment had secured Round Hill.[15] Two demi-culverins were in action at the lane end by mid-to-late morning with the rest arriving by the early afternoon. At about the time the artillery began its ascent, the right wing of the cavalry made its way up the escarpment, probably via

Wheatlands Lane.[16] Their orders were to deploy on Wash Common.[17] If they had succeeded in doing so, the Parliamentary army would have been firmly in control of the common.

At this point most historians who have written about the First Battle of Newbury lose their way.[18] This is largely because they read the battle through Royalist eyes, and the Royalists were not privy to the Earl of Essex's plans. Clarendon and *Mercurius Aulicus* wrote that Essex's purpose in seizing the edge of the escarpment was to establish his army in a first-class defensive position. In fact it was the other way around. Essex was on the attack, attempting a breakout in order to escape from the trap into which he and his army had fallen. In the event the vanguard of the Parliamentary army was stopped in its tracks, but in a position that fortuitously favoured the defence.

The gist of the plan was clearly explained in the *Official Account*:

> The next day being Tuesday, we marched towards Newbury, and when he approached within two miles of the town we might discover the enemy's party upon a hill, their whole army having prevented us were gotten to Newbury and possessed the town. But the next morning, being Wednesday [20 September] by break of day order was given for our march to an hill called Big's Hill, near to Newbury, *and the only convenient place for us to gain, that we might with better security force our passage.*[19]

Circumstantial evidence supports the breakout hypothesis. The way in which the Parliamentary army was deployed in the southern part of the battlefield only makes sense if Essex's plan was more ambitious than finding a stronger defensive position than that provided by the enclosed countryside around Enbourne and Hamstead Marshall. If his objective had been purely a defensive one, he would surely have stationed his foot behind the hedge that topped the escarpment and left his horse in the valley below rather than ordering both of them to deploy on the open heath land of Wash Common. It is, of course, just possible that Essex was unaware that Royalist cavalry were already present on the Common in some strength, but even if he did not know this until his infantry arrived on top of the escarpment, he could have changed his plan there and then.

Unfortunately the detail of Essex's plan is not given in any of the Parliamentary accounts, but the most likely explanation for the deployment of the vanguard on Wash Common was that it marked the start of the next stage of an operation to reach the safety of enclosed country at Aldermaston by outflanking the Royalist position in and around Newbury using the belt of heath land that lay to the south of the town. If this was indeed the case, the role of Stapleton's cavalry, assisted by the three bodies of infantry, would have been to protect the right flank of the main body of the Parliamentary army, that is, the heavy artillery and carriages and what Digby described as the Grand Reserve, as it marched eastwards towards Greenham Common skirting the ribbon of enclosed country that followed the northern slope of the escarpment. Its left flank, on the other hand, would initially be protected against attack from the Kennet valley by regiments defending the northern spur of the escarpment. If either flank guard came under serious attack, it could be reinforced from the Grand Reserve, something that happened on several occasions as the day progressed. However, once the Grand Reserve reached the top of the escarpment and was proceeding eastwards across the heath, the forces defending Enbourne Lane and the northern spur would presumably have followed in its wake as a kind of rearguard, supported, presumably, by Middleton's cavalry regiments.[20]

The plan, however, had one serious weakness. It was predicated on a slow and uncertain Royalist reaction, but Prince Rupert seems to have seen what Essex had in mind from the start and to have succeeded in persuading the Royalist council of war to take the best measures for countering it, that is defending Wash Common with large bodies of horse and foot, and also with artillery, which, for once in a Civil War battle, could be moved about with ease using the Newbury–Andover road and the track into the common that was, according to Rocque's map, on the line of the present road. Alerted soon after dawn of an enemy advance, Rupert went to look for himself and found Essex's infantry already in possession of part of the northern spur of the escarpment. He then organized an attack using the troops he had to hand, a commanded party of musketeers under Lieutenant Colonel George Lisle, and a few troops of horse under Lord Wentworth drawn from a number of regiments. As it was an emergency, he then left the spur to consult with the king and the other generals, who were in the Kennet valley with the rest of the army, leaving Wentworth in charge.[21] What follows is 'his story' but it cannot be a complete fabrication as it was Wentworth's defence against a charge of misconduct. The only discrepancy between the three Royalist accounts of the first fighting on the northern spur is in the number of musketeers under Lisle's command. Rupert mentions 1,000, Wentworth implies a much smaller body, Lord Byron simply suggests that they were too few in number to hold their position against the enemy.[22]

The Royalist musketeers were ordered to attack, but could make no progress and withdrew, calling on the horse for assistance. After experiencing some difficulty in deploying, the horse helped the foot to drive the enemy out of one enclosure into the next one, which covered most of the hill. There they found a much larger body of Parliamentary infantry, a thousand strong, supported by an artillery piece. At this point the Royalist commander's horse was killed. Somewhat surprisingly, he left the field looking for another one, but only after ordering the cavalry to attack the enemy infantry. He then spent some time in the Kennet valley trying to find a suitable mount. When he set off back up the escarpment, he encountered some of his officers who informed him that Lord Wilmot, the lieutenant general of horse, had ordered them to desist. He therefore returned to the valley where the king ordered him to remain for the rest of the day.[23]

What had happened to Lisle's musketeers in the meantime is uncertain, but if the first encounter had been on Round Hill itself, they had probably fallen back some distance, as the next infantry encounter seems to have taken place on a different part of the spur. However, if this was so, Essex did not seize his advantage and push his infantry regiments as far as the junction of the Newbury–Andover road with Monkey Lane. Instead he concentrated on establishing a defensive line along the hedges and banks lining the north flank of the escarpment to resist an attack on the spur he could see building up in the large field beside the river. This is understandable, but his overall plan would have been much easier to implement if he had also moved troops forward to the junction, as this would have made it far more difficult, if not impossible, for Rupert and Lord Forth to have moved the bulk of the king's army, three of his five infantry brigades and most of his cavalry brigades, from Newbury to Wash Common later in the morning using the Andover road. Already, according to Rupert, the Royalist council of war had taken the decision that it must focus, not on defending the large field by the Kennet, but on sending Essex's vanguard tumbling back down the escarpment.[24]

The second attempt to expel Essex's infantry and artillery from the northern spur of the escarpment was on a much larger scale than the first. Lisle's musketeers were to be supported by the infantry regiments of Charles Gerard and Michael Woodhouse assisted by part of the King's Lifeguard, possibly as many as 1,500 foot, under the command of Sir Nicholas Byron, and the large cavalry and dragoon regiments of Sir John Byron and Sir Thomas Aston, between 800 and 1,000 strong.[25] Their exact line of march up the spur is uncertain, but the differences in the descriptions of the enclosures in the Royalist accounts of the two attacks on the spur make it likely that Byron's assault was not on Round Hill itself but on a small hill 400 yards or so to the east of it.

According to the *Official Account*, Major General Skippon had just climbed the hill 'to be near His Excellency' when he saw great activity in the valley below. Fearing that the Royalists' aim was to cut Skinners Green Lane, thus putting a stop to the attempt to bring the whole Parliamentary army onto Wash Common, Skippon apparently drew reinforcements from the Grand Reserve, namely Lord Robartes's brigade and Colonel Mainwaring's regiment, to defend the northern spur of the escarpment. This took some time to organize, and in the meantime the enemy attack was making slow but steady progress. After suffering some heavy casualties, the Royalist horse and foot occupied the small hill and then moved on to secure a foothold on a lane, possibly Skinners

Green Lane.[26] However, as they saw no sign of Essex's train of artillery, it was more likely to have been Dark Lane, which ran from the Kennet valley to the top of the escarpment between the north-west corner of Wash Common and the Newbury–Andover road.[27] To the Parliamentary generals this was equally worrying as it also threatened the left flank of the army's planned route to Aldermaston.

When the Parliamentary reinforcements arrived, the Byrons retreated or were pushed back from the lane, but Sir Nicholas's brigade apparently retained some control over the high ground it had captured until darkness fell, allegedly in the face of several enemy attacks. However, Mainwaring was quickly moved elsewhere and it is unlikely that Robartes pressed his attacks home with any degree of ferocity. His orders were apparently not only to protect the left flank of the advance onto the Common. He was also to prevent the Royalists in the Kennet valley from getting behind the main body of the army by pushing down Hungerford Lane towards Enbourne, but after midday they had insufficient forces in place to attempt any such thing.[28] The only troops that seem to have been left in the large field beside the Kennet defending the approach to Newbury from the west were Sir William Vavasour's infantry brigade, part of the King's Lifeguard of Foot, and a number of troops of horse, some of which had suffered badly in Sir John Byron's assault on the escarpment. However, there seems to have been a firefight in the valley that lasted until well into the night, making inappropriate inroads into Royalist supplies of gunpowder, as the wagons carrying ammunition are likely to have been close by. Elsewhere in the extreme northern part of the battlefield nothing much happened at any time in the day, apart from the probing attack along the banks of the Kennet mentioned in the section on Middleton's cavalry wing, which probably occurred in the morning rather than the afternoon and was quickly dealt with by the King's Lifeguard of Foot. Nevertheless Sir William Vavasour's infantry brigade suffered quite a number of casualties suggesting that it might have been deployed on one or a number of occasions to ease the pressure on Sir Nicholas Byron's men.[29]

If the left flank of Essex's intended route eastwards was reasonably secure by midday, the same could not be said of the right. As mentioned above, Prince Rupert's control of the Andover road from Newbury to the Monkey Lane junction meant that he was able to deploy the bulk of the Royalist cavalry and quite a number of pieces of field artillery on Wash Common by mid-morning. They were followed some time afterwards by the infantry brigades of Sir Jacob Astley, Sir Gilbert Gerard and John Bellasis released by the council of war. As the right wing of Essex's cavalry began to emerge onto the heath, the king's regiments of horse began to harass them. Stapleton succeeded in repulsing two attacks at brigade strength. At about the same time small parties of horse supported by artillery pieces were attacking the Blue regiment of the Trained Bands with a similar lack of success. However, as soon as all six of Stapleton's regiments had left the lane and entered the common, Rupert led a determined attack against them, probably using almost all the horse he had on the Common.[30]

The final cavalry engagement appears to have taken place towards the north end of Wash Common, as the Red regiment of the London Trained Bands saw nothing of it. The Royalists attacked Stapleton's regiments in the front and the flank. Prince Rupert gave Charles Gerard's brigade the accolade of routing the enemy horse and forcing them back down the lane from which they had emerged, inflicting numerous casualties on them in the process. Stapleton's horse, however, were able to avoid annihilation thanks to the fire of musketeers belonging to Barclay's and Holbourne's brigades, who had left Wash Common and taken up a position behind the hedges that bordered it (after a single cannon ball had been fired at them, according to Rupert).[31] They also defeated any attempt by the Royalist cavalry to force their way down Wheatlands Lane. However, despite what is implied in Parliament's *Official Account*, it seems that the action was quickly over.[32]

According to Digby's account of the principal engagement between cavalry on the common, Royalist foot had also been present but refused to advance, preferring to shelter behind a slight rise in the ground that protected them against enemy fire.[33] However, he was running together a number of points in a single sentence and probably mistook the order in which events occurred and as a result assigned to the morning something that happened on Wash Common much later in the day. It is highly likely that Stapleton had been defeated before the bulk of the Royalist infantry reached the common, as there is no mention of them in the very full Parliamentary account of this phase of the battle. Thus the result of the principal cavalry engagement of the day was stalemate. Stapleton's regiments were unable to deploy on the plateau and thus begin acting as a van or flank guard for Essex's army; Rupert's, on the other hand, were unable to complete their rout by pursuing them down the escarpment. Nevertheless the right wing of the Parliamentary cavalry appears to have taken no further significant part in the battle. The only mention of their later involvement is a comment by John Gwyn, who claimed to have been forced to leap over an earthen bank that separated the heath from the enclosures to escape death at the hands of a wing of enemy cavalry, but this was almost certainly an incorrect recollection or a gross exaggeration. Possibly some of Stapleton's horse did make their way up to the top of Wash Common as they fled from Rupert's men, but not in any numbers and they did not stay there for any length of time. The Parliamentary horse are not mentioned in any of the accounts of the fighting in and about Skinners Green Lane End that took place later in the day written by their own side.[34]

The experience of the Trained Band regiments deployed at the extreme southern end of the Parliamentary line as described by Sergeant Foster and the anonymous soldier of the Blue regiment was a frightful one. Their baptism of fire took place at about eight o'clock in the morning, that is, not long after the failure of the first attempt to drive Essex's vanguard from the northern spur of Biggs Hill, and well before Stapleton's cavalry regiments began deploying on Wash Common. To the admiration of friend and foe alike, the Red regiment endured heavy cannon fire, and the Blue repeated cavalry charges, without giving ground.

After several hours under fire, the pressure on the Red and Blue regiments eased, probably because the Royalist cavalry had moved back up the road towards Newbury to prepare for the final encounter with Stapleton's horse. Seizing its opportunity, the Red regiment, assisted by a regiment in blue colours on their left, possibly Colonel Langham's of Holbourne's brigade, advanced and occupied a rise in the ground to their front, probably part of Trundle Hill. There they remained for only half an hour before being pushed back to their starting point by what, reading between the lines, seems to have been a classic combined arms operation. By that time the Londoners' capacity to resist may have been weakened by the departure of Langham's men, as Holbourne's brigade had been ordered to reinforce the regiments defending the north-western corner of Wash Common. However, Foster claims that the Londoners withdrew in good order, reordered their ranks, and moved forward to attack the enemy once more.[35]

If the timing of the various stages in the morning's fighting as recounted by Foster is correct, the encounters in the southern part of Wash Common were over by 1 p.m. at the latest. What happened to the Red and Blue regiments in the second half of the day, however, is far from clear, as Foster's narrative stops abruptly with their temporary withdrawal from the little hill. He then switches to a discussion of the casualties on both sides, which is odd, given the meticulous attention to detail in his narrative from the start of the expedition to relieve Gloucester up to that point, and his spirited description of a cavalry engagement that took place the following day. One suspects that he brought the narrative to an end because he did not want to tell his London readership what they would not want to hear, namely that the Red and Blue regiments made a further retreat, taking up a position behind the hedges that marked the western boundary of Wash Common, after which they took little further part in the battle. Some support for such a move having taken place comes from the *Official Royalist Account*, which claimed that by the end of the day enemy forces had been expelled from all parts of the common. The reason for the retreat could have been sustained Royalist pressure, but it is more likely that the two regiments were ordered to withdraw. This would have had the effect of reducing the length of the battle line, as Essex had already moved both Barclay's and Holbourne's brigades northwards from their original position along the western edge of the Common.[36] Also, by early afternoon with the right wing cavalry driven back and the Grand Reserve crowding into the approaches to the Common but unable to make any further progress, Essex may have given up on his grand plan, concentrating instead on killing as many Royalists as possible. In such circumstances there was no military logic in continuing to deploy the trained bands in an exposed position in the southern part of the common. To leave them there a moment longer would risk giving the Royalists the chance of annihilating them, as there was no chance of supporting them without risking more of his army.[37]

Up to midday what happened in the First Battle of Newbury is reasonably clear, but considerable uncertainty surrounds what happened in the afternoon. Three of the chroniclers, Byron, Foster and Wentworth, have ceased to chronicle, and the accounts of Sir John Digby and John Gwyn are too focused on their subject's exploits to be of any real value in expanding and elaborating the narrative. The next section is therefore very largely hypothesis. However, the *Official Parliamentary Account* suggests quite strongly that two confrontations took place at the north end of Wash Common, the first soon after midday and the other at about 4 p.m. The author of Rupert's Diary largely confirms the nature of the first attack and its outcome. The second is more elusive, but there is considerable circumstantial evidence for it in writings produced by both sides.

By late morning, the forces that had made their way up Skinners Green Lane were beginning to deploy on Wash Common in such a way as to defend the extension of the lane that ran along the edge of the heath land towards the Newbury–Andover road along which the Grand Reserve and the artillery train would have to march. In doing so, Essex probably made use of the line of tumuli situated close to the highest point of the common, which afforded considerable protection to a force having to defend itself against attack from the south. The defence was initially entrusted to the Lord General's regiment, who still acted as the spearhead of the advance, supported by some field pieces and possibly by a commanded body of musketeers from the London Trained Bands.[38]

The first Royalist assault involving two or three brigades of infantry and several brigades of cavalry coincided with the substitution of part of the Grand Reserve, Mainwaring's regiment and part of Skippon's brigade, for Essex's regiment, which had been in continuous action for at least four hours. The moment was well chosen. The new regiments were forced back a considerable distance losing several field pieces in the process. Reading between the lines of the *Official Account*, two heavy cannon that had been placed beside Skinners Green Lane where it entered Wash Common were also nearly captured.

To restore the situation the Lord General ordered his own regiment up again and also the six regiments that made up Barclay's and Holbourne's brigades from further down the heath. They had almost certainly been heavily involved in protecting the retreat of Stapleton's cavalry regiments, but the fighting there had died down, and they too were in the process of being withdrawn from the line. The counterattack won back some of the lost ground and most of the cannon, and Essex consolidated the position at the lane head by moving up one of the London auxiliary regiments.[39] However, taken together, the decisive defeat of the cavalry on the heath and the setback for the infantry on the edge of the common meant that the Grand Reserve could not proceed towards the Andover road in the way that had probably been planned. Part of the force intended to protect its flank had been routed, and Essex's troops would now have to force their way through well over half the Royalist army in order to make any further progress eastwards.

During the course of the afternoon Essex mustered at least fourteen of his twenty infantry regiments at the top end of the heath or in the approaches to it, which must have made the area exceedingly crowded.[40] In the meantime, after a struggle allegedly lasting six hours, Sir John Merrick had brought the rest of the artillery pieces up to the top of Skinners Green Lane and into the hedges that lined the north-west corner of Wash Common, where they soon began to inflict heavy casualties on the Royalist troops to their front on the heath. In late afternoon, however, possibly goaded by the losses they were sustaining from enemy fire, the Royalists apparently attacked once again with a large force of cavalry supported by musketeers, the intention being not only to chase the enemy from their toehold on the heath, but also to capture some of the enclosures they occupied. However, the assault did not go according to plan. The Parliamentarians were duly driven back, but the Royalists made no progress in the enclosures, allegedly because of the lack of spirit shown by their infantry.[41] This is the argument of both the *Official Royalist Account* of the battle and Sir John Byron's narrative. Whilst praising the performance of the horse, they state in no uncertain terms that the foot refused to leave the shelter of dead ground (provided, presumably, by the tumuli). The two writers also drew a sharp contrast between the behaviour of the infantry on the common and that of Sir Nicholas Byron's brigade on the northern slope of the escarpment. John Bellasis, on the other hand, who had commanded one of the infantry brigades involved, gave a more positive, but probably incomplete, picture of the encounter in his reminiscences, claiming that the Royalist foot drove the enemy from the common, but saying nothing about what happened subsequently. Byron, Digby and Bellasis all had reasons for telling the tale as they did, but it is possible to construct a hypothesis that to a large measure reconciles the narratives: the Royalist infantry obeyed the first part of their orders, that is to assist the horse in driving the Parliamentarians from the heath, but some, it seems, from Bellasis's brigade, refused to attack the enemy in the enclosures because of the weight of hostile fire. However, one regiment that fought on the heath, the Earl of Forth's, did suffer heavy casualties equivalent to those sustained by regiments belonging to Sir Nicholas Byron's brigade on the northern slopes of the escarpment, suggesting that it at least had taken part in an assault against a well-defended enemy position. Sir

Gilbert Gerard's brigade, which had well over 200 officers and men killed or wounded during the battle, may also have suffered badly in the assault. The *Official Parliamentary Account* confirms the bravery of at least some of the Royalist infantry, describing an attack into the enclosures late in the day carried out by 500 or so musketeers, which was repulsed with difficulty by Barclay's and Holbourne's regiments, and which probably formed part of a combined assault involving several cavalry brigades.[42] This second attack has been seen as an attempt to split the Parliamentary army in two,[43] but it seems unlikely, as the steepness of the escarpment and the enclosures that lay behind it would have made it impossible for the Royalist horse to sweep through the centre of the enemy army. One Parliamentary account saw the attack as a defensive move designed to protect the Royalist artillery on Wash Common from being overwhelmed,[44] but this too looks improbable, as the Parliamentary infantry would not have dared to stray far from the enclosures without cavalry support, of which there was none.

Despite the failure of the last Royalist attack of the day fully to achieve its objectives, the advance guard of the Parliamentary army was well and truly stuck. It had made no progress since noon, and in front of it on the heath it could see the Royalist horse and foot still drawn up in good order. Essex's officers and soldiers, it was claimed, were also very concerned to see the enemy bringing up more artillery pieces, presumably so as to be able to plaster their front line before renewing the assault the following day.[45] The advantage at nightfall therefore appeared to lie with the Royalists. Admittedly Essex's army might change the direction of its advance by pushing down the hill towards Newbury and trying to rush the bridge over the Kennet, but this would be no more than a desperate, and probably uncoordinated, dash for safety. The bridge could be held by the cavalry and infantry forces the king still had, stationed on the flat ground to the west of the town, until such time as Rupert's cavalry with infantry support were able to push down the Andover road and take the enemy troops in the rear.

Remaining where they were was also out of the question for Essex's army. There was no water in the enclosures and very little if any food in their knapsacks.[46] According to one account, Essex's army was still 'resolved to force a way through or die', but in two days the troops on the escarpment looking north would see Royalist reinforcements from Bristol marching along the Bath road towards Newbury.[47] Retreat might have enabled part of the army to escape, but only temporarily. Provided that the Royalists did not cut the lane from Enbourne to Hungerford, a breakout to the west was feasible, particularly in the case of the so-called left wing cavalry regiments under Colonel Middleton's command. He might also have been able to cover the withdrawal of the infantry that remained in the Kennet valley and on the northern slope of the escarpment, Lord Robartes's brigade and the Blue Auxiliary regiment of the London Trained Bands. However, there was no safe refuge nearer than

Gloucester or Southampton for those who managed to escape. Both were forty miles away across open country, and the chances of not being ridden over by Rupert's triumphant cavalry would have been small. As for the rest of the army in the enclosures to the south of Newbury, they would have been obliged to surrender in circumstances similar to those that were to occur at Lostwithiel a year later. But for the Lord General there would be no chance, as on that occasion, of escaping by sea.

All the Royalists therefore needed to do was to pin down the Parliamentarians until enemy morale collapsed. However, on the day after the battle the king's army lacked the ability to play any role that required firepower, be it offensive or defensive. During the battle the Royalist foot and horse had allegedly used up eighty barrels of gunpowder, and the earliest that new supplies could arrive from Oxford was a day and a half away.[48] According to Reid, some powder suitable for artillery pieces remained,[49] but the defensive line on the heath could not be defended by cannon alone against a determined attack by thousands of musketeers supported by their own artillery. Rupert allegedly wanted to call the enemy's bluff, but the council of war decided to withdraw their forces into Newbury itself under cover of darkness, their only hope of retaining operational advantage being if Essex had been so decisively defeated on the heath that his army had retreated during the night. However, the Lord General had not lost his nerve. As soon as it became apparent that the Royalists had abandoned their positions, Essex assembled the whole of his army on Wash Common, and then ordered it to set off eastwards across the heath towards Reading. Expecting attack from Newbury, he drew his regiments up in battle formation several times as they crossed Greenham and Crookham Commons, but all the Royalists could manage was the occasional cannon ball fired in their general direction. However, just after reaching the enclosures near Aldermaston, the Parliamentarians allowed their guard to slip. Royalist cavalry, supported by musketeers, launched a most effective attack on the left wing of horse (which had not taken part in the fighting at Newbury and was acting as the army's rearguard) as it traversed a narrow lane. In panic the cavalrymen rode over their own foot soldiers, according to Foster, but musketeers drawn from the London Trained Bands assisted by regimental artillery soon created such a barrage of defensive fire that the pursuers halted for fear of incurring heavy casualties. Clarendon was amazed that the Royalist cavalry did not do more to dispute Essex's army's march across Greenham Common. The reason for this was almost certainly the heavy casualties suffered by Prince Rupert's crack regiments of horse and the exhaustion of the rest in assaulting enemy infantry positions during the previous afternoon.[50] Something very similar happened on the Parliamentary side after Marston Moor nine months later, when Oliver Cromwell's victorious horse were quite unable to conduct any kind of pursuit on the day following the battle.[51]

On the morning of 22 September Parliament's field army reached Reading. There it rested for three days before marching to Windsor, the most westerly garrison defending London, and so to Kingston. The Trained Band regiments returned in triumph to the city on 28 September, and Essex shone in their reflected glory. There was no doubt that he had conducted a successful campaign, even if the fight at Newbury had been a victory by default.[52]

Part III

The Decisive Battles of 1644

Chapter 8

The Battle of Cheriton
Context, Sources and Landscape

Context

The Battle of Cheriton was fought on 29 March 1644 about six miles to the east of Winchester where the parishes of Cheriton, Bramdean, Tichbourne and Hinton Ampner join. For Parliament, despite its victory, the Cheriton campaign ended in stalemate. For the king it destroyed the prospect of conquering the rest of England south of the Thames with its rich resources, not merely potential recruits for the army but also ironworks and gunpowder mills, which is thought to have been his strategic objective for the spring of 1644.[1] The attempt by Sir Ralph, now Lord Hopton, during the autumn of 1643 to establish a strong Royalist presence in West Sussex and Hampshire using half the Royalist army of the west had been thwarted by some very effective campaigning by Sir William Waller in the two weeks either side of Christmas. Hopton's army had been saved from humiliating retreat into north Wiltshire by a heavy fall of snow, which blanketed the south of England for well over a month, but Sir William was ready to set out on campaign by the middle of March catching the Royalists somewhat on the hop. His orders were to reconquer the south-west of England, which he had lost through his defeat at Roundway Down the previous July.

Both armies that fought in the Cheriton campaign were hastily assembled conglomerates. The king's forces comprised an infantry corps and several cavalry brigades belonging to the Western Army, some 4,000 men, led by Hopton, its field marshal general, and a contingent of 1,200 infantry and between 1,000 and 1,300 cavalry belonging to the main field army commanded by the Lord General, the Earl of Forth.[2] Forth had been ordered to march south from Oxford when it became apparent that Hopton was facing an army at least twice the size of his own. Edgar implies that the appointment of Forth was evidence of a lack of confidence in Hopton.[3] He may well have been correct, but there was no other officer of suitable rank available. Rupert was organizing an expedition to relieve the besieged garrison of Newark; Wilmot was busy in the Cotswolds trying to starve Gloucester into surrender; whilst Sir Jacob Astley, the major general of foot, had enough on his hands refortifying Reading where he was garrison commander.

Waller's army was even more diverse. It included regiments of horse and foot raised in Kent, Sussex, Surrey and Hampshire during 1643, some of which had fought at Newbury; a number of cavalry regiments which had been with Sir William since early in 1643 and then been brought up to strength again after Roundway Down; a brigade of London Trained Bands consisting of two regiments of foot that had not fought at Newbury; and some regiments raised in the city during the late summer and autumn of 1643. This was largely the army that had run rings around Hopton during the winter, but in early March Waller received a reinforcement of 1,500 to 2,000 cavalry and dragoons from the Earl of Essex commanded by his lieutenant general, Sir William Balfour. Essex regarded Balfour as taking precedence over Waller in matters of command and thus as the army commander. The intention may have been to humiliate Waller, who had sabotaged the Lord General's spring campaign in 1643 and then been indirectly implicated in attempts to ease him out of his command during the summer, but after what had happened at Roundway Down the earl was probably wary of leaving Waller in sole charge of Parliament's only army defending the southern approaches to London.[4]

On 27 March Waller and Balfour ordered a general rendezvous of their forces on the high downs at East Meon, near Petersfield.[5] Hopton and Forth decided not to wait for them to advance but marched towards East Meon taking the lower route, probably using the road that passed through Morestead and Stephens Castle which kept to the 400-foot contour line. The same day the two armies faced each other some eight miles east-south-east of Winchester with the Parliamentarians on Old Winchester Hill and the Royalists to their south, probably at Corhampton. Hopton claimed that he tried unsuccessfully to entice them from their position using Sir John Smith's cavalry brigade, but then realized that the standoff might be a ruse to enable the enemy to send troops to threaten Winchester by marching across the front of the Royalist army and occupying the small market town of New Alresford, a potentially strong quarter on the Alton road some six miles east-north-east of the city. Scouts duly found Balfour's cavalry making for Alresford, and Hopton set out on a parallel course at full speed. Arriving at Alresford with a large body of horse and dragoons, he occupied the town, and in due course the rest of the Royalist army caught up and quartered on high ground just to the south.[6] Balfour in the meantime had fallen back on the rest of the Parliamentary army, which took up quarters for the night of 27–28 March along the Petersfield–Winchester road in and around the village of Cheriton.

Sources

The printed and manuscript primary sources for the Battle of Cheriton have been available to historians for many years. All were accessible to S.R. Gardiner when he wrote Volume 1 of *History of the Great Civil War*, apart from a report of the Cheriton campaign written by Robert Harley, which was published by the Historical Manuscripts Commission several years later.[7]

The most detailed and structured account of the battle was that written by Lord Hopton.[8] The only manuscript is amongst the Clarendon papers, and it therefore seems likely that Hopton gave it or lent it to Lord Clarendon to assist him in writing the *History of the Great Rebellion*. The earliest date at which the manuscript can have been completed is the spring of 1646, some two years after the Battle of Cheriton.[9] The account therefore appears to lack immediacy, but there is some circumstantial evidence that it was based on a report sent to Oxford immediately after the battle.[10]

Hopton has a reputation for probity that is repeated in book after book, including the new *Dictionary of National Biography*, and he had no obvious political motive from the winter of 1645–6 for covering up earlier mistakes. The natural reaction of the historian is therefore to regard the narrative as a dispassionate account of events,[11] but there is no reason why Hopton should not have sought to present future generations with an account that placed his military career in the best possible light. Also, his reputation owes its origin almost entirely to the pen portrait in *History of the Great Rebellion*, which, not unnaturally, was largely positive, given that Hopton's political and religious opinions were close to Clarendon's own. A careful reading of the text suggests that defending his reputation was one motive for writing his accounts of the war. On three occasions he took care to show that the blame for tactical mistakes did not lie with him, and on three others he was careful to take personal credit for tactical successes. In addition, there is some ground for suspecting that he was being economical with the truth.[12] The most interesting example of this was his claim that it was not he but Lord Forth who was in overall command of the army that fought at Cheriton. Admittedly this is implied in the second major Royalist account of the battle, that of Colonel Walter Slingsby,[13] but it is denied by Lord Clarendon who claimed that Hopton tried to persuade Forth to take overall responsibility, but that the Lord General refused to do any more than give advice.[14] Now, I have a very strong tendency to view anything that Clarendon wrote about the king's generals with suspicion,[15] as they were very largely his political opponents, but this was certainly not the case with Hopton. Forth he seems to have disliked, but he was too old, too infirm and too incoherent to be viewed as an enemy. Second, Clarendon had plenty of opportunity to discuss the nature of the command structure at Cheriton with the two generals concerned and make up his own mind, as he spent almost a year in their company whilst serving on the Prince of Wales's Council in the west of England in 1645 and 1646.[16] The language used in the next chapter concerning command and control on the battlefield at Cheriton will therefore be deliberately neutral in tone to reflect this uncertainty as to who was actually in charge on the Royalist side.

Walter Slingsby's account is different. It was written at Lord Clarendon's request, but Slingsby seems to have been determined to avoid controversy by not criticizing those he was known to dislike. In a paragraph appended to his narrative of Cheriton he refused to describe events surrounding the surrender of Bristol as he and Prince Rupert did not enjoy good relations. This may explain why Hopton is not mentioned once in Slingsby's account of Cheriton. He also had very little to say about his own role in the battle, but concentrated on putting the various stages of the fighting in chronological order. Like Hopton's account, however, Slingsby's was almost certainly not written until some time after the event, and the accuracy of his memory of at least one aspect of the campaign was faulty: the manoeuvres that immediately preceded the battle lasted two days, not six.

The account of the battle in *Mercurius Aulicus* contains nothing of value, but is an interesting example of selective use of material.[17] The early stages of the battle are described in considerable detail up to the first Royalist setback, but then the editor claims Hopton disengaged. He thus missed out a good four hours of the fighting, including the mauling of the king's cavalry regiments. What is also intriguing is the similarity in structure and content, if not in vocabulary, to Hopton's narrative, especially in the description of the options available to the enemy after the capture of Cheriton Wood. This suggests that it may incorporate some parts of a report of the battle, possibly written straight after the battle, which is now lost.[18]

The remaining accounts of the battle from the Royalist side are second-, even third-hand, and both are in the nature of obituaries. The first is Edward Walsingham's hagiographic study of the death of the valiant Catholic, Sir John Smith, who had risen from lieutenant of horse to brigade commander since Edgehill.[19] The second, included in a volume of mini-biographies of famous persons published in 1668, is a brief description of the last fight of Lord John Stuart, the king's cousin, who held the post of lieutenant general of cavalry in the Western Army.[20] Both are narrow in that they focus on the incident in which their hero received his mortal wound, but the little additional information they provide does not show any sign of having been borrowed from another writer.

The principal account of the battle from the Parliamentary side is that of Robert Harley, an officer in Waller's own cavalry regiment. His excited letter to his elder brother Edward, later to be a colonel in the New Model Army, covers the first three weeks of the Hampshire campaign.[21] Robert thought little of his account – 'a confused thing patched up by a short memory'. He advised Edward not to read it if he could find another, but it is written in clear, invigorating language and provides excellent detail concerning the movements of the armies. As is the case with this type of communication between friends or family members, the desire to amuse and divert provides a potential diversion from the path of truth, but Robert Harley's sense of humour is entirely at the expense of the soldiers of the London Trained Bands. In no other respect is there any sign of exaggeration for effect, but a major omission is very interesting. Despite a detailed, well-structured and thoughtful account of an incident in which he had been involved on the day before the battle, Harley has nothing whatsoever to say about his troop's role in the battle prior to the pursuit stage. This suggests that it was in the reserve and played no part in the actual fighting.[22] If so, as Waller's horse was on the left and Balfour's on the right, it would have been stationed in low ground in the Itchen valley or on the rising ground to the immediate south or west, but within cannon shot as his lieutenant's horse was seemingly killed in that manner. Thus Harley would have had a good view of the action to his front, and his account duly confirms major aspects of the fighting on the left wing described in other accounts, including the destruction of Henry Bard's regiment and the final advance of Waller's infantry up the western slope of the southern spur that precipitated the Royalist retreat. It was probably his position as much as his poor opinion of the London Trained Bands which explains his failure to write anything further about what happened on the right wing after the loss of Cheriton Wood.

Two other accounts of the battle survive that were written by officers belonging to Waller's corps of the Parliamentary army. There is a passage describing Cheriton in the memoirs of John Birch, lieutenant colonel in Sir Arthur Haselrig's regiment of foot, written by his servant Henry Roe. Birch was a man who had done exceedingly well out of the events of the 1640s.[23] Having begun the decade as a Bristol wine merchant in a middling way of business, he ended it as a major Herefordshire landowner. The account of Birch's contribution to the fighting at Cheriton differs in no substantial way from the rest of Roe's *Memoir*, in that Birch was invariably in the right. By his active patrolling on the night of 28–29 March he ensured that the Battle of Cheriton took place, despite the misgivings of a more senior officer who did not want to fight. He then restored the situation on the right wing when the battle looked lost. Finally, he gave Waller the good advice on tactics, which brought about the Royalist withdrawal. There is no means of ascertaining how much of what Roe wrote is sheer moonshine, but it is important not to be so contemptuous of his rhetoric as to dismiss the whole of the memoirs as worthless. Moreover, there is no evidence that Roe incorporated any material already in the public domain into the narrative.

The other account is a paragraph in the diary of Walter Yonge, MP for Honiton, describing a report delivered in the House of Commons by Sir Arthur Haselrig a few days after the battle.[24] Like Roe's *Memoir*, it suffers from the disadvantage that information concerning what had occurred on

29 March 1644 had passed through two minds before being committed to paper. Haselrig's military reputation on his own side was a poor one: his insubordination had helped Waller lose the Battle of Roundway Down, and two sources, Roe and Denzil Holles, criticize him for his conduct at Cheriton, which they describe as being unduly cautious at best. The first focuses on his caution on one, and possibly three occasions; the second accuses him of cowardice. However, the précis of the report given by Yonge is straightforward and matter-of-fact, and dovetails neatly with what is recorded in other eyewitness accounts. If Sir Arthur had tried to use the opportunity of addressing the House to enhance his own role in the fighting, Yonge ignored it.

Apart from two passages of little significance in Sir William Waller's spiritual autobiography describing his providential escape from capture or death at Cheriton,[25] the remaining reports on the battle from the Parliamentary side are products of the London press. The fullest account in the weeklies is that in the 5 April edition of *Perfect Occurrences*,[26] but it is of no value. What is not to be found elsewhere is brief, and almost certainly a means of filling up space; it shows no sign of being based on an independent source now lost. However, three of the pamphlets printed soon after the battle were written by participants: Sir William Balfour,[27] Captain John Jones, and E.A. (probably Elias Archer) of the London Trained Bands.[28] Balfour's account is short on detail, allegedly because of post-battle fatigue but possibly because his own cavalry regiments may not have performed well early on in the battle.[29] He does, however, provide extremely interesting detail about the initial deployment of the Parliamentary army. The other two accounts are also brief, possibly for the same reason.[30] Written by London officers targeting a primarily London readership, their principal underlying objective was to rescue the reputation of the Trained Bands, which had not done as well in their second battle as they had at Newbury. They therefore played down the trained bands' failure to hold Cheriton Wood against a Royalist flank attack. Jones did not even mention that London troops formed the majority of the defending force, whilst E.A. implies that the Royalists were already in occupation of part of the wood before the Parliamentary soldiers arrived. In contrast, both emphasize the importance of the Londoners' role on the right wing in the closing stages of the battle. That an advance by the right wing did take place towards the end of the battle is unquestionable, but it is more likely that the White regiment of the Trained Bands and Colonel Birch's regiment merely occupied ground abandoned by the king's infantry as the threat to their own right wing increased. Colonel Appleyard, who led a major assault on Cheriton Wood at the start of the battle, was on the opposite wing by mid-afternoon.[31]

The non-written primary sources for the Battle of Cheriton can be quickly described. There are no contemporary maps of how the armies were deployed at the start of the battle or of the area in which the battle was fought, but the survey of the Bishop of Winchester's lands in Cheriton compiled some forty years before is of value in helping to reconstruct the seventeenth-century landscape,[32] as are the Commonwealth survey of the Dean and Chapter of Winchester's lands in Hinton Ampner,[33] Isaac Taylor's and Thomas Milne's maps of Hampshire, the first edition of the Ordnance Survey map of Hampshire, and the much larger-scale maps of the parishes of Cheriton, Hinton Ampner, Tichbourne and Bramdean drawn in connection with tithe apportionment early in Queen Victoria's reign.[34] However, they cannot answer the two most important questions concerning the landscape as it was in 1644, the extent of Cheriton Wood and the location of heath land in three of the four parishes. Regrettably no systematic archaeological survey of the battlefield has yet been undertaken, and the only report I have to hand is second- or third-hand and very generalized.[35]

Landscape

The Battle of Cheriton was fought across a tract of land measuring about two miles from north to south and a mile and a half from east to west. With the numbers of troops involved there was theoretically plenty of room for deployment, but large parts of the battlefield were enclosed, creating problems for both sides similar to those encountered at the First Battle of Newbury.

The battlefield was bounded on the western side by the shallow valley of the infant River Itchen. Directly alongside it ran a road from Alresford on which were located the settlements of North End, Cheriton and Cheriton itself. On the opposite side of the battlefield was a square block of open chalk downland some 200 feet higher than the valley bottom with sides about 600 yards in length. A detached portion of Tichbourne parish, it was known at the time as East Down.[36] Beyond East Down was Cheriton Wood, linked to the rest of its parish by Cow Down, which was probably already enclosed.[37] Between the wood and the river were three ridges of chalk running roughly east–west. The outer ones curved inwards towards the river, but stopped some hundred yards short of it. Their shape has been likened to an arena or a horseshoe with Cheriton Wood at the toe,[38] but this metaphor has caused many writers to ignore the central ridge, less pronounced than the others on a map, but clearly of significance when viewed on the ground. This points south-south-west in a straight line towards North End, Cheriton, but comes to an end well short of the river.

The extent to which these three ridges and the land between them was enclosed in the mid-seventeenth century is uncertain, but research into the agrarian history of Cheriton and Hinton Ampner suggests that very little of it was open field or heath, as Gardiner and Burne and Young suggested.[39] Unlike many of the chalk downland villages of southern England, Cheriton seems to have lost its open fields quite early. There is no mention of strips in the open field in a survey of the village taken on behalf of the Bishop of Winchester in 1602,[40] and there was not even the need for a consolidating act in the period of

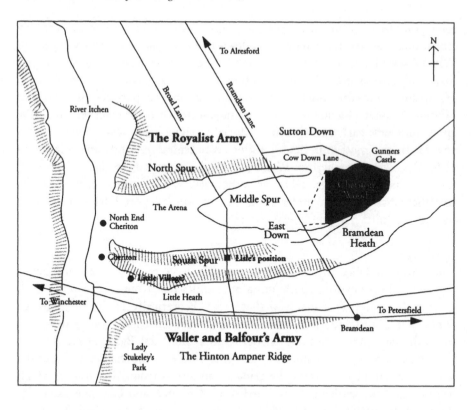

Map 3. The Battle of Cheriton

0 —————————————— miles —————————————— 1

enclosure by Act of Parliament (*circa* 1700 to *circa* 1850) to deal with isolated pockets of common and heath. Moreover, the survey shows that well over a square mile of Cheriton parish was fully enclosed forty years before the battle was fought. This was an area of land large enough to encompass almost the whole of the parish on the east bank of the Itchen between Cheriton Wood and the river itself.[41]

About half a mile beyond the southern spur of the arena, and in Hinton Ampner parish, was a fourth ridge also extending in an east–west direction. Along its northern slope passed the Petersfield–Winchester road. Separating the ridge from the southern spur was a valley through which flowed a tiny stream, the first of the Itchen's tributaries. Gardiner's map in *History of the Great Civil War* fills the valley with small clumps of vegetation that give the reader the impression that it was marshy. However, reference to the table of symbols used in the first edition of the one-inch Ordnance Survey map of the Cheriton area, which he used as his template, shows that what lay in the valley was a small area of rough heath.[42] In 1644, however, the heath may have been larger than in the mid-nineteenth century, stretching possibly as far west as what is now known as Bramdean Lane.[43]

Between the Hinton Ampner ridge and the southern spur of the arena were Lamborough Fields, an area of arable where E.A. claims that the Parliamentary army, or possibly only the London brigade, spent the night of 27–28 and 28–29 March.[44] Their location, however, is problematic. Hopton clearly described Waller's army as being quartered '[ad]joining Lady Stukeley's house in a low field enclosed with a very thick hedge and ditch and their ordnance planted on the rising of the hill behind them'.[45] Lady Stukeley's house was the manor house of Hinton Ampner situated on the summit of the Hinton Ampner ridge looking north. If the park surrounding the house had been the same size and shape as it is today, the artillery pieces would have been drawn up along the Petersfield–Winchester road with the main body of the army below them in what the tithe apportionment map of Hinton Ampner describes as meadow. This would have been enclosed in the way that Hopton described to keep out grazing animals, as winter fodder was at a premium on the light soils of eastern Hampshire in the mid-seventeenth century. However, the Commonwealth survey of the lands of the Dean and Chapter of Winchester in 1651 and the tithe survey of 1841 place Lamborough fields on the south-facing side of the southern spur of the arena. All I can suggest is that E.A. had received the wrong information, as Balfour wrote about a small heath in front of his army's quarters, which would fit the land in the valley between the southern spur and the Hinton Ampner ridge as depicted in the first edition of the Ordnance Survey map.

In addition to the Petersfield–Winchester road, various tracks crossed the battlefield. The most significant one, Bramdean Lane, ran from Bramdean to Alresford, but today it is no more than a bridle path for almost its entire length. It crossed the upper end of the area where fighting took place on 29 March 1644, but does not seem to have had an impact on the shape of the battle other than enabling both sides to move artillery pieces and carriages rapidly from one location to another in its opening and the closing stages. Two other tracks also crossed the battlefield in a roughly north–south direction, namely Broad Lane and Dark Lane. Of these the first was given great tactical significance in the two main Royalist narratives of the battle, as it alone gave access to the heath where the main cavalry encounter took place, but the second may not have been in existence in the seventeenth century as it is not marked on Isaac Taylor's map published in 1759.[46]

Robert Harley identifies a 'little village' as crucial to the viability of the defensive position established by Waller and Balfour on and around the Petersfield–Winchester road.[47] It cannot be Cheriton itself,[48] neither can it be Hinton Ampner or Bramdean, which are too far to the south and the west respectively. Today there are several small collections of houses that lie on or close to the road as it passes between Cheriton and Bramdean. Of these New Cheriton looks the most likely candidate, as the hamlet directly below

Hinton Ampner, which contains at least one house of the right date, is a little too far to the east.

Finally, it is necessary to have a brief word about Cheriton Wood and its environs. Seymour states that the wood may have been a different size and shape from what it is today, and it is highly likely that he was right. By the time Isaac Taylor produced his map, wood (or possibly scrubland) extended as far as Bramdean Lane, as it does today.[49] However, as a result it spilled off the high ground where Cheriton, Bramdean and Bishops Sutton parishes joined into the valley between the southern and middle spurs of the arena. This part of the wood is therefore lower than the two ridges, but at the same time close to the position held by the Royalist advance guard on the night of 28–29 March. Parliamentary troops lining its western edge could not therefore have been described by Hopton as occupying high wooded ground 'commanding the hill' where the advance guard was quartered.[50] I therefore suggest that the western boundary of Cheriton Wood was 400 yards to the east of Bramdean Lane and that much of the lower ground in between was open and formed a continuation of East Down.[51]

*   *   *   *   *

Unlike almost every other Civil War battlefield, there is still some doubt as to the exact location of the fighting. Contemporaries variously describe it as taking place at Alresford, on Cheriton Down, on East Down and on Bramdean Heath.[52] Gardiner was the first to claim that the battle took place in the horseshoe-shaped arena between the northern and southern spurs described above.[53] Burne, Edgar, Young and Holmes, and Reid accepted his location without question,[54] but Seymour maintained that the battle was fought in the more restricted space between the middle and the southern spurs.[55] He is also probably wrong, though the evidence supporting his hypothesis is weightier than is that for the traditional version. Only Adair opts for a location outside the arena, that is the shallow valley that separates its southern spur and Cheriton Wood from the Hinton Ampner ridge and Bramdean, and he is probably correct.[56] However, Adair apparently weakens his case by placing the battlefield too far to the east so as to include the countryside between Bramdean and Cheriton Wood, probably because it was flatter and therefore more suitable for a cavalry engagement.[57] None of the written sources makes specific mention of fighting to the east of Bramdean Lane close to Bramdean village, and this may be borne out by the little evidence there is in the public arena concerning what has been discovered by field walking and metal detecting. A lesser problem with the site favoured by Adair is that, if the Royalist cavalry had been deployed between Cheriton Wood and Bramdean, a well-managed retreat like that known to have happened at the end of the battle would have been impossible, as the wood would have been in their way. However, this would only apply if the wood were the same size as today. If it were smaller, as suggested above, a successful retreat would have been possible, and Adair's location of the cavalry fight on the Royalist left wing would therefore become a much stronger hypothesis.

The principal evidence that the battle did indeed take place in the valley between the southern spur of the arena and the Hinton Ampner ridge is in Lord Hopton's account of military operations on 28 March, the day before the battle, most particularly the position reached by the Royalist advance guard that evening. On the previous night when the Parliamentary army camped near Hinton Ampner, the Royalists took up quarters on a piece of high ground three miles by two, between there and Alresford, the southern limit of which was the north spur of the arena. This is confirmed by Sir Arthur Haselrig, who reported that the Royalists were on Sutton Down, which was situated in the centre of the plateau directly to the north of Cheriton Wood.[58] During the course of the day there was much skirmishing throughout the arena, but before nightfall the Royalists had been able to push forward to a position from which they could see the Parliamentary army encamped in the field surrounded by thick hedges in the low ground to the north or west of Lady Stukeley's house at Hinton Ampner mentioned above. Young and Holmes see the high tide of the Royalist advance as only reaching the middle ridge, but this cannot have been so.[59] At no point is the middle ridge high enough for an observer to be able to see into the valley between the southern spur of the arena and the Hinton Ampner ridge. Gardiner, Burne, Edgar, Seymour and Adair, on the other hand, place its leading edge on the southern ridge, from which there is a clear view to the front, and they are surely right.[60]

To hold the position overlooking the valley between the southern spur and the Hinton Ampner ridge, Hopton brought forward 1,000 musketeers under Colonel George Lisle and placed them in a small wood on top of the spur with 500 cavalry stationed in the lane running alongside it. The wood no longer survives, but the lane was probably Broad Lane, the middle one of the three lanes that cross the spur, if Cheriton Wood was the same size as it is today.[61] If the wood was smaller, it could have been Bramdean Lane.

As a further precaution to ensure that Lisle was not overwhelmed by one of the surprise attacks for which Waller was famous, the rest of the Royalist army stood to arms all night, probably on the northern slopes of the arena rather than in the arena itself, but close enough to be able to respond immediately to any sound of fighting. Balfour and Waller, however, ignored the obvious option of a direct attack. Instead, under the cover of darkness and an early morning mist, they sent a force of infantry and cavalry into Cheriton Wood and its environs, thus outflanking Lisle's position on the east. The Royalists did not realize what had happened until about 10 a.m. on account of the mist; the noise it produced they took to be carriages being prepared for a retreat towards Petersfield. This order of events is described in several of the accounts of the start of the battle written by observers on both sides. However, twentieth-century military historians then take a step in the dark by asserting that Forth and Hopton responded prudently to Waller's occupation of Cheriton Wood by ordering Lisle and his men to fall back on the main body of the Royalist army, which he did without incurring any loss. In the case of Seymour the withdrawal was from the southern ridge to the middle ridge, and in the case of the rest from the southern or the middle ridge to the northern ridge. Next, all historians insist that as Lisle withdrew Balfour and Waller moved the rest of their army forward. By mid-morning they had occupied the whole of the southern ridge of the arena. Thus was the stage set for the battle proper.

However, the assertion that Lisle withdrew from the southern spur goes no further back in time than Volume 1 of Gardiner's *History of the Great Civil War*, but as the withdrawal is not mentioned in any seventeenth-century source, it can be no more than a hypothesis. Indeed Hopton's account of events suggests the exact opposite, namely that the rest of the Royalist army moved forward to join Lisle, thus taking up a position overlooking Waller and Balfour's quarters below Hinton Ampner:

> the enemy ... had in the dark of the night possessed themselves of a high woody ground that was on the right hand of their own quarters, and placed men and cannon in it, that commanded the hill where Sir George Lisle was. Of this he presently advertised the Earl of Brentford, who ... came instantly to him and, seeing the posture the enemy was in, commanded the Lord Hopton to draw up the whole army and cannon up to him to that ground, which he accordingly did ...[62]

Slingsby confirms that the advance took place, adding the information that 'it was (to) the hill where we intended to fight'.[63]

As this new narrative of events of the morning of 29 March 1644 derives from two sources, and is not contradicted by any other contemporary account of the battle, there is a strong case for arguing that the bulk of the fighting took place not in the horseshoe-shaped arena immediately to the east of Cheriton North End, but in and around Cheriton Wood, on the southern spur, and in the valley in Hinton Ampner and Bramdean parish that lay beyond the spur to the south. There are, however, three caveats. Sir William Ogle placed the battle on downland in Cheriton parish, whilst Captain Jones described the fighting as taking place on East Down.[64] Ogle, however, was mistaken, as, with the possible exception of Cow Down to the east of Bramdean Lane, the only downland in Cheriton parish in 1642 was on the west bank of the Itchen. Captain Jones, on the other hand, may have been right if in the mid-seventeenth century East Down, Tichbourne extended further to the east over the area now covered by part of Cheriton Wood, which would have formed a corridor joining East Down to downland in Bramdean parish to the south of

Cheriton Wood, whose existence at some time in the past is attested to by field name evidence.[65] However, this is no more than surmise on my part, as the written evidence, though supportive, is largely circumstantial in nature.[66]

Another possible weakness in my hypothesis is the allegation that the distribution of musket balls and other military artefacts in the area between the River Itchen and Cheriton Wood supports the site traditionally allotted to the battle.[67] However, if all this means is that the bulk of the commonest finds, musket balls, were discovered in and around Cheriton Wood or to the east of Cheriton village with nothing being found in the fields to the south of the wood or to the east of Bramdean Lane in Bramdean parish, the pattern would fit the battle being fought where I have suggested or where Seymour or indeed Burne and Young have placed it. In all three scenarios the main concentrations of infantry artefacts should be located not in the middle of the battlefield but on the fringes, because that was where the main infantry engagements took place.

Finally it could be argued that the valley between the southern spur of the arena and the Hinton Ampner ridge is too narrow to accommodate the kind of cavalry encounter described in Lord Hopton's account and implicit in some of the others. In fact the width of the valley is similar to that of Wash Common as portrayed in Rocque's map of Berkshire, and its potential as a battleground is very apparent from the aerial photograph included as Plate 17 in Adair's study of Cheriton. Moreover, Balfour does not refer to it as anything other than a little heath, whilst David Lloyd in his biography of Lord John Stuart appears to describe the lieutenant general as taking care that one of the later cavalry engagements of the day took place to the east of the battlefield where the ground was more suitable, namely Bramdean Heath.[68]

However, for me what finally tips the balance of evidence against both the Seymour and the traditional hypothesis is the topographical information contained in Sir William Balfour's and Walter Slingsby's accounts.[69] Balfour stated that the principal cavalry encounter took place immediately in front of the Parliamentary quarters, whilst Slingsby claimed that the position taken up by the Royalist army after evicting the Parliamentary troops from Cheriton Wood gave them an excellent view half a mile to the rear of the enemy army where several bodies of troops could be seen leaving the battlefield.[70] He also claimed that the hill on which the Royalist army deployed for battle was nearer to Waller's quarters of the night of 28–29 March than it was to the Royalist ones. These descriptions cannot apply to the north ridge or to the central ridge of the arena.

Chapter 9
The Battle of Cheriton Narrative

Thus, on the night of 28 March 1644 the Parliamentary army lay encamped close to the Petersfield–Winchester road, the Royalists a mile and a half or so to the north, but with an advance guard of brigade strength on the southern spur of the arena under the command of George Lisle. The number of cavalry in each army was very similar. Waller and Balfour had about 3,000 horse, but the Royalists may have had 200 or so more.[1] In infantry, however, the Parliamentary generals had a distinct numerical advantage, and this was to have a very significant effect on the course and outcome of the battle. Adair accepts Sir Arthur Haselrig's estimate of 7,000 musketeers and pikemen, but this seems very much on the large size. Using Adair's own estimates of the strengths of the seven infantry regiments that fought at Cheriton, 5,000 to 5,500 would be a more credible estimate. In addition Waller and Balfour had two regiments of dragoons, size unknown.[2] According to Hopton, he and Forth had 3,200 foot soldiers. They comprised his own troops 2,000 strong, and 1,200 that Forth had brought with him from Oxford. Sir William Ogle described the Oxford contingent as the Queen's forces, that is infantry Henrietta Maria had brought from the north in May and July 1643, but it apparently included a contingent from the Oxford garrison, and also some troops from the Reading garrison, as George Lisle was colonel of one of the regiments stationed there.[3]

The encounter stage of the battle, which began early the following morning as soon as the mist cleared, was initially an extension of the feint and counter-feint that had characterized the previous day's skirmishing. Roe claimed that the general officers and colonels had decided to retreat at a council of war held on the evening before the battle, but Waller and Balfour seem to have decided to stand their ground, not to retreat. However, there remains a slight element of doubt. Balfour's use of language in his post-battle report can be read as an attempt to pre-empt any rumours that the initial decision had been to retreat rather than to defend the Hinton Ampner ridge: 'We having taken a resolution (by reason of your Excellency's and the Committee of Both Kingdom's commandments) to be wary and cautious to engage ourselves in a fight with the enemy but on advantage, yet we finding them resolved to put us to it ...'. Possibly a decision to retreat had been overtaken by events if, as Roe suggests, energetic patrolling during the night by Birch's regiment made it impossible to separate the two armies the following day. On the other hand the occupation of Cheriton Wood suggests resolution, not indecision, unless, of course, the intention was not to encourage Lisle's advance guard to fall back but to secure the left flank of the Parliamentary army as it retreated towards Petersfield.[4]

The force in Cheriton Wood was made up of 1,000 musketeers from Colonel Potley's and the White regiment of the London Trained Bands supported by a regiment of horse and two pieces of regimental artillery. Waller and Balfour had also sent another body of musketeers to defend Harley's little village that commanded the pass between the far end of the southern spur of the arena and the high ground on the west bank of the River Itchen. This may also be seen as a move to secure the other flank of the army in case the Royalists, denied the chance of attacking its right wing by the forces in Cheriton Wood, launched an assault against the left wing instead.[5]

Cheriton Wood lay to the right of George Lisle's position, but overlooking and flanking the southern spur of the arena along which the Royalists intended to deploy if, as suggested in Chapter 8, the wood was smaller than it is today. It was not until the mist began to lift, about two hours after sunrise according to Hopton, that the Royalist generals became aware of what had happened, but continuing with the policy of aggressive defence they had employed throughout the short campaign, they almost certainly moved the entire Royalist army forward to the southern ridge to support Lisle's brigades of horse and foot. The line of battle extended from the end of the ridge adjacent to Cheriton to a point some way to the east where their troops were within range of Waller's musketeers in Cheriton Wood. Hopton's infantry occupied the part of the line nearest to the wood, Forth's that nearest to Cheriton, but Hopton took care to draw up his infantry and cavalry in dead ground, possibly on the slope of the middle ridge where they could not be shot at by the enemy in the wood. Where the rest of the Royalist horse were deployed at this time in the morning is uncertain, but they are unlikely to have been on the right flank of the army. The valley of the Itchen and the arena were full of enclosures, and thus most unsuitable for cavalry fighting. It can therefore be assumed that the cavalry brigades were drawn up somewhere to the east, but in a position from which they could be brought quickly forward to harry the enemy army as it retreated. Sir John Smith had apparently been sent orders the night before to be ready to lead the pursuit with 1,000 horse.[6]

After the Royalist army had been put into battle formation, Hopton apparently ordered 1,000 musketeers from his own corps under Colonel

Matthew Appleyard to expel the enemy from Cheriton Wood. However, on emerging onto the open hillside from the dead ground, the fire they experienced from the western edge of the wood was so intense that there was every possibility that they would be forced to fall back if they remained where they were. Hopton therefore ordered one of Appleyard's four divisions to move up the dry valley between the middle and northern spurs of the arena and attack Cheriton Wood from the north or the north-west with artillery support.[7] This would have been easy to arrange if, as seems likely, the train of artillery was using Bramdean Lane to move from Sutton Down to the southern spur of the arena.[8]

This assault from an unanticipated direction supported by cannon fire was too much for the brigade defending Cheriton Wood. It quickly took to its heels, but not so quickly as to necessitate the abandonment of its artillery pieces. There were few casualties, but Colonel George Thompson, the commander of the cavalry, may have had his leg shattered by a cannon ball at this point rather than later in the battle. The Royalists probably gained the impression that a disorderly withdrawal was getting under way, as 'we could discern several companies of thirty, of forty, and more in some, running over the fields in the rear of their army half a mile and as well discern their horses spanned in their carriages and to their artillery'. Hopton claimed that he was keen to take advantage of the confusion by launching an attack from the environs of Cheriton Wood against the rear of Waller's army with 1,000 foot and 1,000 horse. Forth, however, advised against it and Hopton claims to have been 'very satisfied' to accept his opinion.[9]

The Lord General would have had good reason for waiting on events. With their left flank now totally secure, the Royalists' position on the southern spur of the arena was so strong that the enemy were almost caught in a trap. In order to escape from it, Balfour and Waller had a number of choices any one of which could have ended in disaster. They are unlikely to have considered advancing down the Petersfield road towards Winchester, as their army's march would have been across open downland with no protection against the enemy. Taking a more southerly route towards the city, on the other hand, would have involved moving across difficult country, more downland but interspersed with wooded valleys, where they could easily fall into a trap sprung by the Royalist cavalry operating with infantry support. Moreover, in both cases the enemy's falling in behind them would have completely cut their best line of retreat back into Sussex. Other alternatives were little better. They could have ordered a general attack, but to do so most of their troops would have had to move across open ground towards an enemy drawn up in an excellent defensive position. Alternatively they could have fallen back towards Petersfield, which risked the army falling into disorder and brigades being cut off and destroyed.

However, there was probably another reason for Lord Forth's caution, though it is not mentioned in any of the Royalist accounts, namely the disparity in numbers between the force he and Hopton commanded and the one led by Waller and Balfour. The Royalist generals would have been well aware of this, as they had a very good view of the whole of the Parliamentary army from George Lisle's position on the southern spur of the arena. A swift advance towards the Petersfield–Winchester road at Bramdean by 2,000 of Hopton's troops, a body only a fifth the size of Waller's army, which threatened to cut off the latter's best escape route, might be very risky. If the Parliamentary generals kept their heads, they could easily reinforce their right wing and possibly inflict great damage on Hopton's men before Forth could send support.

Eyewitnesses are rather hazy about what happened next on the morning of 29 March, but a conflation of the reports of observers on both sides results in quite a high level of consensus on how thrust and counter-thrust led to a fully fledged battle developing that neither side seems to have wanted. It appears from Sir Arthur Haselrig's account of the battle to the House of Commons, and from an estimate of the time it would have taken Lord Hopton to re-deploy the Royalist left wing in and around Cheriton Wood, that a period of between one and one and a half hours elapsed before the next significant development. Balfour claimed the Parliamentarians decided to remain where they were after the loss of the wood because the enemy was determined to fight them, and this was as good a decision as any, given the dangers they faced if they tried to move away. He therefore drew up his horse in the small heath to the north of the Petersfield–Winchester road, that is, between the enemy and the rest of his army, thus shielding it from attack by the forces on the southern spur of the arena.[10] The cavalry were nevertheless in a very exposed position, but behind and above them was the massed firepower of the Parliamentary artillery and most of Waller's musketeers. The length of the Parliamentary line is uncertain, but it is doubtful if it stretched in one direction as far as Bramdean village. The western end, however, was anchored in the little village mentioned by Robert Harley, and this was essential for the security of the entire army. If the Parliamentary musketeers lost control of it, not only would Forth and Hopton have turned Waller and Balfour's flank, the enemy infantry would also be in a position to pour devastating fire into the regiments at the western end of the Parliamentary cavalry line.[11]

When all these arrangements were complete, Waller and Balfour had as strong a position defending the Hinton Ampner ridge as Forth and Hopton had defending the southern spur of the arena. Meanwhile, on the Royalist side Hopton had drawn up his corps in a defensive posture covering all the approaches to the wood and to East Down, whilst the Lord General's troops clustered around the position that Lisle's brigade had occupied during the night. Forth's infantry may even have moved down the slope of the southern spur as far as a substantial hedge that probably marked the boundary between fields on the southern spur of the arena and the heath where Balfour had deployed the Parliamentary cavalry. What is certain at the start of the next stage of the encounter, however, is that Waller's army was in the bottom or on the north-facing slope of the Hinton Ampner ridge, and that the Royalists could look down upon them.[12]

The exact circumstances surrounding what happened next, however, are a mystery. The key, I believe, is to appreciate that Waller and Balfour were behaving in a way that the Royalist generals had not anticipated. Instead of retreating or attacking, they had remained exactly where they were, but deployed their army in a defensive formation, which, as Harley commented, involved facing north rather than west. The only vaguely offensive move, apart from the brief occupation of Cheriton Wood, had been sending musketeers to defend the little settlement in the pass by the Itchen.[13] There followed the Royalists' first tactical mistake, but one from which Hopton was very careful to disassociate himself in his narrative. Having put the Royalist left wing into a defensive posture, he was making his away along the brow of the hill to consult with the Lord General when he saw to his amazement Forth's troops 'too far advanced, and hotly engaged with the enemy in the foot of the hill, and so hard pressed, as when he came to Lord Forth he found him much troubled with it for it seems the engagement was by the forwardness of some particular officers without order'. The form of words is interesting. Not only is Hopton saying that it was no responsibility of his, he is also hinting ever so slightly that Forth had ordered the attack by his use of the word 'seems'. Colonel Slingsby was much more forthright. He stated in no uncertain terms that 'we were ordered to fall on from both wings', and thus, by implication, by somebody holding a higher rank than his own. This cannot have been Hopton's major general of foot, Sir John Paulet, who was carrying messages between Hopton and Forth, and who had no jurisdiction over Forth's troops. As Sir Jacob Astley, the major general of the Oxford army, was not present at Cheriton, the officer concerned can only have been the Lord General himself.[14] The behaviour of the enemy during the night and early morning suggested that enemy generals were considering retreat as one of several options. This view would have been further strengthened if Forth had received intelligence from Hopton's wing after the capture of Cheriton Wood on the lines of the passage from Slingsby's account reproduced above. If so, it would surely have crossed Forth's mind that all that was needed to induce Waller and Balfour to withdraw was a thrust against their other wing which, if successful, would render their position along the Petersfield–Winchester road untenable.

What Hopton saw from the brow of the southern spur was almost certainly the final stage of the engagement when some Royalist troops hurrying to help their fellows were being cut to pieces by enemy cavalry. The incident is described in considerable detail by eyewitnesses on both sides, and there is no doubt that the formation being destroyed was under the command of Henry Bard, colonel of a regiment of foot that had arrived from the north as escort for the first great munitions convoy of May 1643. According to Slingsby, Bard 'leading on his regiment further than he had orders for, and indeed with more youthful courage than soldier-like discretion, was observed by the enemy to be a great space before the rest and out of his ground, who incontinently thrusts Sir Arthur Haselrig's regiment of cuirassiers well armed between him and home and there in the view of our whole army kills and takes every man'. Slingsby's identification of the attacking force is incorrect. Harley is very clear about the identity of the attackers. They were a commanded party of 300 men drawn from several of Sir William Waller's cavalry regiments, including two troops of his own regiment and probably all four of Colonel Norton's. Moreover, Sir Arthur's account of the battle delivered to the House of Commons as reported by Yonge makes no mention of his own regiment's involvement in the destruction of Bard's infantry. Instead Haselrig claims to have taken ten men out of every troop of Waller's horse to create the shock force. This is an unlikely story. The chance of destroying Bard's regiment can only have been seen at the last moment, leaving insufficient time to complete such a complex reordering of the cavalry. Possibly Yonge misunderstood what he was hearing. It is also interesting that Royalist cavalry did not intervene, either because there was none on or close to the right wing at that juncture, which seems most unlikely as the cavalry engagement had not yet begun, or because it was all over in the flash of an eye, as may have been the case if Bard's men were entirely musketeers or if the speed with which they advanced broke up their close order, something that could easily happen to infantry formations crossing rough ground.[15]

The background to the incident on the left wing in which Bard's regiment was destroyed is given only in Robert Harley's account, but it is supported in general terms by Slingsby, Haselrig, and the writer of the report in *Mercurius Aulicus*. Harley wrote that a party of 1,600 Royalist foot, which, even allowing for exaggeration, must have comprised almost the whole of Forth's infantry, had attacked the 'little village'. This was probably at about 10 or 10.30 a.m., that is after Hopton had received Forth's rejection of his proposal to attack the rear of the Parliamentary army from Cheriton Wood. At first the Royalists made good progress, according to Harley, driving the enemy from their hedges and setting fire to a barn, but Waller sent in reinforcements, the wind changed direction, sending smoke into the eyes of the attackers, and they began to fall back. Such an outcome is not at all surprising. Allowing for the fact that Bard's regiment was not involved at this point, Forth could only have committed a maximum of 1,000 foot soldiers to the assault on the little village, as Hopton's infantry regiments were all on the left wing of the Royalist army. The formation he was attacking, on the other hand, was probably much larger. Harley described the original force as 'very strong', and Waller drew a further 600 (Haselrig) or 1,200 (Harley) foot soldiers from the reserve to support the left wing when the attack began. The length of the engagement is uncertain, but it may have been quite lengthy as Balfour implies that he did not deploy his cavalry in the heath until after the attack had begun, and it was from the heath that the assault against Bard's regiment was launched.[16]

The fact that Bard's regiment was not involved from the start suggests that it was Forth's infantry reserve, possibly guarding the artillery.[17] Bard therefore behaved in an appropriate manner in one respect. Seeing the main infantry body under attack, he had launched his regiment towards the fray, probably with the intention of attacking the advancing enemy foot in their right flank. The trouble was that in his determination to hit them hard, he almost certainly cut corners. First, instead of making his way to the village using the hedges that covered the slopes of the western end of the southern spur and the valley beyond, he led his men across a corner of the heath. Second, he advanced across open ground without a cavalry escort, taking a route that would have taken him to within a few hundred yards of where Balfour had drawn up Waller's regiments of horse. If this was Bard's most direct route towards the fighting, his regiment was almost certainly positioned in the centre of the Royalist front line rather than on the right. Otherwise a march through the enclosures followed by a short hook to the left over open ground just before he reached the enemy would have been more appropriate. That he had erupted from the centre of the Royalist line is apparent from Slingsby's remark that the whole of the army could see the destruction of Bard's regiment. If it had met its fate any further to the west, it would have been hidden from Slingsby's line of sight by the gentle northward curve of the southern ridge of the arena as it neared Cheriton village. The corollary of this is that Bard's regiment must have been close to Forth's own position, which makes one wonder why the Lord General did not order it to halt as soon as the attack began.[18] Possibly Bard was also under orders, but had exceeded them in his enthusiasm to get at the enemy. This may possibly explain Hopton's statement that Forth was 'much troubled with it, as the engagement was by the forwardness of some officers without orders', which can be read as if it was Bard's forwardness and its probable effects that caused Forth such concern, not the original attack.

The destruction of Bard's regiment seems to have had a highly significant effect on morale, raising the spirits of the Parliamentarians whilst dampening those of the Royalists. However, Forth and Hopton had only suffered a reverse, they had not yet lost the battle. Indeed, Forth was able to stabilize the situation in the Itchen valley, possibly by withdrawing infantry from Cheriton Wood, possibly by drawing his own retreating infantry behind hedges on the south-west corner of the southern spur, as nothing much seems to have happened on the Royalist right wing for some hours. However, elsewhere the battle flared into life. According to Hopton, Lord Forth's response to the setback on the right was to order Hopton to launch a cavalry attack, probably against the centre of the enemy position on the heath. The decision seems an irrational one, as the southern slope of the ridge and the heath beyond were not good cavalry country – first enclosures, then a hedge line and finally a small, narrow piece of rough heath, which would have made it difficult for the Royalist horse to maintain close order in a charge, and where the Parliamentary horse were already drawn up under the cover of their artillery and musketeers. Moreover, for the king's horse at Cheriton as for Sir Phillip Stapleton at Newbury and Sir Thomas Fairfax at Marston Moor, there was only a single entrance into the heath, which meant that his regiments could not deploy in close order until they had passed the hedge line. Slingsby goes so far as to say that they did not have time to deploy, as the Parliamentary horse were upon them as soon as they emerged from the entrance. However, this is not confirmed by any of the Parliamentary sources, which is rather surprising if it had had a major effect on the outcome of the battle. Possibly Hopton managed to stop it as soon as he realized it was happening by moving down some musketeers to provide sufficient firepower at the entrance into the heath to deter the enemy. There were certainly Royalist foot in the valley when the cavalry fight was under way, but this still leaves unanswered the question of why Forth ordered a head-on attack on the enemy horse, backed as they were by the firepower of their musketeers and artillery pieces.[19] A possibility, but no more than that, is that the resources committed to the attack on the little village and the fierce enemy reaction to it combined with Hopton's defences in and around Cheriton Wood left very few infantry in the centre of the Royalist line. To make matters worse enemy horse and foot were drawn up on the little heath and on the slope behind it in such a way that they could easily move forward and divide the Royalist army in two.[20] Thus, as at the northern edge of Wash Common during the First Battle of Newbury, cavalry were required to plug a gap caused by shortage of infantry at the critical point in the battle line, with attack being seen as the best form of defence.[21]

To carry out the Lord General's orders, Hopton chose Sir Edward Stowell's brigade, 1,000 strong. It fought bravely for almost half an hour before falling back, 'broken and routed' in Hopton's words, leaving the brigadier in enemy hands 'with five wounds upon him' after he had managed to penetrate their gun line. Another brigade commanded by Sir John Smith apparently attacked the left of the Parliamentary cavalry formation. The evidence for this is slight, but his biographer wrote of 'both lanes and hedges lined with musketeers', which fits the part of the battlefield around the little village better than any other.[22] However, the brigade's performance apparently left much to be desired. When Smith was wounded, all except his own troop made a disorderly retreat. This may explain why none of the other Royalist accounts describe the encounter, but it may have been only a tiny episode inflated into something bigger by his biographer Edward Walsingham. Parliamentary accounts of the battle only portray the enemy horse in an unfavourable light when they retreated from the southern spur at the end of the battle. Jones in particular commended the Royalists for their valour and Harley praised them for their desperate and bold charges.[23]

From this point onwards the traces of the past, almost always less common for the middle part of a battle than one would wish, become highly fragmentary. They are often no more than brief snapshots of the fighting, which are not only impossible to relate to one another but also rarely capable of being allotted a specific place in the timeline of the battle. On the Royalist left wing the rest of Hopton's command may have been more successful than Stowell's brigade. Slingsby wrote of the left wing as well as the right being ordered to advance after the capture of Cheriton Wood, and E.A., the writer of one of the Parliamentary reports, describes a defeat suffered by some or all of Waller and Balfour's cavalry in that part of the battlefield:

> The enemy presently came on with their main body of horse very powerfully, and were met courageously, yet being of the greater number (for our whole body was not then together) forced ours to a disorderly retreat, at which time the day was doubtful if not desperate, our foot all the while being engaged on the left wing.

This cannot be either the episode in which Smith was mortally wounded, or the one in which Stowell was captured, and the clear implication is that it took place on the Parliamentary right.[24]

Slingsby also recounts an episode that occurred on the Royalist left wing soon after the battle became general, but it is not the encounter that E.A. described. Hopton's regiment of infantry repulsed an enemy cavalry charge on three separate occasions by performing classical parade ground drill for pike and musketeers. There is enough detail in the account to show that the regiment was positioned on open ground some way in advance of the crest of the spur. Lord John Stuart then sent the Queen's regiment of cavalry down to its assistance, but it made 'an unhandsome charge', after which the cavalry action became general. Interestingly, Stuart's obituary talks of his receiving his mortal wound in an action that took place in a large open low-lying expanse of ground, not a hill full of hedges and bushes. This description neatly fits the lie of the land to the south and east of Cheriton Wood as I have depicted it.[25]

A series of engagements lasting for between three and four hours then ensued across the centre and east of the battlefield, which seems impossibly long for what appears to have been primarily a cavalry engagement. Possibly the situation in the valley in front of Hinton Ampner became completely chaotic by midday, with a seething mass of horsemen pushing backwards and forwards across the small heath under no control, a scene first suggested by Burne and taken up by many historians since. However, it is more likely that fighting was intermittent, but such as to force both sides to feed in all except their last reserves. Initially, the Royalists were on the offensive pushing back the enemy cavalry to the foot of the Hinton Ampner ridge but, as we have seen, they were unable to break through. When the brigades commanded by

Stowell and Smith fell back in disorder,[26] the Parliamentary horse appear to have gained complete control of the heath, but they in their turn found difficulty in making progress against enemy infantry drawn up behind the hedge that marked the northern boundary of Balfour's Little Heath. Haselrig indeed uses very similar words to those used by Hopton in describing Stowell's difficulties in breaking through the Parliamentary position in the centre: 'their horse were surrounded by musketeers who lined the hedges and beat us back always when we drove them back.'[27]

The nature of the landscape in which the heath was set, that is, with enclosures both to the north and the south, probably explains why neither the Royalist nor the Parliamentary cavalry was able to achieve a breakthrough. It may also explain why those accounts of the battle written by Parliamentarians had very little to say about the part their horse played in the major cavalry action. The report of Sir William Balfour, Essex's lieutenant general of horse, was completely silent about the cavalry actions, but this may be because Essex's regiments had failed to distinguish themselves yet again.[28] However, in the end, inspired, E.A. says, by some London Trained Band musketeers, the right wing of the Parliamentary cavalry accompanied by some infantry appears to have pushed back a weak Royalist cavalry screen and gained the brow of the southern spur of the arena somewhere near Cheriton Wood.[29]

Long before the cavalry and infantry moved forward on the right, however, the tactical manoeuvre that would decide the outcome of the battle was under way on the opposite side of the battlefield. In mid-afternoon Waller's infantry and dragoon regiments supported by some of the London brigade began pushing around the west side of the cavalry mêlée safe in the knowledge that they would not be attacked. Moving out of the Itchen valley, they began to ascend the slopes of the southern spur of the arena from the direction of Cheriton village, where they were successful in pushing back the Royalist infantry, a body which by then included troops that had earlier taken part in the attack on Cheriton Wood, as it was here that their commander Colonel Matthew Appleyard was wounded.[30]

The advance of the enemy foot on both flanks put the Royalist army in great danger of being surrounded. Hopton took the credit for securing the retreat of the shattered brigades of horse and their supporting infantry from the heath using a small body of Oxford army cavalry, with which he successfully defended the entrance into the enclosures on the southern spur of the arena. That the withdrawal from the heath was successfully accomplished is confirmed by other sources, but Hopton's role in it rests on his testimony alone.[31]

Initially Forth and Hopton attempted to make a stand on top of the southern spur, probably where it was crossed by Broad Lane, but the fire coming from the Parliamentary infantry and dragoons making their way along the southern spur towards them was too strong, and they decided to retreat to the place where the Royalist army had camped on the night of 27 March, the high ground to the south of Alresford.[32]

There followed a pause of anything up to an hour, which gave the Royalist generals time to collect most of their infantry into a body and also some of their horse, and to plan their army's escape to Basing House, eighteen miles to the north. Eventually Waller's artillery commander, James Wemyss, brought some cannon into play, and the Royalist army ran for cover. The artillery train started off in the direction of Winchester, but then quickly turned northwards into a landscape of woods and valleys that made cavalry pursuit difficult, whilst the infantry with a small cavalry escort pursued a parallel course using a lower route with plenty of passes to delay the enemy. A small body of foot remained behind in Alresford to win the rest of the infantry and the artillery train time to reach the safety of the woods. Some were killed or captured, but most also managed to make their escape. Finally the horse took off over the downs, pursued for some miles by the enemy. All three sections of the army arrived safely at Basing House just after midnight.[33] Both Harley and Birch's biographers blame senior commanders for showing too much caution once the battle was clearly won, but Adair is probably right to absolve Waller (and by implication Balfour) from blame. Even if Harley's own troop was fresh, and keen to harry the Royalists as they retreated, the rest of the Parliamentary cavalry were probably too exhausted and too scattered to do much against an enemy that had not broken and run.[34]

The immediate reaction of the London newspapers and of the Parliamentary officers who had fought at Cheriton and written reports of the fighting was that through God's mercy the army led by Waller and Balfour had snatched victory from the jaws of defeat. However, once under way, the battle had been an uninspired slogging match, which appeared to develop its own momentum (or lack of momentum) after the initial Royalist error of attacking Parliament's left wing with too small a body of infantry. To Birch's biographer Roe it was 'the worst prosecuted battle I ever saw'. It is therefore surprising that only he was of the opinion that there was a logical order of events, beginning with the decision not to retreat and ending with the infantry advance on both wings at about 4 p.m.[35]

Chapter 10

The Battle of Marston Moor
Context, Landscape and Sources

Context

The Battle of Marston Moor marked the culmination of military operations which began in mid-April with the collapse of the Royalist northern command. The bulk of the Marquis of Newcastle's army had spent the first four months of 1644 in County Durham trying, with some success, to hold back a Scottish army over twice its size. To defend the southern part of his command against attack from the Yorkshire Parliamentarians under Lord Fairfax and his son Sir Thomas, Newcastle had left an infantry corps under John, now Lord, Bellasis and a large cavalry brigade in a fortified camp at Selby. Whilst much of the cavalry were absent, the Fairfaxes surprised the town on 11 April and captured Bellasis and most of his force. Newcastle then fell back very speedily from the Tees valley to York, placed his infantry in garrison there, and sent his cavalry to Newark to seek help from the king or Prince Rupert. A few days later the Scottish and the Yorkshire armies set siege to York.

Prince Rupert, who was forming a new army in the Welsh Marches capable of operating in support of either the king or the Marquis of Newcastle, was keen to mount a relief expedition, probably via Newark or Sheffield, but was frustrated by the deterioration of the military situation in the Thames valley caused by the defeat at Cheriton and the imminent appearance from winter quarters of the Earl of Essex's army. This necessitated a visit to Oxford between 24 April and 5 May to discuss strategy. When Rupert returned to the Welsh borderland, he quickly drew together an army and marched it eastwards to the Newcastle under Lyme area, but the loss of Cawood Castle, eight miles to the south of York, which guarded the crossing over the River Wharfe, on 19 May, and the arrival of the Earl of Manchester's Eastern Association army in the lower Trent valley within easy marching distance of the Allied forces besieging the city soon afterwards, meant that relieving York from the south would be far more difficult than it had been a month earlier. The only solution was to lead his army into north-west England, where the Earl of Derby had promised him he would find many new recruits, and then to approach the city from the west.

Rupert's army left north Staffordshire on 22 May, crossed the Mersey at Stockport three days later, captured the enemy garrisons of Bolton and Liverpool, and after meeting the Northern Horse at Bury on or about 4 June set about recruiting in Lancashire and in Cumbria, but there was very little time to spare. His uncle's orders in early June were to relieve York as quickly as possible, to destroy the enemy armies that had been besieging it, and then to return to the south without delay. Moreover, intelligence from Yorkshire suggested that York was about to surrender. Reuniting with the northern cavalry under George Goring at Skipton on the 26th, Rupert approached York from the north-east completely wrong-footing the Allied armies, which were drawn up in battle array on Marston Moor guarding the approach to the city from the west. On 1 July York was liberated, but instead of resting and awaiting the arrival of reinforcements from Northumberland and Durham under Sir Robert Clavering, Rupert immediately set off in pursuit of the Allies, determined to carry out the king's orders to seek out and destroy the enemy as quickly as possible.[1]

Landscape

The Battle of Marston Moor was fought on the evening of 2 July 1644 on a tongue of low-lying land immediately to the west of York bounded by the rivers Nidd and Wharfe slowly winding their way towards their confluence with the Ouse, five miles to the north and ten miles to the south of the city respectively. There is no dispute about the location of the battle. Royalist and Allied eyewitnesses agree that it took place on open moorland between the villages of Tockwith and Long Marston. The only differences between them are in the name they use to describe it – Marston Moor, Hessam Moor, Marston Field. All are correct. Fighting was concentrated in Marston parish but in the closing stage of the battle it spilled over into Hessay, its neighbour to the north-east, as the triumphant Allied cavalry pushed the fugitives from Rupert's and Newcastle's armies towards York.

The moorland where the fighting took place was very largely lowland heath resting on a subsoil of clay. It was also almost totally flat, and therefore waterlogged in places with some bog but also some pockets of lighter soil.[2] On the heath there was at least one ditched enclosure where one of the most famous incidents in the battle took place, the last stand of the Marquis of Newcastle's infantry regiment, the so-called Whitecoats. Newman has shown convincingly that the traditional site, White Syke Close, almost certainly did not exist before the moor was enclosed in the middle years of the eighteenth century. However, he is mistaken to bring hedges into his narrative, as no contemporary source mentions anything other than ditches.[3]

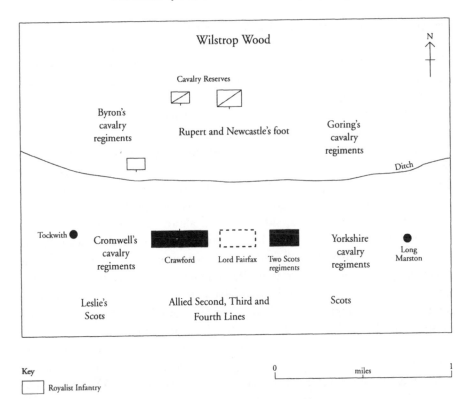

Map 4. The Battle of Marston Moor

Beyond the battlefield to the north was Wilstrop Wood and beyond that the River Nidd, but neither had anything other than a marginal effect on how the battle was fought and won. The wood provided a safe refuge for some of the defeated Royalists, as they were out of reach of the rampaging Allied cavalry. It is therefore possible that the 1,500 or so who were taken prisoner[4] were largely captured there, as the wood was a cul-de-sac with the Nidd cutting off escape to the north and the west.

Beyond the moorland to the south was a ridge known as Braham Hill,[5] on which the Allied army deployed before the battle. Major Lionel Watson, Manchester's scout master, and the Allied generals in their reports, described the position as constricted, possibly because the tongue of land between the Nidd and the Wharfe narrowed as the Nidd turned south on the far side of Tockwith, but almost certainly they were referring to terrain on and around the ridge.[6] The allied infantry drew up in a large field or fields covered knee-deep in corn on the slope facing across Marston Moor towards the Nidd.[7] The highest point was no more than 100 feet above the moor on which the Royalist army deployed, and it was divided laterally by a slight depression.[8] Near Tockwith the ridge faces due north, but as it approaches Long Marston it curves gently towards the east. As a result the left wing of the Allied army was facing north-eastwards, not eastwards as stated in the printed version of scout master Lionel Watson's description of the battlefield. The ridge, however, provided little advantage or disadvantage to either side.

The only element in the landscape of any importance in determining the shape of the battle was a line of hedges and ditches that ran east–west across the battlefield separating the two armies. De Gomme portrays them as a continuous line across the battlefield, but this was probably not the case. Newman, on the other hand, although he is almost certainly right in seeing them as following the line taken by the present road between Tockwith and Long Marston rather than that of a post-enclosure hedge somewhat to the north, is quite wrong in portraying them as being an insignificant obstacle.[9] This is not what the traces of the past have to say. Admittedly the evidence is scrappy, but it is highly probable that the only gap in the ditch was directly in front of the position occupied by the Earl of Manchester's infantry on the left-centre of the Allied line. Parallel to the ditch ran a hedge, a necessary precaution for keeping the animals grazing on the moor away from the cultivated land on the ridge. It extended from close to Long Marston village, where the right wing of the Allied cavalry was deployed, probably as far as the position between there and Tockwith, where the regiments that were in the centre of the first line of the infantry formation were drawn up. This hypothesis is based on what was recorded in Parliamentary and Scottish sources that were in print within three weeks of the battle being fought, and it is largely confirmed by Royalist sources written three to four years later.[10]

Newman cites Lionel Watson's account published on 17 July as evidence that the ditch was almost non-existent on the Allied left wing, but the passage reproduced in full suggests a very different interpretation, namely that it may have been small but was still a significant enough obstacle to disorder advancing infantry and cavalry:

> about five of the clock we had a general silence on both sides, each expecting who should begin the charge, there being a small ditch and bank betwixt us and the moor through which we must pass if [we] would charge them upon the moor, or they pass it if they would charge us in the great corn field and closes, so that it was a great disadvantage to him that begun the charge being the ditch must somewhat disturb their order, and the other would be ready in good ground and order to charge them before the [sic] could recover it.[11]

There were also hedges hemming in the Parliamentary position at both ends, and also, it seems, on the slope.[12] Pioneers were apparently occupied in removing some of these hedges during the afternoon of 2 July,[13] and as a result of their efforts the line of battle was extended almost as far as Tockwith, a length of two and a half miles, not one and a half as in the printed version of Watson's report.[14]

A number of lanes entered or crossed the battlefield, but only two were of any significance to the shape and outcome of the battle. The first entered Marston Moor from the east just to the south of Wilstrop Wood, and was probably used by the Marquis of Newcastle's infantry as they arrived on Marston Moor from York early in the afternoon of 2 July. The second, Moor Lane, led in a north-westerly direction from Long Marston into the moor. It is possible, but by no means certain, that Lord Fairfax's cavalry used Moor Lane in its attempt to deploy on the moor itself, but this detail is only mentioned in the account of 'Captain Stewart'; its claims to be an accurate and impartial description of the battle are discussed below.[15]

Another feature of the battlefield was a rabbit warren on the edge of the moor close to the Tockwith end of the Allied line. This area was the scene of skirmishing in the early afternoon of 2 July, during which a mixed force of Royalist cavalry and infantry were apparently driven from the western end of the ridge.[16] The rabbit warren does not seem to have had any significance thereafter. Barratt's assertion that the pioneers removing the hedges probably levelled it in order to improve the surface over which the left wing cavalry was to charge is highly unlikely.[17] However assiduous the pioneers had been, the cavalrymen would not have been able to judge which former rabbit holes could support the weight of horse and rider and which could not. They would therefore have been unlikely to risk moving across the warren at a rate any faster than a gentle trot.

Sources

Although the accounts of the Battle of Marston Moor by contemporaries are almost as numerous as those for Edgehill, and they embody three perspectives, Royalist, Parliamentarian and Scottish, there is more of an imbalance between them than for any other of the decisive battles and a greater level of incompatibility. All the Royalist accounts of the action, apart from Prince Rupert's very brief report, were written by officers in the Marquis of Newcastle's army or people who were not present at the battle, and most display some antipathy towards the regiments and commanders Rupert had brought with him. This factor, combined with inconsistencies between some of the Parliamentary and Scottish accounts caused by the scramble to earn credit for the victory, means that, although the main outline of the battle is reasonably clear, much of the detail is unsubstantiated and therefore classifiable only as opinion, whilst much of what is said or not said in terms of comment on the fighting in such accounts must be viewed with a quizzical eye.

The principal Royalist account is that of Sir Hugh Cholmley, the commander of the garrison of Scarborough, but, though apparently an observer of the discussions between the Royalist commanders immediately before and after Marston Moor, he did not fight in the battle.[18] Newman's assertion that he can be regarded as objective is not at all convincing.[19] A close examination of the text shows that its principal underlying message was that the Marquis of Newcastle's troops fought bravely, whilst those Prince Rupert brought with him under-performed. The other lengthy description from a northern perspective is that of Sir Henry Slingsby, who, though commander of an infantry regiment that remained in York, nevertheless witnessed the battle.[20] On the surface it appears to be a balanced and even-handed account, like his account of the Battle of Naseby, but it too is inflected by hostility towards the Midlands army. Slingsby, like Cholmley, states that Rupert's cavalry regiments were quickly routed. Parliamentary writers, however, maintain that they were not.[21] It is possible to envisage a London journal editor seeing some propaganda value in claiming that Cromwell's horse had to fight harder than they did, but when three Allied observers of the battle make almost exactly the same point, it seems very likely that it is their assessment, not that of the two Royalist writers, that is the correct one.

A third contemporary Royalist account is that of Arthur Trevor, who was somewhere between Skipton and York on 2 July but well aware that a battle was taking place because of the hordes of soldiers fleeing northwards.[22] His letter to the Marquis of Ormond, the king's commander in Ireland, is therefore dependent on what he was told at York by the survivors. The information it contains is therefore second-hand, and thus probably influenced by special pleading from commanders looking for somebody to blame and garbled by confused thinking on the part of people who had just suffered a catastrophic defeat. Not surprisingly, some of the detail Trevor provides is incorrect, as, for example, when he places Prince Rupert on the left wing rather than the right. However, to be fair to Trevor, he described his account as provisional. He promised to write a better-informed description and assessment in the future, but if he did so the letter does not survive. If Trevor himself had doubts about what he had written, then it is incumbent on historians to be even more wary. Nevertheless, information provided by the letter is central to a widely held hypothesis, now almost orthodoxy, to the effect that the Marquis of Newcastle's infantry regiments were still arriving on the field as the battle started.[23]

I place far more trust in the Margaret Cavendish, Duchess of Newcastle's account, even though she was not herself there and did not compose it until almost twenty years after the battle.[24] It has been rubbished,[25] but its strength lies in the fact that it is to all and intents and purposes the marquis's memoirs.

Margaret was a dutiful wife, and would not have gone into print without her husband's total and absolute approval of what she had written. In addition he paid for its publication. Also, her narrative dovetails very nicely with evidence from Parliamentary and other Royalist accounts without owing anything to them as sources, and it contains no obvious errors. Finally, Newcastle's immense regard for his personal honour makes it unlikely that he would have allowed incorrect factual information to be published, as others at Court could easily contradict it, thus damaging his reputation, for which he had the highest regard. However, Newcastle's influence ensured that the account was extremely anodyne. The reason is explained in the duchess's preface. She had obeyed to the letter her husband's instructions that the narrative should not include anything critical of other Royalists with whom he had disagreed about the conduct of the campaign.[26] As a result little can be learned about mis-understandings or differences of opinion between himself and Rupert or himself and Charles I, or indeed between General King, his principal military adviser, and Prince Rupert.

The Prince's report on the battle and his assessment of the strategic effects of its outcome, which reached the king on 12 July, does not survive, though its generally positive tone can be gauged from Lord Digby's reply to it in the king's name. The account in *Mercurius Aulicus* also probably draws on the report.[27] The commentary in Rupert's Diary on the events of 1 to 3 July is very slim and so tersely written in places as to be almost ambiguous. Nevertheless, it contains a defence of the management of the opening phase of the battle, placing much of the blame for the defeat on Sir John, now Lord, Byron, who commanded the right wing of the cavalry:

> Then the Prince drew his forces into a strong posture making his post as strong as possible. Lord Byron then made a charge upon Cromwell's forces. Represent here the posture the Prince put his forces in and how by the improper charge of the Lord Byron much harm was done. After the enemy had broken our horse, the foot stood till night. Some of them came off after the Prince and General King had drawn up as many as he could.[28]

In the autobiography of King James II, Byron's guilt is developed still further:

> But instead of maintaining his post, as he ought in duty to have done, when the enemy had only drawn two or three field pieces and with them played upon him, he suffered himself to be persuaded by Colonel Hurry to march over the morass and charge them, by which inconsiderate action he gave them the same advantage which he had formerly over them; for they charging him in his passage over the ground already mentioned he was immediately routed.

However, it must be remembered that James was not present at Marston Moor, and that his judgements were based on listening to others, almost certainly including his cousin Rupert, coloured by his own experience of leading troops in battle later in the century.[29]

Byron does not appear to have written in his own defence. His only known comments on Marston Moor were that there had occurred 'such gross errors as I have not patience to describe', and that it was 'our own wilfulness and neglect that overthrew us', but an account may come to light some day, as he wrote spirited descriptions of two of the other battles in which he fought, Roundway Down and the First Battle of Newbury, and also of his defence of Chester where he was governor for the latter part of the war.[30]

The other Royalist accounts printed by Peter Young in *Marston Moor* contain little of significance, and the accuracy of the transcription of the longest of them, Mr Ogden's report of what Dr Lewens told him straight after the battle, cannot be checked, as it was destroyed in a fire at Wrottesley Hall many years ago.[31] The letter in the Musgrave mss at Carlisle discovered by Newman is highly generalized,[32] and as full of pro-Northern Army bias as Cholmley's or Slingsby's accounts. Sir Phillip Monckton's *Memoirs*, on the other hand, focus entirely on his own experience in the battle. However, the twentieth-century printed versions are no more than copies of a highly selective précis. The early eighteenth-century version is far more informative.[33] Finally, there is the account of the battle by Lord Clarendon. He begins with a passage that draws heavily on Sir Hugh Cholmley's account, which was and still is amongst the papers he collected prior to writing the *History of the Great Rebellion*, but he then adds some tactical and strategic observations of his own that may derive from memories of discussions with his former colleagues on the Prince of Wales's Council, Sir John Culpeper and the Earl of Forth, which took place in the west of England almost thirty years before. Needless to say, Rupert and Newcastle are both heavily criticized, and his condemnation of the prince hints strongly that it was Rupert's impetuosity, not the king's orders, that led to a battle being fought at all:

> after the murder of the king he produced a letter ... which he understood to amount to no less than a peremptory order to fight upon what disadvantage soever ... but as the king's letter would not bear that sense, so the greatest cause of the misfortune was the precipitate entering upon the battle as soon as the enemy drew off.[34]

Finally there is the second account of the battle in *Mercurius Aulicus*, dated 13 July.[35] As suggested above, this was probably based on Rupert's report, which is known to have reached the king the day before, probably via Oxford.

It includes an element of special pleading, but the extent to which this was the informant's work or that of the editor cannot be ascertained. However, it does contain some interesting comments, which merit serious consideration.

* * * * *

There are three Scottish accounts of Marston Moor written by officers who fought in the battle, Major General John Lumsden's, second in command of the Scottish infantry, 'Captain Stewart's' and Lieutenant Colonel John Somerville's, and another by Robert Douglas, the Earl of Leven's chaplain, who was on the battlefield. Lumsden wrote his report three days after the battle, addressing it to Lord Loudoun, who did not lead his regiment at Marston Moor but sat on the Committee of Both Kingdoms, the Allied war cabinet. Lumsden's report was printed in Edinburgh, but probably not in London. The damaged original, which also includes a rough sketch, is kept in the library of York Minster. For once, the editorial interference with the text was minimal. Lumsden's main purpose was to explain the behaviour of the Scottish troops during the battle, which had been patchy at best, but his account is by no means a whitewash. It also praised the army of the Eastern Association for its role in the victory.[36]

The relative importance of the contributions of Scots and English troops towards victory was to become a bone of contention in the weeks that followed the battle, as a result of very early claims that Cromwell's men alone were responsible for victory. In a letter written to Robert Blair on 16 July, Robert Baillie alleged that the major of Cromwell's own cavalry regiment, Thomas Harrison, had ridden straight to London to bring the news that the Eastern Association army 'had done it all their own alone'. The Scots, however, had done nothing to show up 'the vanity and falsehood of their disgraceful relation' for several more days. However, within a fortnight of the battle the Earl of Leven's spin on what had happened on the battlefield was on sale in London in what is popularly known as Captain Stewart's account.[37] Firth saw it as a composite work produced in London from a number of sources to enhance the Scots' role in the battle, but this cannot be proved. A passage about casualties similar to that contained in the three generals' report to the Committee of Both Kingdoms is as likely to have been entered into the account at York as in London, and a passage about General Leslie's role in the battle may simply be a piece of clumsy editing at the composition stage. Instead it is probably the 'large letter to Sir John Seton' mentioned by Baillie in correspondence with Lord Eglinton, the commander of the cavalry regiments on the Allied right wing, with its Scottish turns of phrase altered so as to make it easy for English readers to understand.[38]

'Captain Stewart's account' provides a full description of the achievements of some of the Scottish troops without trying to exonerate those who had not performed well, and it did not disparage the achievement of the Eastern Association troops. However, some of the detail does not inspire confidence, most particularly the description of the difficulties that faced the Allied left wing as it tried to reach the moor. Newman attempted to identify these features in the landscape, but was hampered by the fact that Sir Thomas Fairfax's own account tells a different story about the topography of the area to the west of Long Marston village.[39] Stewart's is also the only account to describe the ditch that separated the armies as disappearing in front of the Eastern Association infantry.[40]

Robert Douglas's diary contains a lively account of his personal experience on the fringes of the fighting, but it was not written up until three weeks or so after the battle. As a result it is also reflective and contains some data, such as the size of the Allied armies, which probably comes from Lumsden's report of the battle. It does, however, supply details that are not mentioned elsewhere, such as a chronology for the collapse of the Allied centre and right wing, and the Earl of Manchester's role in the battle's closing stages.[41]

Finally, there is Lieutenant Colonel James Somerville's florid account, which was compiled at least seven years after the event, as he refers to Cromwell subsequently inflicting God's wrath on 'three rebellious nations'. Somerville claimed to be well informed, as he was serving as a volunteer, having laid down his commission, and thus had 'opportunity and liberty to ride from the one wing of the army to the other to view all their several squadrons of horse and battalions of foot, how formed and in what manner drawn up, with every other circumstance relating to this fight'. It is therefore surprising that the only episode described in great detail is the last stand of Newcastle's regiment of infantry. The rest is very generalized and the little detail it contains could have been taken from material that was already in print when Somerville took up his pen.[42]

*   *   *   *   *

The earliest accounts of Marston Moor from the perspective of the Yorkshire and the Eastern Association armies were written on 3 and 4 July. Several were short, official despatches designed to scotch rumours that the Allies had lost the battle. The letter written to the Committee of Both Kingdoms, the Allied equivalent of a war cabinet, by the three army generals gave the bare facts. It did nothing to conceal the fact that parts of the combined armies had fought badly.[43] That by the Earl of Manchester to the Earl of Denbigh, the commander of the Midlands Association, is even briefer.[44] Briefest of all is Lord Fairfax to Mr Farrer at Halifax, which does not directly mention the poor performance of the Yorkshire forces during the battle, though the request to send up troops to York may be an oblique reference to rounding up soldiers who had fled into the West Riding during the disastrous middle stage of the battle.[45] The much longer letter that Farrer himself sent from Halifax the following day draws on sources of information other than Lord Fairfax's letter, but has little more to say about the battle.[46]

There are two other short documents that can be classed as immediate post-battle reports. The first is William Fairfax's short letter to his wife written on 3 July informing her that he was safe. Its significance is that it describes the battle as beginning several hours earlier than any other account. The original cannot be traced, but there may be an error in transcription as the date appended to the letter is given as 13 July rather than 3 July.[47] The second is Oliver Cromwell's exultant letter of 5 July to his brother-in-law, the MP Valentine Walton, which provided no details of the battle but left no doubt in the reader's mind as to which Allied army had routed the Royalists.[48]

The first long account of Marston Moor to enter the public domain was that of Thomas Stockdale written on 5 July. It was read to the House of Commons three days later and reproduced in full by Sir Simon D'Ewes in his Parliamentary diary.[49] A clear and straightforward account, it provides the fullest description of Royalist successes in the first hour of the fighting, but is adamant that victory was very largely won by the Eastern Association infantry and cavalry. Apart from a single regiment of foot, the entire Scottish army had fled from the battlefield.

Even worse for the military reputation of the Scottish army was the very long letter from Lionel Watson, Manchester's scout master. Although not printed until 17 July, it was written on the 3rd and probably circulated in manuscript in London well before it appeared in print. One of these manuscript copies found its way into the More of Linley collection. It is subtly different from the printed version, which contains a number of errors, and is in one or two respects a toned down version. For example, the pamphlet describes the right wing of the cavalry and the whole of the Scottish and Yorkshire infantry as retreating fast towards Tadcaster and Cawood an hour into the battle. The manuscript version describes them more bluntly as running away.[50]

A third long account, written by a member of the Eastern Association army, Simeon Ashe, who was Manchester's chaplain, is similar in content, though not language, to Watson's, but it gives a little more credit to some of the Scottish commanders and is more reflective on the impact of the battle. Although published a few days after Stewart's account, it should not be seen as a counterblast from Cromwell's supporters, as Ashe was of the Presbyterian persuasion. Nevertheless, Baillie saw it as giving more praise than was due, given that Ashe was supposed to be a friend, not an adversary.[51]

The last report that historians regard as having been written by a witness in the immediate aftermath of the battle is the letter of Captain W.H., who claimed to have fought in Manchester's army. It is probably not an authentic first-hand account but one put together in Cambridge, where it was printed, using information culled from a variety of sources. Like others of that type, it is highly generalized, contains a number of errors, ignores W.H.'s own role in the battle (which would have been considerable whatever branch of the army he belonged to) and has nothing specific to say about officers killed or wounded in the Eastern Association army (which would have been of great interest to readers living in the Cambridge area).[52] Moreover, there is no evidence that anybody with those initials held the rank of captain in that army at the time of the Battle of Marston Moor. W.H.'s letter will not therefore be used to corroborate information provided by any other trace of the past.[53]

The reports of the battle published in the London weeklies contribute little of interest. The only important item that may be of a factual nature is a claim that troops in the first line of the Allied infantry, having pushed back the enemy to their front, fled from the battlefield when they heard shouts of 'They run in the rear'.[54] This sounds like an attempt to explain what had happened to a lay audience, but may contain a grain of truth.

Several Parliamentary sources were written long after the battle, but only one is of any real significance, the *Short Memorial of the Wars 1642–44*, written by Sir Thomas Fairfax after retiring from military command.[55] The detail it provides about Marston Moor, however, is highly focused on the fighting on the Allied right wing, its prime concern being, seemingly, to exonerate Sir Thomas from blame for what had happened there.[56] Denzil Holles's attack[57] on Cromwell for cowardice and lack of resolution at Marston Moor may or may not have been merited, but the extent to which the tale Holles told was a fabrication is a matter of irrelevance in so far as the battle narrative is concerned. It was the Eastern Association troops, not Cromwell, who won the battle, a fact that he himself fully acknowledged in his letter to Valentine Walton.[58] A not dissimilar attempt to set the record straight is to be found in *Truth's Manifest*, David Buchanan's lengthy justification for the intervention of the Scots in England's affairs, which was written early in 1646. His narrative of Marston Moor was based on a range of primary sources, some of which no longer apparently survive. As it made David Leslie rather than Oliver Cromwell the architect of victory, *Truth's Manifest* caused great resentment amongst Cromwell's English supporters, and almost certainly caused Nathaniel Fiennes and others to write counterblasts. These are clearly polemics and should be used with care. Their arguments are interesting, but the quality of the evidence on which they are based is questionable.[59] Third, there is Edmund Ludlow's account, which has already been discussed and discounted as a source.[60] Finally, the description of Marston Moor in Whitelocke's *Memorials* is derivative and inaccurate, and contains nothing new.

The two contemporary or near-contemporary depictions of the deployment of the armies at Marston Moor are of value, but neither is a complete portrait of how the armies were drawn up. General Lumsden's hurried sketch, which contains no topographical information and nothing about how the Royalist formations were deployed, must have been compiled very soon after the battle

1. The Edgehill battlefield: the hill on which Essex's army deployed from the Radway to Tysoe Road.

2. The Edgehill battlefield: the hill in profile from the south-west.

3. The Edgehill battlefield: the landscape to the north of the Kineton to Banbury road.

4. The First Newbury battlefield: Round Hill and the northern spur of the crescent from the south-west.

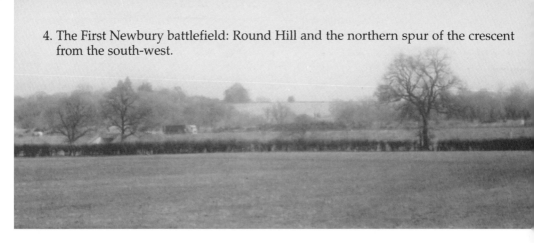

5. The First Newbury battlefield: the steep ascent of Skinners Green Lane.

6. The First Newbury battlefield: one of the tumuli on Wash Common.

7. The Cheriton battlefield: the southern spur of the arena with the northern spur on the horizon from the Hinton Ampner ridge.

8. The Cheriton battlefield: Cheriton Wood and the site of Bramdean Heath from the Hinton Ampner ridge.

9. The Cheriton battlefield: looking towards the northern side of East Down, Tichbourne.

10. The Cheriton battlefield: the probable site of Sir William Balfour's 'Little Heath' and Sir Edward Stowell's charge.

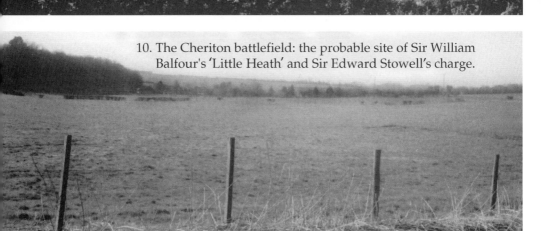

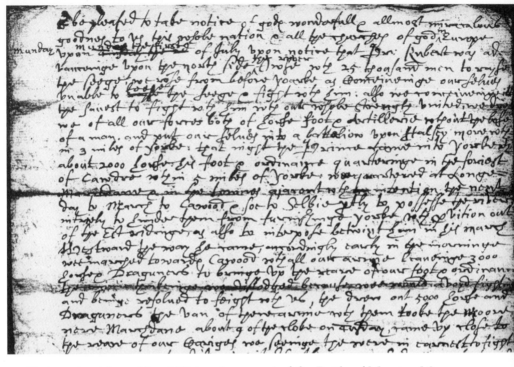

11. An extract from Lionel Watson's account of the Battle of Marston Moor.

12. The Second
Newbury battlefiel
the gatehouse of
Donnington Castle

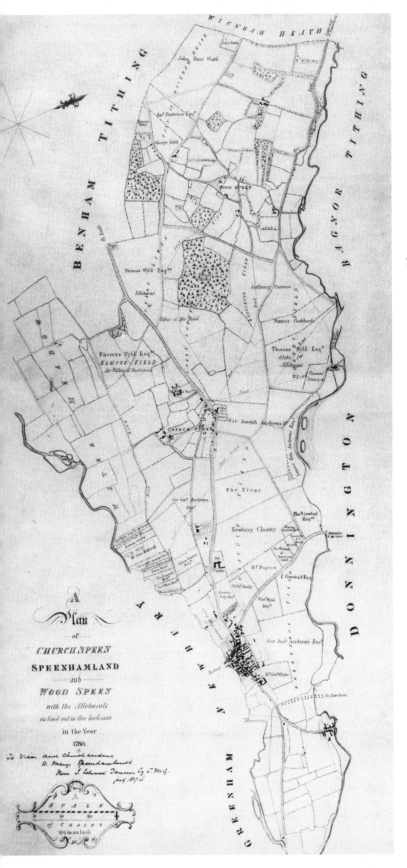

13. The Second
Newbury
battlefield: the
enclosure map of
Speenhamland
1780.

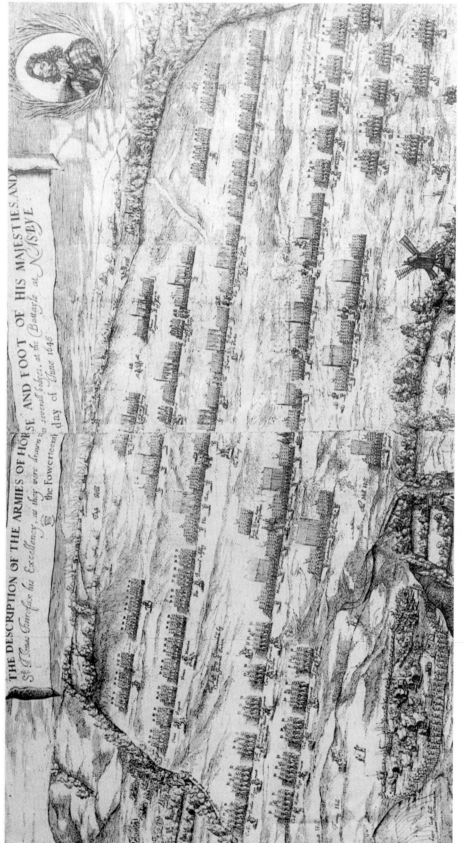

THE DESCRIPTION OF THE ARMIES OF HORSE AND FOOT OF HIS MAJESTIES, AND
Sr Thomas Fairefax his Excellency, as they were drawn into severall bodies, at the Battayle at NASBYE
the Fowerteenth day of June 1645

14. The Naseby battlefield: Robert Streeter's depiction of the deployment of the two armies.

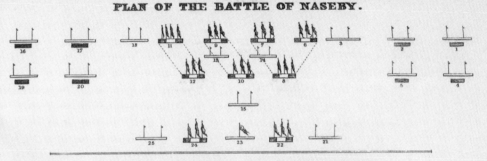

PLAN OF THE BATTLE OF NASEBY.

Order of Battle drawn up by His Majesty's Command on the 14th June 1645, for his forces, consisting of 3500 Foot & 4000 Horse, with 12 pieces of Cannon, in the Action fought with the Parliamentary Army, led by Sir Tho: Fairfax at Naseby Field near Harboro: Prince Rupert commanded in this Battle as General of His Majesty's Army.

Baron de Gomme, fecit.

(The original of this Plan is written in Dutch...De Gomme seems to have been the same with De Gomez, the Engineer who accompanied) Prince Rupert into England.)

The first line of the right wing consisted of 3 divisions of Cavalry under Prince Maurice supported by 100 Musketeers.
1. Prince Rupert's & P. Maurice's Troops.
2. Prince Rupert's Regiment.
3. The Queen's & P. Maurice's Regiments.
The second line of the right wing consisted of 2 divisions of Horse, with 100 Musketeers.
4. The Earl of Northampton's Regiment.
5. Sir William Vaughan's Do.
The Infantry inclusive of the Reserve consisted of nine divisions.
Sir Barnard Ashley's force comprised 3 divisions, viz.

6. Duke of York's Regiment.
7. Colonel Hopton's Do.
8. Colonel Byel's Do.
Sir Henry Baerd's force, two divisions viz.
9. Sir Henry Baerd's & Col. Thomas's Regt.
10. Sir John Owen & Col. Gerrard's Regt.
Sir George Lisle's force, two divisions viz.
11. Sir C. Lisle's & St. George's Regt.
12. The Shrewsbury Foot, commanded by Col. Smith.
13. Three divisions of Horse
14. commanded by Col. Howard.
15. placed between the divisions of Foot.

The first line of the left wing consisted of 3 divisions of Horse with 100 Musketeers.
16. Commanded by
17/18. Sir Marmaduke Langdale.
The second line of the left wing consisted of 2 divisions of Horse with 100 Musketeers, commanded by Col. Carey.
19. Colonel Carey's Regiment.
20. One of the Yorkshire Regt. of Horse.
The Reserve comprised
21. Two divisions of Horse, commanded
25. by Sir Richard Willis.
22. His Majesty's Regt. of Foot.
23. His Majesty's Life Guards (Horse)
24. Prince Rupert's Regt. of Foot.

15. The Naseby battlefield: de Gomme's pre-battle sketch of the deployment of the Royalist army. From E.G.B. Warburton, *Memoirs of Prince Rupert and the Cavaliers*, vol. 3.

16. The Naseby battlefield: the putative Royalist position at East Farndon from the south-west.

17. The Naseby battlefield: the putative Royalist position at Great Oxendon from the south.

18. The Naseby battlefield: the shallow valley behind the New Model Army position on Closter and Shadden Hills.

19. Ridge and furrow in profile below the Edgehill escarpment.

as it follows on directly from the narrative in the manuscript of his account of the battle. However, the units making up the first line of the Allied infantry formation are not as described in 'Captain Stewart's' account. Stewart placed two Scottish infantry brigades in the centre with two of Manchester's brigades to their left and Lord Fairfax's foot to their right. In Lumsden's sketch Fairfax's men are in the middle of the line with the Scots to their right. Second, the sketch has been quite severely damaged.[61] Finally, Lumsden made no effort to draw formations to scale.

De Gomme's watercolour, like the rest of his battlefield representations, was painted many years afterwards.[62] Newman alleged that it was based on a sketch of the intended rather than the actual battle formation, noting that two brigades of Northern Horse were missing.[63] He then assumed that de Gomme did nothing to revise the sketch before completing the watercolour. This cannot be proved one way or the other, but nevertheless Newman then went on to change the east–west orientation of the battle line, thus downplaying the significance of the ditch and the hedge that divided the two army groups. He then went on to reconfigure the deployment of the Northern infantry regiments. The revised plan of the Royalist deployment that resulted from this, however, has very little support from seventeenth-century accounts of the battle. Tincey, on the other hand, has recently argued quite convincingly that de Gomme's depiction is an accurate portrayal of the Royalist deployment at Marston Moor.[64] Nevertheless, as in the case of de Gomme's watercolour of Edgehill, the omission of some Royalist regiments is a cause for concern, and Newman was right to draw readers' attention to it.[65]

The archaeological record of the battlefield is potentially a very interesting one. Newman's early work clearly shows a heavy concentration of musket balls on the moor immediately in front of where Sir Thomas Fairfax's cavalry regiments were deployed.[66] More wide-ranging work undertaken recently shows another concentration of artefacts to the rear of the Allied position on Braham Hill behind Long Marston village, but this almost certainly represents the site of the pillaged Parliamentary baggage train, not an important engagement during the battle. Surprisingly, the survey discovered very few artefacts at the western end of the battlefield near Tockwith village where the cavalry fight between Rupert's and Cromwell's cavalry regiments took place.[67] However, pistol shot has been found just to the south of Wilstrop Wood. As both sides were reserving pistol fire for the mêlée phase of the cavalry encounter, this is not easy to explain. However, it is possible that some of it was dropped by Royalist cavalrymen as they fled the battlefield, and also that the soil on that part of the moor where the mêlée took place was acidic enough to destroy pistol balls, which are, of course, much smaller than musket balls.

Chapter 11
The Battle of Marston Moor
Narrative

Having failed to prevent Prince Rupert from relieving York, the Allied generals decided to re-deploy along the line of the River Wharfe between Tadcaster and Cawood, with the aim of blocking Rupert's way if he tried to return to the Midlands via Newark or Sheffield. By retiring behind the Wharfe they also claimed that they would prevent the Royalists obtaining supplies from the East Riding or returning the way they had come, although it is difficult to see how the latter could have been a consideration, as the Wharfe was to the south, not the north of the city. Finally, quartered at Tadcaster and Cawood, they would be able to cover the approach of reinforcements from Lancashire and the north Midlands under Sir John Meldrum, which were just crossing the Pennines.[1] What they almost certainly did not expect was for Rupert to opt for a set-piece battle at the earliest opportunity.

The Marquis of Newcastle was also surprised.[2] Intelligence from the enemy camp indicated that there were differences between the Allied army commanders with regard to future operations. If left alone, the three armies would therefore probably soon go their separate ways. His advice to Rupert was therefore that the Royalists' best course would be to wait on events, but to use the time profitably by re-provisioning York and integrating the Northern infantry and Clavering's force into the army Rupert had brought with him. However, Rupert brushed aside these arguments. The king's orders were that he was to defeat the enemy armies as soon as possible and then to march back into the south of England. However, evidence supplied by Sir Hugh Cholmley, and also the contents of a letter Newcastle wrote to Rupert on the afternoon of 1 July, suggest that Newcastle changed his mind later in the day, possibly after listening to his officers. Initially he had had no advice to offer.[3]

The slowness with which the Northern infantry got ready for battle was seen in the aftermath as a response to Rupert's ignoring the Marquis's advice, but it may not have been the principal cause. Other reasons cited at the time were that the soldiers were too busy plundering the enemy siege lines, or that they refused to leave the city until they had been paid some of their wages. It was also alleged that they had over-indulged themselves celebrating the ending of the siege. Nevertheless the prince managed to get most of his own army into the field by mid-morning on 2 July using a bridge of boats the enemy had built across the Ouse but failed to destroy when they abandoned the siege of York.[4]

During the morning of 2 July Rupert deployed what regiments he could on a large tract of lowland moor to the west of York where the villages of Long Marston, Tockwith and Hessay had commoning rights, but half deployment was the worst of both worlds, as it made the Allied generals rethink their decision to withdraw behind the River Wharfe. If Rupert had merely harassed their retreat using one or two cavalry regiments, as he had done in the case of the Earl of Essex's army after the Battles of Edgehill and Newbury, they would probably have brushed them off and continued on their way. They had certainly taken textbook precautions against such an eventuality by using 3,000 cavalry as a rearguard to protect their infantry against attack. However, Rupert was also deploying infantry on Marston Moor, suggesting that he was preparing to make a full-scale assault on the armies as they retreated. This would require the Allied cavalry to make a stand, which could only be effective if supported by infantry firepower. Alternatively, by deploying on Marston Moor but not attacking the rear of their column of march, Rupert was possibly signalling his desire to engage the Allied generals in a conventional battle in open country, something they had been hoping for two days earlier as his army approached York. Lords Leven, Fairfax and Manchester therefore ordered their infantry to head back towards York and to join the cavalry rearguard on the best defensive position between the Rivers Nidd, Ouse and Wharfe, namely the shallow ridge of Braham Hill between the villages of Long Marston and Tockwith described in Chapter 10.[5] This necessitated the eviction of Royalist troops from their forward position on the western edge of the ridge close to Tockwith village. The manoeuvre was also a complex one, but it seems to have been completed by early afternoon.[6]

At about midday Rupert seems to have abandoned his initial idea of attacking the enemy that day, probably because of the failure of the Northern infantry to arrive on the moor. Instead he ordered his troops to deploy in a defensive formation. In his own words: 'When the enemy saw the prince ... did not pursue them, they returned ... Then the prince drew his forces into a strong posture making his post as strong as possibly he could.'[7] The same impression is created by de Gomme's watercolour of the deployment of the Royalist armies, in which small bodies of musketeers were placed between the cavalry squadrons, which was normal practice if the enemy were expected to charge first, though Fairfax claimed that they were only deployed in that manner facing the Allied right wing. In addition two infantry regiments were stationed close to the ditch on the other side of the battlefield immediately adjacent to where the cavalry encounter between the Royalist right wing and the Allied left would take place. The intention, according to King James II, was for the musketeers to fire into the flank of the enemy horse as they tried to move off the cultivated land onto the moor.[8] Rupert may indeed have decided that using two of his best infantry regiments in this way was the best means of disrupting the close order of the Eastern Association horse as they charged, but the formidable reputation of Oliver Cromwell's cavalry regiments had yet to be forged. It was Fairfax's horse that had played the active role at Winceby in Lincolnshire in the previous October. The Eastern Association horse had merely held the main body of the enemy in check, whilst Cromwell himself had been knocked off his horse early on and played no significant part thereafter in routing the enemy.[9] Finally, the position of the cavalry reserve in de Gomme's plan also suggests that the prince was thinking defensively, as it was placed in the centre/rear of the army, not directly behind the two wings, thus making it easier for Rupert to move it wherever it was most needed as the battle progressed.

By mid-afternoon the two army groups had deployed in textbook configuration for a battle fought in open country, that is, with the infantry regiments in the centre and the horse primarily on the two wings,[10] but despite the two contemporary battle plans historians have posed numerous questions about their accuracy and about the exact position of individual regiments when fighting commenced. This is not surprising as only half of Lumsden's sketch survives and de Gomme's is probably incomplete. Recent books on Marston Moor devote much space to this,[11] but the debate will never reach a satisfactory conclusion for immediately an error or omission is identified in one contemporary depiction or the other, the whole of the depiction is brought into question.[12] They should therefore be regarded as guides to the ways in which the regiments were deployed, nothing more.

There have also been disputes about the size of the two army groups. However, in this case the primary sources are extensive and robust enough for one to say with a high degree of certainty that the Allied armies outnumbered the Royalist armies by a considerable margin.[13] Most historians agree that much of the advantage was in infantry,[14] but numerical superiority in infantry at the start of the battle was of no real significance in determining its outcome. That is not to say, however, that infantry were irrelevant to its outcome. An hour into the battle the eventual victors probably had fewer foot soldiers left on the battlefield than the vanquished, but the considerable numerical advantage the Allied armies enjoyed in cavalry and dragoons by that stage enabled them to mount a highly effective series of combined operations against the remaining Royalist troops still in formation, and thus win a significant victory. Allied success at the Tockwith end of the battlefield earlier in the evening also owed something, possibly everything, to superior numbers.[15]

De Gomme shows the left wing of the Royalist cavalry consisting entirely of the troops Goring added to Rupert's army in June. They were drawn up in two lines, the first under George Goring himself, the second under Sir Richard Dacre. The East Midlands contingent formed part of the front line, the rest being made up of Northern Horse. A single regiment, Francis Carnaby's, guarded the exposed flank, a necessary precaution in open country whether the battle formation was primarily a defensive or an offensive one. Drawn up on the right wing was almost the whole of Prince Rupert's horse, also in two lines, with Lord Byron commanding the first and Lord Molyneux the second, and a single regiment of Northern or Newark horse under Colonel Samuel Tuke guarding the exposed flank.

The reserve on de Gomme's plan was made up almost entirely of the Marquis of Newcastle's horse. The larger of the two brigades, Sir William Blakiston's, was positioned directly behind the second line of infantry. The other, under Sir Edward Widdrington's command, together with Rupert's Lifeguard, was in the centre rear of the army, and thus well placed to be committed where there was greatest need once the initial enemy attack had taken place. The two brigades missing from the plan were almost certainly not in the reserves. According to Sir Phillip Monckton, Sir Marmaduke Langdale's was in the front line of Goring's wing. It is impossible to say where Sir John Mayne's brigade was deployed, but Goring's front line seems the most likely spot, as they were in a good enough condition to escort the Marquis of Newcastle and a party of his officers to Scarborough on the day after the battle.[16] If this was the case and de Gomme's estimate of 6,000 Royalist horse at Marston Moor is correct, Goring is likely to have commanded getting on for 3,000 horse and Byron just over 2,000, with just short of 1,000 in the reserve formations.

Facing Byron and Molyneux was the Eastern Association cavalry, drawn up in two lines, the first led by Oliver Cromwell as Lieutenant General of the Eastern Association army, the second probably by Colonel Bartholomew Vermuyden, a Dutch professional soldier. Directly behind them was a reserve of three regiments of Scottish cavalry under Lieutenant General David Leslie. This deployment, similar to that employed by the Royalist commanders at Edgehill, suggests an attack formation in which the first line, or the first and the second lines if the resistance hardened, were to punch a large and fatal hole in the enemy formation. In such circumstances the reserves needed to be in close support to provide immediate assistance if necessary, and if unnecessary, to carry out a vigorous pursuit of the fleeing Royalists. For this task the Scots were well suited. Their cavalrymen, lightly armoured and mounted on small but swift horses, were best fitted for skirmishing or rapid movement across the battlefield, not a firefight, as in the Dutch model, or a charge in which discipline and momentum were important, as in the Swedish model. The other wing, commanded by Sir Thomas Fairfax, was also drawn up in three lines, two of Northern Horse and the third line, as on the left, comprising three Scottish cavalry regiments led by Lord Eglinton. The cavalry on both wings were flanked by regiments of dragoons, and their combined strength is unlikely to have been less than 8,000 horse.[17]

According to de Gomme, the main body of Royalist infantry was drawn up in two and a half lines, with the Anglo-Irish regiments that Rupert had brought with him from the north-west Midlands making up most of the front line. Two of the formations towards the right of the eight-brigade formation, however, belonged to Sir Thomas Tildesley's regiment. Raised in Lancashire, it had fought at Edgehill and Newbury as Lord Molyneux's regiment. When it marched north with Lord Byron in November 1643 it is unlikely to have been much more than 200 strong. At Marston Moor therefore its ranks must have been full of new recruits, which at that stage in the war are likely not to have been volunteers but men impressed by commissioners of array on the authority of the Royalist parliament, which had met at Oxford during the winter. This was certainly true of two of the Anglo-Irish formations made up of regiments that had been severely mauled at the Battle of Nantwich six months earlier. These included some Cheshire men recruited for the march to York who were wounded at Marston Moor and applied for annual pensions at or soon after the Restoration. However, having been recruited in the early spring, they are likely to have received more extensive training than the Lancashire levies.[18]

The Marquis of Newcastle's infantry, drawn up in seven divisions, occupied the right and centre of the second and the whole of the short third line. De Gomme does not attempt to regiment them but estimated that they comprised some 3,000 foot, as did Sir Hugh Cholmley. The rest of the second line consisted of the regiments from Derbyshire and the north-west of England that had joined the army in Lancashire. It is doubtful if these amounted in total to more than 2,000 men, and most were either newly raised or garrison troops with little or no battle experience. The remainder of the Royalist infantry were used to support the cavalry, as described above.[19] Its overall strength is impossible to assess, but nearer to 11,000 than 12,000 is probably a fair estimate, with 4,000 in each of the first two lines, 2,000 in the third and another 1,200 to 1,500 supporting the cavalry.[20]

The infantry belonging to the Allied army, between 15,000 and 20,000 men, was drawn up in three full lines with the beginning of a fourth, as befitting its greater size and complexity and the constricted nature of the ridge on which it was deployed. Five of the six Eastern Association regiments of foot under the command of Manchester's Major General Lawrence Crawford were stationed on the left of the allied front line immediately adjacent to their own cavalry.[21] In the centre, according to Lumsden's plan, were two brigades of Lord Fairfax's foot, whilst four Scottish regiments, also drawn up in two brigades, filled the gap between them and the right wing of the Allied horse.[22] According to the so-called Captain Stewart account, however, the Yorkshire regiments were on the right adjacent to their own horse, whilst the Scots were in the centre of the line. The second line was apparently made up entirely of Scottish infantry, eight regiments drawn up in four brigades.[23] The third line, or reserve, was similar in composition to the vanguard, but with the Earl of Manchester's large Eastern Association regiment probably on the right, and two Scottish regiments in the middle forming a single brigade.[24]

*   *   *   *   *

As well as being the Civil War battle in which the largest numbers were engaged, Marston Moor is unusual in being fought during the evening. There is no doubt whatsoever about this. The Allied sources are almost unanimous, and there is no reason why they should have wanted the world to believe that the fighting began later than it actually did. The Royalist sources are less precise about the timing, but circumstantial evidence suggests that their generals were settling down for the night convinced that nothing further would happen until the following day, when the enemy attacked. The Marquis of Newcastle, for example, was alleged to have returned to his coach to wait for the morning.[25] However, the afternoon had not been free from incident, as there had been a short artillery barrage, which did little damage and stopped at about 4 p.m. What surprised Sir Henry Slingsby was that the Allied armies did not launch an attack immediately afterwards. On this point Allied sources are unforthcoming. However, the most important reason was probably that the generals were waiting for Rupert to attack, confident that their superior numbers and good defensive position on Braham Hill would enable them to defeat him without any difficulty. Only when it became apparent that he had no intention of doing so did they decide to take the initiative. However, their offensive deployment suggests otherwise. Sir Hugh Cholmley suggested that a Scottish deserter might have informed the Allied generals that Rupert would not attack until the morning, but by early evening this must have been quite obvious to observers on the ridge. Rupert's soldiers were dismounting from their horses, laying down their pikes and muskets, and lighting fires to cook their evening meals.[26] Another consideration on the Allied generals' part may have been that their troops, having drunk the wells dry in Long Marston the previous night, might be in no fit state to fight if the battle was postponed till morning.[27] It has also been suggested that what stirred the Allied generals into action was the sight of Newcastle's infantry arriving from York, but the evidence for this is too slim and circumstantial for it to be worthy of serious consideration. All it comprises is a throwaway remark by the Duchess of Newcastle in an analysis of her husband's misfortunes, and an extrapolation from Arthur Trevor's account, the shortcomings of which are discussed above.[28] Other sources refer specifically to Newcastle's infantry arriving on the moor at 4 p.m., three hours before serious fighting began.[29] However, the most damning evidence against Newman's hypothesis is a comment in the three generals' letter to the Committee of Both Kingdoms to the effect that the battle only began when 'both armies were in readiness'.[30]

At about 7 p.m. the whole Allied army moved down the slope with the Eastern Association horse in the lead, probably because they had the better going, drawn up as they were on the tongue of moorland immediately to the east of Tockwith village. Ogden's and Cholmley's accounts suggest strongly that Prince Rupert was taken by surprise,[31] but the extent to which the king's armies were caught off-guard by an attack launched so late in the day is impossible to assess. All one can say is that, apart from one probable exception discussed below, the enemy advance does not seem to have bounced the Royalists into making a hasty and inappropriate response. If King James II was right, the front line had instructions issued earlier in the day to wait for the enemy to get into difficulties as they moved onto the moor from the cultivated land before attacking. Rupert's battle plan may then have been to disrupt the front line of the enemy cavalry on both wings with musket fire and then to disperse the rest with a well-timed counter-charge. His outnumbered infantry would presumably have been expected to hold on against superior numbers, helped by the cavalry reserves, until the enemy infantry, realizing that their horse were streaming off the battlefield, broke and ran, heading for the bridges over the Wharfe at Cawood and Tadcaster. As they broke, Rupert would presumably have ordered his uncommitted reserves to ride around the ridge and seize the river crossings, thus cutting off the enemy retreat and forcing them to surrender or be killed. This, of course, is mere speculation. All that one can be reasonably sure of is that the Royalist troops were deployed during the afternoon and evening of 2 July in such a way as to defend themselves against attack, and indeed on the left wing and in the centre the formation Rupert devised was able to absorb the initial assault and then throw the enemy back in disorder. In fact the battle plan was so successful that Rupert drew his troops up in a similar manner at the so-called Third Battle of Newbury. What really matters, however, is that it eventually failed on the right wing and this paved the way for the Allied victory.

The alleged reason for an immediate and serious problem on the Royalist right wing was that, as at Edgehill, Lord Byron disobeyed orders and charged the enemy. This point is made in narrative after narrative from Firth onwards,[32] often with much elaboration based on current military theory and practice, but the supporting evidence from the Royalist side is very limited – a cryptic comment in Rupert's Diary, written after the Restoration, to the effect that Byron had made an 'improper charge' upon Cromwell's forces, which is filled out in James II's memoirs to include Sir John Hurry advising Byron to attack the enemy as they charged.[33] This raises the question of whether Rupert was telling the whole truth. Given that he himself was subsequently criticized for actively seeking to fight a battle against a larger enemy army immediately after relieving York instead of opting for a more cautious strategy, Rupert would have found it very convenient to pin the blame for the defeat not on his miscalculation concerning the enemy's intentions but on the disobedience of a subordinate who was conveniently dead and unable to defend himself. However, there is some support for Rupert's allegation in the language used in the Allied generals' report to the Committee of Both Kingdoms: 'before both armies were in readiness it was near seven o'clock at night, about which time they advanced towards one another, whereupon followed a very hot encounter for the space of three hours.'[34]

If, however, the action on the Royalist right wing did indeed begin in the manner described by King James, why might Byron have disobeyed his orders? The circumstances were very different from those at Edgehill when the Royalists had been on the attack. Despite Byron's reputation for impulsive behaviour, to charge across the ditch and possibly a marsh against an enemy superior in numbers seems totally out of character in a very experienced cavalry commander. Also, if Byron had single-handedly lost the Battle of Marston Moor through disobeying orders, it is impossible to understand why he was allowed to continue commanding troops in the field for at least another three months, and why subsequently Rupert made no adverse comment when informing a close friend that Byron was to be promoted to the post of lieutenant general of cavalry in the main field army.[35] All that I can suggest is that after the battle Byron was able to convince Rupert that he had taken a decision that was justified in the circumstances even though it had meant disobeying orders.

The following chain of events might have provided sufficient justification, though the evidence for it is limited and largely circumstantial. Having spent the whole day in the field, most of Byron's command had left their ranks to feed themselves and their horses. When Cromwell's horse suddenly showed signs of attacking, he led forward a couple of his regiments, probably his own and Sir John Hurry's, that were in some state of readiness.[36] The object of such a desperate spoiling attack of 500 or so horse was to gain precious time. In this he was successful. By sacrificing two regiments Byron failed to prevent the enemy crossing the Tockwith–Long Marston road and advancing onto Marston Moor, but he gave the rest of his command the chance to remount and launch a determined counterattack. It also gave Prince Rupert time to go to the support of Lord Byron, presumably with part of the second line, his Lifeguard and possibly Sir Edward Widdrington's brigade. Apparently they charged the Eastern Association cavalry in the flank but did little more than stop them in their tracks, which may explain why Rupert used the nickname Ironsides to describe Cromwell's men after Marston Moor. This disjointed opening of the fighting at the Tockwith end of the battlefield may explain why both Watson and Stockdale described Cromwell's first clash with the enemy as involving small bodies of horse.[37] However, it must be emphasized that what has just been argued is purely hypothesis.[38] Nevertheless the scantiness and possible bias of the evidence presently available means that the traditional version, in which the cavalry engagement at the western end of the battle line began with an unauthorized charge by Byron's horse, cannot be regarded as anything other than highly probable.

A second uncertainty concerns the length of time the cavalry engagement took to resolve itself. Two of the accounts of the battle claimed that Rupert and his Midlands and Southern cavalry were quickly routed, but they were written by Northern Royalist officers, one of whom was not at the battle. The likelihood that they were prejudiced is discussed above.[39] The most convincing evidence against is that all the major narratives written by members of the Allied armies immediately after the battle, including Lionel Watson's extremely thorough account of fighting from an Eastern Association army perspective, either claim or imply that a long and hard cavalry fight took place at the Tockwith end of the battlefield. Thomas Stockdale's narrative even maintains that after initial success Cromwell's men experienced a distinct setback as the Royalists fed in more troops.[40] The Scottish accounts do not contain such detail, but they do not contradict the picture painted by their allies. The great weight of opinion in sources written immediately after the battle therefore points to the left wing being involved in a mêlée that may have lasted over half an hour. However, the testament of the Northern Royalists cannot simply be ignored. Jamming conflicting accounts together to produce a common narrative is something to be avoided,[41] but there is, however, a chance that what Cholmley and Slingsby described was the routing of a division of right wing horse early on in the battle, which became magnified in the telling, but this can be nothing more than a highly tentative hypothesis.

A third problem concerns the way in which the cavalry fight progressed, ending in the rout of the whole of the Royalist right wing. An exceedingly well-entrenched part of traditional narratives of this part of the battle is an unequivocal statement to the effect that it was the three regiments of Scottish horse in Cromwell's reserve line led by Lieutenant General David Leslie that sealed the Royalists' fate by attacking them in the flank whilst they were heavily engaged in hand-to-hand fighting with Cromwell's Ironsides.[42] However, the first-hand evidence for it is slight, namely a passage in 'Captain Stewart's' narrative, the problematic nature of which has already been discussed.[43] All the other early Allied reports of the action make little or no mention of the Scottish horse on Cromwell's wing other than to say that David Leslie fought well, and it was this that ignited the quarrel between the Scots and Cromwell's faction amongst the Eastern Association officers.[44] Moreover, Stewart's account does not make it completely clear when Leslie's charge took place. Its place in his narrative is such that he could be describing an incident that took place much later in the battle when the other wing of the Royalist horse was put to flight.[45]

Controversy about what had happened on the Allied left wing at Marston Moor revived about eighteen months later, occasioned by the publication of David Buchanan's *Truth's Manifest*, a narrative of the Scottish Revolution and of the Scots' involvement in English affairs. Buchanan reiterated the Scottish view that David Leslie had played a pivotal role in the victory at Marston Moor, but no more. There were two responses to what was deemed 'a scandalous pamphlet', Edward Bowles's *Manifest Truths* and *The Scots Design Discovered*, said to have been written by Lord Say and Sele, the father of Nathaniel Fiennes who wrote an account of Edgehill, and at that time a close political associate of Oliver Cromwell. Both tracts focused not on the tactics employed but on the allegation that Cromwell had left the battlefield early after receiving a minor wound, and that David Leslie took command of the Allied right wing and routed Prince Rupert's horse. Bowles's argument is almost totally concerned with the crucial importance of the Eastern Association horse in winning the battle, whilst explaining that Cromwell had quickly returned to his command after his wound had been dressed. He also claimed not to have found any clear evidence of any charges undertaken by the Scottish horse. The author of *The Scots Design Discovered* takes a similar line to Bowles, but he also argued that the small size of the horses the Scottish cavalry rode meant that they were incapable of anything other than pursuing the enemy, or at best routing a regiment that had already had its ranks broken by another body. This may have been the case, as it fits the role they played in the closing stages of the battle, but the writer does not say categorically that the Scots played no part in the outcome of the cavalry engagement. To be fair to all sides, it is possible that all the Scottish reserve had done was to make their presence known on the exposed right flank of the Royalist cavalry, and that as such they were merely the proverbial straw that broke the camel's back.[46] Nevertheless, it is not a fact but a matter of opinion that a flank attack delivered by Leslie's horse took place, precipitating the collapse of the Royalist right wing.

When the Royalists broke, there was little in the way of a pursuit.[47] What is remarkable is not that the pursuit was so perfunctory, but that the Allied horse were able to keep together in a body and play a further decisive role in the battle. Accounts written by participants on both sides marvel at the way they were able to regain their formation, change their front, and then move across the moor to take a vital part in the next stage of the battle. It was not a trial run for what was to happen the following year at Naseby, where only part of the horse on Cromwell's wing were involved in the first mêlée and the rest used subsequently to attack the enemy reserves. At Marston Moor all the Allied left wing had been involved in the first encounter other than possibly Leslie's regiments. There were no uncommitted reserves to take the lead in the next stage of the fighting. Yet any lengthy cavalry encounter that degenerated into a series of duels between opposing horsemen was likely to end messily even for the victors. The Eastern Association formation, in close order at the start of the mêlée, would have found it difficult not to fray and then to disintegrate as one horseman after another, finding that his opposite number had turned tail, reacted either by bringing his mount to a halt or by urging it forward to pursue and cut down the fugitives. All I can suggest, extremely tentatively, is that the enemy broke very suddenly all along the line rather than falling back slowly and then dispersing randomly, and that the Allied horse, already at a standstill or virtual standstill, were so well trained (or so exhausted) that they remained exactly where they were. The other possible explanation is that the second cavalry fight was so different from the first that the victors did not need to be in close order in order to win it.

Whilst the cavalry engagement was raging to their left, the Eastern Association brigades in the first line of the Allied infantry formation under Major General Crawford were pushing back the enemy facing them. None of the Allied accounts is written from the perspective of Manchester's infantry, but they appear to have routed the last of their opponents at precisely the same time as the cavalry engagement to their left came to an end.[48] If it had taken more time, Cromwell and Leslie's cavalry regiments could have come to their aid by attacking the exposed flank of the enemy infantry; if less, Crawford's pikemen and musketeers could have supported their own cavalry by attacking Rupert's regiments in the flank or rear. Moreover, like the Eastern Association horse, they too appear to have kept their formation and been ready for another engagement.

Having routed the enemy, the officers of the Eastern Association cavalry and infantry and David Leslie conferred about what to do next. The decision that was taken was of crucial significance in view of the almost uniform disaster suffered by the Allied armies elsewhere on Marston Moor, about which they were probably informed by some Scottish horse from the other wing.[49] The prudent move would have been to try to save what was left of the army by retreating across the Nidd and so to Leeds. A fighting retreat would have been possible in that Crawford, Cromwell and Leslie had cavalry and infantry both of which were in good heart. Instead, however, the generals decided to wheel to the right and attack the enemy formations which had routed most of their colleagues in the centre and on the right wing.

On the Long Marston side of the battlefield the Allied cavalry and dragoon regiments under Sir Thomas Fairfax's command had considerable difficulty in deploying on the moor, but the type of hazard they faced is portrayed differently in the various accounts of the action. Sir Thomas himself blamed gorse bushes. The author of 'Captain Stewart's' account claimed that Fairfax's men could only deploy on the moor using a narrow lane that was under heavy enemy fire from the musketeers that were interspersed between the Royalist cavalry squadrons, and that as they emerged from the lane they were charged by the enemy horse. Another account mentions the ditch separating the moor from the cultivated land.[50] The intensity of the Royalist fire is supported by archaeological evidence, in that hundreds of spent musket balls were found when an embankment was levelled in that part of the battlefield in the 1960s.[51] However, deploy his horse Sir Thomas eventually did, as there was a prolonged mêlée at the Long Marston end of the battlefield. Fairfax at the head of a body of 400 horse claimed to have routed the enemy regiment facing him, but thereafter he was unable to control his victorious troopers, who galloped off in the general direction of York in pursuit of the enemy. He then returned to the outskirts of Long Marston where to his considerable surprise he found the Royalists in complete control, the rest of the Yorkshire cavalry and dragoons and their Scottish reserve having seemingly fled in the meantime. Throwing away his white scarf, the badge of the Allied army at Marston Moor, Sir Thomas rode around the rear of the Royalist position where he joined the victorious Eastern Association horse and foot. Having lost his command, he played no further leadership role in the battle, and may have left the battlefield to have his wounds dressed.[52]

The exact circumstances in which the Allied right wing disintegrated are uncertain, but Fairfax's regiments appear to have fled 'suddenly' like Rupert's horse on the other wing. Lord Eglinton's regiment in the reserve line put up quite a fight according to Eglinton himself, but it was put to flight nevertheless. The remaining two Scottish regiments seem to have made their escape whilst Goring's troops chased their Yorkshire colleagues over the ridge and off the battlefield and then set about plundering the Allied baggage train. What was left of the Scottish horse on that wing played little further part in the battle, but according to Stewart's account some joined the left wing.[53]

At about the same time as the Yorkshire horse were fleeing from the battlefield, many of the Allied infantry formations in the centre and the right-centre of the Allied position were also leaving the battlefield. Initially the whole of the front line, not just the Eastern Association foot, had done well. The Scottish regiments crossed into the moorland without any apparent difficulty, aided possibly by the success of Crawford's men to their left. If anything, Lord Fairfax's foot did even better. They captured several enemy artillery pieces, and must have been several hundred yards into the moor when disaster struck. A volley of musket fire from the Marquis of Newcastle's Lifeguard, the Whitecoats, may have brought them to a halt. They were then seemingly charged by a body of cavalry, which, if de Gomme's plan is correct, were Sir William Blakiston's cavalry brigade stationed between the second and third lines of the Royalist formation, which routed them and two of the four Scottish regiments on their flank. This produced panic in part of the second and third line of the Allied infantry, exacerbated by Fairfax's fleeing cavalry riding over some of the infantry regiments in their eagerness to escape from the battlefield. Other infantry regiments, however, appear to have fled of their own accord.[54] Also caught up in the flight were the rest of the Northern infantry belonging to Lord Fairfax's army, together with their general.[55]

Exactly how many Allied infantry regiments took to their heels it is impossible to say, as the sources do not agree. Accounts of the battle written by the Scots do their best to be positive, but there was no escaping the fact that the Earl of Leven himself, after attempting to stem the tide, had deserted his command and ridden to Leeds or Bradford, twenty miles away. At worst only a single brigade in the first line comprising the regiments of Lord Maitland and the Earl of Lindsay stood their ground, and also four or so regiments in the second line under Lumsden's command, but the slow response of the latter when their colleagues in the first line came under attack from Royalist cavalry suggests that they may have been recovering from being run over by Fairfax's horse.[56]

The charge by the Royalist brigade seems to have ended somewhere in the cornfields on Braham Hill where it may have been charged in the flank by the pikemen of the reserve brigade of the Eastern Association infantry and driven back in disorder, but the reserve cavalry had done very well to produce a similar result to that which been achieved at Edgehill by the whole of Rupert's right wing. Moreover, either bruised by the encounter or more likely run over by the Yorkshire horse or by Goring's victorious cavalry, Manchester's brigade also seems to have turned tail.[57]

As if the flight of over half the Allied infantry was not disaster enough, some, but probably not all, the regiments in the second line of the Royalist Northern cavalry under Sir Charles Lucas's command stopped their headlong pursuit of the enemy horse and turned on Maitland's and Lindsay's pikemen and musketeers. In the encounter the feats of endurance performed by the infantry in the open moorland without the protection of either their own cavalry or features in the landscape exceeded even those of the Blue regiment of the London Trained Bands on Wash Common some nine months earlier. They apparently withstood two formidable charges by Lucas's men and then, reinforced by some infantry from the second Allied line, they saw off a third charge and captured Sir Charles Lucas himself, his horse having been killed under him. The Scots infantry regiments had survived, but only just.[58] However, Lucas may have been blamed for making the mistake of attacking infantry without sufficient infantry support of his own.[59] Rupert must surely have learned this lesson from the very heavy casualties suffered by the king's cavalry at the First Battle of Newbury when attacking experienced infantry. It is therefore possible that he had given orders that if the first line was successful in routing the enemy, the second line should follow it and await orders, not turn on the Allied infantry brigades. If this had happened, the last stage of the battle would have been between the left wing of the Allied horse and fresh Royalist regiments, and the result possibly very different. This is the only way that I can make sense of the comment in *Mercurius Aulicus* to the effect that the cavalry battle had been lost partly because the reserves held back. It cannot refer to what happened on the Royalist right or in the centre, but it may, of course, have been a form of words dreamt up by the writer of the report on the battle or the journal's editor, intended to help protect Prince Rupert's reputation.[60]

The general outline of what happened next is very clear. Royalist, Parliamentary and Scottish accounts agree that by nightfall or very soon after, the victorious Allied left wing comprising Cromwell and Leslie's cavalry and Crawford's infantry brigades had destroyed the remaining Royalist formations, and taken thousands of prisoners and the whole of Newcastle's and Rupert's artillery and baggage. However, the stages by which this was accomplished are not clear. The traditional story told by historians from Gardiner to Carpenter[61] is that, having taken the decision not to save what they could by retreating into the West Riding, some or all of the Eastern Association and Scottish cavalry and dragoons moved through the corridor of land between the rear of the Royalist infantry position and Wilstrop Wood and drew up in the place where the Northern Horse had been stationed when battle began, that is facing southwards towards the ridge just to the west of Long Marston village. Goring's troops, which were plundering the Allied baggage train on Braham Hill, marched back down the slope towards the moor and were soundly defeated, possibly by Eastern Association foot as well as horse. This is basically Lionel Watson's account.[62] 'Captain Stewart's' account is on somewhat similar lines, but clearly identifies the enemy horse as those that had attacked the Scottish infantry, not the whole of Goring's cavalry wing.[63] The rest of the accounts written by observers on the Parliamentary side either do not make any mention of a second encounter between the horse at the Long Marston end of the battlefield,[64] or describe it in such terms that it cannot be distinguished from general mopping-up operations,[65] and there is no record whatsoever of any such engagement in any of the Royalist accounts of the battle.

There is then sufficient evidence to indicate that a second cavalry fight took place close to Long Marston village an hour or so after the first, but it may have been a small-scale encounter like that hinted at in 'Captain Stewart's' account. Royalist accounts imply, for example, that only Lucas's men were involved; the rest of the Northern Horse were elsewhere with Sir Hugh Cholmley claiming that initially Goring's men were too scattered to take part in the final stage of the battle. However, they rallied in such numbers, presumably on or behind Braham Hill, that they were ready to charge the Eastern Association troops at dawn, but were ordered to retire to York instead.[66] Monckton tells a similar story, but in much greater detail. His horse was killed in the charge that routed Sir Thomas Fairfax's cavalry regiments, and he had some difficulty in finding a replacement. However,

> when I remounted I went over the slow where I found some 2,000 broken horse, as I endeavoured to put them into order Hurry came galloping through the slough. I rid to him and desired him to assist

me for there was none of them but that knew either himself or me, and if he would bestir himself with me we might regain the field before it was dark, he told me broken horse would never fight and so galloped away to York. I put those horse in order and stayed with them so near the enemy that we could hear them speak until 12 a clock at night and had stayed till morning, but that Sir John Many came to command us of.

Finally, *Mercurius Aulicus*, drawing possibly on Prince Rupert's despatch, claims that Sir Marmaduke Langdale's horse retained control of part of the Allied artillery until well after the battle was over, which gives some support to Monckton's version of events, as he was major of Langdale's brigade.[67] I therefore hypothesize that all Cromwell and Leslie's cavalry did in the final stage of the battle was to chase away the remnant of Sir Charles Lucas's command and help hunt down the fleeing Royalist infantry. They thus won the battle almost by default as the last units still standing.

Evidence relating to the infantry fight in the closing stages of the battle is patchy and to some extent contradictory. Most narratives regard the destruction of Newcastle's Whitecoats as taking place at the very end of the battle.[68] Many years after the battle a man who claimed to have been one of Cromwell's troopers at Marston Moor described his regiment's destruction of the Whitecoats in detail.[69] 'Captain Stewart's' report, however, places the incident much earlier in the battle, but it seems highly unlikely that the Allied left wing cavalry would have been used against infantry formations at that stage if they had an encounter with enemy cavalry still to come. On the other hand, Somerville attributes the destruction of the Whitecoats to Frazier's dragoons, who would have had the firepower to do so.[70] The other point worth commenting on is the hypothesis that the Whitecoats were ordered to sacrifice themselves to cover the withdrawal of the rest of the Royalist army.[71] The evidence for this, however, is entirely circumstantial, and if these were indeed their orders, Rupert gained little from it. Few Royalist infantry were still with him the following day. The scenario is also predicated on the 'last stand' taking place on the north-eastern edge of the battlefield at the very end of the battle. This seems unlikely. Two Parliamentary sources place the Whitecoats' alleged sacrifice in the Royalist centre, not on the fringe of the action.[72]

The fate of the Royalist infantry is therefore problematic. There was no wholesale surrender, as there was to be at Naseby. A second-hand account written by one sea captain to another claims that the men impressed in Wales and the north-west fled without a blow being struck,[73] which may explain why part of the Royalist cavalry reserve was able to carry out such an effective charge through the heart of its own infantry position. However, some of Colonel Chaytor's men marched off the battlefield or quickly returned to their colours, as Rupert left them behind during his march back into Lancashire to help garrison Bolton Castle. Some Northern infantry also managed to reach York where they reinforced the garrison as it prepared for a second siege. So too did some officers and soldiers from the Anglo-Irish regiments of Colonels Tillier and Broughton, as their regiments fought in the king's armies for almost another year.[74] Possibly the escapees were able to take advantage of a window of opportunity when a large gap opened up to the rear of the Royalist position after the Eastern Association cavalry had finished their march from the Tockwith to the Long Marston end of the battlefield. However, once the Allied left wing horse had finished with the remaining enemy formations still in battle array, they were free to deal with fugitives. It is therefore likely that Royalist foot soldiers made up the bulk of the 5,000 to 6,000 or so killed or captured at Marston Moor.[75]

Chapter 12
The Second Battle of Newbury
Context, Landscape and Sources

Context

The last major battle of 1644 took place close to Newbury on 27 October. During the summer the king and his forces in the south of England had fought an effective defensive campaign. Avoiding battle in late May and early June when faced in the Oxford area by the armies of both the Earl of Essex and Sir William Waller, they took full advantage of the Committee of Both Kingdom's over-optimistic appraisal of the strategic situation, which had resulted in Parliament's armies going their separate ways.[1] With Essex and his regiments well on their march towards the Royalist-held south-west of England, the king's generals humiliated Sir William Waller's army at Cropredy Bridge near Banbury at the end of the month. They then combined with Prince Maurice's Army of the West to force Essex's infantry and artillery to surrender near Lostwithiel in Cornwall in late August. His infantry regiments were allowed to return to Parliament's quarters, but the king retained his cannon, arms and other military supplies. In the meantime Rupert, having abandoned the hopeless task of trying to maintain a strong Royalist presence in the north of England without gunpowder, had moved his headquarters to Bristol, whilst quartering his remaining troops in the southern part of the Welsh Marches.[2]

During September the victorious Royalist armies made their way slowly eastwards, their progress delayed by various initiatives designed to enable the four counties of south-west England to defend themselves. The original strategic plan for the late autumn, agreed at discussions with Prince Rupert at Sherborne Castle in Dorset in early October, was for the King's and Prince Maurice's armies to march to Marlborough in Wiltshire, where they would be joined by forces under Rupert's command including the Northern Horse and a new corps raised by Charles Gerard in south-west Wales. The Royalist army group would begin by relieving three besieged garrisons in what can be loosely described as the Thames valley theatre of war, Banbury, Donnington Castle near Newbury and Basing House near Basingstoke, all of which were close to surrendering. It would then march into East Anglia to take up winter quarters.

Opposing the king's forces was a cavalry screen stationed on the Wiltshire–Dorset border composed of elements from Essex's and Waller's armies, and also from Manchester's, which the Committee of Both Kingdoms had ordered to march south just before receiving news of the disaster in Cornwall.[3] By the end of the Sherborne conference, Manchester's infantry regiments were quartered between Newbury and Reading, whilst Essex's infantry were re-equipping at Portsmouth after the long march back from Cornwall into Parliament's quarters.[4]

Within a week of Rupert's return to Bristol, the king was persuaded to try to attack the scattered Parliamentary forces before they could combine. It was a bold plan, but it failed because the royal armies were too slow. Goring's attempt to take Waller's cavalry by surprise at Andover on 19 October was frustrated by the failure of Prince Maurice's infantry to arrive on time, and the king failed by two days to prevent Essex's infantry making a rendezvous with the rest of Parliament's three armies and a corps of the London Trained Bands at Basingstoke on 21 October.[5] Charles's next intention was to relieve Basing House, but to proceed any further eastwards would be like walking straight into the jaws of a trap. The two Royalist armies therefore turned north and set up camp at Newbury where, well supplied with foodstuffs and ammunition and surrounded by friendly features in the landscape – rivers, woods, enclosures and passes – they could spin out the time until either Rupert came to the rescue or the enemy forces withdrew through lack of food, fodder and adequate shelter.[6] Such was the Royalist Council of War's confidence that, having arrived at Newbury and thus relieved Donnington Castle, it sent three of the king's best cavalry regiments under the Earl of Northampton to break up the siege of Banbury.[7] However, the Parliamentary generals, probably aware that the enemy facing them at Newbury was not as numerous as intelligence had earlier suggested,[8] decided on an attack rather than a stand-off.

Landscape
On 25 October 1644 the Royalist armies began fortifying an area of land covering the northern approaches to Newbury. Shaped like a narrow letter V pointing eastwards, it was situated on the opposite bank of the Kennet to the town and to Wash Common and Round Hill where the First Battle of Newbury had been fought. Its sides, some two miles in length, followed the course of the Kennet and its tributary the Lambourn. Between the two was a spur of chalk along the crest of which ran the road from Bath to London. The descent through the village of Church Speen to the Kennet valley was steep, as was the slope between the road and the river. The slope facing the Lambourn, however, was much less steep with a much larger gap between the road and the

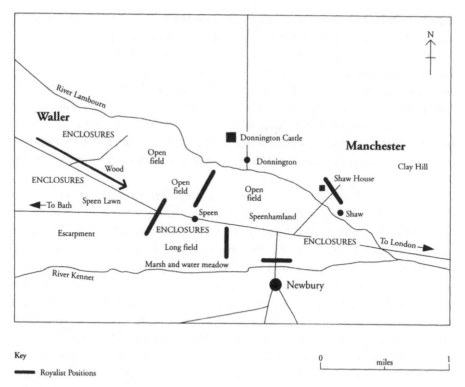

Key

━━━ Royalist Positions

0   miles   1

Map 5. The Second Battle of Newbury

river. Despite John Gwyn's allegation that taking up so restricted a position hampered the king's forces' ability to manoeuvre,[9] the Lambourn in particular was to provide a good line of defence for the royal armies.

Four bridges crossed the Lambourn within the letter V.[10] The most northerly carried the Newbury to Oxford road, which passed through the village of Donnington immediately after crossing the river; the second, which connected Newbury with the countryside to the north-east, carried a road that passed through the village of Shaw in a similar manner. The third, probably no more than a footbridge, was at Shaw Mill. All three were left intact by the Royalists, but they had almost certainly destroyed the large bridge close to the confluence of the Lambourn with the Kennet half a mile to the east of Newbury which carried the Bath road.[11] Small water meadows lined the north bank of the Kennet as far as the only bridge over the Kennet within the V, which led to the town itself. This bridge also remained intact, probably because it might serve as a vital, if narrow, escape route should the fortified area have to be abandoned for any reason.[12]

The side of the letter V facing Donnington and Shaw was defended by two strong-points. A force trying to cross the Lambourn at Donnington bridge would have to face heavy fire from cannon and several hundred musketeers of

Sir John Boys's regiment stationed in Donnington Castle, which was situated on a piece of high ground on the north bank of the river.[13] Also on the north bank of the Lambourn, and a mile or so closer to its confluence with the Kennet, was Shaw House, known at the time as Mr Dolman's house. Close to the bridge that carried the road from Newbury to Shaw, it was described in one of the Parliamentary accounts of the battle as a second castle 'being set about with earthworks, hedges and a dry moat'. Moreover, between Shaw House and the bridge at Shaw were other hedge lines that could provide cover for musketeers and field artillery. All these would have to be cleared of the enemy before an army could cross the river from the east.[14]

The remainder of the north bank of the Lambourn between Donnington and Shaw appears to have been open field arable, but within a short distance the land rose rapidly to Clay Hill, which provided a panoramic view over the whole of the battlefield and a convenient assembly point for a force intending to attack the fortified area from the east. Here a corps of the Parliamentary armies was stationed between 26 and 28 October, and from here two major attacks were launched against the Royalists defending Shaw in the early morning and the late afternoon of the 27th.[15]

However, the strength of the position between the Kennet and the Lambourn was compromised by the decision of the Parliamentary generals to launch their main attack from the west rather than the east, using the ford at Boxford, some two miles above Donnington. Here there was no river to assist the defence, but the third side of what now needed to become a fortified triangle was not that easy to attack. Wickham Heath, the most prominent feature in the landscape between Boxford and Church Speen, was set about with small fields and woods, and no more than half a mile across at its widest point. As a result a large army approaching from the direction of Lambourn or Hungerford would find it impossible to deploy there in conventional battle array without much bunching up of units. Moreover, as it came closer to Speen, it would first have to make its way through some enclosures at Wood Speen and Stockcross, and then pass down a narrow heath in the shape of a funnel known as Speen Lawn. This was a potential killing ground if the Royalists placed musketeers and artillery pieces in the hedges and woodland that surrounded it.

The enclosures also extended in a narrow band around the south of Church Speen, but they were most thickly concentrated to the east of the village along both sides of the Bath road.[16] Beyond these enclosures in the low ground where the Lambourn joined the Kennet was Speenhamland, two large, relatively flat open fields extending from the lane connecting Church Speen with Donnington to the road leading from Newbury bridge to Shaw bridge. Speenhamland's southern boundary for some of its length was the London to Bath road, but as it neared the outskirts of Newbury it crossed the edge of one of the open fields. Its southern boundary then became the hedge that bordered the water meadows which lined the Kennet.

The two open fields were of great advantage to the king's generals as they enabled troops to be moved quickly from one point to another within the fortified area as the military situation developed. Not surprisingly, it was there that they placed their reserves. However, gaps in the defensive perimeter gave an enemy advancing on Speenhamland along the river valleys direct access to the heart of the Royalist position. First, despite the steep slope separating the Bath road from the Kennet, it was possible with difficulty to bypass Church Speen to the south and enter Speenhamland via a long narrow field that separated the enclosures around the village from the water meadows lining the river.[17] However, the narrow field was not ideal cavalry country. The gradient between Speen village and the Kennet, which steepened as it approached Speenhamland, would make it difficult for squadrons riding across the slope to maintain formation.[18]

A second and much more serious problem was caused by the wider corridor of land that lay between Church Speen and the river Lambourn. A body of troops advancing on Speenhamland from Boxford would not have to pass through a wide belt of enclosures and then across Donnington Park, as the first edition of the six-inch Ordnance Survey map of the Newbury area would suggest. Instead most of the route would be across an extensive area of open field arable.[19] This covered not only the whole of present-day Donnington Park, it also extended back past the northern edge of Dean Wood, the principal piece of woodland bordering Speen Lawn, as far west as a thin belt of enclosures at Wood Speen separating Wickham Heath from Worthy Field. It was without doubt the Achilles heel of the Royalist position.

Sources

The traces of the past relating to the Second Battle of Newbury are relatively sparse given the number of troops involved. Little, for example, seems to have been printed in the London journals, possibly because of the disappointing outcome of the battle, possibly because the City Trained Bands played little or no part in the fighting, and there are no contemporary battle plans. However, Rocque's two inch to the mile map of Berkshire published a hundred years later and the map compiled in connection with the enclosure of the open fields of Church Speen in 1780 are of considerable help in removing some misconceptions about the mid-seventeenth-century landscape.[20]

The Royalist sources written soon after the battle comprise a very long account in *Mercurius Aulicus*, several pages in Sir Edward Walker's *Historical Discourses*, and a short but detailed account of fighting in the Kennet valley in the diary of Richard Symonds, who rode in the King's Lifeguard of Horse and wrote up his notes as the campaign progressed.[21] There are also some comments in a letter written by Charles Murray to Sir John Berkeley, the

Royalist governor of Exeter, on 30 October.[22] Unfortunately, however, the two longer accounts bear such a very strong resemblance to one another in terms of structure, content, and even language, that either Walker wrote his using the *Mercurius* account or they both had access to a common source, namely a report written immediately after the battle which has since disappeared. This, then, is a case where cross-referencing between sources cannot be employed to help strengthen the factual content of the narrative, but the overall outline of the battle as they describe it, and some of the detail, is endorsed by Symonds and by several of the Parliamentary accounts.

The other problematic matter is that both the larger accounts were written with an eye to their propaganda value for the Royalist cause. This is obvious in the case of *Mercurius Aulicus*, but the narrative of the 1644 campaign in the south of England and the Midlands in Walker's *Historical Discourses* is not a diary intended to be read by a limited audience of friends and family, or even a judicious appraisal based on mature reflection, but an account written at the king's request, corrected by the king before he set out on the 1645 campaign, and doubtless intended to have a wide circulation.[23] Admittedly, none of the passages in the printed version describing the Second Battle of Newbury is in italics, the sign that Charles I had amended the text, but this can only mean that it gave an account of events that the king found acceptable. Charles himself, not surprisingly, is given a higher profile than in the account in *Mercurius Aulicus*. Walker is also more critical of the behaviour of the Royalist cavalry, most particularly those who fought on the left wing between Speen village and the Kennet, than either the writer of the report in *Mercurius Aulicus* or Richard Symonds, who provides a clear chronology of the fighting but one which naturally focuses on the activities of his own formation, the Royal Lifeguard. However, the weight of the criticism directed against Sir Humphrey Bennett's brigade is slightly suspect, as the passage provides Walker with the chance to include a pen portrait of the king reviving the cavalrymen's spirits with some well-chosen words, after which they enthusiastically re-entered the fray.[24] Nevertheless, Charles Murray provides some support for Walker's spin on events; he wrote that the Parliamentary cavalry had routed most of 'our horse' on the Royalist left wing until such time as the Lifeguard intervened.[25]

Three Royalist accounts of the battle were completed many years afterwards. Sir Richard Bulstrode's description lacks the immediacy of his account of Edgehill, and may have been rewritten by his early eighteenth-century editor, but there is little evidence of Clarendon's *History of the Great Rebellion* in the text. If so, Bulstrode's account would have read like Walker's, as Clarendon used Walker as his principal source. The extent of editorial interference, however, cannot be ascertained, as the manuscript version does not extend beyond the summer of 1644.[26]

The magisterial comments in King James II's memoirs are, as always, highly interesting as the reflections of a former professional soldier on the conduct of war, but they cannot be regarded as anything other than a second-hand account, as James was not present at the battle. The only sign on this occasion that they are no more than an elaboration of Prince Rupert's views is that James blamed Lord Digby, who was 'ambitious of doing something extraordinary', for persuading the king in Rupert's absence to depart from the strategic decision agreed at Sherborne.[27]

John Gwyn's account is problematic for other reasons. It is much less satisfactory than Bulstrode as evidence of the shape of the battle as it lacks narrative structure and is repetitive and on occasions inaccurate. It was committed to paper thirty years or more after the events being described, and as a piece of prose reads even more like a first draft than Prince Rupert's Diary. Gwyn's aim was not to write a narrative, but to be both analytical and reflective. However, his poor memory and lack of language skills meant that the attempt largely fails. On the other hand the account Gwyn gives of the Second Battle of Newbury displays no sign of being anything other than his own work.[28]

All but two of the Parliamentary accounts were written within weeks rather than months or years of the battle being fought.[29] However, the compound failures of the Second Newbury campaign gave rise to such a storm of recriminations in late November and early December amongst those who had fought in it that much of what was written down at that time must be regarded as tainted to a greater or lesser extent by special pleading. First, there are the major denunciations of the Earl of Manchester by Oliver Cromwell and of Cromwell by Manchester. Second, there is the evidence that backs them up, the sworn statements of Cromwell's supporters on the one hand and a pamphlet written by Manchester's chaplain Simeon Ashe on the other.[30]

Fortunately, there are a number of letters and reports produced immediately after the battle, which appear to tell a less emotive story of the battle and its aftermath. The writers were Phillip Skippon, who commanded Essex's infantry regiments and did not contribute to the ensuing debate;[31] Sir William Waller and Sir Arthur Haselrig, who addressed the House of Commons;[32] Colonel Richard Norton,[33] whose account of the day's events had a different slant from the one he gave four weeks later during the great debate mentioned above; the two members of the Committee of Both Kingdoms present with the armies during the campaign, John Crewe and Sir Archibald Johnston;[34] and their civilian aides, Martin Pindar, Thomas Herbert, John Prickman and Stephen White.[35] There is an air of immediacy, most particularly in the account given to the House of Commons by Waller and Haselrig and in the first letter written by Johnston and Crewe, but only in Skippon's letter to the Earl of Essex does the language used imply that he could have said much more.[36]

However, the circumstances of the Newbury campaign mean that even those traces of the past created immediately after the battle are tainted by the fact that a battle that the Parliamentary armies should have won ended in a draw. It is therefore important not to prioritize the first crop of writings as being a set of reports which are unquestionably superior as evidence to those that emerged at the time of the 'great debate', as they are tainted by possible collusion. As suggested above, there were good reasons for presenting a common front to the Committee of Both Kingdoms and Parliament if there was still a chance of bringing the king's forces to battle on a second and more propitious occasion and annihilating them.[37] The best evidence as to the factuality of both sets of sources produced by officers and civilians who participated in the Second Newbury campaign is not the date at which the sources were produced but whether or not Royalist accounts of the battle tell the same story.

Of the weekly journals printed in London, only two include detail not recorded elsewhere,[38] but the most interesting piece of information they provide is problematic. The writer of the entry in *Mercurius Civicus* described the captured Earl of Cleveland as claiming that the poor performance of the king's troops defending Speen was because the king's generals, believing that the principal enemy attack would come from the east, had positioned their best troops facing in that direction. It is, however, impossible to say whether this was Cleveland's declared opinion, or a rumour inflated by the writer's own agenda, putting the Earl of Manchester's corps in a better light by inference.[39]

Sir William Waller's recollections of the Second Battle of Newbury compiled after the Restoration are no more informative than those concerning Cheriton, despite the fact that he commanded well over half the Parliamentary forces in the field. Once again his only comment concerns God's mercy in saving him from being killed, but it does show him leading from the front in a manner that could be classed as foolhardy, rather than managing his extensive reserves so as to exploit the success of the infantry vanguard at Church Speen.[40] Waller's contribution to the spat between Manchester and Cromwell in November included nothing whatsoever on anybody's conduct at the Second Battle of Newbury, possibly a sign that he himself had little to be proud of.[41]

The only other account of Second Newbury from the Parliamentary side completed long after the battle is a passage in Edmund Ludlow's *Memoirs*.[42] The Edgehill account was rejected earlier as a primary source on the grounds that it could have been written using Nathaniel Fiennes's printed narrative. The Newbury account is less closely related to other accounts in terms of its language and structure, but is nevertheless worrying in two respects. First, Ludlow claimed that his horse was killed under him, but Richard Norton writing immediately after the battle claimed that he led Ludlow's regiment into action as their colonel's bridle had snapped.[43] Second, it is most surprising given Ludlow's radicalism, which was already in full flood by 1644, that he does not comment adversely on the Earl of Manchester's conduct during the battle, which came under intense scrutiny from other radicals during the 'great debate'.[44] It could be argued that this is a reflection of his subsequent turning against Oliver Cromwell when the latter assumed monarchical powers in 1653, but if that had been the case one would expect him to have attacked Cromwell's inactivity during the battle rather than to have ignored it altogether. However, the temptation to incorporate evidence from Ludlow's account into the narrative is easier to avoid than in the case of Edgehill. His regiment played little or no part in the battle, as it was with Manchester's corps, and the narrative is dominated by two personal anecdotes, one about the death of his cousin as a result of wounds, and the other about the cunning of one of his officers.[45]

Chapter 13

The Second Battle of Newbury
Narrative

The size of the two army groups that faced one another near Newbury in late October is difficult to assess. Oliver Cromwell's estimate that the Parliamentary armies comprised 11,000 foot and 8,000 horse is almost certainly too large.[1] Other sources suggest the London brigade contained between 3,000 and 4,000 men,[2] Manchester's just over 3,000,[3] and Essex's a similar number.[4] None of Waller's infantry regiments was present.[5] The number of cavalry was probably 1,000 less than Cromwell claimed, but even so the Parliamentary armies outnumbered the Royalists by a substantial margin.[6] On 30 September the two Royalist armies are supposed to have comprised less than 10,000 horse and foot.[7] Since then Northampton's brigade, possibly 800 strong, had been detached to relieve Banbury Castle in cooperation with troops from the Oxford garrison, but 800 infantry had apparently joined the colours, half impressed men from the West Country, the rest musketeers from the Winchester garrison.[8]

It took the Parliamentary generals some time to decide how to attack the Royalist armies. Initially they thought in terms of an engagement to the south of the Kennet. The king's armies appeared to have taken up quarters in Newbury itself, and a clash between cavalry units occurred in the Aldermaston area on 24 October.[9] When the Earl of Manchester and Oliver Cromwell fell out at the end of the Newbury campaign, Cromwell claimed that a great opportunity had been lost by not advancing on the enemy immediately after the rendezvous at Basingstoke three days earlier.[10] However, he was surely mistaken in thinking that the king's army would have risked a battle defending the south-eastern approaches to Newbury. The extensive open heath land around Greenham that came to within a mile of the town would have given the Parliamentarians a major advantage with their superiority in cavalry. Moreover, if the king's forces had been unable to hold their position, a successful retreat to the north bank of the Kennet and so to Wallingford across a single bridge would have been difficult to carry out in a hurry. Falling back along the south bank towards Devizes or Bristol was problematic for another reason. The country between Newbury and Hungerford was enclosed, with plenty of passes to hold up the pursuit, but further west the Kennet valley turned into a bottleneck. There the chalk downs, which extended for miles around on all sides, would provide the ideal terrain for Parliamentary cavalry to hunt down and destroy the king's fleeing infantry.[11] The most logical response of the king's commanders to the threat of a direct attack on Newbury from the south-east would have been to cross the Kennet immediately, knowing that it would be very costly indeed, if not impossible, for the enemy to force their way across the river. Indeed the Royalists may have begun doing so as early as 22 October when a substantial part of the king's forces were drawn up on the north bank to witness the knighting of John Boys, the governor of Donnington Castle.[12]

On learning that the Royalists had in fact crossed Newbury Bridge and were putting up defences in the narrow tongue of land between it and the Lambourn, the Parliamentary generals led their armies over the ford at Padworth and approached Newbury along the Bath road, which hugged the north bank of the Kennet. On the afternoon of 25 October they took up a position on Clay Hill between Thatcham and the Lambourn and less than two miles from the town.[13] The following day the armies were deployed in Shaw fields in the Lambourn valley, but probing attacks revealed the strength of the Royalist position. It was therefore decided to assault it from two directions. The major attack was to be from the west. A force led by Sir William Waller comprising the Earl of Essex's infantry and the London Trained Band regiments supported by at least two-thirds of the cavalry belonging to all three armies was to skirt around the northern flank of the Royalist position and attack it from the general direction of Hungerford. Once fighting had begun, the Earl of Manchester was to lead an assault on the enemy defences in the Lambourn valley. At his disposal were his own infantry regiments, 3,000 strong, and a mixed force of 1,800 or so horse and dragoons.[14] The Earl of Essex played no part in the preparations for battle. Having approved the decision to move the armies to the north bank of the Kennet, he retired to Reading. For the past ten days he had been suffering from stomach problems, and these had suddenly worsened.[15]

Cromwell at the time, and some historians since, have remarked on the risks involved in attempting to assault the Royalist position from diametrically opposite directions.[16] The principal danger, as with all manoeuvres of this nature, was that the two attacks might not go in at the agreed times. If this happened, an alert enemy could use interior lines to throw his entire weight against one pincer and destroy it before the other could make its influence felt. On the Newbury battlefield, however, the risks of this happening were quite small. In the first place, although the plan was for the two attacks to occur almost simultaneously, this was not necessary for success. The force Waller commanded, as large if not larger than the king's two armies combined, had the potential to win the battle on its own.[17] The attack on the enemy position protecting the western side of the Royalists' fortified triangle must therefore have been seen as the decisive encounter. Manchester's force of 5,000 men or less would be too weak to achieve much on its own. Thus its role must almost certainly have been a subsidiary one, as the earl and his supporters subsequently claimed, most particularly preventing the king's generals throwing all their military might against Waller.[18] All the earl had to do was ensure that he was not the first to attack in case they threw most of their resources against him. Second, there was little chance of the assaults getting out of sync with one another. Waller's was to go in first, but the initial bombardment of the enemy position would be the signal for Manchester to throw his troops against the defenders of Shaw, and even if the sound of the big guns did not carry that far, fighting around Church Speen would be easily visible from Clay Hill.[19] Third, although the Parliamentary generals did not know it, the Royalist commanders, confident of the strength of their defences and believing the enemy armies to be demoralized, had no intention of making a pre-emptive strike against either of the pincers.[20]

Waller's force set out from Clay Hill on the afternoon of 26 October, bivouacking for the night at North Heath, halfway along its sixteen-mile journey. Initially it marched in a northerly direction as if Sir William's intention was to block the king's retreat to Oxford via Wallingford. No attempt was made to conceal the march from the Royalists. Writing to Prince Rupert on the morning of 27 October, Lord Digby advised him that a twofold attack was probably under way, but left open the possibility that Waller's march was merely intended to cut the Royalists off from their supplies, presumably in the hope of forcing the king's forces into a Lostwithiel-type capitulation.[21] Suspicion of an attack from the west became a certainty when Waller's force, having crossed the Lambourn unopposed at Boxford, climbed the hill to their front, and turned eastwards to march along Wickham Heath towards Church Speen.

Before nightfall on 26 October the king's commanders took steps to defend the rear of their position against attack. The whole of Prince Maurice's infantry, supported by the Duke of York's regiment of foot from the king's army, about 2,500 men in total, and nine artillery pieces, were ordered to take up a position to the west of Speen village where several tracks converged. Here a formidable barricade was constructed. Its defence was entrusted to 400 musketeers; the rest of the foot were deployed in the enclosures slightly to the rear but in front of Speen village.[22] The exact position of the Royalist barricade, however, is unclear. It could have been immediately to the west of Speen where the road from Wickham met the Bath road, or it could have been half a mile to the west in Stockcross. The former looks the more likely. Sir

Edward Walker's account describes the Parliamentary troops as advancing the last few hundred yards across a small heath with a wood behind them to attack the barricade.[23] This does not fit Wickham Heath, which extended over an area of six or more square miles and could not be described as small. It also did not have a wood adjacent to it in Rocque's map. Speen Lawn on the other hand, to the east of the enclosures that Rocque depicts at Stockcross, was a tenth of its size and bordered by Dean Wood, which has since been cut down. Second, Walker explained that adjacent to the barricade on its south side was a narrow field and then a steep escarpment. This dovetails with the enclosure map of 1780, and with Skippon's description of the engagement at Speen, which implies that there was little ground to the right of his infantry's line of march in which it might deploy when it got close to the Royalist position.[24] Rocque's map, however, shows that a barricade at the Stockcross position would have been a mile away from the escarpment. Moreover, one contemporary stated that the Royalist position dominated all the lanes leading westwards from Church Speen and was within range of the cannon in Donnington Castle, whilst a second portrayed Waller's horse and foot as having an easy march across a heath, then passing with difficulty through lanes and enclosures, and only then having sight of the Royalist barricade a quarter of a mile ahead. These descriptions can only fit the western outskirts of Speen, where the lane from Wickham joins the London to Bath Road.[25]

Thus the Royalist defence line facing westwards appears to have been well sited. However, the king's men apparently had insufficient time or lacked the inclination to improve it by digging trenches. Another near contemporary account was critical of the decision not to try to slow down the enemy advance, but there may be an explanation for this. Walker claimed that Sir James Douglas was sent with a body of 300 horse and 200 foot to hinder the enemy's crossing of the Lambourn, but his force would have been far too small to have much of an impact. Moreover, Douglas appears to have been sent north from Donnington, not west from Speen, and may therefore have failed to make contact with the enemy. The only opposition Waller apparently faced before crossing the Lambourn was even tinier, the Donnington Castle troop of horse.[26]

On the other hand the defenders of the positions at Shaw facing the Earl of Manchester on Clay Hill apparently had all the time they needed to strengthen them still further by filling up gaps in hedgerows and deepening ditches.[27] The two centres of resistance, the enclosures around Shaw village and Shaw House, also had one major advantage over the position at Speen, as they could be easily reinforced from Speenhamland. Their defence was entrusted to 1,200 musketeers and pikemen drawn from the most experienced infantry brigades in the king's army, those of Thomas Blagge and George Lisle. Lisle himself was in command of the troops defending the enclosures, whilst Lieutenant Colonel Page of Sir James Pennyman's regiment was in charge at Shaw House.[28] In support was a single regiment of veteran cavalry, the Prince of Wales's, some 200 strong. The rest of the Royalist horse, apart from some of Maurice's regiments that were at Speen, was kept in reserve on Speenhamland. So also was the third brigade of Royalist foot, Colonel Bernard Astley's, and the pikemen and the remaining musketeers belonging to the other two. However, despite such careful preparations, the opening engagement in the battle, the breaching of the line of the Lambourn, was an unpleasant surprise for the king's commanders.

Early on the morning of the 27 October several companies of Manchester's musketeers made ready to cross the Lambourn somewhere to the south of Shaw village, probably near Shaw Mill but possibly close to Ham Mill situated adjacent to the broken down bridge that had carried the Bath road over the river. The Royalists, possibly heartened by the departure northwards of most of the enemy regiments, were merely patrolling this section of the west bank of the river, which was almost certainly in flood.[29] Crossing it by anything other than a bridge would therefore have been very dangerous, but Manchester's men had brought a portable footbridge with them and were over the river and into Speenhamland in no time. However, foot soldiers belonging to Bernard Astley's brigade, which had originally formed part of Hopton's corps in the Western Army, marched down from Speenhamland and pushed the enemy back across the river, inflicting some casualties.[30] Even if the encounter took place exactly as Simeon Ashe described, he may have been wrong to follow it up with the claim that it had satisfied the primary objective of Manchester's corps, namely to force the enemy to commit his reserves to the less important sector of the battlefield, 'long before our friends on Speen Hill did engage' (with the enemy).[31] Hopton's men are described in another source as being withdrawn from the Lambourn valley in the late afternoon to strengthen the western defences of Speenhamland against a possible attack from the direction of Church Speen.[32]

After crossing the Lambourn Waller's forces met with no resistance in their march towards the barricade to the west of Speen.[33] When they were less than a mile from the barricade, they were drawn up in conventional battle formation for open country, infantry in the centre and cavalry on the wings, but it is most likely that the regiments were stacked up three or four deep.[34] This almost certainly explains why many never appear to have seen action that day, most particularly the London brigade. In Parliamentary accounts they are described as having fought well, but there were no casualties amongst their officers and in Royalist accounts they do not receive a mention.

There are two descriptions of the way in which the infantry of the western pincer of the Parliamentary army was deployed. Samuel Bedford, Sir Samuel Luke's deputy as scout master general and his principal correspondent in the Earl of Essex's army, describes Essex's regiment and two regiments of the London Trained Bands as being on the right. In reserve was Colonel

Aldridge's brigade, and on the left Colonel Barclay's brigade supported by another London regiment.[35] Several days after the battle Skippon described the infantry formation in a letter to the Earl of Essex as follows: the Lord General's own regiment on the right, Colonel Aldridge's brigade and a forlorn hope of about 800 musketeers in the centre, and two London regiments also on the right and behind giving covering fire, with one London regiment and Colonel Barclay's brigade in reserve and apparently to their left.[36] The two accounts, however, are not incompatible. Bedford was describing how Waller's forces were deployed on Wickham Heath a mile before they reached the Royalist line, Skippon their positioning at the start of the assault on the barricade. When Waller's forces emerged from the enclosures at Stockcross and entered Speen Lawn, the fact that the main Royalist defence work was constructed seemingly to the south of their line of advance, namely across the Bath road rather than the lane from Wickham, might have caused Essex's and the two London regiments to veer to the right, thus skewing the entire formation and necessitating some redeployment. This may account for the length of time between the march across Wickham Heath and the attack on the barricade.[37]

The right wing of the cavalry, commanded by Sir William Balfour, included most of Essex's regiments supported by one of Manchester's, the left most of the remainder of the Eastern Association regiments under Oliver Cromwell and Sir William Waller's horse under Lieutenant General Middleton.[38] Waller himself seems to have ridden with the cavalry regiments of his own army instead of managing the reserves, as he specifically states that he charged with 'my troopers'.[39] This seems odd from a command and control point of view, given the strength of the reserves, but he may have thought that the decisive cavalry breakthrough would take place between Speen and the Lambourn where the going was easier, rather than between Speen and the Kennet. If this was indeed the case (and the only evidence for it is Waller's own words) his escape from death in a mêlée that followed a charge by the Parliamentary horse is difficult to place, as other sources state outright or strongly imply that the left wing saw very little in the way of fighting. It is, however, possible that Waller was with the forlorn hope, as described below.[40] As for the Parliamentary artillery pieces, Walker describes them as being deployed in a wood, presumably Dean Wood, which would have been to the left rear of the Parliamentary infantry as it marched towards the barricade, but their deployment in a wood is not confirmed by any of the Parliamentary sources.[41]

The hour at which Waller's troops launched their attack seems to slip backwards in time as divisions emerged between the Parliamentary commanders. Most of the earliest reports of the battle opt for 4 p.m., as does Simeon Ashe; later ones place it between 3 and 3.15 p.m., and Cromwell at 2 p.m.[42] Cromwell was almost certainly lying or repeating the lies of others in order to cast doubt on the commitment of the Earl of Manchester to outright victory. There is no doubt whatsoever that preparations began at about 3 p.m. with an artillery barrage. This is what was reported in Royalist accounts written straight after the battle and they, unlike the Parliamentarians, had no reason for falsifying the time.[43] However, none of the eyewitness accounts says how long the bombardment lasted. The assault itself could therefore have been launched at 3.30 p.m. or even later, as the earliest written report of the battle implies.[44]

Descriptions of the action in front of Speen come primarily from Parliamentary accounts of the battle, but none sets out to provide a comprehensive narrative. Keen to gain some credit for a battle in which so little was achieved, the writers concentrate overwhelmingly on the excellent performance of Essex's veteran infantry, who regained the reputation for bravery that they had gained at Edgehill and First Newbury but lost at Lostwithiel.[45] Of the Royalist accounts Walker and *Mercurius Aulicus* merely mention that the barricade was captured and with it the village of Speen, whilst Murray claimed that the performance of some of Prince Maurice's foot was 'ill'. Bulstrode is less terse. He gives a short account of the stout resistance against overwhelming odds made by the Cornish regiments supported by the Earl of Cleveland's cavalry brigade, until both were pushed back.[46] As Cleveland fought on the right of the Royalist position between Donnington Castle and Speen Lawn, the Cornish cannot have been the defenders of the barricade, despite some claims that they were.[47] Instead they were probably deployed on a small rise in the ground that can be seen immediately to the north-west of Speen village. Circumstantial evidence for this is provided by what Parliamentary accounts do not say about the capture of the barricade. They make much of the retaking of several guns lost in Cornwall and the emotion shown by Essex's foot soldiers as they greeted their lost friends. In such circumstances if the Cornish regiments had been the defenders of the barricade they would probably have mentioned it.

After the artillery barrage a division of the right wing of the Parliamentary cavalry cleared a small brigade of Cornish horse from the heath, thus preparing the way for an infantry assault. According to Skippon Aldridge's brigade carried out a frontal assault on the barricade, whilst Essex's regiment attacked the Royalist infantry position to its right. The assault was apparently delivered with great vigour and valour, but nevertheless it seems to have taken the Parliamentarians about an hour to drive the enemy from Speen village and down the hill towards Speenhamland. Possibly the Royalist infantry continued to resist for some time after the barricade had fallen, thus holding up a general advance. Writers on both sides, however, agree that the retreat stopped at the hedge that separated the enclosures to the east of Speen from Speenhamland itself, but there is no evidence of Colonel Blagge's brigade being drawn in to stop the rout, as Reid claims.[48] Although there would have been at least half an hour's daylight left, Waller did not attempt to storm the hedge. It would have been difficult to feed fresh troops through Speen village into the gathering gloom in the valley below; and there was no sign of the Parliamentary cavalry, whose support Skippon described subsequently as being essential if a full victory was to be achieved.[49]

The left wing of Parliamentary horse, seemingly under Cromwell's overall command, began its advance along the Lambourn valley towards the north-eastern corner of Speenhamland soon after 3 p.m. Its progress was apparently impeded by enclosures, even though these are now known only to have covered a small area of land around Wood Speen,[50] but it then suffered a significant setback for which there is little direct evidence in the traces of the past. Royalist reports provide some detail, but their prime concern is to make the most of one of the more positive features of their armies' performance at Second Newbury.

Bulstrode, Sir Edward Walker and *Mercurius Aulicus* all agree that George Goring, the king's lieutenant general of cavalry, put himself at the head of the Earl of Cleveland's brigade and charged the enemy, but Bulstrode saw the objective as being to relieve pressure on the Cornish regiments defending Speen, whilst for Walker and *Mercurius Aulicus* its purpose was to prevent the enemy horse deploying in a position that threatened the king's reserves on Speenhamland. Cleveland's brigade apparently hit the foremost troop of Cromwell's vanguard in overwhelming numbers as they were in the process of crossing a ditch.[51] Brushing off a counter-charge as they sought to establish a position on the enemy side of the ditch, Cleveland's brigade moved forward under flanking fire from several bodies of enemy musketeers, and then attacked an infantry brigade, possibly as many as three times, without any attempt by the Parliamentary cavalry to intervene. In the process the brigade lost many officers including Cleveland himself, who was captured when his horse was killed under him.[52] Interestingly, the earl was taken prisoner by an officer belonging to Barclay's regiment of foot, which was probably in reserve on the Parliamentary left. This indicates the depth to which Royalist horse had penetrated the enemy position. It also implies that the Parliamentary horse on that wing had fallen back into the enclosures around Wood Speen.[53] Otherwise, they would have been able to charge Cleveland's troopers in the flank as they made their way uphill towards Barclay's brigade, which would have been somewhere near Dean Wood. However, the Royalist push quickly came to an end. Cleveland's brigade, like Sir Charles Lucas's at Marston Moor, did not have the strength to overwhelm a brigade of veteran infantry, whilst the king had insufficient foot to exploit the achievements of his right wing horse without compromising the safety of his troops elsewhere in the fortified triangle.

The earliest Parliamentary accounts of the Second Battle of Newbury had very little to say about the cavalry action that took place between Speen village and Donnington Castle. The first sign of a change is in a letter written by Skippon to the Earl of Essex on 30 October in which he hints that his infantry could have inflicted a heavy defeat on the Royalists had they had cavalry support. When the quarrel over the outcome of the Newbury campaign broke out in mid-November, much more information emerged, but only from the Earl of Manchester and his supporters. Criticizing Cromwell's cavalry for doing nothing at the Second Battle of Newbury was one of the more effective ways of challenging the multiple charges of inaction that were being made against the earl by Cromwell and his allies. However, to be fair to Manchester, there is no evidence in any other primary sources that Cromwell and his Eastern Association cavalry regiments did play a significant part in the fighting. The earl's next allegation, that Cromwell was nowhere to be seen and that Waller's lieutenant general, John Middleton, was unable to persuade the Eastern Association regiments to charge by personally (and unsuccessfully) leading a squadron against a much larger body of enemy horse, is not substantiated by any other report, but it is possible that this is a reference to the unsuccessful counter-charge against Cleveland's brigade mentioned above.[54]

The inactivity of the left wing horse cannot be explained by cannon fire from Donnington Castle.[55] It also seems most unlikely that they were taken at a disadvantage when crossing from enclosed country into open field. The belt of enclosures between Eddycroft Field and Wickham Heath at Wood Speen was narrow, and if the Parliamentary cavalry had been crossing a ditch between enclosed country and open field when the cavalry encounter began, they would have been far to the rear of their infantry brigades, which would have locked horns with the Royalist infantry at the eastern end of Speen Lawn by that time. Moreover, to get at them, Cleveland's brigade would already have outflanked the Parliamentary infantry brigades, and therefore could not have encountered infantry only after crossing the ditch. It therefore seems likely that the ditch followed the line of the old Speen to Bagnor road (now no longer in use), which bisected the present Donnington Park, and probably formed the boundary between Worthy and Claypit Fields.[56]

It therefore seems likely that Cromwell's men were already deployed in open country when the cavalry engagement began, and that they were so severely trounced that they fell back to a position from which it was impossible to take pressure off Barclay's brigade. Later, when Cleveland's brigade had exhausted itself in fruitless attacks on the enemy infantry, a body of cavalry belonging to the Parliamentary left wing helped to herd the Royalists back across the ditch. There is a brief reference to this in the first letter to the Committee of Both Kingdoms from Johnston and Crewe, whilst Symonds describes the encounter on the Royalist right wing as if Goring's charge had not been defeated by infantry alone: 'the Earl of Cleveland before our charge was taken prisoner, most of his officers hurt and killed, his men beaten, being overpowered with horse and foot.'[57] But that was all. If the Parliamentary cavalry regiments had then tried to cross the ditch a second time, the result might have been another embarrassing spoiling attack, as there were still several brigades of uncommitted Royalist cavalry drawn up on Speenhamland.[58]

Most of these comments concerning the performance of the left wing of the Parliamentary cavalry at Newbury commanded by Cromwell, however, are no more than speculation, as the traces of the past are so fragmented and generalized that making correlations between them is well nigh impossible. All that can be said with any degree of certainty is first that the Parliamentary horse on that wing failed to make an assault on the enemy which had any significant impact on the outcome of the battle; second that Cleveland's brigade was able to attack an infantry brigade without initially encountering any opposition from Parliamentary cavalry; and finally that, whilst not retreating entirely under their own volition, Cleveland's brigade was not pursued for any great distance. The extent to which the failure of Waller's troops to push eastwards between Speen and the River Lambourn and thus threaten the centre of the Royalist position was due to the inertia of the troops commanded by Cromwell or to the valour of the Royalists can only be a matter of speculation. However, fighting on that part of the battlefield seems to have begun well before 4 p.m., when there was sufficient daylight for a major cavalry encounter to have taken place and been resolved, and where superiority in numbers and the open terrain would have made a Parliamentary victory a distinct possibility.[59]

Matters were very different on the Parliamentary right wing where Sir William Balfour, Essex's lieutenant general of horse, was in command, if the almost exclusively Royalist accounts of the engagement are not guilty of gross exaggeration.[60] Here, once the Cornish brigade of horse had been driven back, nothing much seems to have happened until after 4 p.m. when the fighting on the left and centre was coming to an end. This was probably because the track linking Speen Lawn with the narrow field that lay between the south side of Speen village and the River Kennet left the London to Bath road at a point that was so close to the Royalists' barricade that it could not be accessed until after their artillery had been silenced and their musketeers driven back.[61] Another problem that would have impeded the quick deployment of Balfour's cavalry in the narrow field was the steepness of the gradient on the track as it descended the escarpment.[62] Nevertheless 500 or so of Balfour's cavalry seem to have been able to make their way into the field, and they were supported by several companies of musketeers, who crept forward under the cover of the hedges separating the water meadows lining the Kennet from the cultivated land.[63] Part of Prince Maurice's regiment of horse apparently failed to see Balfour's cavalry off. Then Sir Humphrey Bennett's brigade of horse fell back before them, though accounts differ as to whether it fled as far as Newbury bridge or simply retired behind some enclosures in order to find ground on which to fight more effectively.[64] However, whatever the reason for its withdrawal, the departure of Bennett's brigade gave Balfour's men the chance to move forward as far as the edge of Speenhamland where they began to deploy.

The danger to the whole Royalist position was obvious, particularly if, as Symonds suggests, the rest of the Parliamentary cavalry on that wing, possibly 2,000 strong, were not far behind the vanguard. Desperate measures were called for. However, intervention by the Queen's regiment of horse, which brought Balfour's men to a halt, followed by a flank attack by the King's and the Queen's Lifeguard led by Lord Bernard Stuart did the trick. If, as seems likely, they were deployed on the most easterly point of the spur between the Lambourn and the Kennet alongside the hedge that marked the western edge of Speenhamland, the Lifeguard would have had the advantage of momentum provided by the slope leading down towards the Kennet, whereas their opponents were strung out across the slope and probably in not as close order as they would have liked.[65] At about the same time Bennett's brigade reappeared and helped in the vigorous pursuit of the enemy during which many of the musketeers, deserted by their cavalry and cut off from the rest of the infantry, were apparently slain.[66] However, that was the end of the matter. The steepness of the slope above the narrow field would have made it impossible for the king's horse to deliver a flank attack against Waller's infantry in and around Speen village.

Having experienced two cavalry setbacks, and stalemate in the infantry battle, Waller seems to have ordered hostilities to cease some time before full darkness fell. His and Haselrig's report to the House of Commons describing the events of 27 October implies that, having driven the king's forces from their prepared positions and reduced their perimeter very significantly, the generals commanding the western pincer were happy to wait for the morrow before settling the issue.[67] However, before discussing why events did not work out as they anticipated, it is necessary to describe the fighting in and around Shaw, which, unlike the cavalry encounters around Speen, is well documented in reports written by witnesses on both sides.

Considerable confusion surrounds the time at which the Earl of Manchester launched his attack. One of the earliest Parliamentarian accounts claimed that it coincided almost exactly with the assault on the barricade to the west of Speen,[68] but once the 'great debate' got under way witnesses swore to an interval of as long as two hours between the two.[69] A gap there certainly was. Four of the five Royalist accounts are very clear about it, and even Manchester's chaplain, who wrote a well-argued pamphlet in the earl's support, admitted to a delay, but without offering a clear justification for it.[70] Manchester's enemies implied that the delay was evidence that the earl had deliberately held his men back, as he wanted the war not to end in outright victory but in a negotiated peace.[71] Elsewhere I have defended Manchester's conduct of operational and strategic matters prior to the Second Battle of Newbury,[72] but traces of the past that explain his inaction are as deficient as those which might explain Cromwell's. All I can offer is surmise supported by nothing more than circumstantial evidence.

A possible reason is that the casualties Manchester's infantry regiments had suffered in the morning attack across the Lambourn were as high as *Mercurius Aulicus* claimed, and that as a result the earl was not prepared to resume the attack until he was certain that things were going very well on the other side of the battlefield. It is also possible that the attack at Speen had gone in much later than originally agreed, and as twilight was imminent Manchester was unwilling for safety's sake to follow suit until he could clearly see that victory was assured.[73] However, whatever the reasons behind his reluctance to order an attack on the Royalist positions at Shaw, Manchester did send his troops in soon after 4.15 p.m., by which time witnesses claim that he could see enemy infantry and cavalry running in panic from Church Speen towards Speenhamland.[74] He may then have thought that the defenders of Shaw and Shaw House would be so demoralized by what was happening behind them that they would quickly abandon their positions. Not surprisingly, after the earl's forces suffered even heavier casualties than they had in the morning, he blamed Waller and his fellow commanders of the western pincer for bringing fighting to a close just when total victory was within Parliament's grasp.[75]

The eastern pincer began its attack with a cannonade, which, like Waller's, was of unknown duration. It was followed by an assault on the hedges adjacent to the bridge over the Lambourn to the south of Shaw house. Initially the Eastern Association foot had some success, the Royalists being driven from one hedge line, but this opened up the Parliamentary flank to devastating fire from Shaw House and the attack petered out. Manchester's next move was against Shaw House itself, but this was completely ineffective and was followed by a counterattack in which the Royalists recaptured the hedge line and in the process took two field pieces, which had been brought forward to support the assault. Manchester's infantry then retreated to the top of Clay Hill pursued by the single regiment of Royalist cavalry deployed on that side of the Lambourn. After darkness had fallen, Manchester's horse tried to recover the cannon their infantry had lost, but were driven off by concentrated musket fire. There had been few losses amongst the defenders, many amongst the attackers. To make matters worse, some Parliamentary formations had fallen victim to friendly fire in the confusion caused by the gathering gloom.[76] The assaults on the Royalist positions defending the eastern approaches to Speenhamland had therefore failed to influence the course of the battle. On the other hand it was unfair of one of Cromwell's supporters to blame Manchester for attacking the Royalists at their strongest point rather than attempting to cross the Lambourn between Shaw and Speen where the river was not guarded.[77] As has been explained earlier, the high levels of water in the river on 27 October would almost certainly have made that impossible.

After dark, fighting died down in all parts of the battlefield, but the situation for the Royalists looked bleak. Despite the resilience of the forces defending the line of the Lambourn, what took place on that sector of the battlefield was no more than a sideshow. The next day the enemy could throw a vastly superior force against the hedge lining the western edge of Speenhamland; Prince Rupert's forces were too far away to provide assistance; and even if the Royalists retained control of Newbury bridge, there was no avenue of retreat southwards or westwards that did not ultimately lead into open country where the Parliamentary generals' superiority in cavalry was likely to be decisive. However, there was an escape plan that had been agreed by the Royalist council of war on the morning of the battle. Before 9 p.m. the king's forces began abandoning their positions defending Speenhamland and Shaw. They then crossed Donnington bridge and assembled in the narrow valley of a tributary of the Lambourn that flowed northwards just under Donnington Castle.

Soon afterwards, the king, who cannot have had much confidence in the plan, rode off with the Prince of Wales and a guard of 500 cavalry to join Prince Rupert.[78] Then Prince Maurice, assisted by Goring, Astley and Hopton, led all the remaining Royalist troops in a march out of the valley and across the Berkshire Downs towards the Thames valley, helped for the vital first few hours by a full moon. Speed was essential if they were not to be caught by the Parliamentary cavalry before they reached the safety of the garrison at Wallingford. The generals therefore left the remaining artillery and the wounded (including the Lord General, the Earl of Forth) at Donnington Castle. Soon after first light the task was successfully accomplished. Both horse and foot reached safety at Wallingford without experiencing the slightest disturbance from the enemy. Crossing to the north bank of the Thames, they headed for the Woodstock area where they had the option of either defending the line of the Cherwell or sheltering in Oxford until Rupert arrived with reinforcements.[79]

But why had the Parliamentary generals done nothing to prevent the Royalists from escaping? Manchester suggested during the great debate that sentries would have heard the king's forces leaving Speenhamland and reported this to their officers, as Cromwell and Waller's horse, the nearest troops to the lane leading to the bridge over the Lambourn at Donnington, were only half a mile away, whilst Essex's infantry on the edge of Speenhamland were nearly as close. Gwyn put them even closer. His brigade retreated, probably from Speenhamland to Donnington, through a narrow filthy pass of puddle and mire just by the hedge side that 'parted us and the two armies ... which were as quiet as if they had taken the same opportunity of drawing off too'.[80] Subsequently, however, it was the Earl of Manchester who got the blame for not noticing the enemy retreating from Shaw on the grounds that his troops were 'little more than a musket shot away'. However, the charge is a spurious one. The earl's troops had returned for the night to Clay Hill.

There is no doubt in my mind that Manchester was right.[81] Waller and Haselrig had given the game away in their report to the House of Commons in which they stated that they had expected the Royalists to offer battle the following day in a position directly under Donnington Castle.[82] Another Parliamentary source written immediately after the battle is more explicit. It admitted that the generals knew the Royalists were abandoning their defensive triangle, but this information was hidden from contemporaries and historians, probably through the actions of Lord Wharton.[83] Putting the two together, there is now very clear evidence that the generals commanding the western pincer knew before 9 p.m. that the Royalists were falling back, but were probably delighted that they were heading northwards across the Lambourn rather than southwards towards Newbury. If they crossed the Kennet breaking down the bridge behind them, it might take days before another confrontation took place. By marching in the opposite direction the enemy was heading straight into a trap. The valley to the north of Donnington, like that of the Kennet beyond Hungerford, led straight into open downland where Waller may have seen himself inflicting on the Royalists a carbon copy of the disaster they had visited on him at Roundway Down in July 1643, namely the routing of their cavalry followed by the surrender of their infantry. What, of course, the Parliamentary generals did not anticipate was that the Royalists would withdraw so far and so fast.

Part IV

The Decisive Battles of 1645 to 1648

Chapter 14

The Battle of Naseby
Context, Landscape and Sources

Context

A very public quarrel between the generals who had commanded the Parliamentary armies at Newbury led to Parliament deciding to create a single field army, the New Model, in December 1644. The army was to comprise twelve full regiments of infantry, eleven full regiments of cavalry and a regiment of dragoons, whose commanders could be relied on to obey the instructions of the Committee of Both Kingdoms. The officers and men of Essex's and Manchester's armies were to provide the core of the new army. In the case of the cavalry there were more than enough troopers on the existing muster rolls to supply 500 per regiment. The infantry regiments were below strength, but the shortfall in numbers was to be met by impressment.

The establishment of the New Model Army was accompanied by an almost clean sweep of the senior officers. All who were members of the House of Commons and the House of Lords lost their commands by the provisions of the so-called Self-Denying Ordinance, though temporary exceptions were allowed in times of emergency. The new commander in chief was to be Sir Thomas Fairfax, formerly lieutenant general of horse in the Northern army; the major general of foot Phillip Skippon, who had held that rank in Essex's army. The post of lieutenant general of horse was left vacant, but a few days before Naseby Cromwell, whose right to command troops had been allowed to continue beyond the date at which the Self-Denying Ordinance became law, received a temporary commission to command the cavalry in chief.[1] However, the process of remodelling had not been an easy one. The House of Lords demanded extensive changes in the lists of officers proposed by Fairfax; almost at the last moment four Scottish colonels resigned their commissions; some of the old soldiers were unhappy with their new officers; and impressing men to fill up the ranks of the infantry regiments proved difficult.[2]

In the king's army, there were few changes.[3] Some senior commanders were removed, with Prince Rupert replacing the Earl of Forth as Lord General,

Prince Maurice succeeding his brother as lieutenant general in Wales and the Marches, and George Goring taking over from Prince Maurice in the West Country, though with reduced powers. Large numbers of new foot soldiers were impressed in Prince Maurice's command to increase the size of existing infantry regiments, but there is no evidence as yet that small regiments in the field army were disbanded and their men added to other regiments. Moreover, the turnover in colonels was no greater than in previous winters. Finally, Maurice's corps of the Western Army was not combined with the Oxford field army as Hopton's had been in the spring of 1644. It was first employed in an independent capacity in Hampshire. It was then sent to assist in the siege of Taunton, an operation that absorbed the manpower of the south-west of England, which should have been used to recruit the Oxford army for the 1645 campaign.

By mid-April Taunton was on the verge of being captured, and the New Model's first task was to march to its relief. This was successfully accomplished in early May, but at the cost of leaving four regiments behind in Somerset to strengthen the garrison.[4] In the meantime the king's army had taken the field and was marching northwards. After first causing Sir William Brereton to abandon the siege of Chester and then capturing Leicester by storm, it took up quarters in the Daventry area for the first ten days in June, waiting, it was claimed, for forces from the west of England to join it. This is now known to be incorrect. The siege of Taunton had resumed, and in early June the king was content to wait for it to come to a successful conclusion before calling for reinforcements for the field army. The New Model Army appeared to be committed to besieging Oxford, which a prominent deserter to Parliament, Lord Savile, claimed might be surrendered through the treachery of a group of dissident Royalist commanders. However, on hearing of the fall of Leicester, the Committee of Both Kingdoms ordered Fairfax to abandon the siege and pursue the king. In north Buckinghamshire he was joined by 2,000 or so cavalry, mainly of the New Model Army, which had been sent beyond the Trent a fortnight earlier to encourage the Scottish army to move southwards. On 12 June cavalry patrols clashed just to the west of Northampton. The Royalist field army set off northwards from Daventry towards the Trent valley, but failed to open up much of a gap between itself and the New Model. Two days later, after spending the night quartered in and around Market Harborough, it prepared for battle, the king having been persuaded by some of his advisers that the New Model was so shot through with faction and discontent that it would be no match for his own troops.[5]

Landscape

The Battle of Naseby took place in classic open field country, and there is no dispute as to its exact location. The Royalist and Parliamentary armies drew up facing one another on a small kite-shaped plateau of wold land about five

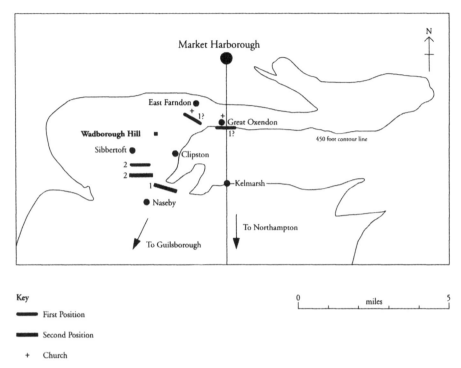

Key

━━━ First Position

━━━ Second Position

+   Church

Map 6. The Battle of Naseby: First and Second Positions

miles by three. This formed the northernmost part of the Northamptonshire uplands, a ribbon of land some 550–700 feet above sea level stretching between the valleys of the Welland and the Cherwell. On the plateau were situated the villages of Naseby, Sibbertoft and Cold Ashby and the deserted medieval village of Sulby. Where the uplands came to an end to the north and east of Naseby and Sibbertoft, there was a steep escarpment intersected by narrow valleys. On the plateau itself, described accurately by a Parliamentary observer as 'a place of little hills and vales', several low ridges ran in an east–west direction.[6] The Royalist army occupied Dust Hill, the more northerly of the ridges, which was in Sibbertoft parish. It was partly open heath and partly planted with corn. The van of the New Model Army was drawn up in Naseby parish on Closter and Sheddon Hill, the ridge directly to the south of Dust Hill, and a mile and a quarter from the village. The rest of the New Model Army filled the space between there and Naseby, an area unimpeded by hedges, walls or ditches, as it was the site of one of the village's three very large open fields, which was lying fallow in the summer of 1645.[7]

Between Dust Hill and Closter Hill is a flat-bottomed valley 400 yards wide known as Broad Moor, along the length of which ran the Sibbertoft–Naseby parish boundary. According to Symonds but no other witness it was full of furze bushes.[8] The slopes of Broad Moor, although rising no higher than

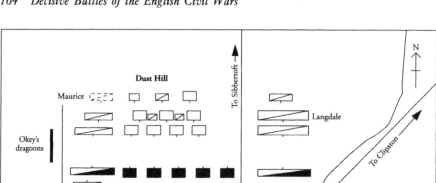

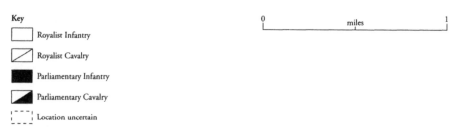

Key

☐ Royalist Infantry

▨ Royalist Cavalry

▰ Parliamentary Infantry

◣ Parliamentary Cavalry

⌐ ⌐ Location uncertain

Map 7. The Battle of Naseby

60 feet above the valley bottom, are quite steep across almost the whole of the battlefield, providing the New Model Army in particular with a better defensive position than modern maps would suggest. Only in the west was there a distinct flattening out of the landscape. Here a tall hedge, which followed the parish boundary between Sulby and Naseby, imposed a clear north–south limit to the fighting, as behind it were small enclosures that made it impossible for one side's cavalry to attack the other's in the flank.[9] One account written by a Parliamentarian described the land on the battlefield side of the hedge as being full of pits and ditches. However, this may be an exaggeration, as it was cited as a reason for the poor performance of some of the New Model Army cavalry regiments.[10]

A contemporary depiction of the battle strongly suggests that there was a barrier similar to Sulby Hedges on the north-eastern side of the battlefield behind and to the left of the Royalist position, namely a very substantial hedge made up of large bushes, trees and possibly small stretches of woodland.[11] There was indeed an area of difficult country in Naseby parish on the north-eastern edge of the escarpment, characterized by steep slopes covered with furze bushes and by waterlogged areas in the valley bottoms,[12] but this was probably more of a problem for Sir Thomas Fairfax than for Prince Rupert as map 7 shows. Indeed the Parliamentary position was so constricted that the infantry was seemingly not drawn up in the customary chequerboard formation but in two parallel lines with small gaps between the regiments.[13] To make matters worse there was a rabbit warren on Cromwell's wing which should have restricted his ability to deploy and manoeuvre.[14] However, as it is now known that the infantry regiments varied in size between 600 and 1300 men, each line may have been deployed in battalions in chequerboard formation, which could well have reduced the congestion noted by Foord.[15]

Sources

Naseby is as well documented a battle as Edgehill and Marston Moor, but none of the narratives written by Royalists is contemporary with the battle. They are also imbued with personal prejudice, which is scarcely surprising considering the calamitous outcome. Sir Edward Walker's dislike of Prince Rupert pervades his account of Naseby, as it does the whole of the 1645 campaign. Lord Clarendon used Walker in *History of the Great Rebellion* to write an even more hostile assessment of the Prince, but to be fair the version of Walker's memoirs to which he had access used more emotive language than the one that was eventually published.[16] The writer of Rupert's Diary provides a balanced and convincing explanation of the Prince's actions, but he makes one point in Rupert's defence that is unique and must therefore be treated with caution. Lord Bellasis, on the other hand, can be absolved from the charge of defending his corner, as he held no formal command at Naseby, but in one section of the narrative his powers of recall let him down, as they also did in his account of Edgehill.[17] Richard Symonds of the King's Lifeguard of Horse, normally a meticulous recorder of events, contented himself with a brief description of the battlefield and a comment on 'this dismal Saturday', which is not surprising given the ignominious part the Lifeguard had played in the action, seemingly through no fault of its own. Finally, Sir Henry Slingsby's diary, though very full, was written well over a year after the battle took place, and includes an account of the performance of the Yorkshire brigade in which he fought which places it in a more favourable light than do other accounts.[18]

The only observations concerning the Battle of Naseby written within a few days of the battle are bound up with the ongoing conflict in the king's council of war between Prince Rupert and Lord Digby. It takes the form of two letters written by the participants to Will Legge, the governor of Oxford, and Legge's reply to Lord Digby. Rupert's letter is no more than a warning to his friend not to listen to what others will tell him about his own role in the defeat. Digby's is a none too subtle attempt to dent Legge's trust in Rupert, but it does contain some very interesting details that confirm some aspects of what the Parliamentary accounts have to say about the battle.[19] Legge's reply is a spirited defence of Prince Rupert against all the charges and insinuations made against him. Letters to the Prince of Wales's Council either did not get through or were destroyed subsequently, whereas the only official report to survive does not provide any detail.[20] *Mercurius Aulicus*, poleaxed by what had happened, failed to produce an edition for the week that included 14 June 1645.[21]

The Parliamentary sources for Naseby are many and varied. Factional interest is less to the fore than in the aftermath of the Battle of Marston Moor. However, the wide range of opinion concerning the circumstances surrounding the defeat of the left wing of Fairfax's cavalry under Henry Ireton, one of Cromwell's protégés, probably reflects the extent to which the individual writer agreed or disagreed with Cromwell's politico-religious programme, outright victory in the war and toleration for the Protestant sects.

The reports of the battle written by Sir Thomas Fairfax and Oliver Cromwell immediately after the battle display the same traits as their accounts of Marston Moor. Fairfax's is laconic in the extreme, but contains some useful information. Cromwell writes from the heart, full of sentiment, politically charged if you accept that the closing paragraph was his own rather than added at a later date, with no detail as to how the battle was won. However, for those who see Cromwell as the astute politician rather than the weak and feeble instrument of God's providence, the label he himself preferred, the language he uses with regard to Fairfax is interesting. The last paragraph of Cromwell's letter to William Lenthall, Speaker of the House of Commons, begins, in customary manner, by attributing victory to God alone. Cromwell then continues: 'The general served you with all faithfulness and honour; and the best commendation I can give him is that I dare say he attributes all to God and would rather perish than assume to himself, which is an honest and thriving way, and yet as much for bravery may be given to him in this action as to a man.'

This passage is clearly written in a way that only those with prior knowledge would be able to interpret it. Without such prior knowledge deconstruction must be cautious in the extreme. However, it appears to assure the Speaker of the House of Commons that the general was indeed 'one of us', whilst suggesting by its condescension that it is Cromwell, not Fairfax, who is in overall command. Indeed the sentiments, if not the language, are almost those of a Second World War battalion commander writing to his divisional commander about the performance in battle of a company commander. Finally, if Cromwell meant to use the phrase 'any man' rather than 'a man', Fairfax's bravery, which he had displayed on many previous situations in open fighting, is acknowledged, but certainly not prioritized. He had fought well, but no better than anybody else. If the word used truly represents the message Cromwell wished to convey, the implication is that Sir Thomas's bravery had been outstanding.[22]

The two civilian commissioners who accompanied the army, Harcourt Leighton and Thomas Herbert, took no part in the fighting and therefore contented themselves with describing what happened before and what happened afterwards. Somewhat surprisingly, they found it necessary to state that all the generals had fought well.[23] This was certainly self-evident in the case of Skippon, who had been severely wounded but stayed at his post and rallied the New Model infantry when they were under extreme pressure. Possibly it was intended to protect Fairfax, who had not apparently played a conspicuous part in the battle until almost the end when the Royalist reserves came under attack, or possibly even Cromwell. Although his cavalry on the right wing of the New Model had been largely responsible for winning the battle, he had not fought at their head. However, the comment is more likely to have been made in defence of Henry Ireton, the newly promoted Commissary General, who, although wounded, could have been accused of losing the contest on the other wing by prematurely attacking the flank of the king's infantry.

The reports printed in London immediately after the battle fall into several categories. First, there are those that appear to be eyewitness accounts. Quite a number, such as *A Letter from a Gentleman in Northampton*, J.W. and G.B., need to be handled with care.[24] Although their authors claim to have been at Naseby, it is odd that they have nothing specific to say about their own or their unit's role in the battle, and that the information they do provide about the fighting is frequently of a generalized nature but with the occasional unique piece of information. This raises the suspicion that at best the writers were members of the press corps who viewed the battle from a distance, but managed to construct interesting narratives by listening to those who had been there and then filling in the gaps using their journalistic imagination and preconceived notions about how battles were or should be fought. In an intermediary position is a breathless, disorganized account by a civilian, possibly John Rushworth, at the time Fairfax's secretary, written on the night after the battle.[25] Its account of the chronology differs from all the others, probably because the writer did not have time to absorb and correlate the various reports he had received.

The only eyewitness whose identity is absolutely certain is John Okey, colonel of the only regiment of dragoons in the New Model Army, and his account is totally different in content.[26] The description he gives of happenings on the western fringe of the battlefield is full and straightforward, but his recollection of the timing of specific incidents may be slightly wrong and the topographical information he provides is not always as precise as one would have wished. Although obviously concerned to put his own regiment in the best possible light, it is interesting that he does not make much of the dragoons' contribution to the battle highlighted by other accounts, namely firing from Sulby Hedges into the flank of Prince Rupert's cavalry regiments as they charged.

Second, there are the numerous descriptions of the battle printed in the London weeklies that draw on a range of evidence. Their descriptions of the main stages in the fighting and their outcomes differ little from one another, and the language employed often shows which first-hand accounts they had used.[27] Rarely do they contain any significant detail not to be found elsewhere, and when they do there must always be some concern about its provenance. One such piece of information states that Colonel John Fiennes's regiment, which fought in the third line of Cromwell's wing, attacked and routed both the infantry regiments in the reserve line of the Royalist army, but the claim is improbable. The attack on Rupert's regiment is attributed by first-hand sources to other regiments, whereas attacking the King's Lifeguard on the diametrically opposite side of the battlefield would have necessitated a ride through a milling mass of infantry.[28] The most likely assailants of the king's regiment were Okey's dragoons.

Three full accounts from the Parliamentary side were written some time after the battle. The first in order of composition is a passage in a description by Captain Thomas Wogan of the whole of the fighting in England in 1645 written for the Marquis of Ormond, commander of the English army in Ireland,[29] but it is problematic in a number of respects. As a result I have tended not to make much use of it in writing the narrative. Although a captain in Colonel Okey's dragoons, Wogan has nothing at all to say about the regiment's very interesting and varied experience at Naseby other than where it was positioned at the start of the battle, which suggests that he was not there. Wogan also claims that the king's horse never rallied after their defeat on the battlefield, but several accounts written by men who fought on both sides declared that they did, only retreating when faced by the entire enemy army as it advanced out of Broad Moor.[30] Finally, the letter is written to amuse, which should always be grounds for suspicion.

The second was written by Joshua Sprigg, Sir Thomas Fairfax's chaplain. It is by far the longest account of the fighting, and the hidden agenda is the army's concern in the winter of 1646–7 that the victorious Parliament had forgotten the debt it owed to the New Model for bringing the war to a quick conclusion.[31] It is not an autographical fragment, like Chaplain Robert Douglas's account of Marston Moor, but a polished narrative compiled from a variety of sources, some of which were Royalist. It is therefore tempting to see it as Fairfax's memoirs, which come to an end to all intents and purposes in January 1645, but the dedication shows very clearly that it was not. It would, of course, be most unlikely for Sprigg not to have acquired some of his information from the general in the course of normal conversation, but some of the comments Sprigg makes about Fairfax would surely not have met with his approval, most particularly a passage that implies that the wounds he had suffered earlier in the war had an effect on his subsequent abilities as a communicator.[32]

The third is to be found in John Rushworth's *Historical Collections*, published at the end of the seventeenth century, which was advertised as an impartial account of the events of the 1630s and 1640s. Although Rushworth had been dead for some years, the printers maintained that he had prepared it for the press, but this does not necessarily mean that there had not been some editorial interference with the text. Indeed the punctuation suggests a very considerable degree of interference had taken place. However, the language used is exactly what one would expect from a man who had been educated early in the second quarter of the seventeenth century. What is most interesting about the account of Naseby is that the author used Sprigg's *Anglia Rediviva* and some material from other printed sources, but not what is claimed to be Rushworth's own report written straight after the battle. However, he does include some material not to be found elsewhere, including a suggestion that some of Cromwell's cavalry regiments were severely shaken by an enemy charge at the start of the battle.[33]

As with Marston Moor there are detailed contemporary or near contemporary depictions of the way in which the armies were drawn up at the start of the battle. One, an engraving by Robert Streeter, was printed a year or so after Naseby to illustrate Sprigg's narrative. According to Rushworth, the way in which Streeter portrayed the Royalist army was confirmed by a sketch of its intended deployment signed by the Royalist commanders, which had belonged to Lord Astley and was in Rushworth's possession.[34] However, Streeter depicts the Royalist army in such a way as to make it appear larger than the New Model. He also indulged in an amount of artistic licence in so far as the landscape was concerned. In the first place, the battlefield was foreshortened so that the fighting appeared to have taken place much closer to Naseby village than it did. Second, as noted above, his engraving spread the battle over two of Naseby's open fields rather than one.[35]

The other contemporary depiction of the Naseby battlefield is yet another of Bernard de Gomme's watercolours. Although completed no earlier than 1658, it was based on a sketch of the intended deployment of the Royalist army he had made before the battle on Prince Rupert's orders. The latter is probably what was redrawn for inclusion as an illustration in Warburton, *Memoirs of Prince Rupert and the Cavaliers*, published in the 1840s.[36] The principal differences between the watercolour and the version of de Gomme's sketch in Warburton are that the captions were originally in Dutch, and that it does not show how the New Model Army was deployed. Second, like the watercolours of Marston Moor and the Third Battle of Newbury, it grossly underestimates the strength of the king's army, but this must be seen as a reflection of the image of Civil War battles that Stuart propagandists wished to convey after the Restoration of the monarchy in 1660 – the kings' armies lost because they were grossly outnumbered, not because of enemy superiority in other respects. Finally, the watercolour contains limited information about the landscape over which the battle was fought. This, strangely enough, is a help rather than a hindrance to understanding, as the tract of country between Naseby and Sibbertoft was far more featureless in the seventeenth century than it is today. The three copses on the eastern side of the battlefield, for example, postdate the enclosure of the parish in the 1820s, as do the farmhouses and possibly the road that bisects the battlefield in a north–south direction.

De Gomme's depiction of the deployment of the New Model Army regiments in the watercolour is almost exactly the same as Streeter's,[37] but this is not surprising as Sprigg's *Anglia Rediviva* had been published some years before. There are also some significant differences between the two in the way in which the Royalist cavalry and its supporting musketeers are portrayed. First, Streeter depicts the Royalist reserve as much smaller than de Gomme and made up entirely of infantry, namely the King's Lifeguard and Prince Rupert's Bluecoats. The King's and the Queen's Lifeguards of Horse do not appear at all, whereas the two brigades of Newark horse, stationed on the wings of the reserve in de Gomme's sketch and map, are both placed in Langdale's second line. Second, the musketeers shown as intermingled with the horse in both de Gomme's depictions are not shown at all in Streeter's. There is no clear indication in other sources as to which of the two is the more accurate portrayal of the way in which the armies were drawn up at the start of the battle. However, the sketch that de Gomme used as a basis for his watercolour may have been compiled several days before the battle. On the day the plan for deployment may well have been modified in response to circumstances, such as the desire to maximize the firepower of the main body of the army. However, Colonel Okey's account implies that Royalist musketeers were operating with the right wing of the king's cavalry at the start of the battle.[38] As for the Newark horse, Sir Philip Warwick mentions a quarrel between Langdale and their commander which took place just as the battle was about to begin, which implies that most if not all were on the left wing.[39] However, Sprigg's complicated account of the cavalry fighting on the Parliamentary left suggests that Rupert's victory was only achieved through the intervention of some of the king's reserves some way into the action, and this provides circumstantial evidence that part of the Newark horse were where de Gomme placed them.[40]

Field walking assisted by metal detecting as an aid to understanding the Civil War battlefield has made more progress at Naseby than on any other Civil War battlefield, and the results are of outstanding interest. We now know that the major infantry confrontation took place on Closter Hill, not on Broad Moor; that the last Royalist infantry brigade to put up a serous fight may have met its end just to the west of the Naseby–Sibbertoft road on the south-facing slope of Dust Hill; and that an engagement of some kind took place on Wadborough Hill, some two miles to the north of the battlefield.[41] However, as explained above, the interpretation of the archaeology of a battlefield can only draw on the evidence that survives today and is accessible using current techniques. It is also subject to the distortions, imperfections and blemishes discussed in Chapters 2 and 3. At Naseby, with a modern road passing through the length of the battlefield, an additional impetus is given to the dispersal of archaeological materials. I can distinctly remember as a child in another Northamptonshire village being one of a small gang of proto–archaeologists who regularly walked the fields in the winter months picking up potsherds and fossils, and as regularly emptying their pockets of the less interesting finds on their way home via the Doddington to Wilby footpath or the Wollaston to Wilby road by tossing them over the hedges into the adjacent fields. I therefore wonder if something like this, rather than a measured retreat by the king's musketeers, explains the narrow ribbon of finds that follows the line of the Naseby to Sibbertoft road.[42]

Chapter 15
The Battle of Naseby
Narrative

On the morning of 14 June the Royalist army assembled on top of a slight ridge in what was primarily open field country two miles or so to the south of Market Harborough.[1] Previous writers have placed the rendezvous at East Farndon[2] or between East Farndon and Great Oxendon,[3] but what looks on the map like an excellent place from which to confront an enemy advance from the south is much less impressive when viewed on the ground.[4] Almost as far as Great Oxendon village the slope of the ridge facing the enemy is gentle, but immediately behind where the Royalist army would have deployed the slope is so steep that, in the event of a setback, an orderly retreat would have been impossible. The Royalist rendezvous may therefore have been not where others have placed it but at Great Oxendon,[5] where the road from Northampton, now known as the A508, passes over the eastern end of the ridge.[6] The Great Oxendon position had several advantages if the enemy, who were known to be less than six miles away the previous evening, had drawn closer to Market Harborough overnight in the hope of catching the king's army off-guard.[7] The south-facing slope was much steeper than elsewhere on the ridge and the north-facing one less so; its convex shape enabled the reserve formations to be deployed out of the enemy's line of sight; and the right flank was protected by enclosures on the ridge at Little Oxendon.[8]

Soon after dawn Rupert apparently sent his scout master Francis Ruce to look for the enemy but he found no sign of them. The result has been dismissed as sheer incompetence or worse, but as it derives from a single source hostile to the prince, it is *ipso facto* suspect.[9] Nevertheless, if Ruce had pushed further down the A508 towards Northampton, as would have been the case if the king's army had been at Great Oxendon, he would have discovered nothing at all. The New Model Army had taken a different route northwards from Northampton, the A5159 Welford road, possibly in the belief that the Royalists were marching from Daventry towards Leicester.[10] Finding them at Market

Harborough was probably an unpleasant surprise, as Fairfax would now have to march his army across country to catch them.

Whilst the king's army was drawing up in battle formation, Slingsby claimed that enemy horse were spotted three miles away between Clipston and Naseby on the escarpment that formed the northern edge of the plateau identified in the previous chapter.[11] A reconnaissance in force led by Rupert showed up the difficulty of attacking such a position – an approach march across a landscape of 'burts[12] and water' followed by a very steep climb.[13] On the other hand if the Royalists remained where they were, they might lose the initiative, as the enemy showed signs of falling back, not preparing for battle.[14]

The Royalist army, still in battle formation, made a half turn to the right with the intention of gaining access to the plateau so as to fight the New Model Army on more equal terms or to gain a better view of the countryside to the west if it was indeed retreating. This necessitated marching in column across the front of the New Model, but far enough away from the enemy for the Royalists to be able to turn and face them should Fairfax try to attack them in the flank.[15] Reaching the plateau via either the westwards extension of the East Farndon–Great Oxendon ridge[16] or the Clipston to Sibbertoft road,[17] the king's army assembled on Dust Hill about a mile and a half to the north of Naseby village. There they found that Fairfax was not retreating but hurriedly deploying the New Model in battle array facing them.[18]

Unlike some other Civil War battles, there is sufficient contemporary evidence to be reasonably confident about the respective strength of the two armies at Naseby. Historians differ as to the number of troops on the battlefield, but there is a very strong likelihood that the king had just over 5,000 horse and just under 5,000 foot, and Fairfax probably between 7,000 and 8,000 foot and 6,200 to 6,500 horse and dragoons.[19] This gave Parliament's general a considerable numerical advantage over Prince Rupert, though Fairfax does not seem to have been aware of it until a day or so before the battle at the earliest.[20]

The depictions of the battle produced by Streeter and de Gomme agree that the two armies were drawn up in the conventional manner for an encounter in open field country with the infantry in the centre and the cavalry on the wings. Rupert also followed his 1644 practice of retaining a strong reserve line and incorporating cavalry into the main body of the army. Keeping so many regiments in reserve, however, meant that it was essential for Rupert to position himself so as to be able to direct them to the place on the battlefield where they were most needed once the action had started. The prince had tried to do this at Marston Moor, but the early collapse of the right wing probably forced him to involve himself directly in the fighting rather earlier than he had intended. At Naseby, however, the story hinted at by Walker but developed much further by Clarendon is that the prince put himself in command of the right wing but did not return to the battlefield with his cavalry until well over an hour later, by which time the battle was lost. By implication, the reserves had been left to fend for themselves.[21] However, Prince Rupert's Diary tells a different story. Prince Maurice, not Prince Rupert, was in command of the right wing, and Rupert, having given his orders to the reserves, merely accompanied his brother to ensure that all went well. Why this should have been necessary, the Diary's author does not say.[22] The significance of the passage for understanding the outcome of the battle will be discussed below.

With Maurice on the Royalist right wing was a total of about 1,500 to 1,700 horse made up of his own and his brother's Lifeguards, four or so regiments of veteran horse from the Oxford army, and the Anglo-Irish regiment of Sir William Vaughan, which had fought at Marston Moor. They were drawn up in two lines and, according to de Gomme, were supported by 200 musketeers. Behind them in the third line may have been a body of 400 Newark horse, but the only evidence for this is in de Gomme's two depictions of the battlefield.[23] What was certainly in reserve were the King's and the Queen's Lifeguards.[24] De Gomme places them in the centre of the third line flanked by two infantry regiments,[25] and this is confirmed in general terms by Sir Edward Walker.

Facing Rupert and his men was the newly appointed Commissary General of the New Model Army, Henry Ireton,[26] who had no previous experience of managing anything larger than a regiment. Ireton may have had 2,500 horse under his command, also drawn up in two lines, that is five regiments belonging to the New Model supplemented by some Eastern Association horse. In support was the New Model Army's only dragoon regiment, commanded by Colonel Okey. These were positioned along the line of Sulby Hedge at right angles to the Royalist cavalry's line of advance. According to Okey, this deployment had taken place under Cromwell's direct supervision, but there was nothing new about it in a tactical sense. The Earl of Essex had used dragoons in a similar way at Edgehill.[27]

The Royalist left wing was drawn up in a similar manner to the right with Sir Marmaduke Langdale in overall command. It included the whole of the Northern Horse (1,500), the single cavalry regiment of Colonel Horatio Carey (200), which may have belonged to the Bristol garrison, and either half or the whole of the Newark horse. In de Gomme's plan the left wing like the right was supported by the firepower of 200 musketeers stationed in the first and second line and by 400 Newark horse in the reserve line. De Gomme provides some information about the composition of the first two lines. Sir William Blakiston's brigade, consisting of cavalry regiments from north of the Tees, were in the centre and on the left of the front line, with half of Langdale's Yorkshire brigade to their right next to the infantry. The other half of the Yorkshire brigade was positioned to the right of the second line in support of their comrades, with Cary's regiment to its left.[28]

Opposing Langdale were four regiments of New Model Army horse, Colonel Rossiter's Lincolnshire regiment, which was later placed on the New Model establishment, Colonel Fiennes's, which was not, and the other half of the Eastern Association horse. This wing was under Oliver Cromwell's direct command, and probably totalled well over 3,000 men drawn up in two and a half lines, the first of which was led by Colonel Whalley. Cromwell seems initially to have remained in the rear, the best place for managing the cavalry engagement effectively.[29] As at Marston Moor there were no Parliamentary cavalry reserves behind the main infantry formation, suggesting that Fairfax's intent was to attack on both wings.

The main body of the Royalist infantry, like the cavalry, was drawn up in two lines. The second was slightly smaller than the first, comprising three brigades rather than four. The two regiments in the reserve line were the king's regiment of foot and Prince Rupert's Bluecoats, some 700 to 800 men in total.[30] Between the first and the second line, and also possibly between the second and the third, was Colonel Thomas Howard's cavalry brigade, between 800 and 900 strong drawn up in two or three squadrons in a similar manner to Blakiston's brigade at Marston Moor and the so-called Third Battle of Newbury.[31] This was a new formation consisting of several garrison regiments stiffened by Howard's own regiment of 'old horse'.[32] Their intended or actual role in the battle is not mentioned in any Royalist account, but given that they had no room to charge, they were presumably intended to provide close support to the infantry.[33]

Fairfax's infantry, though much stronger than the enemy's, was also drawn up in two lines, with five regiments in the first line (Major General Skippon's, Sir Hardress Waller's, Colonel Pickering's, Colonel Montague's and Fairfax's own) and three in the second (Colonel Harley's, Colonel Hammond's and Colonel Rainsborough's). Given their numerical superiority over the enemy, it is not surprising that they overlapped the Royalist first line, most particularly on the far right where Fairfax's regiment may have had no enemy formation immediately to its front.[34] They were probably deployed in a chequerboard pattern, not bunched together in regimental formation as in Streeter's map.[35] However, the intention may have been to deceive the enemy into thinking that the formation they first encountered was the two lines already closed up together.

The second line was drawn up on the reverse slope of Closter Hill and was thus out of sight of the Royalists. This may have been to shield it from enemy artillery fire which never materialized, but possibly Fairfax wanted to conceal the size of his army in the belief that Rupert would not fight if he knew how large the New Model was. The only evidence in support of this, however, comes from Royalist comments made in the special circumstances of post-battle recriminations. Fairfax himself apparently saw the deployment on the reverse slope of Closter Hill as a stratagem for concealing from the enemy 'in what form our battle was drawn and any confusion therein'.[36] Finally, behind the second line was a small part of Colonel Harley's regiment, described as the reserve, helping to defend the train of artillery, which had apparently drawn up just to the west of Naseby village in a small valley, though the only source for its exact position is Streeter's map.

The battle began at about 10 a.m. with an all-out Royalist attack. With almost twelve hours of daylight still to come a repeat of Second Newbury was most unlikely. For once, the fighting was not preceded by much of an artillery bombardment. The Royalist heavy artillery was probably not ready for action because of the speed of the advance.[37] Fairfax's guns also contributed little to the battle. Walker claimed that they fired over the heads of the Royalist troops, and Parliament's generals having, it was said, little faith in the value of a bombardment were happy to keep it short.[38]

Despite the uphill slog, the small Royalist infantry brigades managed to cause considerable disorder in the enemy first line.[39] On the extreme left General Skippon's regiment suffered at least 150 casualties,[40] but it held its ground apparently with some help from a squadron of Ireton's cavalry.[41] The regiment immediately to its right, Hardress Waller's, had very few wounded, possibly because it fell back immediately. The next regiments in line, Pickering's and Montague's, were allegedly pushed back and retreated behind their reserves. Robert Baillie, one of the Scottish representatives in London, reported with relish that these two regiments commanded by Independent rather than Presbyterian colonels had disgraced themselves, but this may not have been that much of an exaggeration, as the shock experienced by the New Model front line is vouched for by other sources.[42] However, probably much to their surprise, the Royalist foot soldiers then found themselves facing a second line of infantry almost as strong as the first.[43]

It is very noticeable how few losses were sustained by the regiments in the New Model second line, the only company to suffer significant casualties being Lieutenant Colonel Hewson's, in which nine men were wounded. This suggests that the Royalist musketeers were unable to make effective use of their weapons at their second encounter with the enemy infantry. Some would have discarded them at the start of the hand-to-hand fighting or damaged them by using them as clubs in the fight with the first line. Alternatively the musketeers had become so disordered that they could not regroup so as to produce an effective barrage. What they are most unlikely to have done is run out of ammunition, given that they would only have had time to fire once or twice before coming into contact with the New Model first line. What is much more surprising is the failure of the Royalist commanders to commit their infantry reserves once the enemy second line came into view. Both Prince Rupert's regiment and the king's regiments of foot appear to have remained on the forward slope of Dust Hill, possibly in obedience to Prince Rupert's orders for the conduct of the battle, which are discussed below.[44]

Rupert and Maurice led the first line of the Royalist right wing towards Commissary General Ireton's regiments. As they advanced Okey's dragoons fired on them from behind the hedge separating Sulby and Naseby parishes, but possibly to little effect, as the only source to mention fire from Sulby Hedges as causing significant casualties amongst the Royalist horse was written by Sir Henry Slingsby, who fought on the opposite wing of the king's army.[45] All that can be said with any certainty about the fighting on the west side of the battlefield is that it probably lasted some time, and that it ended in some kind of Royalist victory. The reason for this is that the primary sources display such a wide range of opinion, ranging from a complete rout to the claim that only two regiments suffered some loss, and that the whole wing was able to play an active role later in the battle.[46] Only Sprigg provided a clear blow-by-blow description, but not of the last stage of the fighting[47] and sadly there is nothing in any of the Royalist accounts to either support or challenge his account.

Sprigg's narrative begins with a Royalist charge that faltered before it even reached the Parliamentarian first line. As they began to pick up speed again, Ireton's men attacked, but only the third and the fifth squadron from the left made any real progress. The fourth did not move, whereas the advance of the first and second squadrons was apparently impeded by ditches and waterlogged ground. Possibly taking confidence from the fact that one of his squadrons had routed its opponents in the enemy second line, Ireton used his own squadron, the sixth, to charge an adjacent enemy infantry brigade in the flank, which was threatening to destroy Skippon's regiment and roll up the first line of New Model infantry. In the engagement Ireton himself was wounded and temporarily taken prisoner. His squadron then may have recoiled having halted but not routed the Royalist brigade, but at that instant more of the king's cavalry moved forward and passed straight through both lines of New Model cavalry in circumstances that Sprigg does not explain in any detail. Some chased enemy horse from the battlefield in the direction of Northampton, whilst the rest led by Prince Rupert expended an inordinate amount of time and energy attacking the New Model artillery train, whilst the king's chance of victory ebbed away in engagements that were taking place elsewhere on the battlefield.[48]

Thus Sprigg does not record the exact circumstances in which the Royalist horse penetrated and then passed through or routed Ireton's second line. However, this could not have happened if substantial parts of the New Model regiments had still been in a condition to fight.[49] Although part of Ireton's wing may have come together as a body later in the battle, they were almost certainly not in close order again until after the prolonged pause that occurred right at the end. Until then they appear to have been incapable of doing anything more than shadow Maurice's cavalry as it returned to the Royalist lines.

Rupert's Diary tells a different tale. The prince did not take part in the attack on the artillery train. Instead he returned to the reserve line on Dust Hill as soon as Maurice's wing had won its victory,[50] but there is nothing to verify his account of what happened. Although the passage was probably composed as a defence of the prince's conduct during the war,[51] it seems most unlikely that the prince would have made this episode up when so many officers who were witnesses to his actions at Naseby were still alive. Admittedly, Rupert's story is contradicted by Parliamentary sources, which claimed that he himself had called on the baggage train to surrender. However, all the baggage guard saw was a resplendently dressed officer, who could equally well have been Prince Maurice. Such misidentification was common: after the battle one of the dead was confidently but quite wrongly identified as the Duke of Lennox.[52]

The fact that Maurice or Rupert did not order their victorious cavalry to halt and attack the enemy infantry (rather than to all intents and purposes writing it out of the battle), has almost universally been taken as evidence of Rupert's inability to train and discipline his horse, and his reputation vis-à-vis Cromwell has suffered as a result.[53] It also ran contrary to one of the current maxims about how to win battles, namely not to pursue the enemy or indulge in plunder until victorious in all parts of the battlefield.[54] On the other hand, one can understand why attacking the New Model infantry might not have featured in Rupert's plans. In the first place, this could be a recipe for disaster. Sir Charles Lucas had attempted something similar at Marston Moor but as a result he was taken prisoner and his brigade was in no condition to face Cromwell's horse in the final stage of the battle.[55] Second, halting a victorious cavalry wing, reordering it and then delivering a second attack on the enemy was something that a commander only achieved on one occasion in the battles discussed in this volume, namely on the Allied left wing at Marston Moor, and under circumstances that may have been highly fortuitous.[56] Moreover, it is by no means certain that the Royalist cavalry commander did indeed lose control of his men. There may have been another explanation for the attack on the enemy baggage train.

In his criticism of Rupert's tactical mistakes at Naseby, Lord Digby drew on information from Sir William Vaughan, who commanded a regiment in Maurice's second line, to the effect that Fairfax had a reserve of 3,000 men, whom the Royalists could not see from Dust Hill.[57] Sir William can only have been referring to Fairfax's second line drawn up in the dip behind Closter Hill, and he could not have seen them until after Ireton's wing had been routed. This raises the possibility that Maurice's initial orders were to sweep around the rear of the New Model Army causing alarm and despondency, and possibly to attack Cromwell's wing in the rear, but that he found a mass of enemy infantry blocking the way. Maurice might then have led his horsemen in a wider loop towards the New Model right wing that took them into the broad valley just short of Naseby village. There they encountered the enemy artillery train blocking their way, a less formidable obstacle than 3,000 infantry, but one that needed to be disposed of if the transit to the other wing was to be successfully accomplished. The Royalist commander therefore ordered it to be attacked. All of this is speculation, but the landscape would have allowed a Royalist advance from the left rear to the right rear of the enemy position, a manoeuvre that the Ironsides had performed with such success in the final phase of the Battle of Marston Moor. An unsuccessful attempt to attack the New Model Army from the direction of Naseby may also explain some oddities in some of the Parliamentary accounts of the battle. Colonel Okey, for example, makes no mention at all of the Royalist right wing cavalry returning to Dust Hill past Sulby Hedges. This he would surely have done had it happened, given the level of detail in the rest of his report on what happened in his part of the battlefield,[58] unless, of course, he wanted to draw a veil over the fact that he had not attacked them. Alternatively, his dragoons may have already been committed elsewhere by the time Maurice's men rode back to their own lines.[59]

A similar paucity of traces of the past pertains to the cavalry fight on the eastern side of the battlefield, with little that can be classed as knowledge and much that is only classable as opinion. The beginning and end are very clear, the Parliamentary accounts of the action being validated by a passage in the diary of Sir Henry Slingsby, who fought in the Northern Horse at Naseby.[60] The Royalists led by Sir Marmaduke Langdale charged first, and Cromwell's front line, comprising his own and Colonel Whalley's regiments with half of Sir Robert Pye's, moved forward to meet them. There then followed a mêlée of uncertain duration after which the whole Royalist left wing fled back to Dust Hill and the Clipston–Sibbertoft road but no further. But the process by which Cromwell's squadrons managed to overcome Langdale's brigades is by no means certain. The following paragraph is therefore entirely hypothetical, and hopefully not too fanciful.

Whalley's regiment and part of Pye's, stationed on the left and in the centre of the cavalry line along what is now the Naseby–Sibbertoft road, charged down the steep slope towards Broad Moor encountering head-on that part of Langdale's Yorkshire brigade deployed in the front line as it made its way up the slope. The rest of the New Model front line, comprising the two squadrons of Sir Thomas Fairfax's regiment, moved downhill more cautiously as it negotiated first the rabbit warren and then the furze bushes in Broad Moor, through which Sir William Blakiston's brigade was also slowly making its way towards them. As a result, at the extreme eastern edge of the battlefield, neither body of cavalry was able to build up any momentum, and a static sword fight ensued in the bottom of Broad Moor. The cavalry engagement on the better ground was hard fought according to Sprigg and Slingsby.[61] This is supported by evidence from the Commonwealth Exchequer Papers to the effect that Whalley's and Sir Robert Pye's regiments had twice as many wounded after the battle, fifty and forty-four respectively, as any other regiments on the New Model right wing. This suggests that the troops belonging to Pye's regiment deployed in the second line were also drawn into or ordered to join the mêlée, as the profile of wounded across all seven of his troops was similar to that of Whalley's.[62] The check experienced by the New Model right wing, if check it was, was probably no greater than this. Once some second-line troops had been committed, Langdale's men gave way, whereupon the victorious Parliamentary cavalrymen seem to have wheeled to the right to take Blakiston's men in the flank, who then also fled. What happened to Langdale's second line is not certain, but they too must have been driven back. Some of Langdale's horse were apparently able to shelter behind the Royalist infantry reserves, but the rest fell back between a quarter and half a mile and then rallied, possibly to their surprise. They did not need to retreat any further as they were not being pursued.[63] Instead Cromwell ordered some of his squadrons, presumably those that had been involved in the mêlée, merely to keep a watch on them to prevent their re-entering the fray.[64]

In the circumstances Langdale's wing had not done too badly.[65] Such a verdict, however, seems to be contradicted by the comment in Prince Rupert's Diary that 'the Yorkshire horse was gone without fighting', and by a passage in the letter allegedly written by John Rushworth just after the battle to the effect that 'Langdale's brigade ran away basely and lost the king the day'. A possible explanation of all of this is that the Yorkshire regiments in the Royalist second line failed to provide effective support to their colleagues in the fight with Whalley, leading to the collapse of the entire wing.[66]

The role of the reserve cavalry in the events that had happened on the Royalist left wing now needs to be examined. Rupert's Diary makes it very clear that the prince's plans for the reserves had been ignored during his absence on the right: 'The King had sent away by somebody's persuasion about him all his horse to charge the wing of the horse of the enemy, whereas if they had stayed till Rupert came back and marched horse and foot together they had probably beaten him.' Leaving aside the interesting insight into Rupert's plans for running the battle, it seems likely that the Newark horse had been committed to supporting the Royalist left wing when it got into difficulties, but had been swept away in their defeat. Charles then personally led the Royal Lifeguards in a charge against Cromwell's cavalry regiments, hoping, presumably, for a repetition of what had happened at the Second Battle of Newbury, where they had prevented a similar disaster by a timely charge delivered against the flank of the advancing enemy horse. No sooner, however, was the charge under way than the king aborted it, apparently as a result of the Earl of Carnwath's seizing his reins and bellowing in his ear that he would be going to his death if he persisted. The Lifeguards then wheeled off in considerable disorder. Rupert was, of course, incensed, but must carry some of the blame for not foreseeing that victory on the right might take some time to achieve, and that something untoward might occur elsewhere on the battlefield in the meantime which might make his orders redundant. But what had been the prince's plans? An attack by infantry and cavalry was apparently intended, and this combination of shock and firepower could have stopped Cromwell's squadrons already involved in the fighting on the left wing in their tracks, and possibly put them to flight. However, Cromwell and Fairfax still had 1,000 horse and Lord Fairfax's infantry regiment uncommitted. The outcome for the Royalists would still therefore have been problematic, but possibly Rupert hoped his brother would have distracted the uncommitted enemy regiments by attacking them in the rear in the manner discussed earlier.[67]

The situation when Rupert returned to Dust Hill was that the Royalist cavalry regiments on the right wing had disappeared behind Closter Hill and were therefore out of contact with the fighting for the moment. On the other wing the Royalist horse had been defeated and broken, but were still on the fringes of the battlefield. In the centre the New Model Army infantry had been shaken by the initial Royalist attack, but the second line had brought the enemy to a halt and probably driven them back a short distance, but not as far as Broad Moor.[68] On the eastern side of the battlefield some of Cromwell's cavalry were keeping a watch on the Northern Horse, but Fairfax still had in hand a sizeable force uncommitted, the third and part of the second line of Cromwell's horse and his own regiment of foot. Although not originally designated as a reserve, this is what they had become. All the Royalist commanders apparently had left in reserve were two regiments of infantry, Prince Rupert's and the king's, and the King's Lifeguard, which seems to have been utterly demoralized by its failed charge against the enemy right wing.[69]

Sir Thomas Fairfax's next move was to attack the one remaining body of Royalist foot of brigade size that was still intact. This was probably Prince Rupert's regiment, which was 500 strong, roughly the size of the other Royalist infantry brigades. The formation was described as the Bluecoats, and his regiment was possibly the only large unit dressed in blue uniforms.[70] The very dense concentration of musket balls on the lower slope of Dust Hill close to where the Naseby–Sibbertoft road now runs is almost exactly where the regiment would have been had it moved slightly forward from the position in which it is depicted in Streeter's battle plan.

However, the archaeological evidence is not what one would have expected from contemporary accounts of the form of attack to which the last intact brigade of Royalist infantry was subjected. Three of the four sources that describe the action in any detail agree that cavalry alone were involved, but an engagement between infantry and cavalry would not have produced such a concentration of musket balls, unless, of course, they were Royalist discards. If so, one would not expect there to have been a single concentration, as both maps of the battlefield portray the Royalist infantry brigades as comprising stands of pikes sandwiched between two bodies of musketeers. The fourth source describes an infantry assault by Sir Thomas Fairfax's regiment following unsuccessful cavalry attacks on the Royalist brigade from front and rear, but there is no mention of a firefight. Instead, the New Model musketeers attacked the enemy using their weapons as clubs.[71] Possibly the concentration of musket balls on the lower slope of Dust Hill merely represents the final resting place of an ammunition wagon.

The fate of the other reserve regiment is less clear. A concentration of musket balls at and adjacent to the north-east corner of Sulby Hedges is quite close to where de Gomme and Streeter place the king's regiment of foot at the start of the battle. Its most likely assailant would have been Okey's dragoons. Okey, however, claimed to have mounted his men and charged an infantry brigade, not a body of only 200 men.[72] Another candidate is Colonel Fiennes's regiment of horse. A brief description in a London journal of the fighting undertaken by that regiment claims that it destroyed both the Bluecoats and then the king's regiment of foot.[73] Neither of the incidents is described in detail in any of the Royalist sources, but the defeat of the whole of the reserve foot is implicit in the passage describing Naseby in Prince Rupert's Diary: 'Lindsey commanded the Guards and Russell Rupert's regiment of foot. After the reserves were beaten, Rupert faced again with his horse but the men were not in condition to do much.'[74]

With the reserve line destroyed, the main body of the king's infantry came to realize the hopelessness of their position, surrounded as they were with enemy foot to the front and enemy horse on their flanks and now in their rear cutting them off from contact with their own horse.[75] They therefore surrendered to avoid further casualties, officers and men alike, though some of the colonels managed to escape, presumably on horseback.[76] A pause then followed as Fairfax ordered the New Model to regroup before attacking all that was left of the king's army, his cavalry, which were trying to reorder themselves in a new position near Sibbertoft, possibly in front of their baggage train.[77] In a masterly display of the control Fairfax's officers had over their men, the New Model Army did not attack immediately but drew up in battle array on Dust Hill facing north with horse on both wings and infantry in the centre, as if to begin the battle all over again. When all was ready, they advanced as a body, whereupon the Royalist horse merely broke and fled. This is not surprising. Not only were they outnumbered, they also had no firepower on which to draw, and firepower was essential for any hope of success against an enemy force comprising well-trained horse and foot. Fairfax then unleashed part of his cavalry, which chased the king's men almost as far as the walls of Leicester by day's end. Whilst the New Model horse pursued the fugitives, the foot plundered the Royalist baggage train, wounding or killing many women who followed the army, an untypical but nonetheless inexcusable episode.[78]

What did not happen in the closing stages of the battle was a fighting retreat of the main body of the king's infantry culminating in a bloody encounter on and around Wadborough Hill, two miles to the north on the edge of the escarpment. This hypothesis, first proposed by Foard, and then taken up most enthusiastically by Reid, Marix Evans, Burton and Westaway, and Marshall,[79] is based on new and exciting archaeological evidence, which is, however, open to a number of interpretations. In the present state of research it must be admitted with regret that their theory is romantic but almost certainly wrong, on account of the overwhelming preponderance of written evidence from combatants on both sides that the king's infantry surrendered almost to a man on or close to Closter Hill.[80]

However, having walked over Wadborough Hill with Peter Burton, I am convinced that an engagement involving infantry took place there, and that the distribution of musket balls cannot represent the demise of an ammunition wagon – but who were the infantry involved? One possibility is that they were Prince Rupert's regiment, if they were not the regiment of Bluecoats destroyed in the penultimate stage of the battle. However, the testimony of Rupert's Diary, and the unanimous testimony of all the sources, which describe the composition of the Royalist force facing the New Model at the end of the battle, that it consisted entirely of cavalry, cannot be lightly dismissed. It is more likely that the finds made on Wadborough Hill[81] represent the last stand of infantry who were never on the battlefield in the first place, the prime contender being the regiment whose designated task was to protect the train of artillery, the gunpowder, the munitions and the cannon.[82] Once they realized that the battle was lost, the natural response of its officers and men would have been to try to escape down one of the cwms leading down from the escarpment into the Welland valley, but they were pinned down on Wadborough Hill by enemy horse before they could make much progress. Subsequently New Model Army infantry or dragoons arrived to finish the job. It is not at all surprising that a small engagement of this nature at the end of the battle failed to attract the attention of any of the eyewitnesses. It is also possible that Royalist writers preferred to draw a veil over the episode, as the regiment could have been seen as indirectly responsible for the slaughter of the women of the baggage train. However, the really important point is that whatever happened on Wadborough Hill was at best a sideshow. The fate of the king's army had been decided in and around Broad Moor an hour or so earlier.

Chapter 16

The Battle of Preston
Context, Landscape and Sources

Context

The Battle of Naseby destroyed the king's infantry and with it the means with which to conduct a successful military campaign. Desperate attempts were made to raise new regiments in south Wales in early July and ship them to Somerset to build Goring's army up into a body large enough to challenge the New Model in the field, but these failed through lack of time. Despite some strategic shilly-shallying by Parliament and a near mutiny because of lack of pay, Sir Thomas Fairfax quickly marched the New Model into the south-west of England. Less than four weeks after Naseby he dispersed Goring's forces at Langport as they were retreating from one defensive position to another, but he failed to destroy them. The Royalists then fell back into Devonshire, where-upon Fairfax quickly captured Bridgewater and Sherborne, thus completing a string of Parliamentary garrisons across the south-western peninsula, which effectively penned in Goring's not inconsiderable army until the New Model had time to deal with it. To satisfy MPs it first laid siege to and captured enemy garrisons in south-central England – Bath, Devizes, Bristol, Basing House and Winchester. Not till October was it ready to march westwards once more.

Elsewhere in England and Wales, Royalist garrisons surrendered one by one, whilst the king wandered ineffectively from Yorkshire to mid-Wales to Huntingdon until almost the end of 1645, accompanied by a dwindling escort of cavalry. Hopes of help from Scotland ended with the destruction of the Marquis of Montrose's army at Philiphaugh in the Borders in the early autumn. Garrison troops enabled the king to create small armies from time to time, but they were quickly scattered by local and regional commanders, as at Rowton Moor outside Chester in September, at Denbigh in November, and at Stow-on-the-Wold the following March. The New Model secured the surrender of the Royalist Western Army at Truro also in March. With the Confederate Irish unwilling and the Scottish Royalists unable to help him,

Charles left Oxford on 5 May 1646 and rode northwards, where he gave himself up to the Scottish commanders whose army was besieging Newark. Soon afterwards almost all the king's remaining garrisons followed his example and gave up the struggle.[1]

However, the end of fighting did not bring peace. The Parliamentary side had always been a coalition bound together by a common interest in defeating the king and forcing him to accept changes in church and state. However, the demands of individual members of the coalition were often at odds, particularly in matters of religion, and as the king spun out negotiations for a peace settlement, the coalition began to fall apart. The Scottish leadership, having achieved their constitutional and religious ends before the war began, were primarily concerned with defending what they had obtained. All they wanted was security for their Presbyterian Church, but they saw its monopoly being threatened by the growth of the Independents and other sects in England, who wanted a measure of toleration for Protestants who were not Anglicans. They were perceived to be particularly strong in the New Model Army, where they enjoyed the patronage of Lieutenant General Oliver Cromwell, who was seen by some Scots as far more dangerous to their interests than the defeated king. Other Scots, however, wanted Charles to commit himself wholeheartedly to Presbyterianism before they would fight for him against his English subjects. Some English Presbyterians were also torn between distrust of the army that Parliament had created and the need to preserve a common front against the king and his supporters, who, though defeated in the field, were still a power in the land. In the event the Scottish noblemen who were prepared to trust the king, though opposed by most of the Kirk, seized control of the levers of state power in Scotland, and determined to destroy the New Model Army in the name of restoring Charles to his rightful position in England. Meanwhile groups of ex-Royalists rose in rebellion, supported by a few officers who had fought for Parliament in the first war. There was little co-ordination between the uprisings, and the neo-Royalists were not only less well armed than in 1642 but also facing a much more formidable military force than the Earl of Essex's army. However, they had two advantages. First was the promise of a Scottish invasion, and second the fact that the New Model was badly stretched because of the general threat of unrest, with small contingents quartered in almost every part of England. However, by the time the Scottish army was ready to take the field most of the Royalist uprisings in England and Wales had been repressed or contained. Even in the far north, where the Royalists led by Sir Marmaduke Langdale had begun well by capturing Berwick and Carlisle, Colonel John Lambert had driven them back against the Scottish border, thus rendering them incapable of combining with the Yorkshire Royalists, who had seized Pontefract castle. A brief resurgence followed when the Scottish army led by the Duke of Hamilton duly invaded, but the string of engagements in Lancashire between 17 and 20 August ensured that the Second Civil War, like

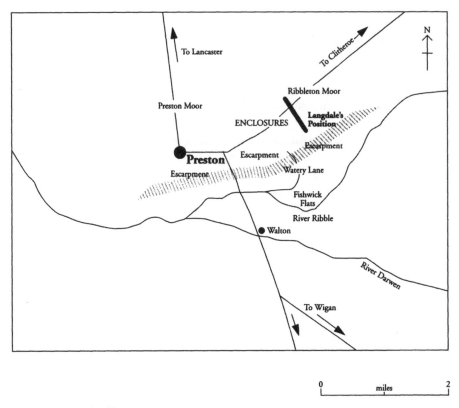

Map 8. The Battle of Preston

the First, spluttered out in a number of sieges.[2] The focus for the next two chapters will be on the first of these engagements, the Battle of Preston.

Landscape

The Battle of Preston comprised two engagements, one lasting from about midday to 6 p.m. and the second for the next two hours until darkness fell. They took place in adjacent but very different locations in landscape terms. There were therefore two distinct battlefields, but there is no dispute as to where the engagements took place. The first was fought in enclosures on either side of the Preston to Clitheroe road, which runs north–eastwards from Preston roughly parallel to the River Ribble. The enclosures began at the western end of Ribbleton Moor and extended almost as far as the town itself, a distance of between one and two miles. The whole area, both enclosures and moorland, is now covered in buildings even more intensively than are Wash Common and Speenhamland on the Newbury battlefields. The only feature of the seventeenth-century landscape easily visible today is the steep slope between the road and the river, which extends from two miles to the east of Ribbleton to the other side of Preston.

The second encounter took place just to the south-east of Preston town centre in and around the bridges over the Ribble and the Darwen, which carried what is now the A6 road in the direction of Chorley. This area is less intensively built over, but nevertheless what is there today bears no resemblance to the open landscape on the south bank of the river in the seventeenth century, which was described by one contemporary as being devoid of even a single bush. The steep slope on the north bank and the advantage that elevation gave to Cromwell's musketeers is mentioned in one account of the battle, but it is now no longer lined with hedges and covered by just a scattering of houses.[3]

Neither of the battlefields could be seen as favouring conventional cavalry warfare. Cromwell did indeed draw his horse up on Ribbleton Moor prior to the most intensive fighting in the first phase of the battle, but they found progress up the lane that bisected the enclosures impossible until the infantry had cleared the ground of enemy musketeers and pikes. Their only role subsequently was the traditional one, pursuing the defeated enemy. Preston was unquestionably an infantry battle.

Sources

Sources for the Battle of Preston are remarkably few.[4] Each has a different angle on the fighting, but there is little conflict between them other than that caused by the writers' attempts to pin the blame for the defeat on one party or another. Not surprisingly, the most partisan account is in Clarendon.[5] He used Sir Marmaduke Langdale, commander of the English corps, as his major and possibly his only primary source, but the description of the shortcomings and misdemeanours of the Scottish military leadership is expressed far more stridently than Langdale does in his *Impartial Relation*. Anxious to drive home the point that the Scots ignored accurate intelligence of the enemy's movements provided by Langdale's cavalry, Clarendon claimed that this wrong-headedness stretched over several days. Langdale, on the other hand, focuses on the morning of the battle itself, implying that a piece of intelligence he provided three days before had been accepted as correct. However, it is possible that Sir Marmaduke in later years told Clarendon more than he put down in writing, and that this informs the *History of the Great Rebellion* and the *History*.

Langdale's *Impartial Relation* is carefully written and was completed only a week after the battle, but there are problems with it as an account, as it exists in several forms. Three versions survive in the Clarendon manuscripts alone. Another, sent to the Marquis of Ormond in Dublin, was published in the early eighteenth century. The fifth, reproduced in a biography of Langdale written in the 1920s, is unreferenced.[6] There are subtle differences between the five versions caused by editorial errors, but that is not all. For example, the comment in the version in the biography to the effect that 1,000 Scottish foot would have enabled Langdale to beat off his attackers is missing from the Ormond version.[7]

The second major early account from a Royalist perspective is the so-called *Letter from Holland* written at Rotterdam in September 1648 and published in London the following month.[8] The author is unknown, but he was an Englishman unable to gain a command in the Scottish army because he was disliked for his stance in the First Civil War. Nevertheless he was very close to Hamilton, and may have been a volunteer in the duke's Lifeguard. His dislike of the Scots for their incompetence and for their plundering shines through, and his delight that he was able to escape to Rotterdam because he spoke English rather than Scots is the one bright moment in the account. However, he does not go quite as far as a revived *Mercurius Aulicus*, for whom the Scots' defeat in the Preston campaign was condign punishment for their treachery to the king in the First Civil War.[9]

The only two accounts written from the Scottish perspective were compiled well after the Restoration. They are both very well crafted, but Bishop Gilbert Burnet's *Lives of the Dukes of Hamilton*, which was produced at the behest of the 3rd Duke in the early 1670s, is little more than an apologia for his two predecessors.[10] It is therefore essentially a secondary work written in compliance with a preconceived agenda, and thus in a similar category to Clarendon when the latter was writing about battles at which he had not been present in person. Burnet has also been criticized for being overly reliant on Sir James Turner's *Memoirs*. He certainly had access to these, and some passages are no more than a more elegant version of what the old soldier had written, but Burnet also used the reminiscences of other Scottish officers who fought at Preston. These could have been a valuable addition to the primary source material on the battle, but as he does not cite his informants other than on a single occasion in a letter to Sir James, it is impossible to ascertain how much of the non–Turner part of the narrative is based on their evidence and how much on his own imaginative reconstruction of what happened.[11]

Turner's highly colourful *Memoirs* were concerned with paying off old scores against English and Scottish commanders alike, but he at least had the advantage of having fought at Preston. Nevertheless, the account was not written until the early 1670s.[12] Sir James claimed in his final paragraph to be fit in mind and body, and to have a prodigious memory, but he was obliged to rely exclusively on his memory in writing up his memoirs, as 'I never used to keep notes in writing'. Not surprisingly, they contain some factual inaccuracies and a number of generalizations that are clearly based on hindsight. Burnet tactfully reminded him of some of the latter, sending him at least one account written by another officer to see if it would reawaken his memory about the intelligence Hamilton had in his hands prior to the battle. Despite Turner's reputation as an irascible old man, he cannot have reacted badly to Burnet's questioning his powers of recall. The tone of a letter he received from Burnet two months later suggested that they were still very good friends.[13]

The fullest accounts of the Preston campaign from the Parliamentary side are in the elegant letters written by Oliver Cromwell between 17 and 20 August to the Speaker of the House of Commons and to the County Committees of Lancashire and Yorkshire.[14] The letter to the Speaker should be seen as the official account of the battle, and it shows Cromwell probably underestimated the size of his own force and overestimated that of the enemy. He was also a little hazy about the intelligence he received, but there is little else that is clearly spin, and he does full justice to all the units under his command, including the local forces. However, what is amazing about the letters is the contrast with most of his earlier battlefield accounts, which are short on military detail but long on religious enthusiasm and written in a homespun style. At times the old Oliver peeps through as, for example, in the final paragraph of the longest letter to the Speaker, but there is nevertheless a strong suspicion that almost all the rest was written by somebody else at the general's behest.

The second major source is Lieutenant John Hodgson's account of the first engagement between the armies, in which his own regiment, Colonel John Bright's, appears to have distinguished itself.[15] It does not conflict in any way with Cromwell's accounts, with the relevant parts of Langdale's *Impartial Relation*, or indeed with an anonymous letter printed in the issue of the *Moderate Intelligencer* for 17–24 August 1648, which is well informed about both engagements, yet not overwhelmingly influenced by the 'official account'.[16] There is, however, another account of the battle published in London immediately after the battle, which is a complete fabrication. Entitled *The Bloody Battle of Preston*, it shows no evidence in the glib generalizations it makes about the fighting of being based on anything other than writer's common sense.[17] According to him there was a single engagement at Preston, not two, and the enemy were exclusively Scots. There were no enclosures and no bridge, but there were cannon, ten of which were captured at the end of the battle, even though the Scottish artillery pieces were with General Monro at Kirby Lonsdale, thirty miles north of the battlefield. Unfortunately, this bogus source is used unquestioningly by a number of historians, including Gentles and also Bull and Seed in the most recent accounts of the battle.[18] There are also two minor sources, the diary of Captain Samuel Birch of the Lancashire brigade, which is much fuller on the campaign than on the battle, and two pages in *A Discourse on the Wars in Lancashire*, written in 1655 probably by Major Edward Robinson. The latter is not completely correct in the details it provides, but is well informed about the countryside over which the battle was fought, which is not surprising as Robinson lived only six miles from Preston.[19]

Chapter 17

The Battle of Preston
Narrative

The Scottish army commanded by the Duke of Hamilton crossed the border on 8 July and joined forces with Langdale's corps at Carlisle a day or so later. Lambert, heavily outnumbered, fell back into the Vale of Eden, and then after some encounters in the Penrith and Appleby area in which his forces suffered casualties, withdrew to Barnard Castle in Teesdale on 18 July.[1] There followed a fortnight of almost complete inactivity, whilst Hamilton waited for supplies and for the arrival of a large brigade of Scottish troops under Major General Monro, what was left of the expeditionary force that had sailed to Ulster in 1642 to help suppress the Catholic uprising. In Lambert's words, 'no action hath been between us'.[2] However, the Scottish siege of Appleby Castle, taken together with Hamilton's establishing his army headquarters at Kirkby Thore on the road from Carlisle to Stainmore, suggested that the Duke's next move would be to cross the Pennines into North Yorkshire and advance on London by the most direct route. On 2 August, however, the Scottish army moved forward to Kendal and on 9 August to Hornby, whilst Langdale's corps, about 4,000 strong, quartered at Settle. This made it look as if the duke had decided on the west coast route, but he still had the option of making a thrust into the West Riding by way of Upper Ribblesdale and Craven.

At Settle Langdale was separated from the Scottish army by thirty miles of difficult country, but Lambert refused to be tempted, even though his force was much larger than Langdale's, comprising two veteran regiments of infantry and four of cavalry, supplemented by troops from Lancashire, Yorkshire and the north-east. This behaviour seems unduly cautious given Lambert's reputation for active campaigning, but Cromwell, who had helped put down an uprising in west Wales and was on the march northwards with several thousand more New Model Army horse and foot, had ordered him to remain on the defensive.[3] Moreover, Barnard Castle was a safe billet if the whole Royalist force tried to engage him in battle before Cromwell arrived, as the Northern corps could avoid an encounter by falling back on the strongly held garrison of Newcastle.[4] The duke, on the other hand, has been criticized for not trying to destroy Lambert's corps before it could be reinforced,[5] but he had tried to do so once at Appleby, and it was most unlikely that he would be more successful on a second occasion, with the preponderance of slow-moving infantry in his army. The decision to wait for reinforcements from Scotland before taking any further action therefore seems judicious in the circumstances.

On 2 August Lambert sprang into action, moving his corps from Barnard Castle to Richmond and then to Ripon. One reason for this was almost certainly that he knew that Cromwell's main body, three regiments of New Model Army infantry, was well on its way north, as most of the Lieutenant General's cavalry had already arrived. It also made sense to close the gap between them as quickly as possible, as new intelligence indicated the duke was about to move off in a south-easterly direction, which would take his forces towards Leeds and so into the Vale of York, rather than eastwards towards Stainmore or south into Lancashire. Lambert thought the enemy's aim was to attack an easy target, some newly raised troops which were besieging the Royalist garrison at Pontefract Castle, but he may have thought that Hamilton was hoping to block Cromwell's passage northwards, a not impossible task if he himself remained in the Tees valley.[6]

By the time the two Parliamentary generals met at Wetherby on 12 August, Parliament's field army in the north probably comprised between 8,000 and 9,000 men, most of whom were New Model Army veterans.[7] The size of the forces under Hamilton's command is, however, a matter of conjecture. Some of the Parliamentary sources provide estimates that are wildly exaggerated. Hodgson, for example, gave a figure of 46,000, the *Moderate Intelligencer* 27,000.[8] A better guess, and it cannot be any more than a guess, begins with Cromwell's estimate of the number of soldiers killed or taken prisoner in the various engagements between 17 and 20 August. To this needs to be added the numbers that avoided the engagement or managed to escape from it, that is, Monro's infantry and an indeterminate number of horse. Taken together, this would give Hamilton and Langdale a strength of about 18,000 men, plus or minus a thousand, that is, about double the size of Cromwell's force.[9] Even this may be an overestimate. The only Royalist to chance his arm, the anonymous writer of the *Letter from Holland*, opted for 10,000 foot and 5,000 horse 'if altogether', figures that presumably were intended to include Monro's brigade.

Even though the invading army was much the larger, the respective battle experience of the two forces was very different. Admittedly Cromwell's army included several regiments of provincial troops, but the only ones he used at Preston, Colonel Assheton's Lancashire brigade and John Bright's Yorkshire regiment, performed as well as any of the regulars. As for Hamilton's army, the veterans of the wars against the Irish Covenanters, Monro's force, never saw action. He did have with him contingents from at least three of the five regiments of the Scottish field army of the First Civil War, retained when the rest were demobilized early in 1647. Although it had been thought unwise to use them against fellow Scots a month earlier,[10] they might perform better against the English. There were also veterans from the first war in Langdale's corps and in the other Scottish regiments of horse and foot, but the rest of the foot, probably well over half the total, were newly raised men. Sir James Turner implies that the pikemen were reasonably competent soldiers, but he had considerable reservations about the musketeers. He made more optimistic noises about the cavalry, but it is unlikely that Hamilton's cavalry were sufficiently well trained to take on Cromwell's veterans in open country.[11] Most would also have been newly raised, as the Scottish New Model contained few horse, but some would probably have been veterans of the First English Civil War, as would some of their officers.[12]

Cromwell's army set out from Wetherby on 13 August, marching at a great pace in a westerly direction to 'attend the enemy's motion'. Speed was only possible because it had been decided to leave the artillery behind. Cromwell subsequently claimed to have known that 'the enemy were advanced with their army into Lancashire', but the intelligence he had obtained cannot have been based on anything more than rumour. The decision of Hamilton's council of war to take the west coast route into England was not made until the following day at Hornby.[13] Only Langdale and Turner give an account of the points made for and against the Lancashire and the Yorkshire options. Langdale claimed to have recommended the Lancashire option on the grounds that the enclosed countryside would favour an army like theirs that was strong in foot. Turner, however, criticized the decision 'which led to our ruin'. In his *Memoirs* he argued that the open country of central Yorkshire would have enabled the Scots to make good use of their horse, not the most convincing of arguments as explained above, and 'come sooner to push of pike'. He also described Hamilton and Langdale's musketeers as 'raw and undisciplined', whereas Cromwell and Lambert's were 'experienced and well trained soldiers and excellent firemen'. Their behaviour in battle points in two directions. Hodgson described his men, not surprisingly, as taking heart when Sir Marmaduke's musketeers fired over their heads in the first engagement at Preston, but it still took some hours to drive them from the hedge lines they were defending.[14]

Sir Marmaduke claimed not only to have learned that Cromwell's force had left Wetherby almost as soon as it had left, but also to have informed Hamilton when he met him at Hornby on 14 August. Woolrych maintains that the information 'did not identify them as Cromwell's',[15] and implies that it was therefore dismissed as of little importance, but Langdale wrote that the enemy 'were gathered together and marching towards us', which strongly suggests that he knew Lambert and Cromwell had joined forces.[16] When he returned to Settle, Sir Marmaduke pushed his corps down the Ribble valley towards Preston taking the road through Gisburn and Clitheroe. Cromwell was a day's march behind and thus unable to intercept him, but the direction of Langdale's march convinced Cromwell's council of war that Hamilton was concentrating his forces. Cromwell also claimed that his army's quick march was occasioned by the intelligence that Monro had landed and was marching towards Lancashire. However, this must have been old intelligence, as Monro was at Kirby Lonsdale, half a mile from the border of Westmoreland with Lancashire, by the time Oliver said he received the news. The Parliamentary army initially followed the same road from Gisburn down the Ribble valley as that taken by Langdale, but on the evening of 16 August at Hodder bridge, the last one before Preston, the question was raised of whether it might be better to take the road via Whalley towards Manchester instead. This was rejected, probably because clashes between New Model cavalry patrols and Scottish troops that day showed that the enemy were still to the north of the Ribble.[17]

At this point an element of uncertainty creeps in both with regard to the intentions of the Duke of Hamilton and to the quality of the intelligence he possessed about enemy movements, as Royalist accounts of the campaign become increasingly influenced by special pleading. By early on the morning of 17 August the bulk of the Scottish infantry had assembled on Preston Moor just to the north of the town. The rest of the army, however, was very scattered. Langdale's arrival with some 4,000 men, most of whom were infantrymen, was imminent, but, as stated above, Monro's Irish veterans were at Kirby Lonsdale, some thirty miles to the north-east. Their orders were to wait for more ammunition to arrive from Scotland before advancing with the artillery, whilst several other regiments had been detached from the army to garrison Carlisle and to blockade Lancaster Castle. The military justification for Monro's absence is an understandable one, but it may not have been the only reason why his corps was so far behind the main body of the army. One source claimed that his force was separated from the rest because a dispute over precedence in command between Monro and Hamilton's generals made it advisable to keep them apart.[18]

As for the Scottish cavalry, a few were with Hamilton and some in scattered quarters to the north of the river, but most were close to Wigan, some twenty miles to the south of Preston, with their commander John Middleton, Waller's former lieutenant general. It was normal practice for an army on the march to employ its cavalry as vanguard and rearguard and to protect its flanks,[19] but having the vanguard so far in advance of the main body, and the rear-guard spread across the countryside between the Lune and the Ribble, seems foolhardy in the extreme, even without the advantage of hindsight. The explanation given at the time was that shortage of food and fodder caused by the inclement weather and a poor harvest the previous year forced their officers to allow them to disperse far and wide for fear of mutiny.[20]

With regard to intelligence, both Woolrych and Reid claim that Langdale failed to keep Hamilton fully informed about the movements of the enemy until the evening before the battle.[21] Admittedly Langdale's account of the information he supplied to the council of war at Hornby rests on his testimony alone, as explained above, but their assertion arises from an incorrect, though understandable, reading of Turner. Sir James informs his readers that one of Langdale's tasks was to supply 'good and certain intelligence of all the enemy's motions', and that want of intelligence 'whether by our fault or his neglect helped to ruin us'. This does not pin the blame exclusively on Sir Marmaduke, but leaves it open to doubt.[22] Moreover, Hamilton had another source of intelligence about Cromwell's movements, namely General Monro at Kirby Lonsdale.[23] However, the most telling evidence that Hamilton knew Cromwell was on the march westwards well before the fight at Preston is provided by Dachment, one of Bishop Burnet's sources for his biography of the first two Dukes of Hamilton. Dachment was with Hamilton a day or so before the battle when the Duke read out loud a letter from Langdale informing him that the enemy forces, including Cromwell's contingent, had reached Otley. This indicated that the whole Parliamentary army was heading for the Ribble valley and central Lancashire, not Manchester and the valley of the Mersey.[24]

By early morning the bulk of Langdale's force was probably in and around Longridge, four miles to the north-west of Preston, though Parliamentary accounts describe it as being chased down the road from Hodder Bridge towards Preston by Cromwell's advance guard.[25] The Duke of Hamilton's aim that day was to pass all his troops over the Ribble, which flowed immediately to the south of the town, and to head for Manchester, which he apparently hoped might declare for the king.[26] The river crossing was about to begin when the duke received a visit from Sir Marmaduke, who reported that there was fighting along the Clitheroe road, and that he was facing the whole of Cromwell's army. Hamilton apparently hesitated for the moment, but was then persuaded by the Earl of Callendar that Langdale was only faced by a few skirmishers. The crossing of the Ribble then resumed,[27] but some troops were sent to assist Langdale. What these reinforcements were was a matter of dispute. In one passage in his account Langdale stated that he received no reinforcements apart from a troop of Scottish lancers. This type of cavalry unit was of value in pursuing a defeated enemy in open country, but of little use in the enclosed landscape to the east of Preston. If, however, he had been sent 1,000 infantry instead and some more gunpowder for his musketeers, he claimed that he might have been able to hold the enemy off. Elsewhere in his account, however, he acknowledged that some Scots appeared towards the end of the fight along the Clitheroe road, but did nothing to assist him: 'neither did the forces that were left for my supply come to my relief, but continued in the rear of mine, nor did they ever face the enemy but in bringing up the rear.' Sir James Turner, on the other hand, claimed to have sent a body of commanded men and some ammunition to assist Langdale, 'but to no purpose for Cromwell prevailed so that our English first retired and then fled'. Langdale's narrative seems the more likely of the two.[28] Scottish lancers, but no other Scottish troops, were noted in enemy reports as defending the eastern approaches to Preston, and the length of time taken up by the encounter on the Clitheroe road would have given plenty of time for commanded men and ammunition to travel the distance between the Scottish assembly point on Preston Moor and the enclosures at Ribbleton.[29]

Why was so little done to reinforce the position on the Clitheroe road? All the Royalist accounts emphasize that Hamilton was not convinced that Langdale was facing the whole of the enemy army until it was much too late. Langdale, not surprisingly, and the writer of the *Letter from Holland*, blamed the duke's advisers for rubbishing the intelligence Langdale brought with him, a point Turner does not deny. However, one can understand why Hamilton's advisers thought Langdale was mistaken given the tactics employed by the enemy, namely using a small vanguard of some 600 men to push the Royalists down the Clitheroe road towards Preston, with the rest of the army four miles or so behind trying to keep pace. As the latter were hidden from view, the activities of the vanguard could be read as a noisy diversion and nothing more. Only when the vanguard ground to a halt in the enclosures just beyond the western edge of Ribbleton Moor in the face of heavy Royalist fire, and the rest of the army began to catch up and deploy on the moor, did it become fully apparent that Langdale had been right, but by then it was probably too late to give him much help. The bulk of the Scottish infantry regiments were already across the Ribble.[30]

In mid-afternoon after several hours or so of skirmishing Cromwell's army was ready to attack.[31] Langdale's position made effective use of a series of hedge lines on both sides of the road, which was narrow and muddy. He also chose to defend a narrow front, mainly, it seems, to the south of the road, thus ensuring that if retreat were necessary it would be in the direction of the bridge over the Ribble not of Preston itself, or even worse to the north of the town onto Preston Moor where his soldiers would easily be cut down by enemy horse. Cromwell's attack began, according to Hodgson, with an attempt to rush the enemy position using the cavalry of the advance guard, a tactic that had been most successful at Langport against the rearguard of another army intent on retreat, but if this was the aim it failed. Langdale had apparently stationed a stand of pikemen in the road itself some way back from the hedge bordering Ribbleton Moor; Cromwell's infantry had not made enough progress in clearing the hedges lining the road to prevent Royalist musketeers delivering effective flanking fire into cavalry as they advanced; and a troop of Scottish lancers were in position to conduct a counter-charge, which was initially successful.[32] The assault troops that took over as the advance guard fell back seem to have comprised three New Model infantry regiments to the north of the road, Pride's, Overton's and Deane's, and one to the south, Fairfax's own, supported by Colonel Bright's Yorkshire regiment. The Lancashire brigade was in the second line together with a regiment of horse. Two regiments of New Model Army horse, Harrison's and Cromwell's, were deployed in the centre, ready to charge down the road if an opportunity offered, but Cromwell's account suggests that they either did not do so or were obliged to fall back by the intensity of enemy fire. Possibly the road was already blocked with dead and dying horses belonging to the advanced guard; there is a slight hint of it in one of the accounts. The rest of the cavalry was placed in reserve, presumably so that they were ready to exploit a breakthrough when it occurred.

After at least an hour or so of intensive fighting, in which the New Model troops suffered considerable casualties, little progress had apparently been made. Two of the three regiments to the north of the road had no Royalists in front of them but were apparently unable to swing round and attack Langdale's position in the flank. The two to the south of the road may have been in difficulties, at which point Lambert ordered the Lancashire brigade forward to assist them. This did the trick. The enemy retreat became a rout, probably because the push to the south of the road achieved almost immediate success by blocking Langdale's escape route from the escarpment to the bridge over the Ribble. Many of his foot were captured or killed on the spot. Some managed to reach Preston, but they were quickly winkled out by two regiments of Cromwell's horse. Langdale's cavalry, which had apparently played no part in the engagement, almost certainly fled northwards with the Scottish rearguard towards Monro's position at Kirby Lonsdale, pursued by two more regiments of New Model horse.[33]

In the valley below Preston town, all was confusion when the New Model Army and its auxiliaries overran Langdale's position. The Duke of Hamilton was nowhere to be seen, having become trapped in Preston trying to gather up the last of the Scottish cavalry as they streamed into town from the north. Middleton's cavalry were still at Wigan. At the bridge over the Ribble a breastwork had been built or possibly refurbished, but the Scottish and Royalist accounts differ as to how the bridge was defended and it is impossible to reconcile them. The *Letter from Holland* mentions two brigades of infantry being detailed to defend the bridge, but Turner's account implies very strongly that initially there were no troops at the bridge, that the two brigades were somewhere else on the north bank of the Ribble, and that they were destroyed before the battle for the bridge began.

According to Scottish and Royalist accounts Preston bridge quickly became indefensible. As soon as the enemy occupied the hedges and houses on the escarpment to the north of the river, they began pouring heavy musket fire into the area surrounding the bridge, which became a killing ground because there was no cover. It also made it impossible to reinforce the defenders. Burnet describes an attempt to do so, which stalled because of the intensity of the incoming fire, and was then overtaken by events as the defenders of the bridge fled their posts.[34] However, all the Parliamentary accounts other than

Hodgson's, which has nothing to say about the matter, describe a long and bitter struggle lasting for two hours that was only decided by the pikes of Fairfax's and the Lancashire regiments rushing the bridge and capturing it. Immediately afterwards they also captured the bridge over the Darwen, a tributary of the Ribble, which joined the river about half a mile or so to the east of Preston bridge. Pursued for a short distance by enemy horse and foot, what was left of the defence fled back to Walton Hill, a mile to the south-east, where the rest of the Scottish infantry had taken up quarters for the night.[35] With darkness falling, Cromwell ordered his men to halt and then, it seems, to fan out along the banks of the Ribble to prevent the Scots trying to cross to the north bank by a ford before daybreak.[36] This seems an unnecessary precaution given the demoralized state of the Scottish army, but he did not want a repeat of what had happened four years earlier at the Second Battle of Newbury.

At that point Hamilton rejoined his army, having swum the Ribble on horseback, but too late for his presence to have any effect on the tactics employed in the final hour of the battle. However, he took part in the discussion that evening at which the council of war agreed that the army should not remain where it was, but should make its way as silently as possible towards Wigan to link up with Middleton's cavalry. After that they were to continue marching south in the hope of joining Lord Byron, who was trying to win over North Wales for the king. The troops Hamilton still had under his command in south Lancashire were probably outnumbered by Cromwell's horse and foot, and they were dismayed and demoralized by what had happened to their comrades and by the prospect of a night march over atrocious roads. To make matters worse, the need to be as quiet as possible in order not to alert the enemy meant leaving their baggage train behind including all their undistributed gunpowder, and without gunpowder the eventual fate of the infantry at least was sealed, even if sufficient had been distributed for the musketeers to deliver some kind of barrage at the next encounter. This is Turner's story, but Cromwell's account implies that his troops captured the enemy supply train some time before nightfall.[37]

The Scottish army made its way south as best it could over the next three days, harried by Cromwell's forces. There were several skirmishes and a further major infantry engagement at Winwick where the Scots suffered heavy casualties. What was left of the infantry, still several thousand strong, surrendered to Cromwell at Warrington on 20 August; they had lost the wherewithal as well as the will to fight, having exhausted all their remaining ammunition at Winwick. Whether or not knowledge that Byron's efforts in North Wales had largely failed entered into their calculations is not known, but the cavalry fled in a south-easterly direction, hoping eventually to turn northwards in the direction of Pontefract, the nearest friendly garrison. However, exhausted by the effort of the past week, they were easily rounded up by local forces. Hamilton himself surrendered at Uttoxeter in Staffordshire with the largest party on 25 August, whilst Langdale reached the outskirts of Nottingham before being captured.[38] The former suffered the fate of the king his cousin; the latter managed eventually to escape to the Continent, as did the Earl of Callendar, whom Langdale, the writer of the *Letter from Holland*, and Gilbert Burnet believed to be largely responsible for the disaster in Lancashire.[39]

Their verdict has been accepted by historians who wrote about the battle in the second half of the twentieth century,[40] but it is possible to offer a defence against some of the charges against Callendar, namely advising Hamilton to disregard Langdale's intelligence at the first sign of fighting to the east of Preston, and recommending that the army should continue crossing the Ribble despite the fighting that was taking place along the Clitheroe road. A reason why Callendar responded so negatively towards Langdale's intelligence report on the morning of 17 August has been suggested above. The second charge is also difficult to sustain when critically examined. If the enemy approaching from the east were merely a diversionary force, Langdale would have sufficient troops to deal with it. If it were the whole of Cromwell's army, it would be foolish to deploy on Preston Moor, even if there were space to do so. Most of the Scottish horse were with Middleton at Wigan and the rest, arriving in dribs and drabs from their scattered quarters around the town, would easily have been swept from the battlefield by Cromwell's veteran cavalry.[41] At least if the bulk of the infantry could transfer to the south bank of the Ribble, there was a fair chance that a balanced army could be formed provided that Middleton arrived in time. Callendar's biggest blunder was the one identified in the Sunderland version of Langdale's account.[42] Given the large number of foot soldiers in the Scottish army, it would have been very easy to provide Sir Marmaduke when he arrived in person on Preston Moor with a brigade to reinforce the English corps. Langdale, however, was probably mistaken in thinking that 1,000 musketeers would have been sufficient for him to be able to defeat Cromwell.[43] Nevertheless, if with the support of Scottish infantry he had been able to hold out for an hour or two longer, there would have been insufficient daylight left for Cromwell to launch an assault on the bridge over the Ribble that day, thus allowing Hamilton time to position his troops in such a way as to be able to attack the enemy as they tried to cross the Ribble the following morning.[44]

Cromwell had triumphed in the only decisive Civil War engagement in which the smaller army was victorious, but he had been lucky. Turner blamed the Scottish defeat on poor intelligence, though the real problem was that good intelligence was rejected.[45] There is, however, not much evidence that Cromwell knew any better. Although he was apparently aware that Monro and Langdale were marching to join Hamilton,[46] none of the contemporary accounts suggests that he knew that the rest of the Scottish army was strung out along twenty miles of what is now the M6 motorway between the northern outskirts of Preston and Wigan, and he would certainly not have known about what was going on in and around Preston itself on the morning of 17 August. In fact Cromwell took an enormous gamble,[47] something that he was to repeat at Dunbar when similarly outnumbered, but clean contrary to the caution that marked his behaviour in the First Civil War. It marks a significant change in Cromwell's generalship, probably reflecting his increasing confidence that he was God's instrument and therefore could not lose whatever the odds.

Chapter 18
Conclusion

It is abundantly clear that, if the procedures described in Chapter 3 are applied to the relevant primary sources, and if knowledge is defined as what happened on the battlefield as opposed to what might have happened, far less is known about the seven decisive battles of the English Civil Wars discussed above than has traditionally been thought. We do not know, for example, exactly how the Royalist army was deployed at Edgehill; we do not know where the Royalist army deployed at Cheriton; we do not know if it was Sir Thomas Fairfax who first brought news to Cromwell of the defeat of much of the rest of the Allied armies at Marston Moor, or if Newcastle's Whitecoats were ordered to sacrifice themselves so that what was left of the Royalist armies could escape from the battlefield; we do not know whether the main body of Royalist infantry conducted a fighting retreat from Naseby to Wadborough Hill before surrendering; and we do not know the contribution of the Scottish infantry to fighting on the north bank of the Ribble at the Battle of Preston. When there is a loss of certainty about what happened on a battlefield, the explanation of why the battle was won or lost becomes correspondingly more speculative. However, if some certainties have been removed, hypotheses of a more or less tentative nature have been proposed concerning the Earl of Essex's plans for the First Battle of Newbury, the Earl of Forth's intentions at Cheriton and Prince Rupert's at Naseby; the varied fortunes of the Royalist infantry brigades at the Battle of Edgehill; the circumstances under which the Royalist army escaped from the battlefield on the evening of the Second Battle of Newbury; and what happened to the Marquis of Newcastle's cavalry during and after the final hour of the Battle of Marston Moor.

The new narratives of the decisive battles of the English Civil Wars presented above represent, in my judgement, a significant improvement on previous narratives including my own, with regard to both the accuracy of the language used to distinguish fact from opinion and the level of critical evaluation applied to the traces of the past which illustrate or underpin the argument, *but no more than that*. The use of the first person in the last sentence is deliberate. As argued on many occasions above, the primary sources that survive are not sufficiently robust for the historian to be able to reconstruct a Civil War battle in its entirety. All that one can do is place in the public arena a hesitant narrative composed mainly of hypotheses as opposed to facts. Moreover, although I strive towards objectivity, like everybody else I am incapable of writing narratives that are not skewed one way or another because of where I am situated in time and space and because of the influence of my upbringing, character traits, gender and life experience on my approach to the study of the Past. Fully mindful of these important caveats, I revert to the question posed at the very beginning of this book – to what extent can what happened on the battlefield contribute to discussion of why Parliament won and the Royalists lost the English Civil Wars?

At one level the answer is that the impact of what happened on the battle-field on the outcome of the wars was enormous and blatantly self-evident: the supporters of Parliament triumphed because they won the more important battles. However, for many historians currently writing on mid-seventeenth-century English history, military factors are second order types of explanations: once Parliament had survived the first year of the war, victory was inevitable because of its overwhelming superiority in resources.[1] Frank Jones and I have argued elsewhere that such a remorselessly determinist explanation is insufficient on its own to explain why the wars ended when they did and how they did.[2] However, such is the domination of the determinist explanation that most studies of the English Civil Wars written recently by military historians assume that it is set in stone and cannot be challenged, and that there is therefore little or no justification in searching for a wider significance in what happened on the battlefield.

The neglect of purely military explanations goes back a very long way. One has, for example, to search very hard in Gardiner to find any direct comments on military considerations, though the genius of Cromwell can clearly be discerned behind his narrative of Naseby, associated as it is with words and phrases carefully chosen to imply that Fairfax was in a slightly different league. However, Gardiner does describe the New Model Army as having a better cavalry officer. He also commented on the numerical advantage the New Model enjoyed at Naseby, with the implication that the rest of the army under-performed.[3] Woolrych's remarks are similar to Gardiner's, but a little more forthright, suggesting that Parliament's victory at Naseby, like that at Marston Moor, owed much to the cavalry that Cromwell himself had trained. The rest of the New Model, however, given its size advantage over the king's army, had performed 'neither better nor worse than might have been expected', composed as it was of 'reluctant conscripts and the disgruntled remains of older and less happy armies'.[4] Other historians are much less forthcoming. Reid's conclusion in *All the King's Armies* is no more than a brief

survey of the period that followed the ending of hostilities.[5] Young and
Holmes are more analytical, but they focus on weighing up the merits of the
principal generals.[6] Barratt has something new to say about the development of
Royalist cavalry tactics on the battlefield in *Cavaliers*, but in *Royalist Generals*
he attributes the New Model's victory in the field to 'good luck, excellent
generalship, and enemy mistakes', all of which are matters of debate rather than
incontrovertible explanations.[7] Anderson, on the other hand, like Woolrych,
focuses on Cromwell's cavalry, whose courage matched Rupert's cavaliers and
whose discipline outshone them.[8]

The most popular explanation of Parliament's armies' success in the field in
the works mentioned must be quickly qualified. The allegation or implication
that excellent cavalry was all a general required to win battles is half right but
no more than that. If it had been so, the Royalists would have won the First
Battle of Newbury. Instead, the confused fighting and heavy casualties that
occurred in and around Skinners Green Lane Head and on the slope of the
northern spur facing the River Kennet showed that cavalry could not be used
as a substitute for infantry. Only in unusual circumstances were cavalry able to
achieve overall victory on their own. Even if they drove the enemy cavalry from
the battlefield, they needed infantry and/or artillery support to provide the
firepower to break up the enemy infantry. There are, however, two principal
exceptions to this generalization about seventeenth-century warfare. First, if
the opposing infantry were raw recruits, they might be disrupted by cavalry
alone, as appears to have happened at Edgehill to a regiment in Richard
Fielding's brigade in the king's army and possibly to several regiments in
the Earl of Essex's army, and at Marston Moor to much of Lord Fairfax's
infantry. In neither case, however, did the encounter have a decisive effect
on the outcome of the battle. Second, in theory cavalry could surround and
then browbeat enemy infantry into surrendering. The weakness of the linear
battlefield formation of the mid-seventeenth century was its vulnerability in
open country to attack from flank or rear by the enemy horse once the latter
had won its victory on the wings. Escape in such circumstances was only
possible under cover of darkness, as at the Second Battle of Newbury, or into
wooded and enclosed country, as at Cheriton.[9] However, some regiments of the
London Trained Bands during the Gloucester and Newbury campaign in
1643, and Lord Lindsay's and Lord Maitland's regiments at Marston Moor the
following year, had the discipline to resist cavalry attack in open country.[10]
Moreover, at Marston Moor the destruction of the Royalist regiments of foot
in the closing stages of the battle appears to have been more the work of
Crawford's infantry and the Scottish dragoons than of Cromwell's horse. Even
at Naseby it is by no means certain that cavalry alone destroyed any of the
Royalist infantry brigades. However, combined operations on the battlefield
required a judicious mix of units. At the First Battle of Newbury some Royalist
infantry formations, which were almost certainly full of new recruits, refused to

advance head-on against enemy troops protected by hedges and banks, leaving Rupert's cavalry to attempt the impossible, whereas at the Second Battle of Newbury the thrust between Speen village and the River Kennet, which came within a hair's breadth of turning the whole Royalist position, failed ultimately because Waller did not commit sufficient infantry to the undertaking despite his huge superiority in that arm. To sum it all up, all the decisive battles of the English Civil Wars that ended in outright victory – Cheriton, Marston Moor, Naseby, and the first, crucial fight at Preston – involved infantry as much as or more than cavalry in their climactic moments. This is well known to writers whose origins lie in re-enacting or in the academic field of War Studies, but it is rarely appreciated in books written by political historians. In the public domain it is therefore a relatively unfamiliar notion that battles could not be won without infantry.

Disparity in the numbers of combatants on the battlefield was most significant in some of the decisive battles. Royalist setbacks during the First Battle of Newbury and the Battle of Cheriton can be attributed directly to lack of infantry, as can the loss of the defences of Speen village at the Second Battle of Newbury and the inability of the foot to exploit their initial success at Naseby. Only in the case of Second Newbury can such setbacks be attributed to poor strategic planning. Even if the king had managed to draw Goring's and Gerard's infantry into his army before fighting the battle to end all battles in the English Midlands in July 1645, Sir Thomas Fairfax would have had time to assemble an even larger force from the provincial regiments that were converging on the New Model Army from all over central England. He would also probably have been able to combine forces with the Scottish army, which was marching rapidly southwards. Similarly if Rupert had waited for Clavering's men before attacking the Allied armies in July 1644, the numerical disparity between the two army groups would have been even greater due to the arrival in south Yorkshire of 6,000 additional Parliamentary troops from the Midlands and the north-west. Moreover, the shortage of Royalist infantry on the battlefield cannot be attributed to the incompetence or bad luck of the generals in command in the provinces, the loss of infantry brigades in Gloucestershire in March 1643 and in Hampshire in the winter of 1643–4 being balanced by Parliamentary losses at the Battle of Roundway Down in July 1643 and the relief of Newark by Prince Rupert in March 1644. The prime causes for the imbalance between the infantry components of the Parliamentary and the Royalist armies were probably the low population of most of those parts of the kingdom that the king's armies controlled, the tying down of the resources of the well-populated West Country in protecting the region against Parliamentary garrisons situated within it, and possibly the lack of appeal of the Royalist cause for those social groups likely to have joined, or been forced to join, the infantry as opposed to the cavalry.

However, this argument should not be taken too far. At Naseby, for example, the Royalists' shortage of both horse and foot has rightly been seen as crucial, but their commanders made the situation even worse by the way in which they used the forces they had. At Marston Moor, on the other hand, the large advantage in numbers the Allied army had at the start of the battle was dissipated within half an hour of its start. By that time the Royalists probably had an advantage in infantry and the Allies an advantage in cavalry, but here again the former made poor use of their resources, possibly because Prince Rupert's flight from the battlefield early on left the king's armies rudderless, as it deprived the Royalist troops of an overall commander.[11] Sir Charles Lucas should have called on infantry support in his attack on the two remaining regiments in the Allied vanguard, but he did not do so or perhaps he tried to and was refused support. Cromwell, Crawford and Leslie, on the other hand, used their depleted resources with great skill. At the Second Battle of Newbury, the disparity in size between the two army groups was even greater, but here the Parliamentary generals were tactically at fault converting a near-certain victory into an embarrassing draw. They failed to exploit their advantage, not only because the attacks on the Royalist position came too late in the day and were apparently not synchronized, but also possibly because of logjams caused by having too many troops milling in and around Speen village and by the curious behaviour of Cromwell and Waller's horse. In the string of engagements in south Lancashire in the Second Civil War, the Scots and their allies outnumbered Cromwell's forces by at least two to one, but failed to deploy their forces in a satisfactory manner around Preston because of lack of fodder, faulty intelligence and the alleged arrogance and wrong-headedness of the Earl of Callendar. They were then defeated in detail, despite the enclosed nature of much of the countryside, largely through loss of infantry firepower when the wagons carrying their gunpowder were captured on the evening of the first day of the fighting.

Finally there is the question of how military doctrine evolved during the English Civil Wars and the impact that this had on the manner in which battles were fought. At first sight it is difficult to see any significant development other than that Parliament's generals gradually abandoned what is generally described as the Dutch tactics of requiring their cavalry squadrons to remain stationary to receive the enemy charge. Oliver Cromwell's description of the encounter at Grantham in May 1643 suggests strongly that his decision to charge the enemy horse came about through accident rather than design, but from then onwards he applied the tactic consistently.[12] Another development that is less certain is that Cromwell's men were more heavily armoured than the Royalists they faced in battle. In consequence they could charge at a more moderate speed with all that meant in terms of retaining close order but without experiencing any loss of momentum. Moreover, the argument that he purposely trained his troopers to halt when the enemy horse fled and to await further orders is based on a misunderstanding of the primary sources. The control displayed by the Eastern Association horse at Marston Moor was probably achieved more by luck than judgement, whilst at Naseby Cromwell merely husbanded his resources, with the result that few if any of his cavalry units were called upon to charge more than once. Combined operations by infantry and cavalry were also nothing new, and the direct involvement of many of the fighting, as opposed to figurehead, generals in man-to-man combat was as characteristic of many of the First Civil War battles as it had been in the Wars of the Roses. However, Cromwell, after initially leading from the front, led from behind at Naseby and in every subsequent battle in which he fought. Whether this was a case of learning from experience or the natural response of an elderly commander to lucky escapes at Winceby and Marston Moor, it had a profound effect on battle management and should perhaps be placed with his training of cavalry as a major achievement of his career as lieutenant general of horse. However, Skippon, who held the parallel command in the infantry, behaved in a similar manner at Naseby. He did not fight with his regiment in the front line but led up the reserve line when the vanguard began to give way. The behaviour of both may therefore be the result of reflection during the winter of 1644–5 as to the battlefield role of the seconds in command. However, the lesson may first have been learned by Skippon at the First Battle of Newbury, where he played a mobile role feeding in reinforcements as and when necessary.

Army generals also, with the exception of Sir William Waller, tended to hold themselves back until the climactic moment of the battle,[13] but this seems already to have been well-established practice in 1642, as it was recommended in various military manuals, including the recently published treatise written by that great Protestant hero, Henri, Duc de Rohan.[14] Sir Thomas Fairfax, though apparently popping up wherever needed at Naseby, does not appear to have led a charge until the end of the battle, but Essex apparently behaved in a similar manner at Edgehill and First Newbury.

In the management of infantry, a greater flexibility can be discerned in the use to which they were put. Musketeers were often separated from the rest of their regiment and used for specific jobs where speed was essential and pikes would have been an encumbrance as, for example, at Cheriton in the fighting in and around Cheriton Wood and in Waller's reinforcement of the Parliamentary right wing slightly later in the same battle. However, the possibility that musketeers' flexibility led to their becoming a higher and higher proportion of an infantry regiment as time passed is probably a chance effect of what traces of the past happen to survive into the present. The argument that Parliamentary infantry regiments at the end of the First Civil War had a higher ratio of muskets to pikes than Essex's infantry regiments in 1642 rests on evidence concerning orders for sending muskets to south Hampshire in September 1644 to replace those the field army had lost at Lostwithiel a month earlier. However, as nothing is known about the number of pikes that were already in the magazine at Portsmouth, it proves nothing.[15]

The conclusions reached have no claims to be anything other than provisional. New written sources will be discovered in the future; old ones will be read in different ways; re-enactment will yield more information about what brigades and lesser formations in Civil War armies were or were not capable of achieving; and field archaeology combined with archival research will shed more light on where specific encounters on the battlefield took place. Hopefully protocols similar to those laid down in Chapter 3 will be applied consistently and refined through usage.[16] However, in complex battlefield situations, sad though it is, definitive narratives and definitive explanations are unattainable.

Notes

Abbreviations

BL	British Library
Bodl.	Bodleian Library
CRO	County Record Office
CSP	Calendar of State Papers
HMC	Historical Manuscripts Commission
ms, mss	Manuscript, manuscripts
TT	British Library, Thomason Tracts

Chapter 1. Introduction

1. Wanklyn and Jones, *Military History of the English Civil War*, pp. 11–24.
2. Carpenter, *Military Leadership in the British Civil Wars*.
3. Gardiner, *History of the Great Civil War*.
4. Wanklyn and Jones, *Military History of the English Civil War*, pp. 188–91.
5. Ibid., pp. 126–7.
6. Ibid., p. 4.
7. See, for example, Gentles, *New Model Army*, pp. 404–9.

Chapter 2. Civil War Battles: The Primary Sources

1. Jenkins, *Re-thinking History*.
2. e.g. Warwick, *Memoirs*, pp. xi, xiii; Clarendon, *History of the Great Rebellion*, book 1, 1–4.
3. Cavendish, *Lives of [the] Duke [and Duchess] of Newcastle*, pp. xxiv–xxv. By gazettes the duchess almost certainly meant weekly journals, which were produced by both sides during the war.
4. Bodl. English ms 132, 13–14. The wording in the printed version of the *Memoirs* is given in square brackets where it departs from the original.
5. Wedgwood, *The King's War*, p. 253.
6. Worden, *Roundhead Reputations*.
7. Firth, 'The "Memoirs" of Sir Richard Bulstrode'.
8. Bodl. English ms 132, 1–18. For one of the few changes in meaning, see note 4 above.
9. See Chapter 7, p. 74 and Chapter 12, p. 142 for further discussion of Gwyn's *Memoirs*.
10. TT E127 28.
11. TT E420 35.
12. The term was coined by Eliot Warburton in his *Memoirs of Prince Rupert and the Cavaliers* (1849).
13. Wiltshire CRO 413/444Ai.
14. Ibid., ii.
15. See Chapter 6, pp. 63–4.
16. The principal criticisms of Clarendon's objectivity are to be found in Firth, 'Clarendon's History of the Great Rebellion'; Wanklyn, 'The King's Armies in the West of England 1642–46', University of Manchester MA; and Hutton, 'Clarendon's History of the Great Rebellion'.
17. e.g. Barratt, *The Battle for York* and Roberts, *First Newbury 1643*.
18. Cholmley, 'Memorials', p. 348. See also Chapter 10, p. 112.
19. Carlyle (ed.), *Cromwell's Letters and Speeches*, vol. 1, p. 289 claims knowledge of the Scots army's march into Lancashire before it had been agreed by the Duke of Hamilton and his Council of War. See also Chapter 17, p. 193.
20. TT E69 10.
21. Bruce and Masson (eds), *Manchester's Quarrel*, pp. 63–4; CSP Domestic 1644–5, p. 75. The explanation was disseminated more widely by the editor of one of the London weekly journals, probably for the same reason (TT E22 10).
22. TT E54 19.
23. Bodl. Carte ms XII, 223. The transcription in Thomas Carte's *Original Documents and Papers*, pp. 55–7, appears to be completely accurate, but the manuscript volume is too tightly bound for some words to be read.
24. See, for example, Chapter 4, p. 40, Chapter 10, pp. 113–14 and Chapter 14, p. 165.
25. TT E69 15.
26. Warburton, *Memoirs of Prince Rupert*, vol. 2, p. 163; Carte (ed.), *Original Documents and Papers*, vol. 1, pp. 20–3.

27. Bodl. Clarendon ms 28; Walker, *Historical Discourses*, p. 125.
28. Shropshire CRO 455/278.
29. HMC Ormond ms n.s. II, 380–4; Roe, *Military Memoir*.
30. BL Lansdowne ms 988, 205–6.
31. Laing (ed.), *Letters and Journals of Robert Baillie*, vol. 2, p. 209.
32. CSP Domestic 1644–5, pp. 75, 76–7; Holmes, *Eastern Association*, pp. 206–7.
33. Sir Robert Walsh's account of Edgehill was also probably published in Holland. (Young, *Edgehill*, pp. 292–4.)
34. Wiltshire CRO 413/444A, i, 59; Warburton, *Memoirs of Prince Rupert*, vol. 3, p. 31; Morrah, *Prince Rupert of the Rhine*, p. 170.
35. Wanklyn and Jones, *Military History of the English Civil War*, pp. 223–4; Bodl. Tanner ms 62, 232.
36. See Chapter 10, p. 110, n 8.
37. See, for example, the period given in full in Chapter 6, p. 65 which describes itself as a model of clarity.
38. Young, *Marston Moor*, p. 236.
39. This was the practice in the earlier volumes of the appendices to the reports of the Historical Manuscripts Commission. Charles Murray's account of the Second Battle of Newbury discussed in Chapter 12 (HMC 4th Report, p. 297) provides a good example of a battle narrative treated in this way.
40. Warburton, *Memoirs of Prince Rupert*, vol. 3, pp. 29–30; BL Additional ms 18981, 312.
41. The earliest complete text, early eighteenth century in date, is BL Lansdowne ms 988, 205–6.
42. Money, *The Battles of Newbury*, pp. 33–6.
43. Reid, *All the King's Armies*; Wheeler, *The Irish and British Wars*.
44. R.F. Hunniset, *Editing Records for Publication*, Archives and the User 4, British Records Association (1977).
45. Carlyle (ed.), *Cromwell's Letters and Speeches*; Warburton, *Memoirs of Prince Rupert*.
46. *Inventories of Worcestershire Landed Gentry 1536–1786*, Worcestershire Historical Society n.s. 16 (1998).
47. See Chapter 3, p. 29.
48. His map of Berkshire covers both the Newbury battlefields.
49. See Chapter 14, p. 169 and Plate 14.
50. BL Additional ms 16370, 57–63; Young, 'The Royalist Army at Edgehill'.
51. Foard, *Naseby*, pp. 210–18.
52. Hampshire CRO 53 M67/1.
53. Warwickshire CRO CR2917, C10, 135.
54. See in Chapter 8, for example, a discussion of the value of the tithe maps of Bramdean, Cheriton and Hinton Ampner to the study of the battlefield of Cheriton.
55. Foard, *Naseby*; Scott, Turton and Von Arni, *Edgehill*. See also Chapter 4, p. 37 and Chapter 15, pp. 182–3.
56. Foard's narrative of the closing stages of the battle is accepted without question by Reid in *All the King's Armies* and further developed by Marix Evans, Burton and Westaway in *Naseby: June 1645*.
57. Pistol shot, being of a smaller calibre, are said to be more likely to have decayed away to nothing, but their comparative rarity maybe a function of the infrequency with which pistols were fired. Their short range meant that from mid-1643 at the latest they were reserved for the mêlée, and there would have been no opportunity to reload in such circumstances.
58. Newman, *Marston Moor 1644*, pp. 3–4, 94.
59. See below, Chapter 14, for a fuller discussion of the distribution of finds on the Naseby battlefield.
60. It may seem odd to describe the results of practical exercises as a primary source, but re-enactment follows on logically from discussion of field archaeology and it has no other obvious home.
61. Less use has been made of experimental archaeology in examining how cavalry fought. The reason for this is primarily the problem of assembling large bodies of cavalry in the twenty-first century. However, re-enactors must be praised for reminding everybody of the crucial importance of cavalry remaining in close order when charging an enemy which had some battle experience and was still in formation.
62. Bodl. Clarendon ms 1738, 5; TT E69 15. For the Trained Bands, see Chapter 6, note 1.
63. Something of this nature may have happened on the Allied right wing at Marston Moor.

Chapter 3. Civil War Battles: Narrative

1. My own choice of the analogy between the jeweller and the historian probably derives from my family background, but I have a shrewd suspicion that I have seen a somewhat similar metaphor elsewhere in a text explaining the postmodernists' critique of the aspirations of historians to reconstruct the past.
2. Roy and Porter, *A Century of History at King's*.
3. Gardiner, *History of the Great Civil War*, vol. 1, p. 378.
4. e.g. Young and Holmes, *English Civil Wars*, pp. 199–200; Barratt, *The Battle for York*, pp. 124–7; Kitson, *Prince Rupert*, p. 195. See also Chapter 11, pp. 127–8.

5. Hobbes, *Leviathan*, Part 1, ch. 30.
6. Scott, Turton and Von Arni, *Edgehill*, pp. xi–xiii.
7. See Chapter 5, pp. 42–3.
8. For the untypical way in which Foard largely ignores the principal written sources when explaining his contention that the Royalist infantry made a fighting retreat from the battlefield at Naseby, see Chapter 15, pp. 182–3.
9. See pp. 42–3 for two contrasting judgements concerning the shape of the Royalist infantry formation at the start of the Battle of Edgehill.
10. Wanklyn, 'Royalist Strategy'. A fuller appraisal is to be found in Wanklyn and Jones, *Military History of the English Civil War*, pp. 92–4, 125–8.
11. Reid, *All the King's Armies*, pp. 150–1.
12. See Chapter 11, p. 129.
13. Reid, *All the King's Armies*, p. 151.
14. TT E54 19. See also Chapter 11, p. 134. The incident described in Stewart's account probably took place much later in the battle during mopping up operations.
15. See for example Chapter 2, p. 15.
16. Markham, *The Great Lord Fairfax*, p. 173; Gardiner, *History of the Great Civil War*, vol. 1, pp. 380–1.
17. An honourable exception is Barratt, *The Battle for York*.
18. Fuller, *Worthies of England*, p. 641; Maseres (ed.), *Select Tracts*, vol. 1, pp. 437–8.
19. Reid, *All the King's Armies*; Roberts, *First Newbury 1643*; Barratt, *First Battle of Newbury*. The Diary is discussed in Chapter 2, p. 10.
20. I am most grateful to Martin Marix Evans for introducing me to a useful term to describe what I had recommended to students in seminar ever since we first began reconstructing what happened at the Battle of Cheriton as an aid to learning in the early 1980s. The perils of not adopting the timeline approach to reconstructing what happened in a complex battle are to be found in the confused description of the fighting at Naseby in Marshall's *Oliver Cromwell, Soldier*, which is in many other respects the best informed military biography of the Lord Protector we have to date. Similarly Reid uncharacteristically failed to establish a timeline for the Battle of Preston with the result that the Duke of Hamilton's reversal of his decision to halt the crossing of Preston Bridge comes not when Langdale first came under heavy attack in the position covering the Clitheroe road, but when Cromwell's horse were already storming through the streets of the town (*All the King's Armies*, pp. 229–30).
21. The best example of this is in Walter Yonge's account of the first battle-winning move taken by the Parliamentary commanders at the Battle of Cheriton as given by Sir Arthur Haselrig to the House of Commons. He places it at 4 p.m., everybody else at about midday (BL Additional ms 18779, 87).
22. It has been suggested that we should not expect seventeenth-century witnesses to be anything other than very vague in their expressions of time, but it is wrong to think that the generals and their staff would not have had some kind of timepiece in their possession. Moreover, the precise way in which they write about time should give us confidence that they were not simply plucking figures out of the air, and that concrete notions such as 3 o'clock or 5 o'clock would have some significance in their readers' minds.
23. TT E69 15. See also Chapter 6, pp. 74–6.
24. TT E126 24, E70 10; Sprigg, *Anglia Rediviva*, pp. 38–43.
25. TT E54 19.
26. See, for example, Scott, Turton and Von Arni, *Edgehill*, pp. 52–3.
27. Young and Holmes, *English Civil Wars*, pp. 199–200; Shropshire CRO 455/278. Kitson takes exactly the same line citing Young's earlier book on Marston Moor as his evidence (Kitson, *Prince Rupert*, p. 195).
28. The origin of this tradition in writing about Civil War battles seems to lie in the series of monographs published by Roundway Press in the 1970s. It is not a feature of the writings of Gardiner, Burne or Woolrych.
29. See, for example, the complex account of the fight between Cromwell's and Rupert's cavalry at Marston Moor in Marshall's, *Oliver Cromwell, Soldier*.
30. See Chapter 5, p. 43 for a discussion of a situation in which the collateral evidence is not strong enough to convert opinion into fact.
31. Burne, *Battlefields of England*, pp. xix–xx.
32. See Chapter 7, pp. 66–7.
33. e.g. Seymour, *Battles in Britain*, vol. 2, p. 75.
34. Roberts, *First Newbury 1643*, p. 91.
35. Tincey, *Marston Moor*, p. 6.
36. After the draft of this chapter had been written I found to my great surprise that Scott, Turton and Von Arni had devised a set of protocols and included it in the appendix to their book on Edgehill. Theirs, however, relate primarily to the investigation of the landscape.

Chapter 4. The Battle of Edgehill: Context, Landscape and Sources

1. Gough, *History of Myddle*, pp. 39–40.
2. Malcolm, 'A King in Search of Soldiers', pp. 257–68; Wanklyn and Young, ' "A King in Search of Soldiers": A Rejoinder', pp. 147–54.
3. Wanklyn and Jones, *Military History of the English Civil War*, pp. 42–8.
4. TT E124 26; E126 13, 38; E128 20.
5. Scott, Turton and Von Arni, *Edgehill*, p. 73.
6. This was too small a space for Essex's army to deploy in a linear formation, and may explain why his infantry were deployed with two brigades in front and one behind.
7. TT E128 20; E126 38. See Plates 1 and 2.
8. Unfortunately, it is most unlikely that field archaeology will be able to identify the exact position of the various components of the infantry battle. For much of the last century the whole of the hill was occupied by a Royal Ordnance depot, and as a result much of the topsoil was disturbed by building operations. An archaeological survey of the battlefield by the Battlefields Trust supported by the Local Heritage Initiative and managed by Glenn Foard, which will complete its work in 2006, has, however, discovered much of interest, as indicated by the interim report on the Battlefields Trust website (www.Battlefieldstrust.com).
9. The Battlefields Trust website has the armies deployed roughly north–south. This is an improvement on previous depictions, but it should not have Essex's army drawn up diagonally across the little round hill, which would have weakened a position which was already not that strong.
10. BL Harleian ms 3783, 60.
11. The only ditch marked on the pre-enclosure map of Radway, Green Ditch, was just to the north-west of the village (Warwickshire CRO, CR 1596). Old enclosures are clearly marked some way to the north of the Kineton–Banbury road on a map of Oxhill drawn in 1796 prior to the enclosure of the rest of the parish (ibid., CR 1134/1). Beyond them on either side was open land. The land adjacent to the road was portrayed as lowland heath in Yates's map of Warwickshire of 1789. The only lowland heath in Radway parish was a narrow ribbon comprising no more than 100 acres that followed the Radway brook (ibid., CR 1596).
12. e.g. Reid, *All the King's Armies*, p. 22; Young and Holmes, *English Civil Wars*, p. 75.
13. See Plate 3, which is taken from the Radway to Gaydon road looking in a north-easterly direction. This is the landscape across which the Royal Lifeguard would have passed if they had been deployed to the east of the Kineton–Banbury road.
14. BL Harleian ms 3783, 60; TT E124 26; Warwickshire CRO, CR 1596; Bodl. English ms 132, 14.
15. Carte (ed.), *Original Documents and Papers*, vol. 1, p. 9; TT E126 24.
16. Bodl. English ms 132, 14; TT E126 4, 38.
17. TT E124 32.
18. HMC Ormond ms n.s. II, 376, 379–81, 385; Davies, 'The Battle of Edgehill', p. 31n. See further discussion of Bellasis's memoirs in Chapters, 3, 6 and 14.
19. TT E126 24, 26.
20. Clarke (ed.), *Life of James II*, p. 13; Wiltshire CRO 413/444A, i and ii.
21. Hinton's Memoirs, reproduced in Ellis (ed.), *Original Letters*, 4th series, vol. 3, pp. 299–300.
22. Wiltshire CRO 413/444Ai, 21–4; ii, 9; Clarendon, *History of the Great Rebellion*, book 6, 85–6 and p. 79n.
23. Clarke (ed.), *Life of James II*, pp. 9–18.
24. TT E53 10; Young, *Edgehill*, p. 293. (Young's transcription of Walsh's *True Narrative* has been checked against the version in the British Library, which contains nothing else of substance on Sir Robert's Civil War career post-Edgehill.)
25. Ludlow, *Memoirs*, vol. 1, pp. 41–5; TT E126 38. Worden's *Roundhead Reputations* (2001) includes a radical critique of the latter part of the *Memoirs*, showing how the original was rewritten by Ludlow's editor to suit the political climate of the 1690s. Unfortunately, the manuscript covering Ludlow's Civil War career against which the printed version can be checked for editorial intervention no longer appears to exist, and so my comments are grounded on critical analysis of the text, not cross-reference.
26. Bodl. English ms 132, 12–13.
27. Young, 'The Royalist Army at Edgehill', p. 56; Wiltshire CRO 413/444A, i 22.
28. See pp. 45–6.
29. See Chapter 3 for further discussion of this point.
30. See p. 45 for a discussion of the possibility that the Earl of Northampton's regiment may have been elsewhere.
31. Young, *Edgehill*, pp. 224–6; TT E126 13.

Chapter 5. The Battle of Edgehill: Narrative

1. The original is in the Royal Library at Windsor Castle, but there is a photograph of it in Young, 'The Royalist Army at Edgehill' and in his book, *Edgehill* published by Roundway Press. The illustration faces p. 56.

2. TT E124 26; HMC Ormond ms n.s. II, 380.

3. Scott, Turton and Von Arni, *Edgehill*, pp. 109–10.

4. TT E124 26.

5. See Plate 2, a photograph of the little hill in profile from the south-west.

6. I read the three words 'appeared to us' as meaning 'what we could see', not 'what seemed to be'. The meaning of the phrase 'all in front' is not completely clear, but it is difficult to see it signifying anything other than 'in a single line', the formation described by King James II in his account of the battle. It certainly cannot be read as 'in more than one line' (Clarke (ed.), *Life of James II*, p. 11).

7. TT E126 38. See also Plate 19, which shows the ridge about a quarter of a mile to the west of Radway.

8. In their recent book on Edgehill, Scott, Turton and Von Arni present a most interesting hypothesis as to how the regiments were drawn up within the brigade. The authors make appropriate use of material from contemporary military manuals and inherent military probability as suggested in Chapter 3 above, and the end result is very convincing (Scott, Turton and Von Arni, *Edgehill*, pp. 58–9). I cannot, however, agree with their view that the van and the middle brigade were drawn up in a line with no gap between them and with some troops of cavalry behind the middle brigade (ibid., p. 67). If this had been the case, the cavalry would have been swept away when the middle brigade broke and ran early in the battle. Instead they played a pivotal role in turning near disaster into near victory as the afternoon wore on.

9. TT E126 1; Rushworth (ed.), *Historical Collections*, vol. 4, pp. 35–9.

10. Bodl. English ms 132, 13; Warwick, *Memoirs*, p. 253; Young, *Edgehill*, p. 213. The troop numbers are taken from Young's *Edgehill*.

11. TT E126 38; Clarke (ed.), *Life of James II*, p. 12; CSP Domestic 1641–3, p. 393.

12. TT E126 38.

13. Essex and Balfour's regiments had six troops each, but Oliver Cromwell's troop belonging to Essex's regiment was some miles behind the army when the battle commenced. Fielding's regiment may also have had six troops but only four troop commanders are known. Sir Samuel Luke's troop, which was unregimented, is described in one account as having fought well. It would also therefore probably have been on the right wing (TT E124 33; E126 13, 38).

14. See pp. 51–2. The composition of Balfour's force is problematic. The lowest estimate based on troop commanders specifically singled out as doing well is four troops of Balfour's own regiment, the highest eleven troops comprising the whole of Balfour's regiment and all of Essex's regiment apart from Cromwell's troop.

15. Ludlow, *Memoirs*, vol. 1, pp. 42–3; TT E126 38.

16. Bodl. English ms 132, 13.

17. TT E124 22; E126 38; E242 2.

18. Reid, *All the King's Armies*, p. 21; Scott, Turton and Von Arni, *Edgehill*, pp. 70–1.

19. TT E 124 21; E126 13; E127 27.

20. TT E124 14, 32; E126 38; E240 46; E242 2.

21. Young, 'The Royalist Army at Edgehill', p. 58; TT E126 38; CRO, Quarter Sessions files, Trinity 1662, 167, 169; Michaelmas 1662, 94–6.

22. Bodl. English ms 132, 13; BL Harleian ms 3783, 60; TT E124 18; Clarke (ed.), *Life of James II*, p. 11.

23. Bodl. English ms 132, 13; Carte (ed.), *Original Documents and Papers*, vol. 1, p. 10; Clarendon, *History of the Great Rebellion*, book 6, 84.

24. TT E128 20.

25. The factuality of this statement has been recently questioned on the grounds that it only occurs in Rupert's Diary written many years later, and that Lord Clarendon does not mention it. However, the point is also made in general terms in the Royalist Official Account of the battle, by implication in Walsingham's biography of Sir John Smith, and categorically in Bernard Stuart's letter written within two days of the battle. It should also be understood that Clarendon's hatred of Prince Rupert is displayed in the passive as well as an active sense, that is, not only by what he chose to write but also by what he chose to exclude. Clarendon was determined that the world should know that it was the Royalist cavalry that were responsible for nearly losing the battle for the king through their lack of control. Mentioning Byron's mistake would only have redounded to the Prince's credit (Scott, Turton and Von Arni, *Edgehill*, p. 95; TT E126 24; E53 10; BL Harleian ms 3783, 60; Clarendon, *History of the Great Rebellion*, book 6, 85–6).

26. Clarendon, *History of the Great Rebellion*, book 6, 85–6; TT E126 24; Warwick, *Memoirs*, p. 253; Clarke (ed.), *Life of James II*, p. 13.

27. Wiltshire CRO 413/444A, i 22–3; 413/444, ii 9; Clarendon, *History of the Great Rebellion*, book 6, 84.
28. TT E124 20, 26, 32, 33; E126 38.
29. Scott, Turton and Von Arni, *Edgehill*, pp. 112–18.
30. TT E124 26.
31. Carte (ed.), *Original Documents and Papers*, vol. 1, p. 10; TT E126 24; BL Harleian ms 3783, 60. Rupert's Diary claims that Caernarvon's regiment routed a regiment of enemy foot, presumably Fairfax's, as it was the regiment nearest to the enemy infantry formation (Wiltshire CRO 413/422A, ii 9).
32. TT E53 10; Wiltshire CRO 413/444A, i 23; Clarke (ed.), *Life of James II*, p. 13.
33. TT E124 26; E126 24, 38.
34. TT E126 38; Scott, Turton and Von Arni, *Edgehill*, pp. 103–4. The evidence comes from a Royalist account of the battle, not a Parliamentary one, as is implied.
35. Warwick, *Memoirs*, p. 252.
36. There were six or seven troops in Balfour's regiment, but only four are mentioned by name as taking part in the battle – those of Major Hurry and Captains Nathaniel Fiennes, Sir Arthur Haselrig and Lord Grey (TT E124 32, 33; E126 38).
37. He could not 'tell what they did unless they went directly to Kineton to plunder our carriages without charging our army at all'. This shows that his troop must have been well away from the line of approach to Kineton from the left wing of the Royalist army and well to the west of the hill on which Essex's army deployed (TT E126 38).
38. e.g. Reid, *All the King's Armies*, p. 22; Scott, Turton and Von Arni, *Edgehill*, p. 88.
39. TT E126 38.
40. TT E124 32; E126 13, 26, 33, 38; Young, *Edgehill*, p. 307; Carte (ed.), *Original Documents and Papers*, vol. 1, p. 10.
41. TT E53 10.
42. Warwick, *Memoirs*, p. 252; Clarke (ed.), *Life of James II*, p. 13; Clarendon, *History of the Great Rebellion*, book 6, 86; TT E53 10.
43. The official Parliamentary account describes Balfour's group's first charge as taking place 'in the beginning of the day' (TT E124 26).
44. Carte (ed.), *Original Documents and Papers*, vol. 1, p. 10.
45. TT E124 26, 33; Young, *Edgehill*, plate 9.
46. In fact he was wrong. Essex's orange coats were not in the van but in the reserve brigade (TT E124 26).
47. Clarendon, *History of the Great Rebellion*, 78. It is significant that Warwick did not mention Lindsey's discomforture, whilst Bulstrode has him happily agreeing to let Ruthven set out the army in the Swedish style. Young and Holmes, and Scott, Turton and Von Arni accept Clarendon's account, but not Reid.
48. Bodl. English ms 132, 13–14; HMC Ormond ms n.s. II, 379. James puts in Lindsey's mouth words very similar to those reported by Clarendon, who was his father-in-law, but directed against Ruthven, not Rupert (Clarke (ed.), *Life of James II*, p. 10).
49. Van Creveld, *Command in War*, pp. 51–4.
50. Clarke (ed.), *Life of James II*, p. 12; HMC Ormond ms n.s. II, 380; TT E124 26.
51. A systematic survey is now taking place of all the accessible parts of the Edgehill battlefield, but no substantial concentrations of musket balls seem to have been found on the traditional site.
52. TT E124 26; E126 38.
53. Young, *Edgehill*, plate 9; Bodl. Ashmole ms 830, 292; Staffordshire CRO Leveson letterbook 2, 67.
54. One ex-soldier, Richard Thomason of Tattenhall who fought in Fitton's own company, mentions Edgehill together with a number of later engagements when describing his wounds, but his two petitions are too vaguely worded for the reader to be anywhere near certain on which occasions he was wounded (Cheshire CRO Quarter Sessions files, Easter 1672, 137–8; Michaelmas 1673, 113). See p. 54 for the task that Fitton's regiment probably performed.
55. Scott, Turton and Von Arni place the Royalist heavy cannon on Edgehill itself at Bullet Hill, the easternmost point of the ridge (*Edgehill*, pp. 25, 80). This cannot be so. Both Royalist and Parliamentary sources describe the king's cannons' descent of the hill prior to the battle, whereas the *Official Parliamentary Account* has Balfour's force encountering the king's biggest artillery piece, a demi-cannon, immediately behind the Royalist foot (TT E124 26, 33; E126 4, 38; Carte (ed.), *Original Documents and Papers*, vol. 1, pp. 10, 11).
56. TT E124 26, 32; E126 38; Young, *Edgehill*, pp. 217–19, 221–3. That some kind of misunderstanding occurred is acknowledged by Clarendon (*History of the Great Rebellion*, book 2, 353n., book 6, p. 79n.).
57. Carte (ed.), *Original Documents and Papers*, vol. 1, p. 11. However, care must be taken with this source. It was the last in the series of Royalist accounts of the battle written in its immediate aftermath, and on this and another occasion – its account of Balfour's force being missed by Wilmot because it was 'in the corner of the field undiscovered, and so uncharged' – it reads more like a mature reflection or rationalization of what happened rather than a direct observation.

58. TT E124 26; E126 38.
59. Some of the shorter Royalist and Parliamentary accounts run the two together, but the incident involving the Royal Lifeguard recounted by Fiennes could not have taken place as described if there had not been a pause in the action.
60. TT E124 26, 33; E126 38; E127 27; E128 8; HMC Ormond ms n.s. II, 380; Young, *Edgehill*, pp. 131, 225–6.
61. TT E124 26; E126 4; Young, *Edgehill*, plate 9; Clarendon, *History of the Great Rebellion*, book 6, 94; Walsh, 'True Narration and Manifest', in Young, *Edgehill*, pp. 293–4. This appears to have been the Royalist artillery park that was temporarily overrun by Balfour earlier in the day.
62. Some historians refer to there being a hedge in front of Gerard's new position. There is indeed a hedge along the Radway brook on the map of 1754, but the reference to a hedge in the only contemporary account to mention one is part of a metaphor, not a description of a feature in the landscape (Warwickshire CRO, CR 1596; TT E126 38).
63. The big weakness of this hypothesis is that the heavy artillery with a flat trajectory would have fired into the rear of the Royalist infantry. Possibly they could have overcome this by elevating the barrels, and this may explain why one source describes the Royalist cannon balls as burying themselves in the soil instead of executing a series of bounces (TT E126 13). The alternative, leaving a gap between the third and the fourth or the fourth and the fifth infantry brigades through which the cannon balls could pass, seems highly unlikely.
64. See Chapter 7, p. 77.
65. HMC Ormond ms n.s. II, 380; Clarke (ed.), *Life of James II*, p. 13; TT E124 26; E126 38; Staffordshire CRO Leveson Letterbook 2, 67. The inscription on Sir Edward's tomb describes him as guarding the king's artillery.
66. Scott, Turton and Von Arni, *Edgehill*, p. 138.
67. Young, *Edgehill*, p. 123. Those who followed have been much less cautious (e.g. Reid, *All the King's Armies*, p. 26).
68. Young, *Edgehill*, pp. 221–2.
69. HMC Ormond ms n.s. II, 380; TT E124 26; E128 20; Clarke (ed.), *Life of James II*, p. 14; Reid, *Sir Thomas Tildesley*, p. 4.
70. Earwaker, *East Cheshire*, vol. 2, p. 584n.
71. TT E126 38, 39.
72. TT E124 26.
73. TT E124 26; E126 38; E53 10; Clarendon, *History of the Great Rebellion*, book 6, 86; Walsh, 'True Narration and Manifest', reprinted in Young, *Edgehill*, pp. 292–4.
74. Firth, *Cromwell*, pp. 84–5; Clarendon, *History of the Great Rebellion*, book 6, 86; Young, *Edgehill*, p. 308; TT E126 1, 38.

Chapter 6. The First Battle of Newbury: Context, Landscape and Sources

1. The Trained Bands were civilians who had received training in drill and in the use of arms so that they could serve as a local defence force for the counties and the larger towns. They were in continuous existence from the middle of Queen Elizabeth I's reign.
2. Wanklyn and Jones, *Military History of the English Civil War*, chs 6–10.
3. TT E69 10; E250 14; Wiltshire CRO 413/444Ai, 40; Rocque, Berkshire, 1759; Ogilby, *Britannia*, plate 81.
4. BL Additional ms 18980, 120; TT E70 10.
5. See Plate 4. It would almost certainly have been less wooded in the seventeenth century.
6. TT E70 10; Clarendon, *History of the Great Rebellion*, book 7, 210.
7. TT E69 10, 12.
8. Reid, *All the King's Armies*, p. 61; Roberts, *First Newbury 1643*, pp. 63–4; Kitson, *Prince Rupert*, p. 150; all of which to varying degrees lay emphasis on small enclosures and narrow lanes bordered by earthen banks and hedges.
9. Rocque, *Berkshire*, sheet 4; BL Additional ms 18980, 120.
10. The first edition of the one inch to the mile Ordnance Survey Map of England, sheet 78. Roberts, mistakenly, portrays Trundle Hill as part of the crescent (*First Newbury 1643*, p. 74).
11. TT E69 12.
12. TT E69 10; E70 10.
13. TT E69 12; E250 14.
14. See Chapter 12, p. 140 for further discussion of the physical characteristics of the north bank.
15. Kitson, *Prince Rupert*, p. 150.

16. TT E69 10. The identity of the author is not absolutely certain, but it seems utterly improbable that anybody else would have spent so much space in the section on the engagement at Aldbourne Chase describing a minor injury suffered by Lord Digby!

17. See, for example, the appraisal of Royalist sources on the Battle of Naseby in Chapter 14.

18. Clarendon, *History of the Great Rebellion*, book 7, 210–12.

19. TT E69 15.

20. Bodl. Clarendon ms 1738, 5.

21. BL Additional ms 18980, 120. The author was Thomas, Lord Wentworth. The handwriting is very similar to that of letters written by Wentworth to Rupert earlier in the year (ibid., 66, 67b) and Wentworth was identified by Rupert as commanding the horse in the first attempt to evict Essex's troops from the hill (Wiltshire CRO 413/444Ai, 40–1). Rupert also makes it very clear that the officer was Thomas, not the infantry brigade commander at Edgehill, Henry Wentworth.

22. Bodl. Clarendon ms 1738, 5.

23. Wiltshire CRO 413/444Ai, 40–2; ii 4–5.

24. Walsingham, *Hector Britannicus*, pp. 79–80.

25. HMC Ormond ms n.s. II, 383; Gwyn, *Military Memoirs*, p. 53.

26. Wiltshire CRO 413/444Ai, 41; 413/444Aii, 4–5; TT E70 10.

27. *Mercurius Aulicus*, p. 527 (20 September 1643).

28. TT E70 10.

29. TT E69 2, 12.

30. TT E69 15.

31. Reid, *All the King's Armies*, p. 62; Roberts, *First Newbury 1643*, p. 70.

32. See Chapter 7, pp. 72–6.

33. BL Additional ms 18778, 54.

34. TT E250 14.

35. Codrington, *The Illustrious Robert, Earl of Essex*, pp. 32–5.

36. TT E67 38; E68 3, 5; E69 2, 3, 5, 8, 12, 17, 27; E70 7; E250 14.

37. TT E69 12, 17.

Chapter 7. The First Battle of Newbury: Narrative

1. TT E70 10; E69 10. The number of soldiers who fought at the First Battle of Newbury cannot be estimated with any degree of certainty, but the general consensus is that Essex was stronger in foot and the king in horse. Roberts gives Essex about 8,000 foot and 6,000 horse, but he may underestimate the former and overestimate the latter. He gives the king about 6,000 foot and 8,000 horse, (*First Newbury 1643*, pp. 26–30) but the evidence is tenuous in the extreme. I therefore prefer to follow the example of Young and Holmes by refusing to give numerical estimates for the Royalist horse and foot. All that can be said with any degree of certainty is that some of the king's cavalry regiments were very strong indeed. Sir Thomas Aston's, for example, mustered almost 450 men in August 1643 (BL Additional ms 36913, 135–9).

2. TT E70 10. The actual total was probably eleven, as there is no mention anywhere in the text of the Orange regiment of Trained Band auxiliaries, which was the fifth regiment in the London Trained Band brigade that set out for Gloucester on 23 August.

3. Barratt, *First Battle of Newbury*, p. 135; Seymour, *Battles in Britain*, p. 63; Reid, *All the King's Armies*, p. 62; Roberts, *First Newbury 1643*, p. 70.

4. See p. 73.

5. TT E69 10; E70 10; BL Additional ms 18980, 120.

6. TT E70 10.

7. The old route of the Newbury–Andover road, clearly marked on Rocque's map of Berkshire published in 1759, no longer exists even as a minor road in what used to be the lower part of the common.

8. TT E70 10. The maps that have been used to describe the topography of the battlefield are Rocque's map of Berkshire, published in 1759, and the first editions of the one-inch and six-inch Ordnance Survey Maps. The map printed in Gardiner's *History of the Great Civil War* is not used as it is inaccurate with respect to certain important details concerning the extent of the heath land and the enclosures.

9. An account that confines itself to describing what was happening at the other end of the line of battle claims that Lord Robartes's brigade was the first to engage with the enemy, but the official account places this brigade with the artillery when the fighting began. The confusion was probably caused by the fact that Essex's first name was Robert, and he was often referred to as My Lord Robert or Old Robin (TT E69 15; E70 10).

10. TT E69 15.

11. Reid, *All the King's Armies*, pp. 62, 65; Roberts, *First Newbury 1643*, pp. 74, 82; Barratt, *First Battle of Newbury*, p. 135.

12. See note 37 below for further discussion of their deployment during the battle.
13. TT E69 15, 17.
14. TT E69 12, 15; E70 10; HMC Ormond ms n.s. II, 383. A function of the *Official Account*, and also of Foster's account, was to kill the rumour put forth by one of the London weekly journals that the Trained Band regiments were deployed in open country by mistake. Instead the blame for the heavy losses they had suffered was placed on the officer in charge of the regiments' field artillery, which did not arrive until half an hour after the fighting had begun. No explanation as to why the regiments were placed where they were was given in either account, possibly because it was part and parcel of a tactical manoeuvre that had failed.
15. See Plate 5, which shows the difficulty facing artillery pieces trying to ascend Skinners Green Lane. That Essex's regiment was deployed early in the day on the northern spur is implicit in the *Official Account* and confirmed by the Royalist official account (TT E70 10; E69 10).
16. Other studies of the battle imply that they used Enbourne Street Lane (Reid, *All the King's Armies*, p. 62; Roberts, *First Newbury 1643*, p. 73; Seymour, *Battles in Britain*, p. 61), but if they had done so, they could not have retreated down the lane whence they had come under the cover of friendly fire. The exit from Enbourne Common was well to the rear of the Parliamentary front line, and as a result there would have been no Parliamentary infantry stationed there. Moreover, the Red regiment saw no sign of friendly cavalry anywhere near their position, which was close to where Enbourne and Wash Common met. Stapleton's men would have been able to fall back via Skinners Lane Head in the manner described in the *Official Account*, and this is Barratt's preferred option, but there is no evidence of Parliamentary cavalry being deployed at the top end of the common at any time in Parliamentary accounts of the battle (but see note 34 below). In addition, it is difficult to see how Stapleton could have passed six regiments of horse up Skinners Green Lane at a time when it was also being used to get to Wash Common by infantry regiments and by the artillery train (Barratt, *First Battle of Newbury*, pp. 97–8).
17. TT E70 10.
18. The exception is Sir Frank Kitson, who saw what Essex's intention was in very general terms, but failed to explain how it was to have been achieved (*Prince Rupert*, p. 149).
19. TT E69 10; Clarendon, *History of the Great Rebellion*, book 7, 210–11; TT E70 10. The emphasis is mine.
20. TT E69 10.
21. See Chapter 6, note 21.
22. Wiltshire CRO 413/444Ai, 40; BL Additional ms 18980, 120; Bodl. Clarendon ms 1738, 5. The information about Rupert's movements comes from Wentworth's letter. It must be correct as the letter was addressed to Rupert.
23. BL Additional ms 18980, 120. There is no confirmation of the detail of this report, but given the circumstances in which it was compiled, it is most unlikely that the writer would have invented the basic narrative of the first clash to take place on the northern spur. (See also Chapter 6, p. 64.)
24. BL Additional ms 18980, 120; Bodl. Clarendon ms 1738, 5; Wiltshire CRO 413/444Ai, 41.
25. Aston's regiments and Rupert's regiments must each have been well over 400 strong, and Byron's is unlikely to have been much smaller as it lost 100 men in the encounter; the Prince of Wales's regiment was 800 strong when it left Shrewsbury for the Newbury campaign; Gerard's regiment had at least ten companies and had ninety-nine officers and men killed or wounded at Newbury (Wiltshire CRO 413/444Ai, 42; Bodl. Clarendon ms 1738, 5; BL Additional ms 36913, 145–9; HMC Beaufort ms, 39; BL Harleian ms 6804, 92).
26. Bodl. Clarendon ms 1738, 5; TT E69 17; E70 10; Wiltshire CRO 413/444Ai, 41; HMC Ormond ms n.s. II, 383.
27. This is the suggestion of Young and Holmes, *English Civil Wars*, p. 147.
28. Bodl. Clarendon ms 1738, 5; TT E70 10; BL Additional ms 18980, 120.
29. TT E70 10; E69 10; BL Additional ms 18980, 120; BL Harleian ms 6804, 92.
30. Wiltshire CRO 413/444Ai, 41; TT E69 15; E70 10.
31. Wiltshire CRO 413/444Aii, 4; TT E69 15.
32. TT E70 10. See also note 16 above.
33. TT E69 10.
34. Wiltshire CRO 413/444Aii, 4; TT E70 10; Gwyn, *Military Memoirs*, p. 53. See Chapter 2, pp. 9–10 for my disquiet about Gwyn's narrative.
35. TT E69 10, 12, 15, 17.
36. TT E69 10, 15.
37. The most likely final role of the two Trained Band regiments was to act as support troops. The Parliamentary Official Account states that two regiments of Trained Bands were deployed to protect the artillery early in the afternoon (TT E70 10). It is just possible that the regiments referred to were the Orange auxiliaries, which were present at Newbury but not mentioned in any of the accounts as playing any part in the battle, and the Blue regiment, which appear to have left or been redeployed earlier than

the Red (TT E69 15), but the *Official Account* invariably distinguishes between Trained Bands and Trained Band Auxiliaries.

38. TT E69 15. Foster mentions a body of musketeers from the Red regiment being used to reinforce the forlorn hope, but it is quite clear from the text that this was not Fortescue's force in the Kennet valley, as it fought in the field immediately to the left of the Londoners. See Plate 6 for one of the tumuli as it is today.

39. TT E70 10.

40. Indeed so crowded were they that there would have been insufficient space for them all to have deployed around Skinners Green Lane Head in the conventional manner based on the calculations of the number of men per metre worked out by Foard and others from what was recommended in drill books. (Foard, *Naseby*, pp. 236–42; Scott, Turton and Von Arni, *Edgehill*, Appendix 3). One wonders, therefore, if there would have been a measure of bunching up, as described in the narrative of the Second Battle of Newbury in Chapter 13 below. Certainly Essex was able to rotate regiments and brigades, whilst one of the London weeklies claimed that not 'a third of our foot' was engaged (TT E69 12; E70 10).

41. Wiltshire CRO 413/444Ai, 41–2; ii, 4–5; TT E70 10.

42. Wiltshire CRO 413/444Ai, 41–2; Walsingham, *Hector Britannicus*, pp. 89–90; Bodl. Clarendon ms 1738, 5; TT E68 5; E69 8, 12; E70 10; BL Harleian ms 6804, 92; HMC Ormond ms n.s. II, 383.

43. Roberts, *First Newbury 1643*, p. 82.

44. TT E69 8.

45. TT E70 10.

46. TT E69 12, 15. An account of the long outflanking march by Waller's corps, which preceded the Second Battle of Newbury, described the soldiers as carrying three days' provisions in their knapsacks (TT E256 31).

47. TT E69 15; E70 10; Hopton, *Bellum Civile*, p. 61.

48. TT E69 10; Wiltshire CRO 413/444Ai, 42.

49. Reid, *All the King's Armies*, p. 68n.

50. See note 25 above.

51. TT E69 2, 10, 15; E70 10; Wiltshire CRO 413/444Ai, 42; Clarendon, *History of the Great Rebellion*, book 7, 212.

52. TT E69 15; E70 10.

Chapter 8. The Battle of Cheriton: Context, Sources and Landscape

1. This is implicit in Sir Edward Walker's Official Account of the 1644 campaign (Walker, *Historical Discourses*, p. 7).

2. Hopton described Forth's contingent as 1,200 foot and 800 horse, but two other cavalry regiments totalling about 500 men were ordered to join the generals a few days later one of which certainly fought at Cheriton (Hopton, *Bellum Civile*, p. 77; CSP Domestic 1644, p. 54).

3. Edgar, *Sir Ralph Hopton*, p. 156.

4. Wanklyn and Jones, *Military History of the English Civil War*, pp. 142–3; Hopton, *Bellum Civile*, p. 77; CSP Domestic 1644, 33; HMC Portland ms III, 107.

5. HMC Portland ms III, 107–8.

6. Hopton, *Bellum Civile*, p. 79; Roe, *Military Memoir*, p. 9; TT E40 1.

7. HMC Portland ms III, 106–10.

8. Bodl. Clarendon ms 1738, 6. A printed edition was edited by C. Chadwyck-Healey and published by Somerset Record Society (18: 1902). The transcription is accurate in every respect. However, Chadwyck-Healey failed to indicate which words or groups of words were added to the manuscript subsequently.

9. George Lisle is described as Sir George (ibid., pp. 80, 81) but he was not knighted until December 1645 and the title is not in the form of an addition or correction to the text (New *DNB*). Hopton at the time was in Cornwall commanding what was left of the king's armies in the west of England and cut off from Oxford by 200 miles of enemy-held territory. On both counts it seems most unlikely that the manuscript was completed until after the surrender in the West in March 1646.

10. See p. 86.

11. Hutton acknowledges the debt that Hopton's reputation owed to Clarendon. Only Reid refuses to be taken in by Hopton's reputation and his well-crafted accounts of his campaigns in the south of England (New *DNB*, 60, p. 157: Thomas, Lord Wentworth).

12. Wanklyn and Jones, *Military History of the English Civil War*, pp. 137–9.

13. Bodl. Clarendon ms 1738, 7. This was also transcribed by Chadwyck-Healey and printed in Somerset Record Society 18 (1902). See note 8 above for the accuracy of the transcription. An endorsement shows that it was handed to Clarendon in the spring of 1647 (Edgar, *Sir Ralph Hopton*, p. 230).

14. Clarendon, *History of the Great Rebellion*, book 8, 12, 32, 90. The report in *Mercurius Aulicus* also states that Hopton was in overall command.
15. See Chapter 2, p. 11.
16. This may help to explain why Clarendon made very little use of Hopton's account of the battle itself in the *History of the Great Rebellion*, whilst making extensive use of the rest of his narrative.
17. *Mercurius Aulicus*, p. 911.
18. 'If the rebels went off, the Lord Hopton would go near to be their utter undoing; and if they came on, they would undo themselves ...' (*Mercurius Aulicus*, p. 911); [Lord Forth's opinion] 'was that, having now possessed all the ground of advantage on our side, we should not hazard any further attempt, for that he now conceived that the enemy would now be forced either to charge us upon their disadvantage or retire' (Hopton, *Bellum Civile*, p. 82).
19. TT E53 10.
20. Lloyd, *Memoirs of Excellent Personages*, p. 326.
21. HMC Portland ms III, 106–10.
22. Harley described himself as quartering near (Bishops) Waltham wood. That village is well to the south of Waller's army's line of advance, but a narrow tongue of land belonging to that parish cuts into the chalk downs to south of the Petersfield–Winchester road. In such circumstances the troop would have found itself in the rear when the Parliamentary army deployed to face north towards Alresford rather than west towards Winchester.
23. Roe, *Military Memoir*, pp. 8–11.
24. BL Additional ms 18779, 87.
25. Quoted in Adair, *Cheriton 1644*, pp. 133–4.
26. TT E40 22.
27. Waller did not apparently write an official report on the battle. There is a single reference to Cheriton in his memoirs, which is essentially the autobiography of a soul, but this only asserts that he was directly involved in the thick of the fighting.
28. TT E40 1, 12, 13.
29. TT E40 13.
30. TT E40 1 (E.A.), 12 (Captain John Jones).
31. Slingsby, 'Battle of Alresford', in Chadwyck-Healey (ed.), *Bellum Civile*, p. 103.
32. Hampshire CRO 53M67/1.
33. Hampshire CRO Eccles. II/59492. Taylor's map is adequate but the scale is only one inch to the mile, and so it lacks the detail to be found in contemporary maps by Rocque. It is also inaccurate in certain respects. The road from Petersfield to Winchester between Bramdean and the outskirts of Cheriton, for example, loops too far to the north. This has the effect of distorting the layout of the roads and tracks in the eastern part of Cheriton parish. It also places East Down due east rather than south-east of the northern spur of the arena. Taylor's depiction of Cheriton Wood is discussed below in note 49.
34. Hampshire CRO 21 M65/F7/30, 46, 117, 232.
35. See note 49 below. The portion of Tichbourne parish that fell within the compass of the battlefield was chalk down.
36. Hampshire CRO 21 M65/F7/232 1. See also Plate 9.
37. Cow Down is not mentioned in the 1602 survey (Hampshire CRO 53M67/1).
38. Burne, *Battlefields of England*, pp. 397–8. Burne's map, which delineates the arena, has been used by later writers without alteration.
39. Gardiner, *History of the Great Civil War*, vol. 1, p. 324n.; Burne and Young, *Great Civil War*, p. 125.
40. Hampshire CRO 53M67/1.
41. Five downs and two moors are referred to in the 1602 survey of Cheriton, all apparently in the western part of the parish (Hampshire CRO 53 M67/1).
42. Gardiner, *History of the Great Civil War*, vol. 1, p. 322; TT E40 13; first edition of the Ordnance Survey one inch to the mile map of England, sheet 12.
43. See p. 92.
44. TT E40 1; Hampshire CRO Eccles. II, 49592.
45. Hopton, *Bellum Civile*, pp. 81–2.
46. Ibid., pp. 83–4; Hampshire CRO 53 M67/1.
47. HMC Portland ms III, 108.
48. Adair is absolutely convincing on this (*Cheriton 1644*, p. 196).
49. Seymour, *Battles in Britain*, p. 82. Taylor's practice was to give an impression of woodland, not a clear outline. However, he provides sufficient detail to show that Cheriton Wood abutted onto Alresford Lane, had a similar northern boundary to what it has today by its relationship to the road from Alresford Lane to Gunners Castle, and that it did not stretch much further south than it does today. It may not have extended as far to the east, but this would not have had any impact on the shape of the battle. For further circumstantial evidence, see Chapter 9, note 8.

50. Hopton, *Bellum Civile*, p. 81.
51. Two Royalist accounts describing the fighting in and around Cheriton Wood comment on the open nature of the landscape. As for the Parliamentarians, Secretary Roe's account of Colonel Birch's activities in the same area makes no mention of hedges, and neither does E.A.'s description of the routing of the Royalist cavalry on that wing by Colonel Browne, the commander of the London brigade (Lloyd, *Memoirs of Excellent Personages*, p. 326; Slingsby, 'Battle of Alresford', in Chadwyck-Healey (ed.), *Bellum Civile*, p. 102; TT E40 1, 12; Roe, *Military Memoir*, pp. 10–11).
52. TT E53 10; *Mercurius Aulicus*, p. 910; BL Additional ms 27402, 94; Slingsby, 'Battle of Alresford', in Chadwyck-Healey (ed.), *Bellum Civile*. Bramdean Heath was located between Bramdean and Cheriton Wood. Field name evidence (Hampshire CRO 21 M65/30/1, 2) and Thomas Milne's map of Hampshire place it to the east of Bramdean Lane.
53. Gardiner, *History of the Great Civil War*, vol. 1, p. 322.
54. Burne, *Battlefields of England*, pp. 397–8; Edgar, *Sir Ralph Hopton*, p. 160; Young and Holmes, *English Civil Wars*, pp. 167–8; Reid, *All the King's Armies*, p. 167.
55. Seymour, *Battles in Britain*, vol. 2, p. 75.
56. Adair, *Cheriton 1644*, pp. 127, 195–7. For the present-day appearance of this area, see Plates 7, 8 and 10.
57. In making this decision, Adair may have been led astray by Gardiner's poorly captioned map and by the place name Hinton Marsh into assuming that the western end of the valley was marshy and therefore an impossible location for the principal cavalry action. Adair, *Cheriton 1644*, pp. 127, 195–7.
58. Hopton, *Bellum Civile*, p. 80; BL Additional ms 18779, 87.
59. Young and Holmes, *English Civil Wars*, p. 168.
60. Gardiner, *History of the Great Civil War*, vol. 1, pp. 321–2; Burne, *Battlefields of England*, p. 397; Edgar, *Sir Ralph Hopton*, p. 162; Seymour, *Battles in Britain*, vol. 2, p. 73; Adair, *Cheriton 1644*, pp. 123–4.
61. Hopton, *Bellum Civile*, p. 80. Also see above, p. 92.
62. Hopton, *Bellum Civile*, p. 81.
63. Slingsby, 'Battle of Alresford', in Chadwyck-Healey (ed.), *Bellum Civile*, p. 101.
64. BL Additional ms 27402, 94; TT E40 12.
65. Hampshire CRO 21 M65/30/1, 2. In the survey four fields directly to the south of Cheriton Wood in Bramdean parish were given a name that included the word Down.
66. See note 51 above.
67. Foard, 'The Archaeology of Attack', p. 9. I am grateful to Charles Singleton for this reference. A telephone conversation with Alan Turton confirmed that the findings are not yet in print.
68. Adair, *Cheriton 1644*; TT E40 13; Lloyd, *Memoirs of Excellent Personages*, p. 326.
69. TT E40 13. See also Plate 10.
70. Slingsby, 'Battle of Alresford', in Chadwyck-Healey (ed.), *Bellum Civile*, pp. 100, 101.

Chapter 9. The Battle of Cheriton: Narrative

1. Hopton, *Bellum Civile*, p. 77 (2,800); CSP Domestic 1644, p. 54 (the regiments of Lord Percy and Thomas Howard, 'near 500 horse effective'); Adair, *Cheriton 1644*, p. 113. Adair accepts Haselrig's estimate of 3,000 Parliamentary cavalry, which seems a realistic total for sixty-six troops of horse. Also, Sir Arthur was Waller's cavalry commander, and should therefore have been well informed.
2. Adair, *Cheriton 1644*, pp. 113, 181–9; BL Additional ms 18779, 87.
3. Hopton, *Bellum Civile*, p. 77; BL Additional ms 27402, 95–6; Luke, *Journals*, vol. 3, pp. 264–5.
4. TT E40 13; Roe, *Military Memoir*, p. 10.
5. HMC Portland ms III, 108; TT E40 1; Roe, *Military Memoir*, p. 10. See Chapter 8, pp. 91–2 for a discussion of its location.
6. Hopton, *Bellum Civile*, p. 81; Slingsby, 'Battle of Alresford', in Chadwyck-Healey (ed.), *Bellum Civile*, p. 101; TT E53 10. The rank is an odd one for a cavalry officer. Possibly this term rather than commissary general was being used to indicate the second in command of the cavalry, or else he was merely brigade major.
7. Hopton, *Bellum Civile*, pp. 81–2. The detail of this account of the operations in and around Cheriton Wood is drawn very largely from Hopton's account, but his narrative is supported in general terms by Slingsby, E.A. and Haselrig, and it makes sense from a landscape point of view.
8. The traditional position for Hopton's cannon is at Gunners Castle at the north-eastern corner of Cheriton Wood and at a considerable distance from the battlefield. Gunners Castle would have been accessible via Cow Down Lane, which leaves Bramdean Lane several hundred yards to the north of the wood. It is marked on Isaac Taylor's map of 1759 and the variety of bushes making up the hedgerows lining it suggest very strongly that the lane was there in 1644. However, if the wood was as large then as it is today, the cannon would have been very poorly placed for bombarding an enemy lining the western edge of the wood. If, however, the wood had been smaller in 1644, as suggested in Chapter 8, Gunners Castle would have made much more sense as an artillery position.

9. Hopton, *Bellum Civile*, pp. 81–2; TT E40 1; HMC Portland ms III, 108; Slingsby, 'Battle of Alresford', in Chadwyck-Healey (ed.), *Bellum Civile*, p. 101.
10. TT E40 13; BL Additional ms 18779, 87. See Plate 10. A Royalist account describes the enemy cavalry as being drawn up in nine squadrons, probably in echelon formation, a well-tried way of ensuring mutual support (Slingsby, 'Battle of Alresford', in Chadwyck-Healey (ed.), *Bellum Civile*, p. 101).
11. Slingsby, 'Battle of Alresford', in Chadwyck-Healey (ed.), *Bellum Civile*, p. 102; HMC Portland ms III, 108.
12. Hopton, *Bellum Civile*, p. 82; Slingsby, 'Battle of Alresford', in Chadwyck-Healey (ed.), *Bellum Civile*, p. 101; TT E40 12.
13. TT E40 13; HMC Portland ms III, 108. See also Chapter 8, pp. 91–2.
14. Hopton, *Bellum Civile*, p. 82; Slingsby, 'Battle of Alresford', in Chadwyck-Healey (ed.), *Bellum Civile*, p. 101.
15. Slingsby, 'Battle of Alresford', in Chadwyck-Healey (ed.), *Bellum Civile*, p. 102; BL Harleian ms 986, 79; HMC Portland ms III, 108–9; BL Additional ms 18779, 87; TT E53 10.
16. HMC Portland ms III, 108–9; Slingsby, 'Battle of Alresford', in Chadwyck-Healey (ed.), *Bellum Civile*, pp. 101–2; Hopton, *Bellum Civile*, p. 82; *Mercurius Aulicus*, p. 911; TT E40 13; BL Additional ms 18779, 87.
17. This was the task of the regiment of Lord Percy, the General of Artillery in the king's field army. That regiment was not present at Cheriton, but Percy's and Bard's regiments had been brigaded together in the past, as they had both marched down from the north in May 1643 escorting a convoy of ammunition (BL Harleian ms 986, 79; *Mercurius Aulicus*, p. 256).
18. Slingsby, 'Battle of Alresford', in Chadwyck-Healey (ed.), *Bellum Civile*, p. 103; Hopton, *Bellum Civile*, p. 83.
19. TT E40 13. The foolhardiness of sending cavalry against such a strong defensive position was apparently drawn to Lord Forth's attention by Sir John Smith, but we only have Walsingham's word for it (TT E53 10).
20. Slingsby, 'Battle of Alresford', in Chadwyck-Healey (ed.), *Bellum Civile*, p. 102; Hopton, *Bellum Civile*, p. 83.
21. See Chapter 7, p. 77.
22. I am suspicious of Walsingham's allegation that, as Smith was killed by a cuirassier, he must have come up against Sir Arthur Haselrig's regiment in Waller's brigade, which were on the left of the Parliamentary line. At Edgehill Sir William Balfour's Lifeguard were also armoured as cuirassiers (TT E53 10; Scott, Turton and Von Arni, *Edgehill*, p. 99).
23. Hopton, *Bellum Civile*, p. 82; Slingsby, 'Battle of Alresford', in Chadwyck-Healey (ed.), *Bellum Civile*, pp. 102–3; TT E53 10; E40 12; HMC Portland ms III, 109. Another contemporary Parliamentary account of the battle used by Godwin, which I have been unable to trace, claims that 'the ground the enemy horse stood upon was so uneven that they could not march in any order' (*Civil War in Hampshire*, p. 181).
24. Slingsby, 'Battle of Alresford', in Chadwyck-Healey (ed.), *Bellum Civile*, p. 101; TT E40 1. Thomas Juxon in his contemporary chronicle of events claimed that Balfour's horse were defeated. The source of his information cannot be identified, but Juxon's hatred of the Earl of Essex and his supporters would have made him quite capable of indulging in wishful thinking (Juxon, *Journal*, p. 49).
25. Slingsby, 'Battle of Alresford', in Chadwyck-Healey (ed.), *Bellum Civile*, p. 102; Lloyd, *Memoirs of Excellent Personages*, p. 326.
26. The role of the fourth Royalist brigade consisting of those regiments that Forth brought with him is not known, but they may have been divided up between the remainder. The Queen's regiment, for example, appears to have been with Lord John Stuart's brigade, whereas Richard Neville's seems to have been on the right wing, where it helped cover the final withdrawal.
27. Burne, *Battlefields of England*, p. 400; Hopton, *Bellum Civile*, pp. 82–3; BL Additional ms 18779, 87.
28. If Waller's regiments of horse had been deployed largely, if not entirely, on the left of the Parliamentary army, Essex's must have been on the right, and thus the subject of E.A.'s account (TT E40 1). See also note 24 above.
29. HMC Portland ms III, 106–10; TT E40 1, 13; Roe, *Military Memoir*, p. 11.
30. HMC Portland ms III, 109; Slingsby, 'Battle of Alresford', in Chadwyck-Healey (ed.), *Bellum Civile*, p. 103; Roe, *Military Memoir*, p. 11; TT E40 12.
31. Hopton, *Bellum Civile*, p. 83; HMC Portland ms III, 109.
32. TT E40 1; Hopton, *Bellum Civile*, p. 83.
33. Hopton, *Bellum Civile*, pp. 83–4; Slingsby, 'Battle of Alresford', in Chadwyck-Healey (ed.), *Bellum Civile*, p. 103; HMC Portland ms III, 109; BL Additional ms 18779, 87.
34. Roe, *Military Memoir*, p. 11; HMC Portland ms III, 109; Adair, *Cheriton 1644*, p. 136.
35. TT E40 22; Roe, *Military Memoir*, p. 11.

Chapter 10. The Battle of Marston Moor: Context, Landscape and Sources

1. Wanklyn and Jones, *Military History of the English Civil War*, pp. 171–83.
2. Newman, 'Marston Moor: The Sources and the Site'; Newman, *Marston Moor 1644*, pp. 46–53.
3. Newman, *Marston Moor 1644*, p. 48.
4. CSP Domestic 1644, p. 311.
5. This is the term used in Newman and Roberts, *Battle of Marston Moor*, which contains the most detailed topographical account of the battlefield.
6. Shropshire CRO, 455/278.
7. TT E2 1.
8. This has been identified for no particular reason with the glen mentioned in printed editions of Sir Phillip Monckton's account. In fact the glen was a late editorial intervention in the text. It does not appear in the earliest text, which has the word slough. (See Chapter 2, p. 15.)
9. Newman, 'Marston Moor: The Sources and the Site', pp. 29–31; BL Additional ms 16370, 64.
10. Shropshire CRO 455/277; TT E54 19; E2 1; BL Clarendon ms 1764. Near Tockwith there was probably a waterlogged area on the side of the ditch facing the moor (Lumsden's account in Young, *Marston Moor*, pp. 267–8; Clarke (ed.), *Life of James II*, pp. 22–3).
11. The extract is from the manuscript version of the report. The printed version has 'feeling' instead of 'being', a rather weaker word, suggesting opinion rather than actuality.
12. Shropshire CRO 455/277; TT E54 17; Bodl. Fairfax ms 36, 14–15; Slingsby, *Diary*, p. 114; Bodl. Clarendon ms 1764.
13. BL Harleian ms 166, 89–90. Bream probably derives from broom (*OED*), suggesting that the area was overgrown with heathland vegetation and not used for any agricultural purpose other than rough grazing.
14. Shropshire CRO, 455/278.
15. TT E54 19. Gardiner argues convincingly that the author was Lord Eglinton, who commanded the brigade of Scottish horse on the Allied right wing (*History of the Great Civil War*, vol. 1, p. 373).
16. TT E54 19. However, by the time the battle was fought the sun would have been quite close to the north-eastern horizon, and thus shining straight into the eyes of the Allied soldiers, provided it was not obscured by cloud.
17. Barratt, *The Battle for York*, p. 82.
18. Bodl. Clarendon mss 1764. Sir Charles Firth's highly accurate transcription of the Account is in *English Historical Review* 5, 1890.
19. Newman, *Marston Moor 1644*, pp. 6–7.
20. Slingsby, *Diary*, p. 114. A facsimile of the original is reproduced in Young's *Marston Moor*, facing p. 240. It shows that the transcription made by Parsons, the early nineteenth-century editor, was an accurate one. From his account of the flight of the Royalist right wing it appears that Slingsby was at the rear of the Royalist armies. This may also explain why he was able to return easily to York at the end of the battle.
21. Shropshire CRO, 445/278; BL Harleian ms 166, 89; Bodl. Fairfax ms 36, 15.
22. Printed in Carte (ed.), *Original Documents and Papers*, vol. 1, pp. 55–7, an excellent transcription of the manuscript, though the tight binding of the manuscript volume makes it impossible to read some of the words (Bodl. Carte ms XI, 223).
23. See Chapter 11, pp. 125–6.
24. Cavendish, *Lives of [the] Duke [and Duchess] of Newcastle*, pp. vi, xxxvi; Jones, *A Glorious Fame*, p. 159.
25. e.g. Firth, 'Marston Moor', p. 63; Wedgwood, *The King's War*, p. 662.
26. Cavendish, *Lives of [the] Duke [and Duchess] of Newcastle*, pp. xix–xx, xxxvi.
27. Wanklyn and Jones, *Military History of the English Civil War*, p. 190.
28. Wiltshire CRO 413/444Ai, 56. The widely used transcription in Peter Young's *Marston Moor* is accurate in every detail other than where he was unable to read a few words in the text, but none of the unreadable passages occurs in the narrative of the battle itself.
29. Clarke (ed.), *Life of James II*, pp. 22–3; Young, *Edgehill*, p. 274.
30. Young, 'Byron's account of Roundway Down'; Bodl. Carte ms XII, 212; Bodl. Clarendon ms 1738 5; Bodl. Rawlinson ms B200. See Chapter 11 for a full discussion of Byron's role in the battle and possible reasons for his escape from censure.
31. Young, *Marston Moor*, pp. 217–18; Firth, 'Marston Moor', pp. 71–2.
32. Newman, *Marston Moor 1644*, pp. 105, 121.
33. Monckton Papers, pp. 17–24; BL Lansdowne ms 988, 205–6.
34. Clarendon, *History of the Great Rebellion*, book 8, 79.
35. The previous week's publication, based on news of the first hour of the battle that had reached Newark, had described Marston Moor as an overwhelming victory for the prince.

36. A manuscript version of most of the original is reproduced in Young's *Marston Moor*, facing p. 145. The printed version, which is slightly shorter, is also reproduced, facing p. 257 (plate 40). An accurate transcription of the manuscript is to be found on pp. 257–9. All references to Lumsden's narrative in my text are taken from the transcription.

37. Laing (ed.), *Letters and Journals of Robert Baillie*, vol. 2, pp. 204, 209; TT E54 19.

38. Firth, 'Marston Moor', pp. 65–7; Laing (ed.), *Letters and Journals of Robert Baillie*, vol. 2, p. 210.

39. Newman, *Marston Moor 1644*, pp. 52–3, 92–3; Bodl. Fairfax ms 36, 15; TT E54 19.

40. Firth, 'Marston Moor', p. 66; see Chapter 3, pp. 12, 26 for discussion of this point.

41. Reproduced in Terry, *Life of Leven*, pp. 280–3 from an early nineteenth-century printed version. I have not been able to check the accuracy of the transcription against a manuscript version.

42. Somerville, *Memorie of the Somervilles*, printed in Young, *Marston Moor*, pp. 259–63. I have not been able to discover the original.

43. CSP Domestic 1644, p. 311.

44. Warwickshire CRO, CR2017/C10, 135.

45. Shropshire CRO, 455/277. Lord Fairfax wrote a different letter to the mayor of Hull. Extracts were reproduced by Sanford, but the full version is printed in one of the London weekly journals together with another letter from the Earl of Manchester that is as short and uninformative as that sent to the Earl of Denbigh (Sanford, *Studies and Illustrations of the Great Rebellion*, Appendix, p. 612; TT E54 9).

46. Shropshire CRO, 455/277.

47. Markham, *Robert Fairfax*, pp. 19–21. It is also possible that Fairfax saw the preliminary bombardment as marking the start of the battle. This began at about 4 p.m., but it was not immediately followed by an assault by one side on the other (Slingsby, *Diary*, p. 114; Shropshire CRO 455/278).

48. Abbott, *Writings and Speeches of Oliver Cromwell*, vol. 1, pp. 287–8.

49. BL Harleian ms 166, 88. The transcription printed in Young's *Marston Moor* is exemplary.

50. TT E2 14; Shropshire CRO, 455/278. An extract from this source is given in Plate 11. Another version, which combines elements of both accounts, is reproduced in D'Ewes's diary immediately after Stockdale's account. Its author's name is omitted, and D'Ewes commented that it was not read in the House, but came to him 'by a private hand'. He nevertheless included it as it supplied additional detail (BL Harleian ms 166, 89–90).

51. TT E2 1; Laing (ed.), *Letters and Journals of Robert Baillie*, vol. 2, p. 210. See Chapter 2, p. 14 for Baillie's comments on how Ashe's reports should be managed in future for the press.

52. TT E54 11.

53. There are also several very early generalized accounts of the battle published in London from 5 July onwards, one of which bears the paw print of Major Harrison, in that Cromwell is placed first in the list of Allied commanders responsible for the victory (TT E54 3, 4, 7).

54. TT E54 8. There is some circumstantial evidence to support this in Lumsden's report (Young, *Marston Moor*, p. 268).

55. Printed in various places (e.g. Maseres (ed.), *Select Tracts*, vol. 1, pp. 414–40). Manuscript versions are to be found in the Bodleian Library (Fairfax ms 36) and in the British Library (Harleian ms 2135). Another copy in the British Library (Additional ms 25708) ends early in 1644.

56. See also Chapter 3, pp. 26–7.

57. The most easily accessible printed version of Holles's memoirs is in Maseres's *Tracts*, vol. 1, where Cromwell's conduct at Marston Moor is discussed on pp. 199–200.

58. Abbott (ed.), *Writings and Speeches of Oliver Cromwell*, vol. 1, pp. 287–8.

59. TT E343 1; E811 2; Firth, 'Marston Moor'.

60. See above, pp. 9, 40.

61. TT E54 19; Young, *Marston Moor*, pp. 267–9, plate 21. A recent study of the battle shows that the markings in red ink added to it in Young's *Marston Moor* were the Brigadier's own interpolations based on evidence obtained elsewhere (Tincey, *Marston Moor*, p. 23).

62. BL Additional ms 16370, 64. De Gomme's depiction of the Allied armies as drawn up in two rather than three lines suggests that he did not have any real knowledge of how they were deployed.

63. Newman, *Marston Moor 1644*, pp. 43–5.

64. Tincey, *Marston Moor*, pp. 22, 25–33.

65. See Chapter 4, p. 41.

66. Newman, *Marston Moor 1644*, p. 94.

67. Newman and Roberts, *Battle of Marston Moor*, endpaper.

Chapter 11. The Battle of Marston Moor: Narrative

1. CSP Domestic 1644, pp. 287, 311; HMC 4th Report, pp. 267–8.

2. Cavendish, *Lives of [the] Duke [and Duchess] of Newcastle*, p. 60.

3. Cholmley, 'Memorials', p. 347; Newcastle's letter to Rupert, which cannot have been written before midday on 1 July, indicates that his intelligence concerning the enemy's movements was uncertain, and

he could not 'resolve anything, since I am made of nothing but thankfulness and obedience to your Highness', which could be read as acceptance that he and his army were under the Prince's command (Wiltshire CRO 413/377).

4. Wiltshire CRO 413/444Ai, 55–6; Cholmley, 'Memorials', p. 347; Newcastle Cavendish, *Lives of [the] Duke [and Duchess] of Newcastle*, p. 60; Slingsby, *Diary*, p. 215.

5. BL Harleian ms 166, 88; Shropshire CRO 455/278. Two Allied accounts of the battle imply that the generals would have preferred to draw up their forces on the moor, but were unable to do so as the Royalists had arrived there first (TT E2 1; E54 19).

6. TT E54 19; Young, *Marston Moor*, pp. 267–8.

7. Wiltshire CRO 413/444Ai, 55.

8. BL Additional ms 16370, 64 (de Gomme's plan); Clarke (ed.), *Life of James II*, p. 23. Another possibility is that they were deployed so as to prevent the enemy cavalry making use of the only gap in the ditch, which lay adjacent to this spot. This would also explain why the regiments are portrayed as facing to the front rather than to the right.

9. Reid, *All the King's Armies*, pp. 91–2; Young and Holmes, *English Civil Wars*, pp. 155–7.

10. Shropshire CRO 455/278. Newman's hypothesis that regiments of Newcastle's infantry were still arriving on the battlefield in the early evening (*Marston Moor 1644*, p. 65) is discussed below.

11. Reid, *All the King's Armies*, pp. 140–3; Newman, *Marston Moor 1644*, p. 44; Rogers, *Battles and Generals*, p. 142; Wiltshire CRO 444/413Ai, 56.

12. e.g. Reid, *All the King's Armies*, ch. 11; Tincey, *Marston Moor*, pp. 20–31. All I can add is that Marcus Trevor's regiment was apparently 400 strong at Marston Moor and that Sir Marmaduke Langdale's brigade major fought in the front line of the Royalist left wing (HMC Beaufort ms, 42; BL Lansdowne ms 988, 205–6).

13. The figures for the strength of the two army groups' infantry are as follows: Lumsden: Royalist 12,000, Allied not given; de Gomme: Royalist 11,000, Allied not given; Douglas: Allied 16,000, Royalist not given; Watson: Allied not given, Royalist 13,000–14,000. De Gomme estimated the strength of the Royalist army as 19,000 and the Allied 27,000; Douglas as 20,000 and 24,000 respectively. Both Fairfax and Simeon Ashe thought both armies to be roughly equal in size – about 23,000 to 24,000, and 20,000, respectively.

14. Young, *Marston Moor*, p. 99; Newman, *Marston Moor 1644*, pp. 61, 71, 89–92; Reid, *All the King's Armies*, pp. 136–45; Barratt, *The Battle for York*, pp. 88–95. I exclude Woolrych's and Tincey's figures on the grounds that Woolrych's figures are imprecise with regard to the number of horse, and that Tincey's are imprecise for the Eastern Association army cavalry (Woolrych, *Battles of the English Civil Wars*, pp. 70–1; Tincey, *Marston Moor*, pp. 20, 91).

15. Contemporary figures for cavalry are as follows: Lumsden: Royalist 7,000, Allied 6,000 English and 2,000 Scots; de Gomme: Royalist 6,000, Allied not given; Douglas: Royalist not given, Allied 6,000 plus 6 Scottish regiments; Watson: Royalists 8,000–9,000, Allied 150 troops; Stockdale: Allied right wing 4,000. Reid, the only historian to produce roughly equal figures for both sides, perhaps failed to allow for the fact that on one wing at least Lumsden's figures do not include dragoons in the Yorkshire and the Scottish armies. He also seems to have picked an arbitrary figure for calculating the number of horsemen per troop in the Yorkshire and the Scottish armies.

16. BL Additional ms 16370, 64; Newman, *Marston Moor 1644*, p. 6; BL Lansdowne ms 988, 205.

17. Young, *Marston Moor*, plate 21; TT E54 19; Terry, *Life of Leven*, p. 281.

18. Young, *Marston Moor*, pp. 87–8. Over half of the Cheshire maimed soldiers who fought with the Anglo-Irish regiments in England had not fought in Ireland. Richard Jenison of Tarporley, for example, had been impressed for the journey to York. Only one of the others claimed to have volunteered (Cheshire Quarter Sessions Files, 1661–1675; Easter 1669, 127; Easter 1670, 200).

19. Wiltshire CRO 413/444Ai, 56; BL Additional ms 16370, 64; Cholmley, 'Memorials', p. 348.

20. This is the kind of figure given by Lumsden and de Gomme, but there is a possibility that the musketeers intended to deploy on the right wing did not do so (Bodl. Fairfax ms 36, 15).

21. Watson implies that all the Eastern Association foot were on the left, but this cannot be so. Lumsden's plan, Douglas, and Ashe state or imply that one brigade was to the rear, probably Manchester's own regiment, which appears to have left the battlefield in some disorder and suffered more casualties than the remainder. It is also difficult to explain why Manchester himself left the battlefield if he was with his own infantry (Shropshire CRO 455/278; Young, *Marston Moor*, p. 217 and plate 21; Terry, *Life of Leven*, p. 269; TT E2 1).

22. Young, *Marston Moor*, plate 21.

23. Although the Eastern Association foot were in the missing part of the Lumsden sketch, it can be inferred from the code used to identify the formations that all five were in the first line, not divided between the two.

24. This reconstruction, which is different from Young's, draws on 'Captain Stewart' and other sources to fill up the gap in Lumsden's plan (Young, *Marston Moor*, pp. 240–1; TT E54 19; Beaumont (ed.), *A Discourse of the Warr in Lancashire*, p. 154; TT E2 1).

25. It would have been very difficult to see after 9.30 p.m. British Summer Time was not introduced until the First World War.
26. Young, *Marston Moor*, pp. 114, 215; CSP Domestic 1644, p. 311; Cholmley, 'Memorials', p. 348; Shropshire CRO 445/278; Slingsby, *Diary*, p. 114.
27. TT E2 1.
28. Cavendish, *Lives of [the] Duke [and Duchess] of Newcastle*, p. 154; Carte (ed.), *Original Documents and Papers*, vol. 1, p. 55. See also Chapter 2, pp. 12–13.
29. Cholmley, 'Memorials', p. 348; Shropshire CRO 455/278; BL Harleian ms 166, 88.
30. CSP Domestic 1644, p. 311.
31. Cholmley, 'Memorials', p. 348; Firth, 'Marston Moor', p. 71.
32. Firth, 'Marston Moor', p. 43; Woolrych, *Battles of the English Civil Wars*, p. 73; Kitson, *Prince Rupert*, p. 195; Young and Holmes, *English Civil Wars*, p. 199; Tincey, *Marston Moor*, p. 60.
33. Wiltshire CRO 413/444Ai, 56; Clarke (ed.), *Life of James II*, pp. 22–3.
34. CSP Domestic 1644, p. 311.
35. Warburton, *Memoirs of Prince Rupert*, vol. 3, p. 27 (Prince Rupert to Will Legge 16 October 1644).
36. Cholmley mentions Hurry's troop as being the first to run ('Memorials', p. 348).
37. Ibid.; Slingsby, *Diary*, p. 114; Cavendish, *Lives of [the] Duke [and Duchess] of Newcastle*, p. 61; Carte (ed.), *Original Documents and Papers*, vol. 1, p. 57; BL Harleian ms 166, 88; Shropshire CRO 455/278; BL Additional ms 16370, 64.
38. Shropshire CRO 455/278; BL Harleian ms 166, 88.
39. See Chapter 11, pp. 111–12.
40. Cholmley, 'Memorials', p. 348; Slingsby, *Diary*, p. 114; BL Harleian ms 166, 88; Shropshire CRO 455/278.
41. See Chapter 3, p. 28.
42. e.g. Young and Holmes, *English Civil Wars*, p. 200; Tincey, *Marston Moor*, p. 114; Reid, *All the King's Armies*, p. 152; Barratt, *The Battle for York*, pp. 127–8. The honourable exception, as with the site of the Battle of Cheriton, is Seymour (*Battles in Britain*, vol. 2, p. 96).
43. TT E54 19. Somerville reports something of the sort in very general terms, but he wrote some years after the event and is most unlikely not to have known about the two outbursts of controversy about Leslie's role in the success of the Allied left wing (Young, *Marston Moor*, pp. 260–1). A more plausible piece of evidence is the report of Sir Adam Hepburn, the Scottish Commissary General of Horse, to Robert Baillie that Leslie's intervention was decisive when Cromwell's men were on the back foot after the arrival of Prince Rupert's reinforcements (Laing (ed.), *Letters and Journals of Robert Baillie*, vol. 2, p. 218). However, by the time Hepburn wrote his letter Stewart's account was in print, representing the Scottish 'party line'. The two traces of the past are therefore not mutually supportive.
44. See Chapter 10, pp. 115–17.
45. Laing (ed.), *Letters and Journals of Robert Baillie*, vol. 2, pp. 203, 209; Young, *Marston Moor*, pp. 257–8. One of Baillie's later letters amplifies Stewart's account, but was probably derived from it, as it was written some time afterwards (see Chapter 3, note 14).
46. CSP Domestic 1645–7, p. 327; TT E343 1; *The Scots Design Discovered*, p. 78 (printed in 1654 but according to Firth very largely written in 1647: Cholmley, 'Memorials', p. 346). In his memoirs Lord Holles is even more critical of the spin given to Cromwell's personal role in the victory at Marston Moor, but he does not mention the charge of Leslie's horse (Holles, 'Memoirs', p. 199).
47. This is worded in most secondary works as if Cromwell had ordered it, but the only evidence in support comes from *The Scots Design Discovered*, a source that, under a thin veneer of even-handedness, is emphatically pro-Cromwell. The order to halt is not mentioned either by Lionel Watson or in the version of Simeon Ashe's account to be found in the Thomason Tracts (Shropshire CRO, 455/278; TT E2 1). Barratt quotes another version of Ashe, printed in Terry, which describes the front squadrons of the Eastern Association cavalry as chasing the enemy to the walls of York whilst the rest remained in a body, but the episode being described may have taken place at the end of the battle (Barratt, *The Battle for York*, p. 129).
48. Shropshire CRO 455/278; TT E54 19.
49. TT E54 19; Terry, *Life of Leven*, pp. 243, 251. Sir Thomas Fairfax was almost certainly not the bringer of the bad tidings (see Chapter 3, p. 26).
50. Terry, *Life of Leven*, pp. 243, 251; TT E54 19; Bodl. Fairfax ms 36, 15.
51. Newman, *Marston Moor 1644*, p. 94.
52. The narrative of this part of the paragraph relies heavily on Fairfax's own account (Bodl. Fairfax ms 36, 15–16) but some of the detail is supported by comments in other Allied accounts and in Monckton's memoir (TT E2 1; E54 19; Terry, *Life of Leven*, pp. 281–2; BL Lansdowne ms 988, 205).
53. TT E2 1; Shropshire CRO 455/278; Terry, *Life of Leven*, pp. 282–3; Young, *Marston Moor*, plate 21.
54. TT E2 1; Shropshire CRO 455/278; BL Harleian ms 166, 88; Young, *Marston Moor*, p. 258; TT E54 19.
55. TT E2 1; BL Harleian ms 166, 88.

56. Terry, *Life of Leven*, p. 282; TT E54 19; BL Harleian ms 166, 88; Young, *Marston Moor*, p. 258.
57. TT E2 1.
58. Young, *Marston Moor*, p. 258; TT E54 19; E2 1; Terry, *Life of Leven*, p. 282.
59. Unlike Lord Byron, Lucas seems to have been demoted after Marston Moor. Admittedly he spent some time as a prisoner of war, but his next post was as governor of one of Bristol's out-garrisons. By the end of the war, however, he was lieutenant general of horse (Young and Holmes, *English Civil Wars*, p. 266; New *DNB* 34, p. 663).
60. *Mercurius Aulicus*, p. 1084.
61. Gardiner, *History of the Great Civil War*, vol. 1, p. 381; Carpenter, *Military Leadership in the British Civil Wars*, p. 98.
62. Shropshire CRO 455/278. It is tempting to speculate on why it was the Royalists who attacked. Admittedly they had the advantage of the slope, but they must also have known of the difficulties they would face in crossing the terrain that had caused such trouble to Sir Thomas Fairfax's regiments at the start of the battle. Possibly by this time it was too dark to see the size and composition of the force they were attacking, as after sunset light disappears first from low ground. It is also possible that the light of the setting sun impeded their vision or that they were riding to the rescue of their own infantry, whose formations they could see being attacked and broken by enemy foot and dragoons on the moor below them.
63. TT E54 19.
64. e.g. Bodl. Fairfax ms 36, 15; Young, *Marston Moor*, p. 258.
65. e.g. Stockdale, who merely mentions a second charge, which could have been carried out by infantry (BL Harleian ms 166, 88).
66. TT E21; E54 19; Cholmley, 'Memorials', p. 349. There is some slight support for Cholmley's comment in the second account of Marston Moor given in *Mercurius Aulicus*, where Sir Marmaduke Langdale is described as commanding an undefeated detachment of Royalist horse that was still plundering the enemy baggage hours after the battle had commenced. It was this plundering that almost certainly accounts for the mass of artefacts found on Mill Hill, that part of Braham Hill which lies behind Long Marston village. Roberts has it that this represents the site of the final cavalry encounter between Cromwell and Goring in which infantry were also involved, presumably because field archaeologists have found masses of musket balls there. Roberts sees the infantry as being Royalist, but it is impossible to understand how Royalist infantry could have got so far behind Allied lines. Moreover, none of the written accounts describe a combined arms engagement as taking place on Mill Hill. There remains, however, a slight nagging doubt that the infantry could have been dispersed by the remnants of the Earl of Manchester's regiment discussed in note 21 above, which may have returned to the battlefield at the eleventh hour with their general in circumstances described only by Robert Douglas and Simeon Ashe. However, Douglas, who was with the earl, stated that the returning troops were cavalry, not infantry, whilst Ashe does not say whether they were horse or foot (Newman and Roberts, *Battle of Marston Moor*, p. 89; Terry, *Life of Leven*, p. 282; TT E2 1).
67. Cholmley, 'Memorials', p. 348; BL Lansdowne ms 988, 205–6; *Mercurius Aulicus*, p. 1058. Slough occurs as glen in edited versions of Monckton's account and has been misidentified as the relatively flat corridor of land between the summit of the ridge on which the Allied army deployed and the final slope from the ridge to the moor.
68. TT E54 19.
69. Lilly, *Life and Times*, pp. 77–8.
70. TT E54 19; Young, *Marston Moor*, p. 261.
71. Reid, *All the King's Armies*, p. 159; Tincey, *Marston Moor*, pp. 73–4; Barratt, *The Battle for York*, p. 134.
72. TT E2 1; E54 19; Young, *Marston Moor*, p. 261.
73. Young, *Marston Moor*, p. 251.
74. TT E54 11; Young, *Marston Moor*, p. 216; CSP Domestic 1644, p. 311; Carte (ed.), *Original Documents and Papers*, vol. 1, p. 56; Wiltshire CRO 413/444Ai, 56–7; Slingsby, *Diary*, p. 114; Newman, *Marston Moor 1644*, p. 132.
75. The general consensus amongst the Allied sources was that 1,500 enemy soldiers were taken prisoner and between 3,000 and 4,500 slain.

Chapter 12. The Second Battle of Newbury: Context, Landscape and Sources

1. CSP Domestic 1644, pp. 199, 211, 226.
2. Wanklyn and Jones, *Military History of the English Civil War*, pp. 167–70, 190–1, 194–7.
3. Ibid., pp. 197–9.
4. Bodl. Carte ms LXXIV, 160 (a diary of the marches of Colonel Montague's regiment). For Waller's infantry see Chapter 13, note 5.
5. Wanklyn and Jones, *Military History of the English Civil War*, pp. 199–202.

6. BL Additional ms 18981, 297–9, 303, 312, 316.
7. Walker, *Historical Discourses*, pp. 105, 107–10.
8. Ibid., p. 110; TT E14 2.
9. Gwyn, *Military Memoirs*, p. 57; Walker, *Historical Discourses*, p. 111.
10. The River Lambourn was almost certainly in flood (TT E14 14, 16) but this did not prevent Waller's force crossing the river by a ford at Boxford, two miles above the battlefield, soon after midday.
11. The first report on the battle published in the London weeklies reported that immediately prior to the battle Parliamentary pioneers were trying to rebuild Thatcham bridge, as it was known at the time.
12. See note 20 below.
13. See Plate 12.
14. Walker, *Historical Discourses*, pp. 110–11; BL Harleian ms 166, 141.
15. Ibid., pp. 111–13; TT E22 10.
16. Walker, *Historical Discourses*, pp. 110–11; Skippon in Rushworth (ed.), *Historical Collections*, vol. 5, pp. 722–3; BL Harleian ms 166, 140; Rocque, *Berkshire*, sheet 4.
17. Walker, *Historical Discourses*, p. 114; Symonds, *Diaries*, p. 148; TT E14 16.
18. The contours of the slope, which is still open land, are easily observable from the minor road that runs from Speen village parallel to and to the south of the Bath road towards the mid-twentieth-century housing that now covers Speenhamland.
19. Eddycroft and Worthy Fields (Berkshire CRO Q/P116B/28/22/1).
20. Ibid. De Gomme's map of the deployment of the Royalist army preparatory for the abortive Third Battle of Newbury in November 1644 provides useful detail of the water meadows by the Kennet and the approach to Newbury bridge along the north bank of the Kennet (BL Additional ms 16370, 61). The enclosure map is reproduced in Plate 13.
21. *Mercurius Aulicus*, pp. 1233–40; Walker, *Historical Discourses*, pp. 210–14; Symonds, *Diaries*, pp. 145–6.
22. Gwyn, *Military Memoirs*, pp. 57–62; Bulstrode, *Memoirs*, pp. 117–18; HMC 4th Report, p. 297.
23. Toynbee and Young, *Battle of Cropredy Bridge*, p. 114.
24. Walker, *Historical Discourses*, p. 112.
25. Ibid., pp. 111–12; *Mercurius Aulicus*, pp. 1234–5; HMC 4th Report, p. 297; BL Harleian ms 986, 89; Symonds, *Diaries*, pp. 145–6. 'Our' presumably refers to the horse of the Western Army, not the horse as a whole, some of whom fought very well, whilst others were not engaged at all. Other sources describe the defeat of a Cornish brigade at the start of the fighting around Speen, whereas Sir Humphrey Bennett's brigade, which retreated before the enemy advance, were eligible to be described as Western Horse as it had fought in Hopton's army at Cheriton (Hopton, *Bellum Civile*, p. 83).
26. Firth, 'The "Memoirs" of Sir Richard Bulstrode'; Bulstrode, *Memoirs*, pp. 119–18; Bodl. English ms 132.
27. Clarke (ed.), *Life of James II*, pp. 24–5. See Chapter 14 for the rivalry between Digby and Rupert for the king's ear.
28. Gwyn, *Military Memoirs*, pp. 57–62.
29. The exceptions are the accounts of the battle in Ludlow's *Memoirs* and in Waller's *Experiences* (Adair, *Roundhead General*, p. 215), which are assessed at p. 88 above. The section in Whitelocke's *Memorials* on the Second Battle of Newbury contains no original material, whilst the narrative in Rushworth is very largely drawn from TT E14 16.
30. CSP Domestic 1644–45, pp. 146–60; Bruce and Masson (eds), *Manchester's Quarrel*, pp. 58, 62–4, 84–6; TT E22 10.
31. Rushworth (ed.), *Historical Collections*, vol. 5, pp. 722–3.
32. A précis of their report to the House of Commons is to be found in the Parliamentary diary of Sir Simon D'Ewes (BL Harleian ms 166, 140). If the original was printed, it does not appear to have survived.
33. Roe, *Military Memoir*, p. 215.
34. CSP Domestic 1644–5, pp. 75, 76–7. See Chapter 13, note 83 for a discussion of the removal of material dangerous for Cromwell but helpful to Manchester from their first letter written after the battle as reproduced in the letterbook of the Committee of Both Kingdoms.
35. TT E14 16.
36. BL Harleian ms 166, 140; Rushworth (ed.), *Historical Collections*, vol. 5, pp. 722–3.
37. See Chapter 2, p. 14.
38. TT E14 14, 15 1.
39. TT E14 14.
40. Waller's memoirs are quoted in Adair, *Roundhead General*, p. 215. Sir William claims to have fought on Speenfield. If by that he means Speenhamland, it is difficult to understand how the encounter occurred unless he was in the forlorn hope, which got into difficulties crossing a ditch early in the battle (see Chapter 13, p. 152).

41. CSP Domestic 1644–5, pp. 151, 156–8.
42. Ludlow, *Memoirs*, vol. 1, p. 104.
43. Roe, *Military Memoir*, p. 215.
44. CSP Domestic 1644–5, pp. 146–61.
45. See Chapter 2, p. 9.

Chapter 13. The Second Battle of Newbury: Narrative

1. Bruce and Masson (eds), *Manchester's Quarrel*, p. 85.
2. CSP Domestic 1644–5, p. 56. It consisted of five regiments when it arrived at the rendezvous at Basingstoke, but one was left behind to garrison Reading.
3. Holmes, *Eastern Association*, p. 238.
4. The size of Essex's corps is particularly difficult to assess. It had been 6,000 strong in Cornwall in August, but the only precise figure for the Portsmouth re-arming is 800 to 900 men in the Lord General's own regiment (CSP Domestic 1644, pp. 482, 502). Peachey and Turton's estimate of just over 3,000 fit infantry still at Portsmouth in early October seems judicious, as a garrison regiment had been shipped back to Plymouth and a Trained Band regiment allowed to return to London (Peachey and Turton, *Old Robin's Foot*, p. 17).
5. They were used to reinforce the Parliamentary garrisons of the south-west during September (CSP Domestic 1644, pp. 489, 495, 502, 505–6, 516, 523, 537; 1644–5, pp. 13, 36).
6. These figures are slightly larger than those given in Wanklyn and Jones, *Military History of the English Civil War*, pp. 202–3, where we underestimated the size of the City brigade.
7. Walker, *Historical Discourses*, p. 98.
8. Ibid., pp. 109–10; BL Additional ms 18981, 303.
9. Luke, *Letterbooks*, pp. 360–1, 363.
10. Bruce and Masson (eds), *Manchester's Quarrel*, p. 85.
11. There is further discussion of the landscape to the west of Newbury in Chapter 6.
12. Symonds, *Diaries*, p. 143; Walker, *Historical Discourses*, p. 108. John Gwyn suggested another alternative, namely using the artillery train to cover the approaches to Newbury bridge from the south, but this was merely to give the king's armies the best chance of avoiding battle and allowing Prince Rupert time to arrive with reinforcements. It does not take into account the fact that the king's prime purpose in remaining at Newbury was to be in the best possible position to relieve Basing House, which had been under intermittent siege for several months (Gwyn, *Military Memoirs*, p. 59).
13. HMC Braye ms, 155; *Mercurius Aulicus*, p. 1232.
14. Luke, *Letterbooks*, p. 366; Rushworth (ed.), *Historical Collections*, vol. 5, p. 722.
15. HMC Braye ms, 155; Luke, *Letterbooks*, p. 363.
16. Bruce and Masson (eds), *Manchester's Quarrel*, p. 85; Young and Holmes, *English Civil Wars*, p. 216; Rogers, *Battles and Generals*, p. 170.
17. It probably comprised 11,000 to 12,000 men against the Royalists' 9,000 to 10,000.
18. TT E22 10; E903 3; Bruce and Masson (eds), *Manchester's Quarrel*, p. 64.
19. TT E22 10; Bruce and Masson (eds), *Manchester's Quarrel*, p. 86.
20. BL Additional ms 18981, 303, 312; Bodl. Firth ms C7, 217.
21. BL Additional ms 18981, 312. Lord Digby did not mention Bagnor, but by early on the morning of the battle the direction of Waller's march made it most unlikely that the crossing place would be anywhere other than at Boxford ford.
22. Walker, *Historical Discourses*, p. 111; Bulstrode, *Memoirs*, pp. 117–18.
23. Walker, *Historical Discourses*, p. 111; CSP Domestic 1644–5, p. 75; Rocque, *Berkshire*, sheet 4; Willis, *Map of Ten Miles around Newbury*.
24. Walker, *Historical Discourses*, pp. 110–11; Rushworth (ed.), *Historical Collections*, vol. 5, p. 722; Berkshire CRO Q/P116B/28/22/1.
25. CSP Domestic 1644–5, p. 75; Walker, *Historical Discourses*, p. 111; BL Harleian ms 166, 140. An investigation of the distribution of musket balls in and around the two positions might be expected to solve the problem for once and for all, but much, if not all, of the archaeology has been destroyed. The immediate surroundings of Speen are now covered with housing estates, and Stockcross is now a substantial village rather than a crossroads. Moreover the building of the Newbury bypass has destroyed the most likely position for the barricade.
26. Walker, *Historical Discourses*, pp. 111–12.
27. The only evidence for this comes from John Gwyn's *Military Memoirs*, pp. 58–9, but the detail he provides suggests that he himself took part in the fighting there or else drew on a source of information independent of Walker and *Mercurius Aulicus*, which is now lost.
28. Gwyn, *Military Memoirs*, pp. 58–9; Walker, *Historical Discourses*, p. 113.
29. See Chapter 12, note 10.

30. Walker, *Historical Discourses*, p. 111; Bruce and Masson (eds), *Manchester's Quarrel*, pp. 64–5; TT E22 10, 2–3.
31. TT E22 10, 3.
32. They may, however, have been cavalry. At the so-called Third Battle of Newbury a fortnight later Hopton commanded a brigade of horse (Gwyn, *Military Memoirs*, p. 61; BL Additional ms 16370, 61).
33. Walker, *Historical Discourses*, p. 111.
34. See Chapter 12, p. 139.
35. Luke, *Letterbooks*, p. 366.
36. Rushworth (ed.), *Historical Collections*, vol. 5, pp. 722–3.
37. BL Harleian ms 166, 140. The army was deployed in battalia on Wickham Heath by 2 p.m.
38. Luke, *Letterbooks*, p. 366.
39. Quoted in Adair, *Roundhead General*, p. 215.
40. See Chapter 12, note 40.
41. Walker, *Historical Discourses*, p. 111.
42. TT E14 14, E256 30; CSP Domestic 1644–5, pp. 75, 76; Bruce and Masson (eds), *Manchester's Quarrel*, p. 86.
43. Bruce and Masson (eds), *Manchester's Quarrel*, p. 75.
44. Bodl. Carte ms LXXX, 715.
45. TT E14 16; CSP Domestic 1644–5, p. 75.
46. HMC Braye ms. 155; Bulstrode, *Memoirs*, p. 117.
47. e.g. Gardiner, *History of the Great Civil War*, vol. 2, p. 49; Young and Holmes, *English Civil Wars*, p. 219.
48. Walker, *Historical Discourses*, pp. 111–12; CSP Domestic 1644–5, p. 75; Bulstrode, *Memoirs*, pp. 116–17; TT E22 10; Bruce and Masson (eds), *Manchester's Quarrel*, p. 65; Reid, *All the King's Armies*, p. 187.
49. BL Harleian ms 166, 140; Rushworth (ed.), *Historical Collections*, vol. 5, p. 733.
50. CSP Domestic 1644–5, p. 75. See also Plate 13. The enclosures between the tongue of Wickham Heath near Dean Wood and the western border of Eddycroft field were no more than 250 yards in width.
51. For the location of the ditch, see p. 153.
52. *Mercurius Aulicus*, pp. 1235–7; Walker, *Historical Collections*, p. 113; BL Harleian ms 166, 140; Bulstrode, *Memoirs*, pp. 117–18.
53. Rushworth (ed.), *Historical Collections*, vol. 5, p. 733; TT E14 16.
54. Bruce and Masson (eds), *Manchester's Quarrel*, pp. 63–4; TT E22 10.
55. See Chapter 2, p. 12. There is no mention in any Royalist source of part of the artillery train being placed there prior to the battle.
56. The ditch cannot be located on any map, and fieldwork is impossible since the construction of the Newbury bypass. There is a ditch in the south-west corner of Donnington Park, but it is impossible to date and appears to run in the wrong direction.
57. CSP Domestic 1644–5, p. 75; Symonds, *Diaries*, p. 146.
58. Only Sir Humphrey Bennett's brigade, part of the Queen's, Prince Maurice's regiment, and the troops of the Royal Lifeguard seem to have been deployed to the south of Speen in the Kennet valley, whilst only the Prince of Wales's regiment was at Shaw. The whereabouts of the Cornish brigade that had been deployed in front of the barricade defending Speen and chased away by superior numbers is not known. Therefore left in reserve were several regiments belonging to the king's army, and at least two of Maurice's brigades, those of Sir Thomas Aston and Sir Francis Dorrington. Neither of them was Cornish and both were at the so-called Third Battle of Newbury two weeks later (BL Additional ms 16370, 61).
59. Symonds stated that the fight in the Kennet valley between Balfour's horse and Royalist cavalry in which he himself was involved did not reach its climax until after Cleveland had been captured (*Diaries*, pp. 145–6).
60. Ibid. The only reference to it in a non-Royalist account is in the evidence given by Captain Hooper who, during the great debate, described Sir William Balfour's forces as routing the enemy cavalry around Speen 'who fled away in the sight of this examinant and of the Earl of Manchester's forces standing near Shaw' (CSP Domestic 1644–5, p. 149).
61. Rocque, *Berkshire*, sheet 4.
62. Walker, *Historical Discourses*, p. 111.
63. Symonds suggests that they were the vanguard of a larger body of horse, but if this was so the latter took no part in the engagement that followed (*Diaries*, p. 145).
64. Walker, *Historical Discourses*, p. 112; *Mercurius Aulicus*, pp. 1234–5. Some enclosures can be seen on Rocque's map abutting onto the water meadows, but their shape makes it difficult to understand why they should have caused Bennett's officers any concern and they do not feature in de Gomme's watercolour of Third Newbury (BL Additional ms 16370, 61).
65. See Chapter 12, p. 140.
66. Symonds, *Diaries*, p. 145; Walker, *Historical Discourses*, p. 112.

67. BL Harleian ms 166, 140.
68. CSP Domestic 1644–5, p. 76.
69. Cromwell, for example, claimed that the attack went in at 4.30 p.m., half an hour after sunset and two and a half hours after he alleged that the assault on the barricade at Speen had begun (Bruce and Masson (eds), *Manchester's Quarrel*, p. 86).
70. Walker, *Historical Discourses*, p. 112; HMC 4th Report, p. 297; Symonds, *Diaries*, p. 145; *Mercurius Aulicus*, p. 1237; TT E22 10, 4.
71. CSP Domestic 1644–5, pp. 147–60.
72. Wanklyn and Jones, *Military History of the English Civil War*, pp. 200–2.
73. There are hints of this in Manchester's description in which it was claimed that Waller's force was late in setting out due to a last-minute decision to alter its composition. There is also a clear statement in Ashe about impatience at the non-appearance of the western pincer in the morning amongst the commanders on Clay Hill (Bruce and Masson (eds), *Manchester's Quarrel*, p. 63; TT E22 10, 2–3).
74. CSP Domestic 1644–5, pp. 153, 159–60; Bruce and Masson (eds), *Manchester's Quarrel*, p. 86; TT E22 10, 3.
75. TT E22 10.
76. Walker, *Historical Discourses*, p. 113; Gwyn, *Military Memoirs*, pp. 50–1; TT E22 10; Bruce and Masson (eds), *Manchester's Quarrel*, p. 65.
77. CSP Domestic 1644–5, p. 149.
78. Symonds, *Diaries*, p. 146.
79. Walker, *Historical Discourses*, p. 114; Symonds, *Diaries*, p. 146; CSP Domestic 1644–5, p. 76; Gwyn, *Military Memoirs*, p. 58.
80. Gwyn, *Military Memoirs*, p. 59.
81. Bruce and Masson (eds), *Manchester's Quarrel*, p. 64; CSP Domestic 1644–5, p. 150. Manchester claimed that the Royalists retreated 'in great disorder' (implying noisily), that General Skippon and Colonels Bartlett and Davies informed Cromwell's cavalry that the enemy were on the move, and that Cromwell himself had 'knowledge of the enemy's running', but that nothing was done until the following day. It is probably significant that none of the officers he named gave evidence on Cromwell's behalf in the great debate. Moreover, the letter described in note 83 below supports almost all of Manchester's allegations.
82. BL Harleian ms 166, 140.
83. The copy of the first letter of the members of the Committee of Both Kingdoms, who had accompanied Waller on his march to Speen, to their colleagues in London is preserved in the Committee's records in the National Archives at Kew. It is reproduced in full in Bruce and Masson (eds), *Manchester's Quarrel*, pp. 49–50. The original, which I have recently discovered in Lord Wharton's papers, dated 9 p.m. on 27 October, includes the following passage: 'There is a report come presently that the King's forces are drawn away by Donnington Castle which if we find true we resolve presently with all our horse to follow' (Bodl. Carte ms LXXX, 715). Waller and his generals and civilian advisers may, of course, subsequently have been informed that the report was untrue, but at least they had an inkling that the Royalists might be leaving Speenhamland and should have checked and double-checked during the night that such a manoeuvre was not under way. However, the fact that the minuted version was docked suggests that there was something that needed to be concealed, as indeed do the remaining passages which are missing from the Committee's letterbook – an acknowledgement that the Earl of Manchester's corps had attacked 'in seasonable time', the hour at which the letter had been written, and the hope that 'the victory will be consummated tomorrow by the same God who began it so happily'.

Chapter 14. *The Battle of Naseby: Context, Landscape and Sources*

1. The involved process by which Cromwell was able to retain some kind of military command in May and early June 1645 despite the ordinance is elegantly described in Gentles, *The New Model Army in England, Ireland, and Scotland*, pp. 25–7.
2. Ibid., pp. 21, 23, 32–3; Kishlansky, *Rise of the New Model Army*, p. 48.
3. Reid, *All the King's Armies*, p. 193; Wanklyn and Jones, *Military History of the English Civil War*, p. 220.
4. Wanklyn and Jones, *Military History of the English Civil War*, p. 233.
5. Ibid., pp. 235–40, 241–3.
6. TT E288 38.
7. Slingsby, *Diary*, p. 151; Sprigg, *Anglia Rediviva*, p. 38; TT 288 22. There is some uncertainty surrounding the names of the undulations on the ridge on which the New Model Army deployed. I have opted for those used by Foard in his book *Naseby: The Decisive Campaign*, (1995).
8. Symonds, *Diaries*, p. 193. Unfortunately, a contemporary estate map, a photograph of which may be found in Marix Evans, Burton and Westaway's *Naseby: June 1645*, does not show the extent of the uncultivated land.
9. Sprigg, *Anglia Rediviva*, pp. 38, 39; Slingsby, *Diary*, p. 151.

10. Sprigg, *Anglia Rediviva*, pp. 38, 42.

11. For a full discussion of the shortcomings of Streeter's map, see Chapter 14, pp. 169–70 and Chapter 2, p. 18.

12. Marix Evans, Burton and Westaway, *Naseby: June 1645*, p. 73. It is also significant that Sprigg only mentions a hedge on the western side of the battlefield (*Anglia Rediviva*, p. 38).

13. Slingsby, *Diaries*, p. 151; Sprigg, *Anglia Rediviva*, p. 40.

14. Foard, *Naseby*, pp. 236–42.

15. Sprigg, *Anglia Rediviva*, p. 40. The exact location of the rabbit warren has recently been determined by field walking and metal detecting (Foard, *Naseby*, p. 218; Marix Evans, Burton and Westaway, *Naseby: June 1645*, p. 73). It is impossible to say how serious an inconvenience it was, but nevertheless it is curious that Slingsby does not mention the warren in his detailed account of the cavalry fight on the Royalist left wing in which he took part.

16. Walker, *Historical Discourses*, pp. 130–2; Clarendon, *History of the Great Rebellion*, book 9, 35–40; Bodl. Clarendon ms 28, 46–68.

17. Wiltshire CRO 413/444Ai, 69–70; HMC Ormond ms n.s. II, 386.

18. Symonds, *Diaries*, p. 193; Slingsby, *Diary*, pp. 150–3.

19. Staffordshire CRO DW 1778Ii, 54, 56; Warburton, *Memoirs of Prince Rupert*, vol. 3, pp. 119–21. A second letter written by Rupert from Wolverhampton describing the battle had disappeared from the archives of the Earl of Dartmouth, Legge's descendant, by the mid-nineteenth century, as it is not reproduced by Warburton in *Memoirs of Prince Rupert and the Cavaliers*. Its contents cannot be inferred from Will Legge's reply to Lord Digby, and so it may have been intercepted by the enemy before it reached Oxford.

20. Bodl. Carte ms XV, 48 (Lord Digby to the Marquis of Ormond, Bewdley, 19 June 1646).

21. Thomas, *Sir John Berkenhead*, pp. 71–2, 243.

22. House of Lords Journals VII, 433–4; Abbott (ed.), *Writings and Speeches of Oliver Cromwell*, vol. 1, p. 365.

23. TT E288 27.

24. TT E288 21, 28, 38.

25. TT E288 26.

26. TT E288 38.

27. e.g. TT E288 31–7, 40, 46.

28. The source of such information is likely to have been an officer or soldier of Fiennes's regiment, which formed part of the escort accompanying the Royalist prisoners on their forced march to London after the battle. Telling the press was possibly part of a campaign to get Fiennes's regiment incorporated into the New Model Army (TT E289 3; E288 45, 46; Luke, *Letterbooks*, p. 579).

29. Carte (ed.), *Original Documents and Papers*, vol. 1, pp. 128–33.

30. e.g. TT E288 21, 28, 38; Slingsby, *Diary*, p. 152; Sprigg, *Anglia Rediviva*, p. 44.

31. Sprigg, *Anglia Rediviva*, pp. 37–48. There is also an interesting eyewitness report of Cromwell's role in the decision to move from the position on the escarpment facing towards East Farndon and Clipston to the one where the battle was fought. It was printed in 1647 at the height of the conflict between the army and Parliament, and may have been intended to scotch the rumour that Cromwell's role in the victory had been a limited one (TT E372 22).

32. Sprigg, *Anglia Rediviva*, pp. 14, 47, 51 and elsewhere in the text.

33. Rushworth (ed.), *Historical Collections*, vol. 6, pp. 42–4; TT E288 26. Whitelocke's account is clearly a synthesis of a number of printed sources, but he also cites an anecdote concerning the role of Fairfax's Lifeguard in the destruction of a Royalist infantry brigade (*Memorials*, p. 151).

34. Rushworth (ed.), *Historical Collections*, vol. 6, p. 42.

35. See Chapter 2, p. 18. The mistake was not picked up by Childs, whose representation of the battle is severely flawed as a result (Childs, *Warfare in the Seventeenth Century*, pp. 126–7).

36. BL Additional ms 16370, 63; Warburton, *Memoirs of Prince Rupert*, vol. 3, p. 105. The original formed part of the Bennet of Pythouse collection and may be the one recently rediscovered in Bodleian English ms C51. However, the binding of that volume suggests that it was put on some time before the Warburton sketch disappeared from public ken with the sale of Alfred Morrison's collection by auction between 1917 and 1919 (*The Location of Collections documented in the Reports on the Collections Section*, Guide to the Sources for British History 3, HMSO (1982), p. 45). The Bodleian sketch cannot be the Astley/Rushworth sketch, as it is not signed by the Royalist commanders.

37. Foard, *Naseby*, p. 213. The only difference between them is that de Gomme placed the infantry regiments further apart than Streeter.

38. TT E288 38.

39. Warwick, *Memoirs*, p. 316.

40. Sprigg, *Anglia Rediviva*, pp. 41–2.

41. Foard, *Naseby*, p. 276; Marix Evans, Burton and Westaway, *Naseby: June 1645*, pp. 104, 116.

42. See Chapter 2 for further discussion of the archaeological record as evidence of the scale and extent of fighting on Civil War battlefields.

Chapter 15. The Battle of Naseby: Narrative

1. Walker, *Historical Discourses*, pp. 129–30; Symonds, *Diaries*, p. 193; Slingsby, *Diary*, p. 150; Sprigg, *Anglia Rediviva*, p. 36.
2. Reid, *All the King's Armies*, p. 198.
3. e.g. S.R. Gardiner, *History of the Great Civil War*, vol. 2, p. 421n.; Woolrych, *Battles of the English Civil Wars*, p. 121; Young and Holmes, *English Civil Wars*, p. 240; Seymour, *Battles in Britain*, vol. 2, p. 114.
4. See Plate 16.
5. See Plate 17.
6. Slingsby described the ridge as being topped by a chapel. Both East Farndon and Great Oxendon churches are positioned thus, but the former could clearly be seen from Market Harborough as part of a village on the north side of the ridge. There would therefore have been no reason for not describing it as a church. Great Oxendon church, on the other hand, was on its own on the first summit of the ridge some 400 yards in advance of its village, which was on the south-facing side of the second summit and invisible from the church. It therefore seems that Slingsby would have had good grounds for describing Great Oxendon church as a chapel rather than a church (Pevsner, *Northamptonshire*, p. 190; Slingsby, *Diary*, p. 150).
7. One Royalist account claimed that intelligence placed Fairfax's army around Northampton on the night of 13 June, another two only six miles from the king's army (Symonds, *Diaries*, p. 193; Walker, *Historical Discourses*, p. 129; Slingsby, *Diary*, p. 150).
8. Foard, *Naseby*, p. 210.
9. Clarendon, *History of the Great Rebellion*, book 9, 37; Walker, *Historical Discourses*, p. 130.
10. Fairfax's headquarters was at Guilsborough close to the A5159 on the night before the battle (Sprigg, *Anglia Rediviva*, p. 333).
11. *Diary*, p. 150. Walker, on the other hand, claimed only that intelligence of the enemy approach had been received. Their presence on the escarpment was only discovered during the course of the reconnaissance in force (*Historical Discourses*, p. 130).
12. Probably a misreading of butts, an alternative name for the parallel ridges created by the strip system of open field agriculture. The Naseby area today is scattered with corrugated landscapes of ridge and furrow as a result of the open fields being laid down to grass in the fifteenth and sixteenth centuries. The difficulties they posed for cavalry moving across them at speed are fully apparent from Plate 19.
13. Slingsby, *Diary*, p. 151. A pamphlet written in 1647 has Cromwell advising Fairfax that Rupert would not attack up so steep a slope, and that the New Model Army should move elsewhere if it wanted to tempt the Royalists into fighting a battle (TT E372 22).
14. Walker (*Historical Discourses*, p. 130) claimed that what could be seen of the enemy's motions may have suggested this to Prince Rupert, and Slingsby reported that enemy horse were returning up the escarpment towards Naseby village (*Diary*, p. 150).
15. This caused considerable puzzlement to earlier writers, who rightly pointed out that the sources do not clearly show that Rupert was the first to move (Gardiner, *History of the Great Civil War*, vol. 2, pp. 244–5; pp. 386–91, Colonel Ross's observations; Burne, *Battlefields of England*, pp. 444–6). However, the only source that suggests that the New Model Army moved first is Slingsby, who described 'their horse marching up on the side of the hill to that place where after they embattled their whole army', but if Cromwell's horse (probably Okey's dragoons which had spent the night beyond the ridge in Clipston Fields) were using the road from Clipston to Naseby, which goes across the escarpment in a diagonal direction as it heads for Naseby village, to rejoin the New Model, they would have given the impression that they were heading further west towards Sheddon Hill and Broad Moor (Slingsby, *Diary*, pp. 150–1; TT E288 38).
16. Foard, *Naseby*, p. 226. I am grateful to Martin Marix Evans for pointing this route out during a tour of the Naseby battlefield conducted under the auspices of the Battlefields Trust.
17. Walker described the king's army as moving a mile and a half in the enemy's direction from its first position. This would have taken it as far as Clipston village whether it had been deployed at East Farndon, between East Farndon and Great Oxendon, or at Great Oxendon. In all three circumstances the escarpment would have been best climbed using the Clipston–Sibbertoft road rather than backtracking onto the westwards extension of the ridge (*Historical Discourses*, p. 111).
18. Although well able to watch the progress of the king's army from the escarpment, Fairfax seems to have taken as long to deploy his troops on Closter Hill as the enemy did to deploy on Dust Hill. This was possibly because the constricted nature of the plateau around Naseby village produced bottlenecks as regiments arriving from the west encountered other regiments moving northwards from the edge of the escarpment to the new position.

19. I very largely agree with the excellent collaborative account in Foard's *Naseby*, which is based on careful research combined with painstaking and thoughtful discussion. My figure for the Royalist army is slightly larger, as the participants failed to notice that one of the Newark garrison infantry regiments, Colonel St George's, fought at Naseby. It is also possible that the Dudley garrison foot joined the king's army as it passed close to the castle on 16 May rather than at Stow-on-the-Wold a week earlier. Reid, though apparently using Foard's work, argued mistakenly that the armies were much closer to one another in size, but his calculations do not take into account the likelihood that 400 Newark horse left the king's army between the capture of Leicester and the Battle of Naseby, whilst almost 500 Lincolnshire cavalry under Colonel Rossiter joined Fairfax just before the battle began. Gentles, on the other hand, overestimated the size of the Parliamentary cavalry by including the number of horse Cromwell claimed to have raised in the Eastern Association, not the number he actually brought with him (Foard, *Naseby*, pp. 197–209; Evelyn, *Diary*, p. 145. Reid, *All the King's Armies*, pp. 199–201, 205; Gentles, *The New Model Army in England, Ireland, and Scotland*, p. 36; Symonds, *Diaries*, p. 186; Sprigg, *Anglia Rediviva*, p. 35; Young, *Naseby*, pp. 90, 92–3).
20. Wanklyn and Jones, *Military History of the English Civil War*, pp. 241–2.
21. Walker, *Historical Discourses*, pp. 130–1; Clarendon, *History of the Great Rebellion*, book 9, 39, 41.
22. Wiltshire CRO, 413/444Ai, 69; BL Additional ms 16370, 63.
23. BL Additional ms 16370, 63. See also note 28 below.
24. See Chapter 13, p. 170. They were apparently 130 strong at the assault on Leicester, but 500 strong at Naseby. If this was the result of large numbers of new recruits or gentlemen volunteers joining their ranks, it may help to explain what went wrong with their charge (Symonds, *Diaries*, p. 182; Walker, *Historical Discourses*, pp. 130, 131).
25. See below, p. 170.
26. Vermuyden had suddenly resigned as Commissary General on about 7 June after he and his force had joined Fairfax in North Buckinghamshire. He apparently needed to return to the Continent as soon as possible (Sprigg, *Anglia Rediviva*, p. 32), but it seems odd that his resignation was accepted so readily in the middle of a campaign with a battle probably in the offing.
27. TT E288 38; Slingsby, *Diary*, p. 151.
28. Streeter's plan places the whole of the Newark horse on the Royalist left wing. It is impossible to say whether his or de Gomme's is correct. Sir Philip Warwick mentions 'some trivial but pernicious disputes' between Langdale and the commander of the Newark horse that occurred prior to the battle and implies that it had an effect on what happened on that wing. On the other hand, Sprigg's account of the fight between Ireton and Maurice on the right wing suggests that it may have been decided by cavalry from the Royalist reserves, and these cannot have been the Royal Lifeguard (BL Additional ms 16370, 63; Warwick, *Memoirs*, p. 316; Sprigg, *Anglia Rediviva*, p. 42). See also Plates 14 and 15.
29. Sprigg's account indicates that Cromwell did not personally lead the first line in response to Langdale's advance (*Anglia Rediviva*, pp. 40, 48–9) and his description of Cromwell's direct involvement in the fighting is subtly different from those of Fairfax, who was in the thick of the fray, and Skippon, who was wounded leading up the second line of the New Model infantry. George Bishop's account gives a similar impression (TT E288 38).
30. Symonds, *Diaries*, pp. 165–6; Walker, *Historical Discourses*, p. 130.
31. Here again there is a slight disagreement between de Gomme (three bodies) and Streeter (two bodies).
32. Symonds, *Diaries*, p. 182; BL Additional ms 16370, 63.
33. One Parliamentary source suggests that they were placed where they were to push the infantry forward if they hesitated (TT E288 28).
34. Sprigg, *Anglia Rediviva*, p. 41, though this is not apparent from Streeter's plan.
35. See p. 165.
36. Staffordshire CRO DW 1778Ii, 56; Sprigg, *Anglia Rediviva*, p. 38. Phillip Skippon, in conversation with the Earl of Orrery, merely claimed that the front line was ordered to fall back from the northern slope of Closter Hill to the summit because it was better ground (Boyle, *Treatise of the Art of War*, p. 154).
37. Sprigg, *Anglia Rediviva*, p. 31.
38. Walker, *Historical Discourses*, p. 130; TT E288 22.
39. Walker, *Historical Discourses*, p. 130; TT E288 25.
40. Foard, *Naseby*, pp. 409–10.
41. The only direct evidence of cavalry involvement is in Sprigg's account, but the fact that Ireton himself was wounded by an infantry weapon early on in the battle provides a measure of indirect support (Sprigg, *Anglia Rediviva*, p. 41; Walker, *Historical Discourses*, p. 130).
42. Laing (ed.), *Letters and Journals of Robert Baillie*, vol. 2, p. 286.
43. This can be inferred from Slingsby's comment that the lie of the land gave the attacking Royalists a false impression of the size of the enemy army (*Diary*, p. 151).
44. Young, *Naseby*, p. 87; PRO SP23.124, 627; Cheshire CRO Quarter Sessions files, Trinity 1663, 94.
45. TT E288 38; Slingsby, *Diary*, p. 151.

46. TT E288 26, 37.
47. Sprigg, *Anglia Rediviva*, pp. 41–2; TT E288 38.
48. The exact position of the New Model artillery train is a matter of dispute, but it lay somewhere between Closter Hill and Naseby village.
49. Sprigg, *Anglia Rediviva*, p. 43. Admittedly Okey describes Colonel Butler's regiment, which was on the extreme left of the first line, as likely to have been annihilated had his dragoons not provided covering fire from Sulby Hedges, but the text reads as if the cavalry mentioned were fugitives, not ordered bodies of horse (TT E288 38).
50. Wiltshire CRO 413/444Ai, 69.
51. See Chapter 2, p. 12.
52. TT E288 38.
53. See, for example, Kitson, *Prince Rupert*, pp. 243–4.
54. Rohan, *The Complete Captain*, part 3, ch. 7.
55. See Chapter 11, pp. 132–4.
56. Ibid., pp. 129–30. Foard claims that Rupert probably used all his reserves to defeat Ireton including, presumably, any Newark horse behind the right wing. Rupert's Diary does not explicitly rule this out, though he implies otherwise (Foard, *Naseby*, p. 269; Wiltshire CRO 413/444Ai, 69).
57. Staffordshire CRO DW 1778Ii, 56.
58. TT E288 38. See also Plate 18.
59. Carte (ed.), *Original Documents and Papers*, vol. 1, p. 128.
60. Sprigg, *Anglia Rediviva*, pp. 39–40; TT E288 26; Slingsby, *Diary*, p. 152.
61. Sprigg, *Anglia Rediviva*, p. 40; Slingsby, *Diary*, p. 152.
62. Foard, *Naseby*, pp. 409–12 is an accurate transcription of an unfoliated document in PRO SP28.173 that lists the costs of caring for the wounded. This shows that Sir Thomas Fairfax's cavalry regiment had only eighteen wounded despite being in the front line, Sheffield's seven, Fiennes's two, and Rossiter's none.
63. Wiltshire CRO 413/444Ai, 69; Sprigg, *Anglia Rediviva*, pp. 39–41; TT E288 26; Slingsby, *Diary*, p. 152; Walker, *Historical Discourses*, pp. 130–1.
64. Sprigg, *Anglia Rediviva*, p. 43; Walker, *Historical Discourses*, p. 131; TT E288 28; Foard, *Naseby*, p. 411; Rushworth (ed.), *Historical Collections*, vol. 6, p. 43.
65. Sprigg, *Anglia Rediviva*, p. 40; Slingsby, *Diary*, p. 152; Rushworth (ed.), *Historical Collections*, vol. 6, p. 43; Walker, *Historical Discourses*, p. 131.
66. Wiltshire CRO 413/444Ai, 69; TT E288 26, 28.
67. Walker, *Historical Discourses*, p. 131; Wiltshire CRO 413/444Ai, 69; Sprigg, *Anglia Rediviva*, pp. 39–40.
68. The paucity of musket balls found over much of Broad Moor suggests that they did not retreat too far.
69. Circumstantial evidence in support of this Royalist viewpoint is to be found in Okey's narrative.
70. Charles Singleton has suggested that the brigade may not have been Prince Rupert's regiment, but the one belonging to the first or second line, as blue was a common coat colour in the Oxford army.
71. Whitelocke, *Memorials*, p. 151; TT E288 26; Sprigg, *Anglia Rediviva*, p. 43.
72. Marix Evans, Burton and Westaway, *Naseby*, p. 152; TT E288 38; E289 3; Symonds, *Diaries*, p. 166.
73. TT E288 38; Symonds, *Diaries*, p. 166. The sole evidence for their destruction is a brief comment in one of the newspapers published ten days after the battle (TT E289 3). See Chapter 15 note 28 for discussion of the provenance of the source.
74. Wiltshire CRO 413/444Ai, 70. The King's Regiment were frequently described as the King's Lifeguard of Foot.
75. Walker, *Historical Discourses*, p. 131; Slingsby, *Diary*, p. 152; Sprigg, *Anglia Rediviva*, p. 43; TT E288 26.
76. This is very apparent from the list of officers taken prisoner (TT E288 21).
77. Recently it has been suggested that the final stand by the king's cavalry was beyond the Sibbertoft–Clipston road on the northern edge of the escarpment, but it takes a highly eccentric reading of the written sources to reach such a conclusion.
78. HMC Ormond ms n.s. II, 386; Sprigg, *Anglia Rediviva*, p. 43; TT E288 28, 37, 38.
79. Foard, *Naseby*, pp. 275–80; Reid, *All the King's Armies*, p. 203; Marix Evans, Burton and Westwood, *Naseby*, pp. 115–19; Marshall, *Oliver Cromwell, Soldier*, p. 148.
80. The only narrative that might imply that the king's infantry did anything other than surrender en masse on the battlefield is Thomas Wogan's, but it takes a very eccentric reading of the text to make it so. Wogan describes that part of the Royalist cavalry which had routed much of the New Model's left wing (i.e. not the infantry) as retreating to 'the top of the hill toward Harborough', but the context is such that the description almost certainly refers to Dust Hill where the king's army drew up at the start of the battle, which was on the Market Harborough side of the battlefield, not somewhere further to the north. This passage is followed by a brief description of the surrender of the king's infantry as a result of their being deserted by their horse. There is nothing in Wogan's account that conflicts with the other accounts

written by soldiers and civilians on both sides which state that the surrender took place on the battlefield (Carte (ed.), *Original Documents and Papers*, vol. 1, pp. 128–9).

81. For a possible explanation of the musket balls on either side of the road between Naseby and Sibbertoft, see Chapter 14, p. 171.

82. The regiment that had guarded the train in 1644 - Lord Percy's, but by 1645 Colonel Murray's - may have continued in that role. Reid suggests otherwise but does not cite his evidence. Another possible contender is Prince Rupert's firelocks. For reasons of safety the force guarding the main store of gunpowder would not normally have been armed with matchlocks (Reid, *All the King's Armies*, p. 205; Young, *Naseby*, pp. 105-6).

Chapter 16. The Battle of Preston: Context, Landscape and Sources

1. Wanklvn and Jones, *Military History of the English Civil War*, pp. 255-61.
2. Ibid., p. 282.
3. See Chapter 17, p. 196.
4. There are no contemporary sketches of the battle, and no prospect of discovering anything of value from an archaeological survey of the few areas of the battlefield not covered in housing or industrial premises. The two maps of Preston drawn before 1750 are too focused on the town to be of any value.
5. Clarendon, *History of the Great Rebellion*, book 9, 75-7.
6. Sunderland, *Marmaduke, Lord Langdale*, pp. 133-5; Carte (ed.), *Original Documents and Papers*, vol. 1, pp. 159-61; Bodl. Clarendon ms 2862.
7. Sunderland, *Marmaduke, Lord Langdale*, p. 134. This is the version that I use in writing the narrative in Chapter 17.
8. TTE467 21.
9. TT E461 5.
10. Woolrych, *Battles of the English Civil Wars*, p. 192.
11. Burnet, *Memoirs of the Lives and Actions of the Dukes of Hamilton*, pp. 357-60; Turner, *Memoirs*, Appendix, pp. 249-51; TT E467 21.
12. Turner, *Memoirs*, pp. vii-x, 57-68.
13. Ibid., Appendix, pp. 228, 248-9, 252-4.
14. Abbott (ed), *Writings and Speeches of Oliver Cromwell*, vol. 1, pp. 632-9.
15. Blackmore, 'Counting the New Model Army', *Civil War Times* 58, Leigh-on-Sea.
16. TT E420 35.
17. Turner, *Memoirs*. These were published, together with some of Sir James's correspondence, by the Bannatyne Club in 1829, but the editor provides a clear chain of descent from Sir James to the owner of the manuscript in the early nineteenth century. There is no evidence of editorial interference, such as the language and spelling having been brought up to date.
18. TT E460 20; Gentles, *The New Model Army in England, Ireland, and Scotland*, p. 514; Bull and Seed, *Bloody Preston*.
19. HMC Portland ms III, 174-5; Beaumont (ed), *A Discourse of the Wan in Lancashire*, pp.174-5.

Chapter 17. The Battle of Preston: Narrative

1. HMC Portland ms HI 174-5; HMC Brave ms, 168; Turner, *Memoirs*, pp. 61-2; Beaumont (ed.), *A Discourse of the Warr in Lancashire*, p. 64.
2. Rushworth (ed), *Historical Collections*, vol. 8, p. 1211. Woolrych and Reid describe an encounter at Stainmore on 26 July, but do not cite their sources. Bull and Seed cite Hodgson and Carlyle's edition of Cromwell's letters, but these describe the encounter at Appleby, which took place before the withdrawal to Barnard Castle. I cannot find any record of it in the reports of Lambert's despatches to London reproduced in Rushworth (Woolrych, *Battles of the English Civil Wars*, p. 163; Reid, *All the King's Armies*, p. 226). The origin of the rumour appears to have been an anonymous letter reproduced in TT E456 5, and repeated almost word for word in TT E456 13, which was almost certainly composed in London, as it represents Stainmore as a bridge six miles from Barnard Castle, not an extensive upland moor between Barnard Castle and Brough. The only bridge in the vicinity, the one over the Tees, is in Barnard Castle itself.
3. Whitelocke, *Memorials*, p. 326.
4. Ibid., p. 314; HMC Portland ms III, 175.
5. Carpenter, *Military Leadership in the British Civil Wars*, p. 133.
6. Ibid., pp. 174-5; TT E459 2; E525 20.
7. Abbott (ed.), *Writings and Speeches of Oliver Cromwell*, vol. 1, pp. 634, 638; Hodgson, *Memoirs*, p. 114. Lambert claimed that he had 9,000 troops under his command in early August, but this figure included local levies which did not fight in the Preston campaign, and possibly the forces besieging Pontefract and Scarborough (Rushworth (ed.), *Historical Collections*, vol. 7, pp. 1211, 1218).

8. Hodgson, *Memoirs*, pp. 114, 119; TT E460 35.
9. Abbott (ed.), *Writings and Speeches of Oliver Cromwell*, vol. 1, pp. 635–8. Cromwell put the total at 21,000, but this almost certainly included Monro's troops from Ireland, between 2,500 and 3,500 strong, and overestimated the number of horse that had escaped northwards from Preston. Worryingly, he mentioned 24,000 in a letter written the same day (ibid., p. 639). The most recent historians' estimates are just short of 14,000 without Munro's corps (Woolrych, *Britain in Revolution*, p. 416) and 21,000 (Carpenter, *Military Leadership in the British Civil Wars*, pp. 132, 134).
10. Reid, *All the King's Armies*, pp. 225–6.
11. Turner, *Memoirs*, p. 62; Cholmley, 'Memorials', p. 346; Abbott (ed.), *Writings and Speeches of Oliver Cromwell*, vol. 1, pp. 634–5; HMC Portland ms III, 175. They may, however, have been mounted on better horses than they are supposed to have had at Marston Moor (see Chapter 11, p. 129).
12. Reid, *All the King's Armies*, pp. 225–6, 234.
13. Abbott (ed.), *Writings and Speeches of Oliver Cromwell*, vol. 1, p. 634.
14. Turner, *Memoirs*, p. 62; Langdale, 'Impartial Relation', in Sunderland, *Marmaduke, Lord Langdale*, p. 133.
15. Woolrych, *Battles of the English Civil Wars*, p. 166.
16. Langdale, *Impartial Relation*, p. 133. See below for Dachment's confirmation that Hamilton received such intelligence.
17. Abbott (ed.), *Writings and Speeches of Oliver Cromwell*, vol. 1, p. 634.
18. Burnet, *Memoirs of the Lives and Actions of the Dukes of Hamilton*, p. 357.
19. Rohan, *The Complete Captain*, ch. 5 ('Of Marching').
20. TT E467 21.
21. Woolrych, *Battles of the English Civil Wars*, p. 166; Reid, *All the King's Armies*, pp. 228–9.
22. Turner, *Memoirs*, pp. 62–3.
23. Ibid., Appendix, pp. 248–9.
24. Ibid., p. 251.
25. TT E460 35; Hodgson, *Memoirs*, pp. 115–16.
26. Turner, *Memoirs*, p. 62.
27. Ibid., pp. 62–3; Sunderland, *Marmaduke, Lord Langdale*, pp. 134–5.
28. Turner, *Memoirs*, pp. 62–3; TT E467 21.
29. Hodgson, *Memoirs*, p. 117; TT E460 35.
30. This point is made by Burnet (*Memoirs of the Lives and Actions of the Dukes of Hamilton*, p. 359).
31. The time of the day is rarely mentioned in accounts of the battle, but the assault could not have taken place any later than 4 p.m. given what was to follow, a lengthy engagement in the enclosures and another lengthy engagement at the bridge over the Ribble.
32. Abbott (ed.), *Writings and Speeches of Oliver Cromwell*, vol. 1, pp. 634–5; Hodgson, *Memoirs*, pp. 115–18; TT E460 35; Langdale, *Impartial Relation*, p. 134.
33. Hodgson, *Memoirs*, p. 118; Langdale, *Impartial Relation*, p. 135; Beaumont (ed.), *A Discourse of the Warr in Lancashire*, p. 35; Abbott (ed.), *Writings and Speeches of Oliver Cromwell*, vol. 1, pp. 235–6. The intended route for the retreat was probably along the present-day Watery Lane, which leads from the Clitheroe road via Fishwick Flats to the riverside right by the bridge.
34. TT E460 35; E467 21; Turner, *Memoirs*, p. 64; Burnet, *Memoirs of the Lives and Actions of the Dukes of Hamilton*, p. 360. It seems, however, a little surprising that the Scots did not destroy the bridge before Cromwell's infantry occupied the escarpment, but they may not have had any pioneers available. Additionally Hamilton's generals wanted to keep the bridge open so that as many troops as possible could cross to the south side of the river, including the duke himself. Blowing the bridge up with gunpowder was probably not an option. This was in short supply. It should also be remembered that the explosives and technology then available did not make it easy to lay and explode a charge, especially as enemy troops on the escarpment were able to bring intense fire down onto the bridge.
35. Abbott (ed.), *Writings and Speeches of Oliver Cromwell*, vol. 1, p. 365; TT E460 35; Beaumont (ed.), *A Discourse of the Warr in Lancashire*, p. 65.
36. TT E460 35; Abbott (ed.), *Writings and Speeches of Oliver Cromwell*, vol. 1, pp. 633, 635–6.
37. Turner, *Memoirs*, pp. 63–5; TT E460 35; E467 21; Hodgson, *Memoirs*, pp. 120–1; Abbott (ed.), *Writings and Speeches of Oliver Cromwell*, vol. 1, p. 236. Bull and Seed claim that Hamilton also abandoned his artillery at this point, but this is incorrect despite their assertion that there is evidence for this in two accounts written immediately after the battle. The first is the fallacious *Bloody Battle of Preston* pamphlet. The second is the *Moderate Intelligencer*, but this only refers to ammunition and carriages (*Bloody Preston*, pp. 39, 77).
38. Abbott (ed.), *Writings and Speeches of Oliver Cromwell*, vol. 1, pp. 236–7; Beaumont (ed.), *A Discourse of the Warr in Lancashire*, pp. 45–6; TT E421 29; Langdale, *Impartial Relation*, pp. 135–6; Turner, *Memoirs*, pp. 67–8.
39. Langdale, *Impartial Relation*, p. 134; TT E467 21.

40. e.g. Reid, *All the King's Horses*, pp. 228–9; Young and Holmes, *English Civil Wars*, p. 285.
41. TT E467 21.
42. Langdale, *Impartial Relation*, p. 134.
43. Indeed, the fact that it was Lambert apparently who issued the order for the Lancashire brigade to advance at the climactic moment of the battle to the east of Preston, and that Cromwell's defence of the conduct of the two regiments on the right flank was that they had not been involved in the fighting because they outflanked the enemy, may mean that he was exploring the option of redeploying them when the breakthrough came (Hodgson, *Memoirs*, p. 118; Abbott (ed.), *Writings and Speeches of Oliver Cromwell*, vol. 1, p. 635).
44. This is Callendar's advice as described by Burnet, but it is also possible that he did attempt to reinforce Langdale using the two brigades as suggested by Turner. If so, they were probably a scratch force of stragglers who had arrived late on Preston Moor.
45. Turner, *Memoirs*, pp. 62–3.
46. Abbott (ed.), *Writings and Speeches of Oliver Cromwell*, vol. 1, p. 634.
47. Kitson describes it as a calculated risk, based on the uselessness of the Scottish army, but it is difficult to understand how Cromwell could have known at this stage in the campaign that the Scottish army was useless (*Old Ironsides*, p. 153). A contemporary pamphlet is more perceptive: Cromwell was fortunate to fall on the Scots 'in the nick of time' whilst their commanders were arguing about how to quarter their troops (TT E460 23).

Chapter 18. Conclusion
1. See, for example, Smith, *History of the Modern British Isles*, p. 147.
2. Wanklyn and Jones, *Military History of the English Civil War*, pp. 11–24.
3. Gardiner, *History of the Great Civil War*, vol. 2, pp. 249–51.
4. Woolrych, *Battles of the English Civil Wars*, pp. 138, 139.
5. Reid, *All the King's Armies*, pp. 251–5.
6. Young and Holmes, *English Civil Wars*, pp. 334–7.
7. Barratt, *Cavaliers*, pp. 29–30; Barratt, *Cavalier Generals*, pp. 208–9.
8. Anderson, *Civil Wars*, p. 84.
9. Identifying a safe way to retreat was an elementary precaution, and one of the Parliamentary weeklies commented as follows on Rupert's failure to do so at Naseby: 'Why did you fight thirteen miles from a garrison and where there was neither hedges, woods or river to stop us following?' (TT E288 37).
10. Boyle, *Treatise of the Art of War*, p. 180. See also Chapter 9, p. 106 and Chapter 13, p. 157.
11. This is what Lord Byron claimed (Bodl. Carte ms XII, 218: Byron to Ormonde 3 August 1644).
12. Wanklyn and Jones, *Military History of the English Civil War*, p. 272.
13. In Rupert's case it can be argued that his early intervention at Marston Moor was essential to prevent the complete collapse of his right wing and at Naseby because success on the right was essential to his battle plan.
14. *A Particular Treatise of Modern War*, the third part of *The Complete Captain*, translated from the French by John Cruso, printed in Cambridge and purchasable from April 1640 onwards at the sign of the Angel in Pope's Head Alley in the City of London. Since Rohan had been killed three years earlier fighting for the Protestant cause, this is just the kind of book Oliver Cromwell would have purchased to learn more about military matters. It has been neglected by historians, probably because the book appears in library catalogues as if it were merely a commentary on Julius Caesar's *Wars*, but these only form parts 1 and 2 of the book. I first came across a reference to the treatise in the library of the Musée de la Paix at Caen.
15. Reid, *All the King's Armies*, pp. 203–4.
16. Another set of protocols has recently been published in Scott, Turton and Von Arni's *Edgehill: The Battle Reinterpreted*, but these concentrate on how to set about researching a Civil War battle from scratch and how to view the landscape, the latter being the great strength of their book. They therefore complement my set, which focuses primarily on how to manage written texts.

Bibliography

Manuscript Primary Sources

Public Record Office
SP 23 (Royalist Compounding Papers)

British Library
Additional ms 16370, 18778–9, 18980, 18981, 25708, 27402
Harleian ms 166, 986, 2135, 3783, 6804
Lansdowne ms 988

Bodleian Library, University of Oxford
Ashmole ms 830
Carte ms X, XI, XII, XV, LXXIV, LXXX
Clarendon ms 21–25, 28, 1738, 2862
English ms 132, C51
Fairfax ms 36
Firth ms C7
Rawlinson ms B200
Tanner ms 62

Berkshire County Record Office
Q/P116B/28/22/1 (enclosure map of Speen)

Birmingham Reference Library
Battle Farm, Kineton survey

Cheshire County Record Office
Quarter Sessions files

Hampshire County Record Office
53 M 67/1 (survey of the manor of Cheriton, 1602)
M65/F7/30, 46, 117, 232 (tithe apportionment maps of the parishes of Bramdean, Cheriton, Hinton
    Ampner and Tichbourne)
Isaac Taylor, Map of Hampshire and the Isle of Wight, 1759

Staffordshire County Record Office
Earl of Dartmouth mss DW 1778Ii
Duke of Sutherland mss, Letterbooks 2, 3

Shropshire County Record Office
445/277 An account of the Battle of Marston Moor by Ferdinando, Lord Fairfax
445/278 A version of Leonard Watson's account of the battle that appears to predate the one printed in
    London (Thomason Tracts E2 14)

Warwickshire County Record Office
Earl of Denbigh ms CR2017/C10
Maps CR 1134/1, 1596, 2917, c10 135

Wiltshire County Record Office
413/377 Letters to Prince Rupert
413/444Ai Prince Rupert's 'Diary' of the Civil War
413/444Aii Typed copy of notes made by the seventeenth-century compiler of the Diary to supplement the
    narrative, but not included in the text of 413/444a

Printed Primary Sources

Contemporary Biographies, Diaries and Memoirs

Boyle, Roger, Earl of Orrery, *A Treatise of the Art of War*, London, 1677.

Bulstrode, Sir Richard, *Memoirs and Reflections upon the Reign and Government of Charles I and Charles II*, London, 1721.

Burnet, Gilbert, *The Memoirs of the Lives and Actions of James and William, Dukes of Hamilton*, London, 1677.

Byron, Sir John, 'Relation of the Late Western Action', in P. Young (ed.), *Journal of the Society for Army Historical Research* 31, 1953.

Cavendish, Margaret, Duchess of Newcastle, *The Lives of William Cavendish, Duke of Newcastle and of his wife Margaret, Duchess of Newcastle*, London: J.R. Smith, 1872 edn.

Cholmley, Sir Hugh, 'Memorials Touching the Battle of York', *English Historical Review* 5, 1890.

Clarendon, Earl of (Edward Hyde), *History of the Great Rebellion and Civil Wars in England from 1641*, ed. W. Macray, Oxford: Oxford University Press, 1888.

Clarke, J. (ed.), *Life of James II collected out of memoirs written by his own hand*, vol. 1, London: Longman, 1816.

Codrington, Robert, *The Life and Death of the Illustrious Robert, Earl of Essex*, London, 1646.

Evelyn, John, *Diary*, ed. W. Bray, Oxford University Press, 1877–9.

Fuller, Thomas, *The Worthies of England*, London, 1662.

Gough, Richard, *Human Nature displayed in the History of Myddle*, Shrewsbury: Adnitt and Naunton, 1878.

Gwyn, John, *Military Memoirs: The Civil War*, ed. N. Tucker and P. Young, London: Longman, 1967.

Hodgson, John, *Memoirs*, in Sir Henry Slingsby, *Original Memoirs*, London, 1806 edn.

Holles, Denzil, 'Memoirs 1641–1648', in Francis, Lord Maseres (ed.), *Select Tracts relating to the Civil Wars in England*, vol. 1, London: R. Wilks, 1815.

Hopton, Ralph, Lord, *Bellum Civile*, ed. C. Chadwyck-Healey, Somerset Record Society 18, 1902.

Juxon, Thomas, *Journal 1644–47*, ed. K. Lindley and D. Scott, Camden Society 5th series 13, 1999.

Lilly, William, *History of his Life and Times*, London, 1667.

Lloyd, David, *Memoirs of the Lives, Actions, Sufferings and Deaths of the Noble, Reverend and Excellent Personages who suffered for the Protestant Religion*, London, 1668.

Ludlow, Edmund, *Memoirs 1625–1672*, vol. 1, ed. Sir Charles Firth, Oxford University Press, 1894.

Luke, Sir Samuel, *Journals*, 3 vols, ed. I. Phillip, Oxfordshire Record Society, 29 (1947), 31 (1950), 33 (1952–3).

—, *Letterbooks*, ed. H. Tibbutt, Historical Manuscripts Commission Joint Publications 4, HMSO, 1963.

Monckton Papers, *Philobiblion Society*, Miscellany 15, *c.* 1884.

Roe, Henry, *Military Memoir of Colonel John Birch*, ed. T. Webb, Camden Society n.s. 7, 1873.

Rohan, Henri, Duc de, *The Complete Captain III: A Particular Treatise of Modern War*, translated by Captain John Cruso, Cambridge, 1640.

Slingsby, Sir Henry, *Diary*, ed. D. Parsons, London: Longman, 1836.

Slingsby, Walter, 'Accounts of the Campaigns in the South of England 1643–44', in C. Chadwyck-Healey (ed.), *Bellum Civile*, Somerset Record Society 18, 1902.

Somerville, James, Lord, *Memorie of the Somervilles*, Edinburgh, 1815.

Sprigg, Joshua, *Anglia Rediviva*, London: Oxford University Press, 1844 edn.

Symonds, Richard, *Diaries of the Marches of the Royal Army during the History of the Great Civil War*, ed. C. Long, Camden Society 74, 1859.

Turner, Sir James, *Memoirs of His Own Life and Times*, Edinburgh, 1829.

Walker, Sir Edward, *Historical Discourses*, London, 1705.

Walsh, Sir Robert, *The True Narration and Manifest*, 1679.

Walsingham, Edward, *Britannicae Virtutis Imago*, Oxford (Thomason Tract E53 10), 1644.

Walsingham, Edward, *Hector Britannicus: The Life of Sir John Digby*, ed. G. Bernard, Camden Society, 3rd series 18, 1910.

Warwick, Sir Philip, *Memoirs of the Reign of King Charles I*, Edinburgh: Ballantyne, 1813.

Whitelocke, Bulstrode, *Memorials of the English Affairs*, London: J. Tonson, 1732.

Edited Collections

Abbott, W. (ed.), *The Writings and Speeches of Oliver Cromwell*, vol. 1, Cambridge, Mass.: Harvard University Press, 1937.

Beaumont, W. (ed.), *A Discourse of the Warr in Lancashire*, Chetham Society 62, 1864.

Bruce, J. and Masson, D. (eds), *Manchester's Quarrel: Documents relating to the Quarrel between the Earl of Manchester and Oliver Cromwell*, Camden Society n.s. 12, 1875.

Calendar of State Papers Domestic 1641–3, 1644, 1644–45, 1645–47, London: HMSO.

Carlyle, Thomas (ed.), *Oliver Cromwell's Letters and Speeches*, 3 vols, 2nd edn, London: Chapman and Hall, 1846.

Carte, T. (ed.), *A Collection of Original Documents and Papers 1641–60 found amongst the Duke of Ormonde's Papers*, vol.1, London: J. Buttenham, 1739.
Chadwyck-Healey, C. (ed.), *Bellum Civile: Hopton's Narrative of his Campaign in the West and Other Papers*, Somerset Record Society 18, 1902.
Ellis, Sir Henry (ed.), *Original Letters Illustrative of English History 1400–1793*, 3rd series, 4th series, London: Richard Bentley, 1847.
Historical Manuscripts Commission, MSS of the Earl de la Warre (Appendix to the 4th Report), London: HMSO.
—, MSS of the Earl of Denbigh, (Appendix to the 4th Report), London: HMSO.
—, MSS of the Duke of Sutherland (Appendix to the 5th Report), London: HMSO.
—, MSS of A. Morrison (Appendix to the 9th Report, part II), London: HMSO.
—, MSS of Lord Braye (Appendix to the 10th Report, part VI), London: HMSO.
—, MSS of the Duke of Beaufort (Appendix to the12th Report, part IX), London: HMSO.
—, MSS of the Duke of Portland III (Appendix to the 13th Report, part II), London: HMSO.
—, MSS of the Marquis of Ormond new series II (Appendix to the 14th Report, part VII), London: HMSO.
House of Lords Journals, vol. 7.
Laing, D. (ed.), *Letters and Journals of Robert Baillie 1637–1662*, 3 vols, Bannatyne Club, Edinburgh, 1841.
Maseres, Francis, Lord (ed.), *Select Tracts relating to the Civil Wars in England*, 2 vols, London: R. Wilks, 1815.
Roy, I. (ed.), *Royalist Ordnance Papers*, Oxfordshire Record Society 43, 1964 and 49, 1975.
Rushworth, J. (ed.), *Historical Collections*, vols 4, 5 and 6, London: D. Browne, 1721.
Sanford, J. (ed.), Appendix to *The Great Rebellion*, London: Bickers & Son, 1858.
Wanklyn, M. (ed.), *Inventories of Worcestershire Landowners 1536–1785*, Worcestershire Historical Society, n.s. 16, 1998.
Warburton, E.G.B., *Memoirs of Prince Rupert and the Cavaliers* 3 vols, London: Richard Bentley, 1849.

Collections of Newspapers and Pamphlets
British Library, Thomason Tracts (TT) 669f, E2–350.
Thomas, P. (ed.), *The English Revolution III: Newspapers. I: Mercurius Aulicus*, 4 vols, London: Cornmarket, 1971.

Printed Secondary Sources

Books and Pamphlets
Adair, J., *Cheriton 1644: The Campaign and the Battle*, Kineton: Roundway Press, 1973.
Adair, J., *Roundhead General: The Campaigns of Sir William Waller*, 2nd edn, Stroud: Sutton, 1997.
Anderson, A., *The Civil Wars*, 2nd edn, London: Hodder and Stoughton, 2002.
Barratt, J., *The Battle for York: Marston Moor 1644*, Stroud: Tempus, 2003.
—, *Cavalier Generals: King Charles I and his Commanders in the English Civil War 1642–46*, Barnsley: Pen and Sword, 2004.
—, *Cavaliers: The Royalist Army at War 1642–46*, Stroud: Alan Sutton, 2000.
—, *The First Battle of Newbury*, Stroud: Tempus, 2005.
Bull, S. and Seed, M., *Bloody Preston*, Lancaster: Carnegie, 1997.
Burne, A.H., *The Battlefields of England*, London: Penguin, 1996.
Burne, A.H. and Young, P., *The Great Civil War: A Military History of the First Civil War*, London: Eyre & Spottiswood, 1959.
Carpenter, S., *Military Leadership in the British Civil Wars 1642–1651*, London: Cass, 2005.
Childs, J., *Warfare in the Seventeenth Century*, London: Cassell, 2001.
Earwaker, J.P., *East Cheshire Past and Present, or a History of the Macclesfield Hundred*, 2 vols, London: privately printed, 1877, 1880.
Edgar, F., *Sir Ralph Hopton*, Oxford: Oxford University Press, 1968.
Firth, Sir Charles, *Cromwell*, London: Putnam's, 1904.
—, *Cromwell's Army*, London: Methuen, 1962.
Foard, G., *Naseby: The Decisive Campaign*, Whitstable: Prior Publications, 1995.
Gardiner, S.R., *History of the Great Civil War*, 4 vols, Moreton in the Marsh: Windrush Press, 1887–94 (1991 edn).
Gentles, I., *The New Model Army in England, Ireland, and Scotland, 1645–1653*, Oxford: Blackwell, 1992.
Godwin, G.N., *The Civil War in Hampshire 1642–48*, London: Bumford, 1904.
Holmes, C., *The Eastern Association in the English Civil War*, Cambridge: Cambridge University Press, 1974.
Jenkins, K., *Rethinking History*, London: Routledge, 1991.

Jones, K., *A Glorious Fame: The Life of Margaret Cavendish, Duchess of Newcastle*, London: Bloomsbury, 1988.

Kishlansky, M., *The Rise of the New Model Army*, Cambridge: Cambridge University Press, 1979.

Kitson, Sir Frank, *Old Ironsides: The Military Biography of Oliver Cromwell*, London: Weidenfeld & Nicolson, 2004.

—, *Prince Rupert: Portrait of a Soldier*, London: Constable, 1994.

Marix Evans, M., Burton, P. and Westaway, M., *Naseby: June 1645*, Barnsley: Pen & Sword, 2002.

Markham, Sir Clement, *The Great Lord Fairfax*, London: Macmillan, 1870.

—, *The Life of Robert Fairfax of Steeton*, London: Macmillan, 1885.

Marshall, A., *Oliver Cromwell, Soldier: The Military Life of a Revolutionary at War*, London: Brasseys, 2005.

Money, W., *The First and Second Battles of Newbury and the Siege of Donnington Castle*, 2nd edn, London: Simkins, Marshall, 1884.

Morrah, P., *Prince Rupert of the Rhine*, London: Constable, 1976.

Newman, P., *The Battle of Marston Moor 1644*, Chichester: Phillimore, 1981.

Newman, P. and Roberts, P.R., *The Battle of Marston Moor*, Pickering: Blackthorn Press, 2003.

Peachey, S. and Turton, A., *Old Robin's Foot*, Leigh-on-Sea: Partizan Press, 1987.

Pevsner, Sir Nicholas, *The Buildings of England: Northamptonshire*, London: Penguin, 1961.

Reid, S., *All the King's Armies*, Sevenoaks: Spellmount, 1998.

—, *The Finest Knight in England: Sir Thomas Tildesley*, Aberdeen: privately printed, 1979.

Roberts, K., *First Newbury 1643: The Turning Point*, Oxford: Osprey, 2004.

Rogers, H., *Battles and Generals of the Civil Wars 1642–1651*, London: Seeley Press, 1968.

Roy, I. and Porter, S., *A Century of History at King's*, London: privately printed, 1979.

Sanford, J.H., *Studies and Illustrations of the Great Rebellion*, Oxford: Oxford University Press, 1854.

Scott, C., Turton, A. and Von Arni, E., *Edgehill: The Battle Reinterpreted*, Barnsley: Pen & Sword, 2004.

Seymour, W., *Battles in Britain. Vol. 2: 1642–1746*, London: Sidgwick and Jackson, 1975.

Smith, D., *A History of the Modern British Isles 1603–1707*, Oxford: Blackwell, 1998.

Smurthwaite, D., *A Complete Guide to the Battlefields of Britain*, London: Michael Joseph, 1993.

Sunderland, F., *Marmaduke, Lord Langdale*, London: Jenkins, 1926.

Terry, C., *Life and Campaigns of Alexander Leslie, Earl of Leven*, London: Longman, Green, 1899.

Thomas, P., *Sir John Berkenhead 1619–1679: A Royalist Career in Politics and Polemics*, Oxford: Oxford University Press, 1969.

Tincey, J., *Marston Moor: The Beginning of the End*, Oxford: Osprey, 2003.

Toynbee, M. and Young, P., *The Battle of Cropredy Bridge*, Kineton: Roundway Press, 1970.

Van Creveld, M., *Command in War*, Cambridge, Mass.: Harvard University Press, 1985.

Wanklyn, M. and Jones, F., *A Military History of the English Civil War 1642–1646: Strategy and Tactics*, London: Pearson/Longman, 2004.

Wedgwood, C.V., *The King's War*, London: Collins, 1958.

Wheeler, J., *The Irish and British Wars 1637–1654: Triumph, Tragedy and Failure*, London: Routledge, 2002.

Woolrych, A., *Battles of the English Civil Wars*, London: Batsford, 1961.

—, *Britain in Revolution*, Oxford: Oxford University Press, 2003.

Worden, B., *Roundhead Reputations: The English Civil Wars and the Passions of Posterity*, London: Allen Lane, 2001.

Young, P., *Edgehill: The Campaign and the Battle*, Kineton: Roundway Press, 1967.

—, *Marston Moor 1644*, Kineton: Roundway Press, 1970.

—, *Naseby*, London: Century Press, 1985.

Young, P. and Holmes, R., *The English Civil Wars*, London: Eyre Methuen, 1974.

Essays and Journal Articles

Davies, G., 'The Battle of Edgehill', *English Historical Review* 36, 1921.

Firth, Sir Charles, 'Clarendon's History of the Great Rebellion', *English Historical Review* 19, 1904.

—, 'Marston Moor', *Transactions of the Royal Historical Society* n.s. 12, 1898.

—, 'The "Memoirs" of Sir Richard Bulstrode', *English Historical Review* 10, 1895.

Foard, G., 'The Archaeology of Attack', paper presented at the 'Fields of Conflict' conference, 2000.

Hutton, R., 'Clarendon's History of the Great Rebellion', *English Historical Review* 97, 1982.

Malcolm, J., 'A King in Search of Soldiers: Charles I in 1642', *Historical Journal* 21, 1978.

Newman, P., 'Marston Moor: The Sources and the Site', *Borthwick Papers* 53, 1978.

Wanklyn, M., 'Royalist Strategy in the South of England 1642–1644', *Southern History* 3, 1981.

Wanklyn, M. and Young, P., '"A King in Search of Soldiers": A Rejoinder', *Historical Journal* 24, 1981.

Young, P., 'The Royalist Army at Edgehill', *Journal of the Society of Army Historical Research* 33, 1955.

—, 'The Royalist Army at the Battle of Roundway Down', *Journal of the Society of Army Historical Research* 31, 1953.

Theses
Wakelin, A..P., 'Pre-industrial Trade on the River Severn: A Computer-aided Study of the Gloucester Port Books', PhD, Wolverhampton, 1991.
Wanklyn, M., 'The King's Armies in the West of England 1642–46', MA., Manchester, 1966.

Maps
HMSO, *Ordnance Survey Maps of the British Isles*, 1st edn, sheets 11, 12, 52, 53, 54, 63, 64, 89, 91, 93.
Milne, T., *Hampshire*, 1791.
Ogilby, J., *Britannia, or an Illustration of the Kingdom of England and the Dominion of Wales*, 1665 (1939 edn).
Rocque, J., *Berkshire*, sheet 4, 1759.
Willis, J., *Map of Ten Miles around Newbury, Berkshire*, 1768.

Website
www.battlefieldstrust.com – The Battlefields Trust Website, which includes aerial photographs of all the battlefield sites except that of Preston. Some of the battlefield files, however, contain incorrect depictions of the way in which the armies were deployed.

Index